GUATEMALA

HONDURAS

GUATEMALA
CITY

Santa Rosa
de Copán

Jalapa

Comayagua

La Paz

PAN AMERICAN
HIGHWAY

Metapán

TEGUCIGALPA

Lempa R.

Chalatenango

Santa Ana

Suchitoto

Ahuachapán

Sonsonate

SAN SALVADOR

Cojutepeque

San Francisco
Gotera

Acajutla

Nueva
San Salvador

San
Vicente

San Miguel

La Libertad

Zacatecoluca

Usulután

EL SALVADOR

La Unión

Jiquilisco

Choluteca

Puerto El Triunfo

Pacific Ocean

*Gulf of
Fonseca*

NICARAGUA

0   10   20   30   40   50
SCALE OF MILES

DON PITCHER

erto
ezas

Prinzapolca

Caribbean Sea

N

Bluefields

Juan del Norte
reytown)

W   E

SAN JOSÉ

Limón

*PANAMA
CANAL*

**PAN AMERICAN
HIGHWAY**

S

Colón

Golfito

P A N A M Á

**PANAMÁ
CITY**

David

C O L O M B I A

Santiago

VIOLENT NEIGHBORS

VIOLENT NEIGHBORS

El Salvador,
Central America,
and the United States

Tom Buckley

Times
BOOKS

Portions of this book appeared in somewhat different form in *The New Yorker*.

Published by TIMES BOOKS,
The New York Times Book Co., Inc.
Three Park Avenue, New York, N.Y. 10016

Published simultaneously in Canada by
Fitzhenry & Whiteside, Ltd., Toronto

Library of Congress Cataloging in Publication Data

Buckley, Tom.
    Violent neighbors.

    1. El Salvador—Politics and government—1979–   .
2. Central America—Politics and government—1979–   .
3. Revolutions—Central America.   4. Central America—
Foreign relations—United States.   5. United States—
Foreign relations—Central America.   I. Title.
F1488.3.B82 1984   972.84′052   82-40366
ISBN 0-8129-1035-4

Designed by Doris Borowsky

Manufactured in the United States of America

84 85 86 87 88 5 4 3 2 1

For Barbara

Acknowledgments

MANY PERSONS in public and private life in the United States and in the countries that I have dealt with, some of whom asked not to be identified, assisted me in the preparation of this book. To them I extend my thanks. To those of them who have continued, against all the odds, to work and to fight for democracy and social justice, I express my profound admiration.

Contents

VIOLENT
NEIGHBORS

I

An Honest Count

A PRIEST SAT in the departure lounge at Tegucigalpa, serenely reading a paperback book. His Roman collar, short-sleeved black shirt, shiny black trousers, and heavy black shoes marked him as a conservative of the old school. In Central America few priests wear clerical attire in public and often not even in their churches. He was in his sixties, at a guess, a short, round-faced man, with a look of amiability and a natural tonsure of gray hair.

When the flight to San Salvador was announced, he dog-eared the page he was reading and closed the book. As he stood up, I saw the cover. It was not, as I had assumed, a devotional work, but *The Last Mafioso,* a biography of a gangland killer named Jimmy "the Weasel" Fratianno. As we walked to the plane, I caught his eye, pointed to the lurid volume he carried, smiled, and shook my head.

"The book?" he said with an innocent smile. "It's interestin' to me, this stuff. I grew up in Greenwich Village, the corner of Houston and Thompson. I knew a lot of these guys in the old days."

We introduced ourselves. "Call me Father Joe," he said, extending his hand, "Father Joe Napoli." His smile faded, though, when I took a seat within easy conversational range.

"You're a long way from the Village," I said.

"For me, this is like comin' home," he replied, putting aside *The Last Mafioso* with an expression of regret. "I worked down here for 25 years. Panama, Honduras, El Salvador, you name it. Finally I said to myself, 'Enough is enough. You're not a kid anymore.' Now I've got a church in Amarillo. They're Mexican people mostly. Good people. Amarillo is a great place. Everybody gets along with everybody else."

He was a Franciscan, he said, a member of the order founded by the gentle St. Francis of Assisi. In their sandals and rough brown habits,

3

Franciscans marched shoulder to shoulder across Mexico, Peru, and the Spanish Main with the *conquistadores*. They held aloft the cross in desperate battles, shouting, *"In hoc signo vinces* ["In this sign you shall conquer"]," and saved millions of Indian souls.

"I came down to see some old friends, and now I'm on my way to Sonsonate," Father Joe said. "I built the church there. The Canadian Franciscans took it over when I left. Now I hear they're pullin' out. I'm going over there to talk to them. I'm tryin' to make up my mind whether to come back or not."

Sonsonate is a town in western El Salvador. The *matanza,* the great slaughter, of 1932 took place in that area. At least 8,000 peasants, many of them Indians, were murdered after an unsuccessful uprising. Its organizer, Agustín Farabundo Martí, was the founder of the Salvadoran Communist party. The guerrillas of the 1980's fight in his name as the Farabundo Martí Front for National Liberation.

"I heard about the *matanza,*" Father Joe said when I mentioned it. "It was a terrible thing."

Now it was March, 1982, almost exactly 50 years later. I brought up the Salvadoran elections, which were then only a week away.

"I don't follow politics very much," Father Joe said. "You do, and before you know it, you're getting involved, and then you're in trouble with everyone."

"Like the Jesuits?" I asked.

"They're very smart fellas, the Jesuits," he said mildly, "but they get in a lot of trouble."

Relations between the two orders, one noted for intellectual brilliance and the other for humility, have been cool since 1773. In that year, under pressure from France and Spain, Clement XIV, a Franciscan Pope, suppressed the Jesuits. Not until 1814 were they officially permitted to reconstitute themselves.

"What can you do?" Father Joe said with a shrug when I mentioned that event. "They got out of line. Somebody had to straighten them out."

He opened *The Last Mafioso* and began to read with a scowling intensity that suggested that even a gentle Franciscan might revolt if he were interrupted again. But it is only a 25-minute flight, and by then the plane was swinging low over the Pacific and back across the sugar fields of the coastal plain for a landing.

I was on my way to collect my luggage when I saw someone I knew.

He was Mario Redaelli, the secretary-general of the Republican Nationalist Alliance—ARENA, in its Spanish acronym. Redaelli's amiability lowered the tension when the party's founder and leader, Roberto D'Aubuisson, was around. D'Aubuisson, a former major in Salvadoran army intelligence, regarded himself as the fiercest anti-Communist in the country. Robert E. White, the former United States Ambassador, described him as "a psychopathic killer." Not that Redaelli's own anticommunism doesn't run deep. His father, an Italian immigrant, was the only European—that is, white person—to be killed in the uprising that led to the *matanza*.

Six months earlier, when their party was just getting started, I had a pleasant conversation, which is the only kind advisable, with Redaelli and D'Aubuisson. On the strength of that meeting Redaelli offered me a ride to San Salvador in his car. When it failed to appear, we shared a cab. We stopped at a military checkpoint a couple of miles from the airport. It was there, in December, 1980, that four American women missionaries were abducted and then murdered. Some people think that D'Aubuisson ordered the killings, as well as that of Archbishop Oscar Arnulfo Romero nine months earlier. As the taxi halted, a national guardsman looked in the window, saw Redaelli, saluted, and waved us on.

A story had appeared in the press a couple of weeks earlier, while I was in Nicaragua, stating that D'Aubuisson had been slightly wounded in an assassination attempt. The account was blurry and unconvincing. My colleagues there said it sounded like a fake. Promising that I would keep the story to myself until my book appeared, I asked Redaelli what had really happened.

"It *was* a fake," he said, laughing so hard his mustache waved in the breeze. "Bob was being driven back from a campaign appearance up in Chalatenango, I think, when one of his bodyguards' pistols went off. Luckily Bob was wearing his bulletproof vest, and he got only a graze on his arm."

By now the cab was threading its way through San Salvador's rundown central district. There have been so many earthquakes and volcanic eruptions all over Central America that few old and distinguished buildings have survived. Aside from a few earthquake-resistant towers of 10 or 15 stories, new structures are generally kept low and cheap to reduce the investment at risk.

I dropped off Redaelli at his home and went on to the Sheraton Hotel. The Camino Real, where the press stayed, had been full for weeks. The Sheraton, which is situated high above the rest of the city on the slopes of the Volcano of San Salvador, was at least as good but was out of the way, and its star boarders were the American military advisers, intelligence operatives, arms salesmen, and other such transients, most of whom were inclined to be surly and combative toward the press.

Unlike the Camino Real, the Sheraton was heavily guarded, but security seemed to be selectively applied. In January, 1981, José Rodolfo Viera, the head of the Salvadoran Institute of Agrarian Transformation, and two American advisers, Michael P. Hammer and Mark David Pearlman, were murdered in the hotel's coffee shop by men who were later identified as members of the National Guard in civilian clothes. One of the Salvadoran owners of the hotel was later implicated in the murders.

From my room in the VIP tower, a separate building on the far side of the swimming pool, I called René Cárdenas, a Salvadoran who had assisted me on previous visits, and arranged to meet him at the Camino Real. I then dropped in on Mario Rosenthal, the editor and publisher of the *News-Gazette,* a weekly tabloid that appears in both Spanish and English. He had office space at the hotel, which he otherwise could not have afforded, because people like the hotel's owners regard the *News-Gazette*'s viewpoint as wise and fair-minded.

Rosenthal is a stocky, peppery white-haired man of 66. He was born in New York, the son of a Salvadoran mother and an American father, but he has been knocking around Central America most of his life. He worked as a dispatcher for the old United Fruit Company in the 1930's and as a publicity man for an American entrepreneur named O. Roy Chalk, who briefly owned the International Railways of Central America, in the 1960's. Rosenthal was also the author of a less than prophetic book, *Guatemala: The Story of an Emergent Latin-American Democracy,* and collaborated with Miguel Ydígoras Fuentes, the Guatemalan dictator from 1958 to 1963, on *My War with Communism.* He worked as an editor on *El Diario,* a New York daily owned by Chalk. In 1977, his wife, who is Salvadoran, persuaded him to settle in San Salvador. The next year he bought the *News-Gazette,* whose readers and advertisers were already heading for Miami, for a handful of pesos.

"I don't care who wins as long as Duarte loses," he exclaimed, referring to President José Napoleón Duarte. "You know what Duarte said? He said, 'There will be no private enterprise under my government.' "

"When did he say that?" I asked since it sounded out of character.

"Look, right here," he said, burrowing through a pile of back numbers, looking for the damning quotation, while he continued talking. "If the Christian Democrats get a majority, we'll really be heading down the road to a screwball socialism that no one wants."

Rosenthal was still looking for the quotation when I excused myself to meet Cárdenas. While I was waiting for a cab, I read the wall of the hotel. It bore the names of 40 or 50 nations that had sent contestants to the 1975 Miss Universe contest, for which the hotel was the headquarters. The competition turned out to be of greater political than aesthetic importance. Students at the National University demonstrated against the contest as an insult to womanhood and a waste of public funds in a country where malnutrition prevents many bosoms and legs from developing to their full potential and where tooth decay causes smiles to lose their dazzle quickly. The students' march was broken up with bullets and tear gas. A certain number—nobody's count can be relied on—were killed and wounded. Others were arrested, never to be seen again. Not long afterward the left retaliated by murdering the Minister of Tourism.

Tom Brokaw and his retinue of producers, writers, and technicians rolled up in a van. Four bellboys began unloading a mountain of luggage and equipment. Brokaw, who wore a beautifully cut bush jacket and matching trousers, was taller, over six feet, than he appeared to be on television. A couple of days later, after we had been introduced, I mentioned this to him. "Everyone says that," he replied.

Journalists swarmed in the lobby of the Camino Real. The television crews' rented vans crowded the hotel parking lot.

The press was beginning to sulk. They were less interested in the election than in the bloodshed that was expected to accompany it, and nothing much was happening. One or two of the five separate guerrilla groups were making fearsome threats, but the others said the election was too farcical to interfere with. The security forces and the death squads weren't even massacring anyone, although four members of a Dutch television crew had been killed a few days earlier. An army patrol was waiting in ambush at their rendezvous with an armed guerrilla band and shot everyone dead.

American correspondents, even those farther to the left, would probably have been dealt with more considerately, but the Netherlands gave no aid and little sympathy to the Salvadoran government.

7

The death of the Dutchmen also served, as the security forces had probably anticipated, to reduce the enthusiasm of the press for such excursions.

Cárdenas turned up only a little late.

"Hey, pardner, good to see you," he said. *"Qué pasa?"*

Cárdenas is a Salvadoran who served for 29 years in the United States Army, about half of it in the Special Forces. He retired as a sergeant major with the Legion of Merit, a decoration seldom awarded to non-commissioned officers. I met him in the spring of 1981, on my first visit to the country, and he had assisted me as companion, guide, and interpreter when I was caught in the line of fire of machine-gun Spanish. Cárdenas was as conservative as any old soldier, but he was an accurate interpreter, and as it happened, he had admired Duarte since his schooldays. Cárdenas was a freshman at the Liceo Salvadoreño when Duarte was a senior, the president of his class, and a basketball star who was known as Loco because of the way he charged recklessly down the court.

The voters in the election would be choosing the 60 members of a new Constituent Assembly, the first since October, 1979, when it was dissolved after a coup. The new Assembly would name a provisional president, draw up a new constitution, and set a date for a presidential election. Six parties had put up candidates, but it had become a personal contest between Duarte, who was not running, and D'Aubuisson, who was. Both the Marxist rebels and the non-Marxist left had declined invitations to participate, on the reasonable ground that they were likely to be murdered if they tried to campaign.

The Christian Democrats, leading a coalition with the moderate left, won the presidential elections in 1972 and 1977, but the victories were stolen from them by the military and the oligarchy. Even without the left, the Christian Democrats were favored to win a plurality of the Assembly seats but not a majority. Ordinarily a party in that position makes a deal on jobs and policies with one or more of its rivals and forms a coalition. However, ARENA, which was expected to finish second or third, was trying to unite all the other parties to exclude the Christian Democrats from the government if that was the way the election turned out. The key was the third major party, the Party of National Conciliation, or PCN. If it allied itself with the Christian Democrats, Duarte would remain in power, which was what Washington

8

wanted. If it went with ARENA, he and the Christian Democrats might be frozen out.

As it happened, the previous November I had discussed these possibilities with the secretary-general of the PCN, a man named Rafael Rodríguez González. He was the head of the butchers' union, and he had the big belly, thick forearms, heavy thumbs, and false geniality of a purveyor of tough and overpriced cuts. He had worked closely for 20 years with the American Institute for Free Labor Development, a branch of the AFL-CIO that is generally thought to have received funds from the Central Intelligence Agency.

Rodríguez said that the party was no longer the tool of the oligarchy and the military. He even defended, with qualifications, Duarte's land reform. I came away with the strong impression that he favored an alliance with the Christian Democrats. I was probably correct, because only a month or so after our conversation Rodríguez was murdered. There were no arrests. The Salvadoran police are busier committing homicides than solving them.

It was to seek enlightenment on this point that I asked René to lead me to the PCN headquarters. The exterior of the building, which had been in happier times a nightclub, bore many chips and cracks. It had been bombed a year or so earlier. There was no preelection tumult. A couple of secretaries and a half dozen hangers-on dozed on rump-sprung chairs and benches. They said that the party's executive committee could be found at the studios of *Canal Seis,* Channel Six, where they were making a campaign broadcast.

When Raúl Molina, a businessman who had replaced Rodríguez as secretary-general, emerged from the studio, I introduced myself and asked him which way the party was headed.

"The door is still open," he said portentously, drawing himself up to his full height in the manner of Central American statesmen and fixing his gaze high over my head. "I have been talking with your embassy. A couple of weeks ago I was in Washington. I met with members of Congress and officials of the National Conference of Catholic Bishops."

Hearing that, I thought the Christian Democrats' worries were over. I expected to smell victory in the air at their headquarters, which we visited next. It occupied a modest house on a quiet street. Several young men, armed with automatic shotguns and rifles, stood guard outside. They looked more embattled than triumphant. None of the party leaders was around. Many of them, like Duarte, were public officials and were thus prevented by law from taking part in the campaign.

By scrupulously observing this prohibition, for the first time in Salvadoran history, the Christian Democrats thereby cost themselves the services of their most popular spokesmen.

By then it was time to head for the National Gymnasium, where ARENA was holding a rally. The long lines of people filing into the building had the same glazed, cheerful true-believer look as the audiences at Goldwater rallies in 1964 or, for that matter, at Reagan rallies in 1980. They wore plastic ARENA boaters with red, white, and blue bands, and they waved ARENA flags. The crowd was predominantly middle-class and white, rather than *mestizo,* the white-Indian mixture that accounts for more than 90 percent of the population of El Salvador and most of Central America. Women were clearly in the majority. René said they had been attracted by D'Aubuisson's powerful *macho* vibrations. Duarte had received the same sort of female adoration, which transcended politics, in his run for the presidency in 1972.

Every few minutes the crowd, which was growing to 10,000 or 12,000, chanted D'Aubuisson's name—"Daugh-bwiss-*on*"—five times, with increasing speed and a swelling roar, and then: *"Patria, sí! Comunismo, no!"* It stood at rigid attention throughout the playing of a recorded version of the Salvadoran national anthem. El Salvador may be the smallest nation in Latin America, but its national anthem, which has sections that echo the Sextet from *Lucia di Lammermoor* and the Overture to *William Tell,* is as long as Chile.

Three mariachi orchestras—violins, guitars, and a trumpet—competed for a prize for the best song in honor of D'Aubuisson. Pompon girls snake-danced across the floor of the arena. A watermelon was prominently displayed on the podium. For D'Aubuisson it symbolizes the Christian Democrats, being green, their party color, on the outside and red, their true color, on the inside.

When D'Aubuisson finally arrived, he stood before the audience, his hands clasped over his head, turning first one way, then the other, letting the electricity flow into the crowd. The audience rose and cheered and jumped up and down. Women screamed his name in open-throated ecstasy. *"Bobbee! Bobbee! Bobbee!"* D'Aubuisson was then 38 years old. He stands only about five feet seven inches, but he holds himself very straight and wears cowboy boots to add a couple of inches to his height. He is slim, although the bulletproof vest he wore under his Windbreaker puffed him out like the Michelin tire man. He has the bony, flashy good looks of the Frank Sinatra of 25 or 30 years ago. He combs his thick brown hair into a pompadour, as Sinatra used to be able to do. His mouth is wide, and his smile is bright, but his brown eyes are as cold as death.

D'Aubuisson spoke sharply, directly, almost without inflection, as though he were giving orders. His platform, he said, was to destroy every last guerrilla and his allies, and that did not exclude the Christian Democrats.

"We're not going to let the president of Venezuela or the Mexicans or the French tell us how to vote," he declared.

The Christian Democratic government of Venezuela was supporting Duarte. France and Mexico had issued a joint declaration six months earlier, calling the National Liberation Front "a representative political force."

"We're going to make our own decisions," he went on, after the booing stopped, "and we're going to save not only El Salvador but the rest of America from communism as well."

At three the next morning I was awakened by bursts of automatic-weapons fire. They rose to a furious fusillade, died away for five or 10 minutes, and then began again. My room overlooked the hotel parking lot and a street lined with houses that would be in the $100,000 class in the United States. Behind them was one of the *barrancas*, or ravines, that radiate downward from the Volcano of San Salvador. They probe like fingers toward the heart of the city and are often used by the guerrillas as attack routes.

The firing was continuing at first light. I dressed, left the building by the parking-lot entrance, and followed the road downhill for 500 feet or so. An army lorry and several police cars were drawn up. Muzzle flashes winked at the bottom and on the far side of the ravine. The light ripping sound of automatic rifles was punctuated by the slower beat of a heavy machine gun.

A soldier who was sheltering behind a tree said that a group of guerrillas, coming up from the *barranca*, had attacked the headquarters of the Central Elections Commission, which occupied a walled house on the same street. The commission's guards held them off until reinforcements arrived. The guerrillas had then retreated into the ravine. Danger was remote, but the soldier looked unhappy. His body, he said, was in El Salvador, but his heart was in the United States.

The next day, René and I found, across the street from the Sheraton's tennis courts, where a pair of slim, tanned young women in white, attended by a ball boy, were keeping up a polite rally, a path

11

leading down into the *barranca*. Just below street level, the path widened. Huts stood on both sides. They were larger, perhaps 12 feet square, and sturdier than those I had seen in other squatter colonies in San Salvador. Many of them were constructed, at least in part, of brick and had roofs of corrugated galvanized iron or of a deluxe material resembling fiberglass that admits some light, provides insulation against the beat of the sun, and doesn't rust.

The people we spoke to assured us that they had slept through the fighting. The poor in countries like El Salvador long ago decided that their only chance of safety lay in silence and the affectation of stupidity. Even so, we finally found a man who was reckless enough to talk to strangers. He was relaxing in a tattered beach chair close to the bottom of the ravine.

"Sixty families live along this path," he said. "Most of us have been here for many years. It's not bad here. We have a cooperative. We brought in our own electric line, and so we have lights and television. We built a cistern for water, and we have taps that run even now, in the dry season."

He pushed open the curtain that hung in the doorway of his house to show us these amenities. We congratulated him on the pleasant life he had made for his family, and he smiled broadly, but when we asked about the shooting, his smile faded.

"They say the guerrillas come through the *barranca* a lot at night," he said. "I heard that four or five were killed, but there were no bodies. Perhaps the guerrillas carried them away. I do not know. I stayed in my *ranchito* with my wife and children."

To help Duarte realize his goal of holding the first indisputably honest national election in the history of El Salvador, the State Department had been flying in experts for the better part of a year. The best known were Richard Scammon, a former director of the Bureau of the Census, and his associate, Howard Penniman. For more than 20 years, the two of them have been traveling to the most remote and inhospitable corners of the world in the interests of an honest count.

During the week before the election Scammon addressed a luncheon meeting of the Salvadoran-American Chamber of Commerce at the Camino Real. By then only a handful of foreign businessmen of any nationality remained in the country. The rest had departed to avoid the possibility of being kidnapped or murdered by the guerrillas. Their places at the luncheon were taken by their Salvadoran stand-ins. Scammon, a hearty, rubicund man of about six feet five inches, with a shining, absolutely hairless head, towered over his audience like the Volcano of San Salvador. Penniman, by contrast, was short, pale, and worried-looking.

The well-worn contours of Scammon's speech suggested that it had been delivered many times before. Its soporific power was intensified by the pauses that were necessary every couple of sentences for a Spanish interpretation. Scammon defined elections, reviewed their history, described the procedures that would be used, excused past lapses by citing instances of fraud in the United States, and concluded by quoting Winston Churchill to the effect that democracy was the worst system of government except for all the other systems.

As I nodded off, I had an uncanny feeling that, somewhere, I had heard it all before. Suddenly it came to me. It was Saigon in 1967, the rooftop dining room of the Caravelle Hotel, Scammon making his speech, and another delegation of observers on hand to certify the honesty of a presidential election that was rigged from the start, although so clumsily that one candidate got more votes than General Nguyen Van Thieu, the winner, thought appropriate and was sent to prison for several years as a reward.

When I mentioned the occasion to Scammon, he gazed down at me and said if the voting hadn't been honest, the other fellow wouldn't have received enough votes to anger Thieu. I replied that if it had been honest, Thieu would probably have been beaten.

That night I continued my rereading of Joseph Conrad's *Nostromo*. Nearly eighty years after its publication, this great novel remains the best guide to the politics, economics, and society of Latin America. One of hundreds of passages that could be cited is a judgment made by the cosmopolitan son of an old family in Conrad's imagined land of Costaguana:

> There is a curse of futility upon our character: Don Quixote and Sancho Panza, chivalry and materialism, high-sounding sentiments and a supine morality, violent efforts for an idea and a sullen acquiescence in every form of corruption. We convulsed a continent for our independence only to become the passive prey of a democratic parody, the helpless victims of scoundrels and cut-throats, our institutions a mockery, our laws a farce. . . .

Since the Salvadoran newspapers, television, and radio stations did not cover the campaign, or the war, either, for that matter, publishing only the official communiqués and government-released photographs, the parties were required to present their messages as paid advertising. This the Christian Democrats, who were receiving financial support from Venezuela and probably the United States, and ARENA, which had the backing of the Salvadoran oligarchy, did lavishly.

The Christian Democrats not only laid out their positions in excruciating detail but also took the low road by attacking D'Aubuisson not only for crimes of which he was suspected but also for some that he seemed unlikely to be guilty of—for example, of "deserting" his men under unexplained circumstances. ARENA's advertising, which I was told was being placed by a subsidiary of the McCann-Erickson agency, included what were purported to be photocopies of letters exchanged by leading Christian Democrats and functionaries of the Salvadoran Communist party arranging covert visits by the Christian Democrats to the Soviet Union and East Germany. Few persons could have been deceived by them since two different typefaces were used in each letter.

As I was entering the Camino Real the next afternoon, I was almost bowled over by a rush of correspondents out the door and into their vans and cars. It turned out there had been a coup in Guatemala. With no planes available for charter, the quickest way to get there was by road. No longer a deadline slave, I decided to stay where I was. I would be in Guatemala in a week. Meanwhile, there was always a chance that the upheaval might travel down some political fault line into El Salvador itself.

All of Central America had been vibrating ominously since the Sandinista-led rebellion overthrew the Somoza family dynasty in Nicaragua in 1979. For the first time a government led by avowed Marxist-Leninists held power on the mainland. The Reagan administration, fearing the end of the United States' 100-year monopoly of power in the region, had organized an émigré army to harass and, conceivably, overthrow the Sandinistas. Honduras, where the army was based, seemed likely to be dragged into the fighting. Guatemala also had a guerilla uprising on its hands.

Aside from the ideologies involved, there was nothing new about that. Since gaining independence from Spain in the 1820's, Guatemala, El Salvador, Honduras, and Nicaragua have shown a propensity for violence out of all proportion to their size. (With a total area of 157,000 square miles, the four are a bit smaller than California. Their population of 15,000,000 or so is considerably less than that of the New York metropolitan area.) They have fought countless wars with one another, most of them as pointless as drunken quarrels, and in each have occurred rebellions and coups beyond counting.

The other three nations had different histories and fewer immediate problems. Belize had been British Honduras until 1980, and British troops were still stationed there to protect it from the territorial claims of Guatemala. Costa Rica, settled by Spanish farmers and historically the most stable and democratic nation in the region, was at peace, but it had an external debt of $4 billion, the largest in the world on a per capita basis, which threatened its standard of living. Panama, a part of Colombia until it was detached in a rebellion inspired by the United States in 1900, was still dizzy with delight at having regained at least nominal sovereignty over the canal, but there, too, there was an enormous foreign debt.

The American observers held a press conference on the day before the election. Senator Nancy Kassebaum, a Kansas Republican and the daughter of Alfred M. Landon, the party's presidential candidate in 1936, said that she was looking forward to "visiting" with as many Salvadorans as possible during her three days in the country.

Another observer was the Reverend Theodore M. Hesburgh, the president of the University of Notre Dame. He had been one of Duarte's teachers there in the 1940's, and the two men had remained friends. Hesburgh said that in Chicago, a city with which he was familiar, the election day motto was "Vote Early and Often." Under the circumstances, he said, he didn't think the press ought to "nitpick" the Salvadoran balloting. Academe was represented by Clark Kerr, president emeritus of the University of California. Asked why he had been chosen, he replied with a smile, "I'm not sure, but if President Reagan had known about it, I think he would certainly have vetoed me. He fired me, you know, at the first meeting of the university's board of regents after he became governor in 1967."

The Salvadoran government, at the prompting of the United States, had also invited a couple of hundred other observers from 25 or 30 countries. The precise count was unavailable and probably unknown. Most of them came from Latin America and the Caribbean. England was the only country in Europe that sent official observers, Prime Minister Margaret Thatcher having dispatched them to show her support for Reagan's hard-line policy. Both official and unofficial delegations, which represented, for the most part, Christian Democratic and Conservative parties in European and Latin American countries, were put up, gratis, at the most luxurious of San Salvador's hotels, the Presidente. The hotel, which had been closed for a year for lack of patronage, was opened and staffed for the event.

From a corner of the lobby I watched a stream of red-faced and perspiring observers arriving from the airport by limousine and chartered bus. Young women volunteers got them registered, issued credentials, and asked them to pick a city or town to visit on election day. The selection, I noted while standing behind an official of the Conservative party of Norway, was pretty much limited to the western side of the country, which was relatively peaceful.

Dr. Jorge Bustamante, the public-spirited but nonpolitical gynecologist who had assumed the chairmanship of the Central Elections Commission at the request of his old friend Duarte, was chatting with two men he introduced as observers from Venezuela.

"This is quite a party," said Bustamante. "Thank God my work is nearly over and I can get back to what is left of my practice."

René and I made a circuit of the outlying sections of the capital, the *tugurios,* or shantytowns, the bus depots, the factory districts along the highways. Troops were deployed on all the main roads, pulled back from the countryside for the election. On the lower slopes of the Cerro San Jacinto on the other side of the city from the Volcano of San Salvador, a company of the Atlacatl Battalion, picked men trained by the American advisers, patrolled along the paths that ran upward between the huts of squatters and ended in the thick brush and scattered trees above. The men of the Atlacatl were taller, older, more soldierly, and better equipped than other army units I had seen, in which the ranks were filled out by urchins of 14 and 15 in hand-me-down uniforms. The company commander said the guerrillas had pushed into the area on the previous night. Now his men were trying to find them. As in Vietnam, the army and the guerrillas were on different timetables.

No more than two miles away, we stopped briefly outside a factory where 2,000 persons assembled and tested computer components for Texas Instruments. Even though it might have been seen as a symbol of *yanqui* imperialism, Salvadorans, even perhaps the guerrillas, who had done nothing to interfere with it, were intensely proud of this plant. It was at least as efficient as other Texas Instruments plants anywhere else on earth.

In Mejicanos, a shabby and lively district that was a separate town not many years ago, we stopped at the central market. It was the height of *verano,* summer, as Salvadorans call the dry season, a succession of perfect sunny days with temperatures that range between 70 and 80 degrees in the uplands, which runs from December through April. On the sidewalk, as possessively as a flock of hens on clutches of eggs, farm women presided over fragrant pineapples, oranges and bananas, plantains, papayas and mangoes, tomatoes and cabbage, heaped in straw pannikins or laid out on broad, glossy banana leaves. In the dim interior, rice, freshly ground cornmeal, and shiny black beans were sold from burlap sacks.

There were also several small restaurants. René led me to one of them Rosa Neri Santiago's, for a bowl of her famed *sopa de bolos,* drunk soup, so called because it has the power to wash away the most intractable hangover.

"It's good soup even if you don't have a hangover," René said. "Anyhow, it's time for lunch."

We sat down on one of the three splintered wooden benches. René told Rosa, a plump woman in her forties, that we wanted two *especiales.*

"She charges by how much meat you ask for," René said. "The *sopa especial* has the most. It'll cost you five colones."

That was about $1.50 at the free-market rate, and I said I could handle it. Rosa relayed the order to her assistant, who ladled the soup into chipped bowls from a cast-iron pot that was simmering over a charcoal fire. My first taste told me that Rosa's soup meant business. It was a pungent broth in which a pig's foot, a couple of meaty neckbones, and slices of pulpy yucca floated.

Rosa said that anyone could boil up a good pork stock, but that the secret was in the mixture of spices, herbs, and other, nameless, ingredients called *ayote,* and that hers, which brought her a comfortable living, would be disclosed on her deathbed to whichever of her daughters had been most devoted to her.

Three other men were eating Rosa's soup. On the bench opposite us a man of about 50 was spooning it down for dear life. He had a three-day stubble, and his eyeballs looked as though they were dissolving in blood. The other two seemed to be in marginally better shape, and I asked them how they were going to vote.

Campesinos, or peasants, and the squatters in the *barranca* would have looked blank and said they didn't know, but these were city men, and they spoke up. *"La pesca . . . la pesca . . . las manos . . . la pesca."* The fish was the emblem of the Christian Democrats, and *las manos,* the hands—that is, a handshake—of the National Conciliation party, the PCN. When I asked how they thought the war was going, only the man with the murderous hangover spoke up.

"There are guerrillas all over Mejicanos," he said. "They are here every night. In the *campo,* the countryside, it's worse. I'm a truck driver, and I know. On the highways the guerrillas stop you all the time and rob you. They call it making you pay their war taxes. They have burned the trucks of many of my friends who tried to drive to San Vicente. You can't go to that part of the country at all."

From Mejicanos we drove past the National University. It was closed in 1978, when the government decided it was the center from which subversion radiated. The campus, overgrown with weeds, was enclosed by a cyclone fence that was guarded by troops. The three-story buff-colored buildings were smeared with revolutionary graffiti. Many windows were broken. The faculty had scattered, and the university seemed unlikely to reopen until the rebellion had triumphed or had been definitively crushed. From there we circled through the Santa Lucía and San Antonio Abad districts, which lie across the *barranca* from the Sheraton Hotel. The guerrillas slipped through them by night. By day the streets were empty. The houses seemed abandoned. Troops sat on their front steps in the shade and smoked and waited for darkness to fall.

That night I dined at the home of a man I will call Juan Hernández because he has asked me not to identify him. I met him on my first visit to El Salvador and always made a point of looking him up when I returned. Hernández, who is in his middle forties, is an agronomist. He owns and operates a model dairy farm in the broad Santa Ana Valley about 20 miles east of the capital. He also manages an 1,800-acre coffee *finca* for an oligarchy family that was then residing in Florida. The family foresightedly divided it years earlier into separate ownerships that were not large enough, as it turned out, to be expropriated in the land reform of 1980. He and his family live in a $250,000 house in San Benito, not far from the Hotel Presidente.

Hernández, whose late father was a diplomat, spent most of his childhood and youth in the United States. Like Bustamante, Duarte, and many other members of the rising professional middle class, he has a reformist political and social outlook that has far more in common with the viewpoint of the same class in the United States than with that of the old oligarchy or the new entrepreneurial class in El Salvador.

Hernández had been fairly optimistic when I first met him. He showed me around the *finca* and his own farm, and he spoke, tentatively, as is his way, of the possibility that the land reform might help bring peace. Now I found him gloomy, baffled, and angry by turns, worried about his family and wondering if he should sell his farm for whatever depressed price it would bring and emigrate to the United States. Agricultural production was plunging, he said. His area was still quiet, but he sensed that the war was moving closer. Hundreds of farms were being abandoned. What the fighting wasn't destroying, he said, was being choked by governmental interference.

Hernández said he was not yet certain how he would vote. His wife, who usually sat listening demurely, said that she would vote for D'Aubuisson, and so would all the women she knew, because only he could defeat the Communists. Their four children, all in their teens, agreed with her. With their jeans and Top-Siders they wore white polo shirts that were embroidered with the ARENA party emblem, a white cross outlined in red and blue, with the acronym below it. Everybody at their private school had at least one, they said. The Hernández's oldest child, a boy, was a senior at a leading New England prep school. He and his parents discussed the relative merits of Harvard, Yale, Stanford, and the University of Virginia with me. I doubt that it has ever occurred to Hernández or his wife, and I did not mention it, that their son, as well as conscripted peasant boys, had an obligation to help to defend the family's property.

Election day was March 28, a Sunday, the day of the week on which Latin America goes to the polls—when it is permitted to. I had arranged to travel with Peter Arnett, an old friend. In Vietnam, where we met, he was the star of the Associated Press and the Napoleon of correspondents. A couple of years ago he joined Ted Turner's Cable News Network, which does not regard a pretty face and a full head of hair as a journalist's most important qualifications.

More than 700 persons had received press credentials from the Salvadoran government. Minute by minute, scores of vans similar to ours, representing the great television networks of the civilized world, most of which had assigned several crews to the election, rolled out of the hotel parking lot, in a blare of horns and vivid Spanish curses. We sped to a high school where, although it was 7:00 A.M. and the polls had just opened, thousands of persons were waiting to vote. Lines stretched out of the school grounds, down the sidewalk, and even across busy thoroughfares. In a less anarchically inclined country, a gap would have been left to permit the traffic to pass. In El Salvador, unless you stood close enough to your neighbor to pick his pocket, someone was sure to try to push in ahead of you. The voters were middle-class and, hence, voluble supporters of D'Aubuisson. Their attitude toward the American press was summed up by the posters and bumper stickers that ARENA had printed by the thousands. They read, *Periodista: Entrega Tu País, Pero No El Nuestro. Di la Verdad!* Or, "Journalist, Sell Out Your Own Country, Not Ours. Tell the Truth!"

While Arnett's crew was filming the scene, a limousine, escorted by two armored station wagons, pulled up, and Deane Hinton, the American Ambassador, stepped out. He pumped hands, kissed babies, and posed for Arnett's camera, as though he were running for office himself. Hinton, who is tall and spare, looks and sounds like an Indiana feed-and-grain magnate who contributed his way into diplomacy. But the baggy suits and washed-out shirts and the twanging exclamations like "hell and damnation" and "don't you believe it" were camouflage. Hinton was one of the senior ambassadors in the Foreign Service, and those were very cool eyes behind his steel-rimmed spectacles. He was serving in Chile when Allende was becoming unstuck and in Ethiopia when the United States and the Soviet Union were facing off there. His posting to El Salvador was a mark of the White House's confidence in him. Hinton was seen as an East-Wester—that is, one who saw such conflicts in terms of the rivalry between Russia and the United States—rather than as a North-Souther, who saw it as a struggle between the haves and the have-nots.

The voting was taking place at a half dozen tables set up under the covered walkways that connected the school buildings. The procedure was straightforward. The voter presented his *cédula,* the national identity card. To prevent repeat voting, it was marked, as was his hand, with ink that showed up under ultraviolet light. The voter signed the election register or made his mark, literacy not being a requirement, and was given a ballot on which the names and symbols of the six parties were printed in color. He then marked his ballot at a stand with three high sides, which provided adequate privacy, folded it, and dropped it into a transparent plastic box beneath.

These procedures, with one important exception, had been used in previous elections. The exception grew out of a decision by Bustamante and the rest of the elections commission not to try to bring up-to-date the voting registers, which had last been revised in 1972, and instead to rely entirely on the *cédula* as a means of identification. The potential for fraud was recognized. Tens of thousands of counterfeit identity cards were thought to be in use, and many persons were thought to have several. However, there was also an important advantage. Hundreds of thousands of persons who had left their homes because of the fighting would be able to vote wherever in El Salvador they happened to be.

The mechanics of the election may have been familiar, but the guiding spirit was brand-new. Duarte, who had been cheated out of the presidency in 1972, was determined that the election should be honest, even if it cost him his job. Washington also wanted honest elections. With the left refusing to take part, it looked like a no-lose situation. Duarte was clearly the president that the Reagan administration wanted, but it thought it could get along with the rightists, too. As I heard it, Hinton had knocked heads until the military, which would continue running the war no matter who was chosen as president, gave a solemn pledge of noninterference.

After leaving the school, the Arnett crew was struck by a disaster. The cameraman was filming the crowd as he walked forward. In such situations, with his eye glued to the viewfinder, he is unable to see hazards like potholes and small dogs directly in front of him, and it is the duty of the sound man, who walks alongside, to warn him of these. The sound man, a locally hired Salvadoran, let the cameraman walk straight into a lamppost. He got a black eye; worse, his camera was broken.

Arnett held his head in despair. There was nothing to do but to return to the hotel with the paltry film that had already been shot. As it turned out, the other Cable News Network correspondent, Jim Maklashelski, had also just returned to the hotel to drop off tape for beaming to Atlanta by satellite. He kindly agreed to take me out with him.

We hastened to Mejicanos, where fighting was reported. Turning a corner, we saw voters standing in line in a narrow street lined with shops. In the street that crossed it, a block away, soldiers ran and fired and took shelter in a construction site. We walked toward them. The firing was not heavy, but the bullets seemed to be coming from several directions. They broke windows and pitted the pale blue and green

21

walls of shops and houses. An ambulance arrived to pick up a soldier who had been shot in the leg. The voters remained stolidly in line in the street. It may have been fatalism or patriotism that prevented them from seeking shelter, or, more likely, their unwillingness to give up their places in the line.

Not far from where we were standing, a Chilean photographer had been wounded an hour earlier. (He died a couple of weeks later.) The only significant military action around the capital, I later learned, had taken place at dawn, when 15 guerrillas, apparently part of a detachment that had slipped into the city through the *barranca* near the Sheraton, were killed in a fire fight in San Antonio Abad.

Maklashelski returned to the hotel and turned over his crew to Arnett. We then headed for Suchitoto, about 25 miles north of the capital and halfway to the Honduran border. The town had been heavily attacked during the guerrillas' "final offensive" in January, 1981, and they remained dug in in a maze of tunnels and trenches on the slopes of the nearby Guazapa Volcano. This was dry, upland country, 3,000 feet above sea level. The vegetation was burned brown after four rainless months. The people of the area, most of them tenant farmers, had fled or had been removed by the army. Their adobe huts sat empty, many of them burned, in tangles of vines. We passed a few *campesinos* trudging along the shoulder of the highway, some bent under loads of firewood, but there was no wheeled traffic except ambulances and press vehicles. The guerrillas had threatened to destroy everything else.

Troops manned outposts spaced every two or three miles along the highway. They were youngsters, very different from the men of the Atlacatl Battalion. They waved at us and occasionally stopped us with leveled rifles. Their little redoubts were almost worse than useless, being scarcely more than piles of rock roofed with corrugated metal. Bullets or explosives would break off sharp-edged fragments, as dangerous to the defenders as shrapnel. The only sandbags I ever saw in El Salvador fortified the American Embassy.

Suchitoto nodded under the intense light and dry heat of early afternoon. In the central square, with the long white church at one end and the town hall at the other, nothing stirred. The election tables were set up on the veranda of the elementary school. The plastic ballot boxes were well filled. The polls would remain open until 4:00 P.M., but the clerks and poll watchers said that they didn't expect many more voters.

The town's leading citizen, whom I had met a year earlier, stood in the shade, drinking a Coke. He was a stout, graying man named Alejandro Cotto. His brother, a lieutenant colonel in the army, was the secretary to the Secretary of Defense, General José Guillermo García. Cotto occupied the best house in Suchitoto. I had drunk wine in his shaded garden, listening to the splashing of a moss-covered fountain in counterpoint to a Bach invention on his phonograph and gazed down a long hillside at the lake 500 feet below created by the construction of a hydroelectric dam on the Lempa River.

Cotto, who had been an assistant to Luis Buñuel, the great film-maker, in Mexico City in the 1940's, had told me at the time that he was trying to raise the money for a documentary about El Salvador in the grip of revolution.

When I asked him how his project was coming, he shook his head. "My countrymen are fools," he said. "They do not see the importance of telling their story to the world."

From Suchitoto we took a secondary road that met the Pan American Highway about 20 miles east of San Salvador. The highway, the main route across the country, was also empty of traffic except for occasional vans marked, like ours, with the letters *TV* in white tape on the doors and the roof and a white flag flapping from the aerial.

South of the highway lay the broad and fertile San Vicente Valley. The irrigated fields gleamed in shades of green—rice, sugarcane, and thick pasturage in which black-and-white Holsteins grazed. Beyond rose the symmetrical cone of the San Vicente Volcano, haloed by cloud. We turned north onto a rocky track amid small and dusty fields and withered scrub. The road ended at the village of Santa Clara. Arnett said he had roamed the area the week before. The hills behind it, he said, were thick with guerrillas.

Even by Salvadoran standards, Santa Clara was Tobacco Road. The people were thin, and their coppery skins seemed to have a grayish cast. Most of the small children were naked, scabby, and dirty. Their stomachs stuck out, and their eyes were red and sore. Pigs rolled in the mud in the town square. They looked healthier and happier than the people. Most of the men were *jornaleros,* day laborers, who worked in the fertile valley. The only well-nourished people in the place were the dozen or so soldiers who sat on splintered chairs on the porch of the one-room police station. They told us they had driven off a guerrilla attack that morning. Here, too, the election officials, who sat behind a

23

long table on the veranda of the tumbledown village hall, said that the voting had been completed hours before.

We returned to the highway and continued eastward. Rounding a bend, we saw an astonishing sight—hundreds of *campesinos* trudging down the middle of the highway in the blazing afternoon sun. Many were barefoot. Some of the women balanced parcels on their heads and carried infants on slings across their back.

The men and women we spoke to said that they were returning to their settlements, which were too small to have polling places, after having voted in Apastepeque, their market town. They were walking, they said angrily, because the guerrillas had forbidden the buses to run. We asked one man if he thought the vote would change anything.

He pushed back his straw sombrero and rubbed his forehead with his thumb and index finger. "The voting is a very good thing," he said. "The *políticos* say it will end the war, and the soldiers say we must vote, so we vote."

Whom had he voted for? He shrugged and shifted his broad, flat feet, and looked off toward the volcano.

"It is a secret, no?" he murmured, and walked on.

By then it was four o'clock, time for Arnett to be getting back to transmit his tape. We had gone only a mile or two when we saw, standing at a cut where a dirt road from the hills met the highway, three armed men in green uniforms. Two others, lookouts, stood on the hill. I thought at first they were government troops, but their uniforms were a different shade of green and cut differently. They were *los muchachos,* the boys, which is what everyone calls the guerrillas, and we stopped to talk to them. The guerrillas know that they cannot afford to shrink from the cameras in their campaign to win hearts and minds all over the world. They made no objections as Arnett's crew began setting up.

The guerrilla leader introduced himself only as Dico. He had the Che Guevara look—black beret, long, lank hair, a short black beard. He was slight of build. His skin was pale, "European," as they say in Central America, and he wore horn-rimmed glasses. He said he was 27 years old, a native of San Salvador, and a student at the National University until it was closed. He had been a combatant, he said, for two years, but his face, his figure, and his manner, in which diffidence and self-confidence were having their own civil war, were those of the graduate student rather than the soldier. The young men standing with him, who were in their late teens, were darker, *mestizo* rather than Euro-

24

pean, and their smiles suggested that they liked the idea of starring on American television. Their names, they said, were David and Ricardo. They said they came from the San Vicente region and had been to high school, a level of education that *campesino* families cannot generally afford. At a guess, their families kept small shops or owned 20 acres of good land. The only insignia on their cheaply made uniforms were red enamel stars on the collar. Dico and Ricardo carried Belgian-made automatic rifles that they said had been seized from government troops. David carried a Soviet-bloc rocket launcher.

"Our assignment," Dico said, "is to make sure nothing but the press and ambulances move on the highway. So far nothing has. We have seen no troops the entire day. I think they do not want to confront us."

The reason might be, one of us said, that they all were guarding the polling places, where those hundreds of *campesinos* had just come from voting, and Arnett asked him how he explained that long procession.

"They told us that the soldiers told them they would be in trouble if they didn't vote," he said. "We understand. We didn't try to stop them. The voting is all a trick. It makes no difference."

Dico said he was a member of the Popular Liberation Forces, or FPL, the oldest of the five guerrilla forces, and this was the line it had taken. A couple of the smaller groups had warned the public, "Vote in the morning, die in the afternoon," but this was to prove to be an empty threat.

The FPL was founded in 1970 by Salvador Cayetano Carpio after he had resigned as the head of the Salvadoran Communist party. Until 1980 it was a tiny and generally ineffectual organization. By 1982, however, it was thought to be the largest of the five guerrilla groups. The total number was usually estimated at 4,000 to 6,000 by the United States and the Salvadoran government, and at 6,000 to 8,000 by the guerrillas themselves—as many, they say, as they had arms for.

Like the young lieutenants in the Salvadoran army I had spoken with, Dico could rattle off the things he was fighting for. These included the freeing of the country from the imperialist yoke of the United States, the establishment of a policy of nonalignment but fraternal friendship with socialist lands, a true land reform instead of the sham instituted at the orders of Washington, literacy classes, maternity clinics, an adequate diet for the *campesinos,* and the reformation of their social customs to end drunkenness and wife beating. As he spoke,

David and Ricardo nodded and smiled as though they would never tire of hearing this catalog of benefits in much the same way as their Indian ancestors would have been enthralled by the descriptions of heaven that they heard in church.

His unit, Dico said, was encamped in the hills to the north, but he would say nothing about its size, composition, and plans.

"We are doing what we intend to do," he said. "We ambush the army when they try to attack us, and then they run. These rifles were carried by soldiers we have killed. One thing is certain: that is, that the rule of the rich and the army in El Salvador is finished."

In the early evening, I attended a cocktail party that was being given by a New York businessman at his rented mansion a few blocks from the Sheraton. He had a contract to replace the electrical transmission towers that the guerrillas had been blowing up in great numbers. The scotch was gone when I arrived, and the buffet was curling at the edges.

Most of the guests were Salvadorans and Americans of the commercial and social demimonde. They all were strong supporters of D'Aubuisson, and their long afternoon of drinking made them surly and argumentative. A young woman who said she gave card readings at a private club in San Benito spoke incoherently of the tarot and of what it said about the future of her country. She introduced me to the owner of the club. He was a scowling man in his thirties named Robin Dunne. He was, he said, the son of the South African Ambassador, Archibald Gardiner Dunne, who had been kidnapped in 1979 by the FPL, the Carpio group, and murdered.

"I had a Salvadoran wife and a business here, and I was damned if I was going to let those murderous bastards drive me out of the country," he said. "I must admit I never thought you Yanks would turn out to be on their side."

That night I visited Election Central, which was situated in a theater adjoining the Hotel Presidente. The results were telegraphed there, town by town, read out, and chalked up on a big blackboard. By midnight the totals had scarcely reached the low hundred thousands, but a trend had already been established: the Christian Democrats were getting about 40 percent of the valid vote, and the other five parties, led by ARENA, the rest. About 10 percent of the ballots were being defaced, some of them, certainly, as a sign of support for the left.

Bustamante, flanked by other members of the elections commission, sat behind a long table on the stage. After their busy day many of the observers relaxed in the comfortable seats in the cool and dimly lighted auditorium. José Figueres, the former president of Costa Rica, with whom I had spent a morning a couple of weeks earlier in San José, told me, "I don't know who the winner is, but I know who the loser is. The loser is violence."

A little later I heard three men murmuring in posh English accents a couple of rows away. They were, as I supposed, the British observers —Sir John Galsworthy, a retired Ambassador, and a distant relation of the writer, and Professor Derek Bowelt, the president of Queens' College of Cambridge University.

"In one town," Bowelt told me, "Ciudad Arce, I believe it's called, would you believe that we entered the polling place through a hole in the wall?"

"Our terms of reference forbid us to reveal anything that could be construed as an opinion or a conclusion," said Sir John. "That will be done at the discretion of the Prime Minister after we submit our report. In any case, I must say that my impressions are still filtering down through a rather clogged mind."

A couple of English journalists joined us, pelting the observers with questions that Sir John evaded or batted back with diplomatic slice and chop.

"Can't you give me a straight answer?" one of the Fleet Streeters finally asked with some asperity.

"Of course I can," Sir John replied, "but I choose not to."

By noon the next day, the vote had already exceeded the total of 700,000 that Bustamante, Duarte, and the American Embassy had agreed would constitute a great success. The figure was thought to represent the 50 percent of the population of 5,000,000 over the voting age of 18. These were estimates; no census had been taken since 1970.

Before heading home, the American observers issued a statement that said, "The tremendous turnout, perhaps over 1,000,000, underscores the sense of commitment of the people." That 1,000,000 figure was soon reached and for the next several days continued to climb. It finally reached an official total a couple of weeks later of 1,551,687, or more than 100,000 *more* than the estimated total number of eligible voters.

As it was, the trend established on the first night never varied. The

27

Christian Democrats got 35 percent of the total vote and 40 percent of the valid ballots. By the system of proportional representation that was used, they won 24 of the 60 seats in the Constituent Assembly; ARENA got 26 percent of the valid vote and 19 seats; the PCN 17 percent and 14 seats; the three minor parties received the balance, and one of them, Democratic Action, won the remaining three seats.

Even though most of the 160,000 defaced ballots could have been taken as a vote for them, the Democratic Revolutionary Front, the co-ordinating body for all the nonviolent opposition organizations out-side the country, and the Farabundo Martí National Liberation Front, the coordinating body for the guerrilla forces, as well as their support-ers in the United States and Europe, could scarcely conceal their aston-ishment and dismay. It appeared that the campaign to get out the vote, led by Duarte and other government officials, had succeeded beyond anyone's fondest dreams.

A couple of days after the election, the five rightist parties said that they had formed their coalition and that D'Aubuisson would be the provisional president. Both Washington and the Salvadoran military made clear their opposition. Hinton let it be known that the price of installing D'Aubuisson and excluding the Christian Democrats from the government was likely to be the loss of many tens of millions of dollars in aid, a certain percentage of which always slips out of the pub-lic purse and into private pockets. In any case, senior officers preferred being nagged by the Pentagon and the State Department to taking or-ders from a young ex-major.

Several weeks of skirmishing followed. Rumors that D'Aubuisson was planning a coup circulated, but he finally yielded. A nonpolitical figure who had the backing of the military was chosen as provisional president to serve for the 18 months to two years until the election of a president for a full five-year term. He was Álvaro Alfredo Magaña, an economist trained at the University of Chicago in free market princi-ples, a former official of the Organization of American States, and for the previous 17 years president of a Salvadoran bank. The Assembly also voted to create three vice-presidents. The Christian Democrats, ARENA, and the PCN each got one. Cabinet posts were also divided. D'Aubuisson, the only party leader who had run for the Assembly, was chosen as its president.

Mindful of the interim nature of his position and his lack of political power, Magaña said he would proceed cautiously while regarding the Assembly as "the supreme power in the land." That might be so on paper, but nothing had happened to suggest that the armed forces would not continue to direct the war without civilian help and to hold a veto power over important government decisions.

The second anniversary of the murder of Archbishop Oscar Arnulfo Romero fell on March 24, four days before the election. A memorial mass was advertised in the press and then canceled. No explanation was offered, but none had to be. D'Aubuisson had been accused of complicity in his death. A public observance might have led to demonstrations and, possibly, confrontations with both the military and ARENA's strong-arm men. The decision to cancel the mass was made by the acting archbishop, Arturo Rivera y Damas. It cannot have been an easy one, since he was Romero's protégé and the only supporter of his program of social activism among El Salvador's bishops.

The Vatican, it was generally believed, had made Rivera y Damas's permanent appointment conditional on his reducing the church's involvement in temporal affairs. Rivera y Damas was thought to want the post if for no other reason than to prevent its going to a conservative who would do his best to destroy what remained of Romero's legacy. Even so, Rivera y Damas followed orders. When he touched on political and social issues in his Sunday homilies at the cathedral, his voice was muted. Compared with Romero's, it could scarcely be heard at all. Even so, Rivera y Damas let it be known that he favored government negotiations with the left, which was one of the demands of the Democratic Revolutionary Front, and the ending of arms shipments to both sides from abroad, which did not please the Salvadoran armed forces. As though to balance these positions, he countered the left's boycott of the elections by joining the three other Salvadoran bishops, all conservatives, in issuing a pastoral letter, which was read from every pulpit in the country, that stated that Catholics had a moral duty to vote.

A couple of days after the election, Rivera y Damas held a press conference. The dozen or so journalists who showed up were easily accommodated around a conference table. He was taller—six feet or so—than he seemed to be when he presided at the cathedral. His face was plain, padded by the flesh of middle age. He wore spectacles, and his hairline was receding. In his gray tropical suit, bishop's purple dickey and clerical collar, and with his air of serene caution, he seemed like a salesman of afterlife insurance.

Rivera y Damas said that he interpreted the results of the election as a repudiation of the guerrillas, that he did not think that the people

voted out of fear of the military, and that he hoped the new government would continue the reforms begun by Duarte. He denied that
there was any strain between him and the Vatican. He said that the Romero mass had not been canceled but had been held in private to avoid
the possibility of serious disorder at a time when emotions were running high. Someone wanted to know what Romero would be doing if
he were still alive.

He replied, "Things are very different now than they were in Archbishop Romero's time."

Indeed they were. For one thing, so many missionary priests had
been expelled or had left the country under threat that 40 percent of
the rural parishes had been shut down. The *comunidades de base*
(basic Christian communities) set up during Romero's day had virtually
ceased to function. Hundreds of *delegados de la palabra* ("delegates
of the word," or lay ministers) had been killed.

When it became apparent that the Christian Democrats would not
control the Constituent Assembly and would, in fact, be fortunate not
to be frozen out of the government, Duarte announced that he was
ready to yield such power as he held. He thus became a museum
specimen—a Latin American politician who, by conducting an honest
election, had created the circumstances of his defeat. Given the fact
that at that point it looked as though D'Aubuisson or some equally un-
savory character was going to take over, Duarte seemed more than
ever to be a Don Quixote who had slipped away from Cervantes and
found himself in the wrong country and the wrong century—a lost
knight errant trying to rescue the fair lady Democracia.

On the Thursday following the election, Duarte gave his valedictory
to the press. Entering the grand salon of the Presidential Palace with his
shoulders squared and a smile on his face, he said, "I came back from
exile to work for democracy, and this is only the first step on the ladder of democracy. My duty and my responsibility have not ended yet. I
can't just fade away. I made a pledge over 20 years ago, and it is not yet
fulfilled. There are a million tasks to complete, and you are going to see
a lot of Napoleón Duarte in this process. If my party wants me to run
for president, I'll be there. If they want me to sustain the reforms, to
keep democracy running, to protect human rights, I'll be doing it. Until then I am accepting the responsibility of being, humbly, the leader
of the people who believe in democracy."

He said the Assembly would have trouble if it tried to suspend or to reverse the land reform, which was the price he charged the Carter administration for entering the government in March, 1980. He said that he opposed negotiations with the insurrectionists until their actions indicated that they had learned that they could not win through violence. Duarte seemed to believe that his own good faith in giving up the presidency ought to persuade the Democratic Revolutionary Front of the good faith of the new government.

Always agreeable, calm, anxious to explain, sensing perhaps that it would be a long time before 10 television crews and 100 members of the world press gathered to ask him questions, Duarte went on for too long. Well before the press conference ended, two-thirds of his audience had drifted away.

Shortly before leaving El Salvador, I dined with a man who had been unfailingly helpful to me since my first visit and with the woman who was then his fiancée and later that year became his wife. He was well known as a supporter of the democratic left, which made him, as far as the death squads were concerned, no better than a Communist. He had nonetheless remained in the country, teaching and administering a documentation center that collected printed material about the insurrection. It was important that someone do this, he said. Ever since independence, lacunae and great gaps in the record had impeded the study of Central American history. There were many reasons for this— frequent changes of government, a relaxed attitude toward record keeping, continual wars and rebellions in which such archives as existed were often destroyed, the inadequacy of the libraries, and the pervasive corruption, which rendered suspect existing accounts and reports.

We were halfway through our meal when there was a stir among the waiters and diners. We turned to look. A party of eight was being led to a table. The maître d'hôtel and two waiters danced attendance with small skipping steps on one of them, a burly, rough-looking man who wore a pale blue leisure suit. A large gold-and-diamond ring flashed on one thick and hairy finger.

"That's Colonel [Francisco Adolfo] Castillo, the Deputy Minister of Defense," my friend whispered. "There's a street here that they call the *avenida de los coroneles* because so many colonels live on it. They don't earn enough in 10 years to buy a house here, but they manage somehow."

(Three months later the colonel's life-style changed abruptly. The guerrillas shot down his helicopter and captured him.)

For two weeks before the election and a week afterward, the death squads, which had killed at least 25,000 persons, took a holiday, thus making it clear that the killers were controllable and were not of the left. Television crews got no chance to film bodies that at other times could be found at dawn each day. One of the favorite disposal sites was a placed called El Playón, literally the big beach, about 15 miles east of San Salvador. It had long been used as a garbage dump. El Playón is an area of brown and gray volcanic rock and ash, about five miles long and a half mile wide, extruded through a crack in the surface of the earth tens of thousands of years ago. Its desolation is made even starker by the green fields that border it on both sides.

Los buitres, the vultures, presided at El Playón. I had seen them there, their wings of rusty black half-open, their naked necks thrust forward, as they tore at the bodies or parts of bodies that were left there. People went to El Playón to search for a missing son or daughter or husband only as a last resort. While they looked, fearing what they might find, the vultures flapped, hopped, limped a few yards off, staring implacably with yellow eyes. For the death squads, death was not punishment enough. Women and girls, some scarcely into their teens, and even some young men, had been raped. Bodies often bore the marks of torture. It was nothing exquisite—fingers and joints crushed by hammerblows, flesh burned away by blowtorch, large areas of skin removed by the flayer's knife. Then, at last, murder by bullet or machete and, finally, the mutilation of the corpse. At El Playón could be found severed arms and legs, limbless torsos, even bodies that had been split longitudinally. There were severed heads with mouths frozen open in terror and eyes that stared until the vultures ate them.

The Santa Ana highway bisects the length of El Playón, and one morning when René and I were driving by on our way to Juayúa, the village where the uprising that led to the *matanza* of 1932 had begun, we saw a pickup truck parked on the shoulder of the road. A man, a woman, and two young boys, forming a line parallel to the road, walked slowly along, their heads down. We stopped, and the man told us they were not searching for a loved one, but scavenging for scrap metal. The factory where he worked had closed down, and he was without other income. He brought his family to El Playón a couple of times a week, he said. On a good day they could make $8 or $10. Too bad there was no market for the bones. He revealed, with a kick, part of a rib cage under a mound of garbage. A couple of weeks before, he said, soldiers had come to bury the remains that lay about, and since then there had been no fresh ones.

"It was a good thing," he said. "This one here"—he tousled the hair of a boy of about eight—"would see them, and then he would have nightmares."

We asked him to point us toward one of the burial places, and he directed us to a natural declivity about 100 feet from the roadway. We stumbled over the rounded slippery rocks, and then it hit us. The high, hot stench of putrefaction roared out of the ground, as though driven from the furnaces of hell itself. Seeing in my mind's eye what lay beneath a foot of rock and cinder, I felt I was about to vomit. I held my breath and turned and ran back to the highway. The old sergeant major ran just as fast. At our hired car, we caught our breath and then shouted our good-byes to the scavenging family. The man waved back. He made an exaggerated gesture of holding his nose and laughed.

The dry season was ending. The sun still blazed all day; but in the morning and evening there was a hint of moisture in the air, and a few drops of rain fell. The *chicharras,* locusts, sang fortissimo all day long, as they do when Easter is coming. The people say that the three black spots on the insect's carapace are a symbol of the nails that were used in the crucifixion.

2

Under the Flag of Spain

In July, 1502, on his fourth and final voyage to the New World, Christopher Columbus discovered Central America. It was a modest, not to say anticlimactic, conclusion to a great career. Columbus, no wiser than he had been 10 years earlier, was certain that the sodden coast of Honduras, where he made his landfall, was the Malay Peninsula and that he would finally find the passage to India by sailing along the coast to the southeast for a week or two. On December 23, his squadrons of four ships dropped anchor in a fine harbor at the mouth of a swiftly flowing river. The city that now stands there bears the name Colón, the Spanish form of Columbus's surname. It is the eastern terminus of the Panama Canal. The Pacific Ocean, which was unknown to Columbus, lay less than 50 miles away, beyond the rank and malarial swamps and jungled mountains of the isthmus.

By then Columbus was confronted with all the old familiar problems. His ships were being eaten by worms, the sails were rotting, food was giving out, the crews were mutinous, and he was shaking with malaria. The time had come, he decided, to return to Spain. As he beat across the Caribbean, first one ship and then another were lost. In the passage between Cuba and Jamaica, a third began to sink. Columbus managed to beach both ships in a Jamaican cove. There he was marooned for more than 12 months.

When he finally arrived at Seville in November, 1504, he learned that Queen Isabella, his patron, had died two weeks before. Seeking the redress of numerous grievances, real or fancied, he remained with the royal court for 12 months as it traveled from city to city. King Ferdinand, who had never shared his late wife's enthusiasm for the Genoese explorer, rejected most of his demands. In Valladolid, Columbus fell ill, and in May, 1506, at the age of 55, he died.

A settlement was established in Panama in 1508. It was on the point of collapse when Vasco Núñez de Balboa turned up as a stowaway on a supply ship from Santo Domingo. Within months, he had deposed the governor and taken command himself. He treated the Indians humanely, and in the way of simple savages the world over, they happily traded pearls and gold for beads and calico. Balboa had also heard reports of the great ocean that lay nearby. In 1513, he led an expedition across the isthmus. He claimed the Pacific Ocean, which he called the South Sea, and all the lands it touched for Spain. Balboa's discovery finally laid to rest the notion that the islands of the Caribbean lay anywhere near Asia.

In Spain, Ferdinand, having heard the complaint of the ousted governor, ordered Balboa's removal. The arrival of news of his great discovery as well as the king's share, the royal fifth, of the gold and pearls caused the king to change his mind. Balboa was confirmed as the governor of the Pacific side of the isthmus. A courtier, Pedro Arias de Ávila, was sent out to govern the Atlantic side. Balboa and Arias got along for a while as well as any two arrogant and ambitious *hidalgos* could. Balboa even married Arias de Ávila's daughter. Four years later, however, Arias began to suspect Balboa of treachery. Arias lured him to his side of the isthmus, arrested him, tried him, found him guilty, denied his right of appeal to the crown, and had him beheaded.

In 1519, Hernán Cortés, heading a force of 508 men, with horses and cannon, landed at the harbor on the Mexican coast that he named Veracruz. Within two years, aided by Indian allies, he had destroyed the Aztec empire. After that, the conquest proceeded rapidly. Cortés sent Pedro de Alvarado marching south through Guatemala and El Salvador, which he conquered by playing off the warring tribes of the old Mayan nation against one another. In El Salvador, he met Ávila de Arias marching north. The two fought. There were probably fewer than 1,000 Spanish on the mainland, but it was already too small for them.

By the middle of the 16th century, Mexico, Central America, present-day Colombia, Venezuela, and Peru were under Spanish control. The Indians were enslaved in all but name. (Their status was a subject of learned debate at the Spanish court.) Under the whip they were working the great *haciendas* that Ferdinand and his successors awarded to the *conquistadores* and to their appointed officials and were mining the silver and gold that enabled Spain to become the defender of Catholic orthodoxy against the Protestant Reformation and Islam.

35

With the ascension of Elizabeth in 1558, England took the offensive. Privateers, of whom Sir Francis Drake was the most formidable, captured treasure galleons and sacked the ports from which the gold was shipped. There was economic warfare as well. Spain tried to monopolize trade with the colonies, but it remained a backward and feudal country. The goods it sold them had to be purchased elsewhere in Europe. Drake's defeat of the Spanish Armada in the English Channel in 1588 saved England from invasion and cost Spain control of the seas. After that, England, the Netherlands, and France, with the connivance of corrupt colonial officials, sold their cloth, ironware, cheeses, and fine wines direct, eliminating the Spanish middleman.

Meanwhile, the Indian population, and the colonial economy with it, were being destroyed by harsh treatment and diseases like measles and smallpox. They had been unknown before the conquest, and the Indians had no resistance to them. Between 1500 and 1620, the Indian population was wiped out in Cuba and Hispaniola. In Central America and Mexico, which had a population estimated at 25,000,000 to 50,000,000, it fell to 1,000,000 and recovered only slowly.

From the middle of the 16th century onward, the shortage of labor, the playing out of many mines, and the depredations of pirates, privateers, and rival navies steadily reduced the amount of gold and silver reaching Spain. As the treasure declined, so did Spanish power. Nonetheless, Spain continued to govern its dominions in the same old way. Only *peninsulares,* men of Spanish birth, could hold government posts above the rank of clerk. Senior officials had to buy their jobs from the crown, to make their fortunes in five or 10 years by illegal means, and then to return to Spain and give others a chance.

Clerical preferment was also for sale, but only to *peninsulares.* The church grew fat on the revenues from enormous landholdings. The New World was the Big Rock Candy Mountain for the Spanish clergy. By the middle of the 18th century, of Mexico City's population of 60,000, no fewer than 8,000 were in holy orders.

One purpose of this system of government was to prevent officials from identifying themselves as Mexicans or Guatemalans, say, rather than as Spaniards. It was costly otherwise, but on that level it worked for 250 years. However, by the middle of the 18th century, the *criollos,* as persons born in the New World of unimpeachably European parents were called, were noisily opposing this discrimination. From the time of the French and American revolutions, talk of independence was heard more frequently in the Spanish possessions.

Neither *peninsulares* nor *criollos* were even remotely concerned with the welfare of the Indians and *mestizos* who formed the overwhelming majority of the population. From the days of the *conquistadores, mestizos,* a term that derives from the verb *mestizar,* to crossbreed, were the offspring of unsanctified unions between Spanish men, who brought few women of their own with them, and Indian women. *Mestizos* remained on the fringes of society until long after independence. Nowadays, with the decline in the number of unassimilated Indians, persons with some admixture of Indian blood are thought to constitute something like 90 percent of the population of Mexico, Central America, and the northern states of South America. *Mestizos* have been called *la raza nueva,* the new race. That may or may not be so, but persons who can plausibly claim entirely European ancestry still dominate government and society, business and the professions.

Spain was at war, recovering from war, or preparing for war throughout most of the 18th century, and it was almost never a winner. In 1762, for example, Spain invaded Portugal, which was an ally of Great Britain's. Britain, which was already at war with France, declared war on Spain and defeated them both. France ceded Canada to Britain. Spain, in order to retrieve Havana, which a British fleet had captured, gave up its claims to all lands lying east of the Mississippi. By way of compensation, France ceded to Spain the Louisiana territory lying west of the Mississippi. In 1793, Britain persuaded Spain to go to war against revolutionary France. Spain thereby lost the eastern region of Hispaniola, the present-day Dominican Republic. In 1796, Spain allied itself with France against Britain, lost again, and had to give up Trinidad and Tobago. In 1799, Napoleon persuaded Spain to give back Louisiana in exchange for his promise to enlarge the duchy of Parma, which was then a Spanish possession.

And so it went, with Spain bouncing between Britain and France and losing something with every change of sides. In 1807, Napoleon occupied Portugal and parts of northern Spain. The next year, an anti-French rebellion forced Charles IV to abdicate in favor of his son, Ferdinand VII. A French force occupied Madrid. Napoleon, dazzling the world with his diplomacy, required Ferdinand to abdicate in favor of Charles, who then was persuaded to abdicate in favor of Napoleon, who then abdicated in favor of his brother Joseph.

With a Corsican usurper on the Spanish throne, many colonial officials decided, as a matter of loyalty to their deposed monarch, that they had no choice but to seek some sort of independence. They spoke of finding a king of their own among Europe's unemployed princelings. *Criollos,* on the other hand, taking the United States as their model, began to talk not only of independence but also of an end to royal and clerical absolutism. One of the *criollo* leaders was a Venezuelan named Simón Bolívar. He had studied in Spain, France, and Italy and had seen Napoleon's rise to power at first hand. Bolívar returned to Caracas by way of the United States to join the independence movement.

In 1812, the British drove the French from Spain. Ferdinand was returned to his throne. He swore to uphold a new constitution that limited his powers, but after Waterloo, he changed his mind, and restored a bloody despotism. In Spanish America, however, the *peninsulares* could not turn back the clock. In Mexico, a rebellion led by a priest, Miguel Hidalgo y Costilla, had begun in 1810. He was captured and shot, but the uprising spread across the country. Indians and *mestizos,* promised freedom and justice, joined the fight. Ferdinand sent troops to suppress the insurrection, and by 1815, after much of central Mexico had been laid waste, they succeeded.

Venezuela, led by Bolívar, declared its independence in 1811, but the rebellion was put down within a year. The reason for the defeat, Bolívar wrote in his "Cartagena Letter," was dissension among his comrades rather than Spanish power. "As yet our fellow citizens are not in a condition to exercise their rights," he wrote, "for they lack the political virtues which characterize a true republic and which can never be acquired under an absolute government."

In 1814, Bolívar withdrew to Jamaica, trying without success to gain British support. In his "Jamaica Letter," he wrote that he hoped that a few great republics would emerge in Spanish America, but he feared there would be many weak ones. By 1817, Bolívar was back on the mainland, organizing an army. Many of its members were English and Irish volunteers. In 1819, Bolívar entered Bogotá in triumph and proclaimed the republic of Greater Colombia, comprising Colombia, Venezuela, and Ecuador, with himself as president and temporary military dictator.

Ferdinand, like most of the Spanish Bourbons, had turned out to be extremely stupid as well as despotic. (Goya's famous portrait shows a lumpish figure swathed in velvet and ermine, macrocephalic, with a prognathous jaw and dim, suspicious eyes.) He dismissed ministers who told him that Spain lacked the strength to subdue rebellions from

Buenos Aires to Mexico City and that only by sharing power with the colonies might it be able to keep them. The army, aware of the impossibility of the task it had been given, turned against the king. In 1820, the junior officers of an expeditionary force mutinied at Cádiz. The rebellion spread, and within months, the liberals had returned to power and readopted the constitution of 1812.

By 1822, Bolívar and José de San Martín, the commander in Argentina and Uruguay, were victorious almost everywhere. When the two heroes finally met, they loathed each other on sight, and San Martín left for Europe, never to return. In 1825, Bolívar and his deputy, Antonio José de Sucre, defeated the Spanish armies in Peru, their last bastion. Bolívar had written years earlier that he feared peace more than war, and once again, he was proved to be correct. In less than a year, Greater Colombia had begun to dissolve in a corrosive solution of jealousy and greed, personal ambition, and sectional rivalry. In an effort to save his creation, Bolívar again took dictatorial power, and civil war broke out. In 1829, Venezuela seceded from Greater Colombia. In a final effort to reunite the nation, Bolívar convened a congress in Bogotá and called Sucre out of retirement to assist him. The congress failed, and Sucre was assassinated as he returned home.

Already ill with tuberculosis, Bolívar decided to leave for Europe. As he waited on the coast to embark, he received a plea from an old comrade-in-arms, General Juan José Flores, to return to Bogotá. In refusing, he gave his mordant verdict on the people for whom he had gained independence. "After fighting for 20 years," he wrote, "I have reached a few definite conclusions. First, America is ungovernable for us. Second, he who serves a revolution plows the seas. Third, the only thing that can be done in America is to emigrate. This country will fall into the hands of an unruly multitude and then into the rule of petty tyrants."

Unlike the states of South America, which fought for it, Mexico achieved independence by duplicity. In February, 1821, using a shipment of stolen government silver as capital, Agustín de Iturbide, the commander of the royalist army that was hunting down Vicente Guerrero, one of the last of the rebels still in the field, proclaimed Mexico's independence as a monarchy that was to be ruled by a Bourbon prince. Guerrero joined him, and in September, they entered Mexico City without resistance. Iturbide made himself the interim head of government. Deciding that he was as good as any Bourbon, he proclaimed himself Emperor Agustín I in May, 1822. In March, 1823, Guerrero and

Guadalupe Victoria, another of the rebel leaders, forced him to abdicate and proclaimed a republic. Iturbide went into exile. He tried a comeback in 1824 but was quickly captured and shot.

In Spain, the liberal government was soon reduced to squabbling factions. In 1823, Ferdinand's cousin Louis XVIII sent an army to rescue him from the clutches of constitutionalism. A new reign of terror began. Many members of the Cortes, the legislature, were executed. The leader of the military rebellion was hanged, drawn, and quartered. Ferdinand still hoped to restore his rule in the Americas. France and Russia, his allies in the so-called Holy Alliance of absolute monarchies, agreed to help.

George Canning, the British Foreign Secretary, conveyed his country's unalterable objections to the three powers. He conferred with Richard Rush, the Ambassador of the United States. In Washington, his cousin Stratford Canning, the British Ambassador, met with Secretary of State John Quincy Adams. Britain, which already was dominating trade with the new nations, sought a joint declaration of opposition to any attempt by Spain to reimpose its rule. Adams did not believe the new nations would ever amount to much. In arguing successfully for neutrality during their wars of independence, he had stated that he saw "no prospect that they would establish free or liberal institutions of government. Arbitrary power, military and ecclesiastical, was stamped upon their habits, and upon all their institutions. Civil dissension was infused into all their seminal principles."

Anticipating that Britain might someday wish to hoist its flag over the weak and anarchic nations, Adams instructed Rush to seek a joint guarantee against *any* European interference. Meanwhile, France assured Britain that it would do nothing to help Spain. The Holy Alliance was no match for the Royal Navy, which had been supreme since defeating the French-Spanish fleet at Trafalgar in 1805. With the French statement, the threat of invasion ended.

President James Monroe was inclined to accept the British proposal. Adams decided that setting an independent course would not harm his chances for the presidency the next year. At a Cabinet meeting in November, 1823, Adams stated, as he wrote in his *Diary,* "It would be more candid as well as more dignified to avow our principles explicitly to Russia and France, than to come in as a cock-boat in the wake of the British man-of-war." Monroe agreed and said he would announce his new policy in a message to Congress.

In his message, delivered on December 2, 1823, Monroe pointed out that the United States had removed itself from the quarrels of the European powers. He did not mention that any other course would have been absurd and dangerous. The United States was still a poor and thinly populated nation, with no navy to speak of and a standing army about the size of a European fortress garrison. He went on to say, "We owe it, therefore, to candor and to the amicable relations existing between the United States and those powers to declare that we should consider any attempt on their part to extend their system to any portion of this hemisphere as dangerous to our peace and safety. . . ." Monroe said that the European states could keep the colonies they already had, but that any attempt by any European power to oppress the independent states of the hemisphere would be regarded "as the manifestation of an unfriendly disposition toward the United States."

In Europe, as Dexter Perkins notes in *A History of the Monroe Doctrine,* the speech was regarded, given the United States' lack of means, as so much hot air. Moreover, he points out, the newly independent nations probably feared the intervention of the United States more than they did a return of the Holy Alliance. They had already been sounding out Britain as their guardian against both. In the 15 years after Monroe spoke, Washington chose to ignore several instances of European intervention. For example, in 1833, Britain seized the Falkland Islands from Argentina, and in 1838, it enlarged British Honduras at the expense of Guatemala. In neither case did Washington protest. Not until the middle of the century did Monroe's statement acquire the quasi-religious status of a doctrine.

Central America looked on with a certain rustic detachment during the wars of independence. San Salvador, which even then was known as the most troublesome city in the region, was the center of such anti-Spanish agitation as existed. Its leaders were José Matías Delgado and his nephew, Manuel José Arce. Delgado, a priest, was ineligible, as a *criollo,* to become a bishop. He thought his chances would improve with independence.

When Iturbide proclaimed himself emperor of Mexico, Central Americans began to worry. As the successor to the viceroys, he might claim authority over them. A speedy declaration of independence seemed to provide the best chance of preventing that from happening. Thus, in September, 1821, Guatemala, speaking for the states of the captaincy general, cut its ties with Spain and Mexico. Delgado and Arce objected. They didn't want to be ruled by Spain, by Mexico, or, least of all, by Guatemala. So, a week later, they proclaimed El Salvador independent of everyone. When Sonsonate and Santa Ana, the principal towns of the western region, declined to join them, Delgado and Arce sent troops to enforce their decree, but a Guatemalan force, sent to protect the towns, chased them away.

When Iturbide announced in 1821 that he was about to invade Central America, Guatemala quickly agreed to the annexation by Mexico of the territory of the captaincy general. Delgado and Arce once again refused to permit Guatemala to decide their future for them. When Iturbide actually sent troops to Guatemala, Arce and Delgado, clutching at straws, sent an urgent appeal to Washington. They asked for the establishment of a protectorate or, failing that, for outright annexation.

The Mexican force soon reached Guatemala City and kept right on marching. When it arrived in San Salvador, Arce, anticipating events, warned the commander that he probably was trespassing on the territory of the United States. The commander stayed where he was. When several months had passed without a reply from Monroe, Arce decided to present his case in person. No sooner had he sailed than Iturbide was overthrown. The Mexican troops withdrew, Guatemala reclaimed its independence, and Arce took the next ship home.

By then, Central America, which did not yet know that it was being protected by Britain and the United States, was worrying about the arrival of a Spanish army. Union seemed to provide its only hope of survival. So it was that on July 1, 1823, delegates gathered at Guatemala City and proclaimed the formation of the United Provinces of Central America, comprising Guatemala, El Salvador, Honduras, Nicaragua, and Costa Rica. In 1824, a constitution was drawn up. Thomas L. Karnes in *The Failure of Union: Central America, 1824–1960* notes that it bore striking similarities to the Constitution of the United States. The document changed the name of the new country to the Federal Republic of Central America, established a Congress and a Supreme Court, and promulgated a bill of rights. Slavery, titles of nobility, the inquisition, and the most onerous of the Spanish taxes were abolished.

However, the republic turned out to have three fatal defects. The first was that its leading citizens, then as now, did not relate the adopting of laws to the obeying of them. The second was that the constitution described the five former components of the captaincy general as sovereign states rather than as parts of one sovereign state. The third was that the Central American Republic failed to replace the discontinued Spanish taxes with any of its own. It was authorized to issue currency but had almost no sources of income. The Central American Republic, in short, was not a nation and would continue not being one until its dissolution in 1839.

For the moment, the republic could ignore these problems. In 1825, Arce, who by then was styling himself a Liberal, was elected as its first president. His defeated rival, a Guatemalan Conservative, thereupon sounded the cry that has been echoing through the region ever since. He said that he had been cheated and started an uprising. Arce, having no other means of defraying the costs of suppressing the revolt, not to mention the ordinary expenses of government, floated a loan from a London banking house. This transaction was also to be repeated many times down to the present. Because of the risk involved, the amount of cash provided by the lender was considerably less than the face amount of the loan and the interest rate was usurious. On the other hand, the loan was not repaid, and the banking house failed.

Amid the turmoil, Arce did not forget his uncle, but Rome refused to make him, or anyone else in San Salvador, a bishop. Believing that Pope Leo XII had been led astray by enemies in Guatemala City, Arce persuaded the Salvadoran Assembly that it had the power to create the bishopric and put Delgado in the job. It did so, provoking a brief and indecisive war with Guatemala. Delgado continued to wear his dubious robes until 1826, when the Pope declared that he and Arce would be excommunicated and all of El Salvador placed under an interdict unless he ceased his scandalous and impious behavior. Delgado yielded, but once roused, papal wrath was slow to cool. Not until 1842, with the Conservatives in power, was the bishopric granted.

In 1826, the Central American Republic began its slide from confusion into chaos. Arce abandoned the Liberals and allied himself with the Conservatives. The war between El Salvador and Guatemala resumed, and civil war began in Nicaragua. The Liberals found a new leader in a Honduran landowner named Francisco Morazán. He defeated the Conservatives in Guatemala City, their stronghold, and, in 1829, became president of the republic. Conservative leaders were shot or exiled, and the capital was moved to San Salvador.

Morazán, who was fiercely anticlerical, ousted the Guatemalan archbishop, suppressed three monastic orders that he said had fallen into slothful and concupiscent ways, seized church funds, and melted down the altar silver for coinage. Tithing was abolished, and civil marriage and divorce were legalized. For the next eight years, fighting erupted sporadically in all parts of the republic except Costa Rica. In 1831, the Conservatives captured San Salvador but were quickly driven out. Morazán spent most of his time in the saddle, at the head of hastily gathered military expeditions, comprising perhaps 50 white officers, the sons of leading Liberals, and a thousand or two ragged *mestizos* and Indians armed with machetes and rusty muskets. The fighting was as savage as it was primitive. Then as now, prisoners, even the wounded, were, as often as not, shot or cut to pieces.

In 1837, a cholera epidemic struck Guatemala. Priests told the credulous Indians that the Liberals had poisoned the water. One of those who heard and perhaps believed the rumor was the commander of a handful of troops named Rafael Carrera. He was a barely literate *mestizo* of about 25. Ten years earlier, he had been a drummer boy in the Guatemalan army that opposed Morazán. At the head of a mob of angry and frightened Indians, he fought his way into Guatemala City. The sight of a *mestizo* in command of any sort of military force frightened both Conservatives and Liberals, all of whom were, or pretended to be, of pure European descent. They awarded Carrera $1,000 and distributed $10,000 among his troops on condition that he accept the command of the remote district whence he had come.

No sooner had Carrera withdrawn than Morazán turned up at the head of the Liberal army. In their hour of peril, the Conservatives turned to Carrera. He was promoted to general, gathered his army, and took to the field against Morazán. The two ragged bands skirmished indecisively for the rest of 1838, but in January, 1839, Morazán defeated Carrera soundly, entered Guatemala City once again, and restored the Liberals to power. While Morazán was thus occupied, the dominant Conservative factions in Nicaragua and Honduras, encouraged by Guatemala, invaded El Salvador. While Morazán was defending El Salvador, Carrera retook Guatemala City. In March, 1840, it fell to Morazán. Carrera recaptured it the next day. By now, support for Morazán and for the republic had vanished, even in El Salvador. Hotly pursued by Carrera, he made it to the Pacific coast and caught a ship for Panama.

In 1842, Morazán responded to an appeal from Costa Rica to help it remove a self-proclaimed dictator for life. When he succeeded, he was appointed president. Morazán immediately began planning to resume the fight for federation. When the Costa Ricans learned what he was up to, they removed him from office. Morazán raised a rebellion, but it failed, and he was captured and executed.

The best account of the events of 1839–40 is provided by John L. Stephens's *Incidents of Travel in Central America, Chiapas, and Yucatán.* Stephens, a New York lawyer and writer, served as special envoy of the United States to the Central American Republic. He arrived in Guatemala City shortly after Carrera had vanquished Morazán for what turned out to be the last time. After attending a meeting of the Assembly, which, without debate, reimposed tithing, Stephens wrote, "There was but one side to politics in Guatemala. Both parties have a beautiful way of producing unanimity of opinion, by driving out of the country all who do not agree with them. If there were any Liberals, I did not meet them, or they did not dare to open their lips."

Carrera became the region's first *caudillo,* or chief. He ruled Guatemala from 1839, with a three-year hiatus, until his death in 1865. He also used his control of Central America's richest and most populous state to help Conservatives keep power during much of the same period and for many years thereafter in El Salvador, Honduras, and Nicaragua.

From Guatemala, Stephens pushed eastward into El Salvador in search of Morazán, generally arriving somewhere a day or two after Morazán had left. In the course of his search, Stephens encountered a retired officer of the Royal Navy who had been retained by the Central American Republic to survey a canal route across Nicaragua. The man, who complained that he hadn't been paid, showed Stephens his maps, elevations, and cross sections. Stephens, persuaded by him, wrote that the steamboat made an isthmian canal an inevitability.

After seven months of looking for someone to whom he could present his presidential commission, Stephens decided to return home. "I could not conceal from myself that the Federal Government was broken up," he wrote. "There was not the least prospect of its ever being restored, nor, for a long time to come, of any other being organized in its stead."

In 1845, John L. O'Sullivan, a New York lawyer and editor, arguing for the annexation of Texas, wrote that it was the "manifest destiny"— meaning clear, unmistakable, obvious—of the United States to expand to the Pacific. The term caught on and became a guide for action. A year later, the United States acquired the Oregon Territory, which stretched from the California border to the present Canadian border, by negotiation from Great Britain, and in 1848, at the conclusion of the Mexican War, California and the Southwest came under the Stars and Stripes. In 1849, the California gold rush began, and Cornelius

Vanderbilt, the "commodore" from Staten Island who had turned a harbor skiff into a transportation empire, began promoting a shortcut to the Pacific coast. Steamers made the run from New York to San Juan del Norte on the Miskito, or Mosquito, Coast of Nicaragua. From there, passengers and freight were carried on smaller steamboats up the San Juan River and across Lake Nicaragua. The final 30 miles to the Pacific coast, where another steamer awaited them, was done by stagecoach.

Tens of thousands of fortune hunters, all but a few of whom would spend far more gold than they would find, were streaming westward. No matter what fare Vanderbilt charged, his route was certain to be cheaper and faster than the 8,000-mile detour around South America. However, to get his project moving, he needed the approval of Great Britain, the dominant power all along Central America's Caribbean coast, and he went to London to get it. By doing so, he angered President James K. Polk. The President didn't think that British approval was necessary to create the most convenient route to California and Oregon across what, after all, was supposed to be an independent country. With Polk's encouragement, a rival syndicate was formed. Polk also instructed Secretary of State John M. Clayton to tell the British minister, Henry Bulwer, that by enlarging its territories in the hemisphere, Britain was in noncompliance with the Monroe Doctrine. It appears to have been the first time that the doctrine was actually invoked. Britain was inclined to be conciliatory, and in April, 1850, the Clayton-Bulwer Treaty was signed. The two governments agreed to exercise joint control over any Central American canal and to refrain from establishing colonies or imposing their authority over any of the states of the region. In 1860, after quibbling, Britain transferred the Bay Islands to Honduras and formally renounced its protectorate over the Miskito Coast, although it continued in fact for another 30 years.

In 1850, John Lloyd Stephens formed a syndicate of New York bankers and merchants that put up the money for a railroad across the Isthmus of Panama in competition to Vanderbilt's Nicaraguan steamer-and-stagecoach route. The concession granted to Stephens's company by Colombia, of which Panama was then a part, also covered other means of transportation across the isthmus. Stephens took personal charge of construction. Like thousands of others, he was struck down by the virulent fevers that raged there, and in 1852, he died. The railroad was not completed until 1855, three years behind schedule. It cost $8,000,000 for 47.5 miles of single track, six times the estimated figure. It was, nonetheless, enormously profitable. In its first six years of operation, it made back virtually its entire cost. The success of the railroad and the work of its surveyors, which showed that there was a gap in the continental divide only 275 feet above sea level, half the previously estimated height, stimulated interest in Panama as the eventual site of a canal.

Despite the Clayton-Bulwer Treaty, intrigues between Britain and the United States continued in Nicaragua, the former using the Conservatives as cat's-paws, and the latter the Liberals. Like all out-of-power parties throughout Central America's history, the Liberals were plotting a rebellion. Washington encouraged them. The Liberals thereupon hired an odd character named William Walker to help them to seize power. Walker, a Tennesseean who rejoiced in the sobriquet "the grey-eyed man of destiny," had failed not long before in an attempt to establish an independent republic in northern Mexico. With 56 men whom he had recruited in San Francisco and who were armed and paid by Vanderbilt's rivals, Walker landed on Nicaragua's Pacific coast in 1855.

Assisted by a force of Liberals, he captured Granada, the Conservative stronghold, and installed a Liberal president who was immediately recognized by the United States. At Walker's direction, the president confiscated Vanderbilt's business and turned it over to the other group. The Liberals may have assumed that Walker would now pick up his check and go home, but he installed himself as Minister of Defense and sent word to the United States that land and glory awaited men who were willing to fight for them. More than 2,000, many of them veterans of the Mexican War, responded to his call. No one is certain what Walker had in mind. Some historians think he hoped to have Nicaragua admitted to the Union as a slave state. More likely, he wanted to make himself the ruler of Nicaragua and perhaps of all Central America as the viceroy of the United States.

The glow began to rub off Walker's fantasy in 1856. The other Central American states, all of which had Conservative governments, sent troops to oppose him. Britain provided arms and money. When the puppet president resigned, Walker appointed himself to the post. Astonishingly, he was recognized by the United States. Hoping to stimulate southern support, Walker reimposed slavery.

With arms and ammunition available from abroad, the fighting was more prolonged and severe than was usual in Central America. The durability of the anti-Walker coalition was without precedent. A British blockade shut off Walker's supplies, and cholera broke out among his men. In May, 1857, Walker and the last of his American volunteers surrendered and boarded an American warship for return to the United States.

Twice more Walker returned to Central America, the last time in 1860. Britain had just agreed to return the Bay Islands to Honduras. The inhabitants, who didn't want to go, asked his help in establishing an independent republic. Walker gathered a small force and occupied a town on the Honduran coast. British marines were landed. He was captured, turned over to the Honduran authorities, and executed.

3
On to the Isthmus

BETWEEN 1860 and 1890, more or less, while the United States was pre-occupied by the Civil War and Reconstruction, westward expansion, European immigration, and industrial development, Central America had to get by on its own. It didn't do badly. The annual incidence of wars, rebellions, punitive expeditions, vendettas, coups d'état, plagues, and earthquakes stayed about the same, and landowners found a crop they could make money on. It was coffee, for which Europe and the United States were developing an unappeasable craving. Coffee and Central America were made for each other. The altitude of the *meseta,* the central plateau, ranged from 2,000 to 6,000 feet, at which coffee grows best. It also had a frost-free climate, rich volcanic soil, hillsides for shade, and the large labor force required to pick the crop. The harvest increased almost without interruption from 1860 until the start of the First World War. Even so, supply did not overtake demand. The price continued to rise, and profits were enormous.

The coffee boom made Central America a significant part of the world economy for the first time. The old landowners, including the church, had been slow to see it coming. They dozed along, operating self-sufficient *haciendas*, as they had since the land was settled. A new class of men who knew markets and shipping schedules and, most important, had access to European credit, arose. They leveraged land purchases, built the *beneficios* where the coffee was processed, the wharves, and the warehouses, and set up the banks and trading companies. In each of the five countries the new men soon gained control of the old Liberal party, and by the 1870's, the Liberals were in power. The new Liberals were anticlerical, but unlike Morazán and the Liberals of an earlier generation, their opposition to the church was practical rather than philosophical. Some may have invoked positivism, social

49

Darwinism, and progressivism, but what they wanted was the church's land.

The new men argued that the time had come to remove the dead hand of the clergy not only from its control of education and censorship, marriage and divorce but also from agriculture. The inefficient management of clerical properties, they declared, was keeping Central America poor. Laws were passed, decrees issued, and the expropriations took place. When the land was put up for sale, the new men usually ended up with the best parcels, and at remarkably reasonable prices.

Something similar happened with the *ejidos,* the land held in common by Indian communities. Until the 1880's these holdings did not stir anyone's covetousness. They were generally remote from the population centers, hilly and less fertile than the lands of the central plateau. However, they were particularly well suited for coffee. The new men argued that the *ejidos* were also obsolete. The land, they said, should be divided among the members of each community. That way, spurred by the profit motive, the Indians could finally make some money. The trouble was that the Indians did not necessarily grasp the principle of private ownership. They lacked capital, they understood little Spanish, they were improvident, they had a fatal weakness for alcohol, and the new men controlled the government and the courts. Under the circumstances, it was scarcely surprising that much of the divided land was quickly lost, either sold by the Indians for quick cash, foreclosed for debt, or simply taken by the new men's *pistoleros.*

With the dispersal of the *ejidos,* Indian society began to disintegrate, except in the highlands of Guatemala. The Indians became entirely dependent on the benevolence of the owners of the coffee *fincas.* They could count themselves fortunate to get year-round work that provided them with a hut and plot on which to grow corn and beans. Because these jobs had become desirable, the coffee planters gradually abandoned the peonage system. There was no need for it. To get the seasonal labor they needed for harvesting, the new men passed what they called vagrancy laws, requiring the army of landless *campesinos* to put in a certain number of days a year working for them.

Guatemala's first Liberal *caudillo* came to power in 1873. He was Justo Rufino Barrios, a lawyer and commander of troops during the long struggle for power that followed Carrera's death. Carrera had exalted the clergy; Barrios persecuted them. He expelled the Jesuits, who were foreigners, and when the archbishop protested Barrios's seizure of church lands, Barrios expelled him, too. Barrios wanted unification, and since Guatemala was the largest and strongest nation in Central America, he was prepared to bring it about by force if necessary. In 1876, he called a meeting in Guatemala to discuss the matter. Disapproving of the attitude of the Salvadoran delegate, he invaded El Salvador and ousted the government. It made no difference. The other governments were masters of evasion. Agreements were initialed in principle, submitted for ratification, disputed, amended, rejected in favor of substitute proposals, which were tabled for further discussion, until roaches had eaten or dampness disintegrated the very parchment on which they were written.

Barrios bought a shipload of rifles and field guns, established a military academy, and hired the most eminent warriors of Europe as the faculty. In 1885, he issued an ultimatum—voluntary unification or else. Only Honduras, which was going through a period of chain reaction coups, supported him. El Salvador, Nicaragua, and Costa Rica formed a defensive alliance and shouted for help. Porfirio Díaz, the Mexican dictator, who had no interest in being sandwiched between the United States and a potentially less weak and divided Central America, mobilized troops on the Guatemalan border. The United States dispatched five warships to Guatemala's Pacific coast. Barrios was not deterred. He invaded El Salvador at the head of his troops and was marching triumphantly on San Salvador when he was killed by a sniper's bullet. The Salvadorans counterattacked, and the leaderless Guatemalans didn't stop running until they were back home again.

In 1889, the five nations announced that the Republic of Central America had finally been created and would take effect the following year. A few months later the president of El Salvador, a supporter of the scheme, was assassinated. His successor pulled out, the plan collapsed, and Guatemala again invaded El Salvador. In 1895, El Salvador, Nicaragua, and Honduras proclaimed the Greater Republic of Central America, with themselves as members. An ambassador was sent to Washington to request recognition. The Cleveland administration agreed, just as soon as the little matter of the external debts of the three countries was taken care of. Who was going to pay? On that question unity foundered.

Although every imaginable approach and combination of countries had been tried without success, Central American foreign ministries continued to call meetings on unification. From time to time they would announce that they were on the brink of a breakthrough. They weren't, but government officials got a chance to look busy and sound important and to get away from home occasionally at government expense.

In the same way, every fall, while waiting for the coffee to ripen, or in the spring, after it had been picked, the thousands of colonels and generals in the armies of the Central American countries would rally their barefoot militias and set out to vindicate national honor against whatever neighboring nation or nations had most recently outraged it. The number of combinations that can be made with five armies—one against one, two against one, three against one, four against one, and three against two—is in the hundreds. A look at even an incomplete list of Central American conflicts suggests that all of them have been tried at least once. In his *El Salvador,* for example, Alastair White cites a study by a Salvadoran historian who counted 42 conflicts, not counting internal uprisings, in which his country had been involved, from independence down to the Football War with Honduras in 1969.

Between 1870 and 1875, the United States sent seven expeditions to Central America to survey possible canal routes. Both the San Juan River–Lake Nicaragua and the Isthmus of Panama routes had supporters. But no action was taken, and in 1878, the Colombian government sold the Panama concession to a company organized by Ferdinand de Lesseps, the builder of the Suez Canal, and financed by the sale of stock, primarily to the French public.

No sooner had construction begun than the United States began to feel uneasy. American troops had been sent several times, with the permission of the Colombian government, to protect the Panama railroad during periods of civil disturbance. It seemed likely that at some point De Lesseps would also need troops and that he was more likely to request them from Paris than from Washington. Anticipating this possibility, President Rutherford B. Hayes declared in 1880 that the United States would not "surrender" control of the canal to any European power or powers, ignoring the fact that the United States couldn't surrender what it didn't possess.

"An interoceanic canal would be the great ocean thoroughfare between our Atlantic and Pacific shores, and virtually a part of the coastline of the United States," Hayes stated. "Our merely commercial interest in it is greater than that of all other countries, while its relations to our power and prosperity as a nation, to our means of defense, our unity, peace, and safety, are matters of paramount concern. . . ."

The French government made clear its displeasure, but De Lesseps was overjoyed. He interpreted Hayes's statement to mean that the United States was prepared to defend the canal, presumably without charge, when the formality of building it had been attended to. By 1882, the great earthmovers had been shipped to Panama, tens of thousands of workers, mainly West Indians and Chinese, had been hired, and construction had begun. De Lesseps continued to radiate optimism, but it was clear within a couple of years that the canal was in trouble. The planning had been faulty, the financing inadequate, and the death toll, caused mainly by yellow fever, was disastrously high. By 1887, the company, after having spent $287,000,000, went bankrupt.

For the United States, preventing any other power from controlling an isthmian canal turned out to be a matter of greater urgency than building one. New commissions were appointed to consider sites and to discuss the plan of construction. In 1890, Alfred Thayer Mahan had published *The Influence of Sea Power upon History,* a work that attracted worldwide attention. Mahan stated that the Caribbean was "America's Mediterranean," and that a canal was essential if the country was to fulfill its destiny as a world power. When the United States finally got around to building it, he said, bases would be needed in the Caribbean for its defense.

The American Mediterranean was subject to political squalls, especially in the vicinity of Hispaniola. Nonstop civil war raged in Haiti and the Dominican Republic. Loans negotiated by earlier governments fell into arrears, bringing bill collectors from Germany and France who arrived in warships. Cuba, on which Washington had looked covetously since the 1840's, had been becoming increasingly dissatisfied with autocratic and inefficient Spanish rule. Armed uprisings became frequent in the 1850's. Southern politicians urged the annexation of Cuba, with its millions of black slaves, as a makeweight against the North. In 1868, after an attempt to secure reforms in Madrid had failed, the island rose in rebellion. The insurgents were not united on their objective. Some sought autonomy within the Spanish empire; others, independence; still others, to become part of the United States.

The fighting went on for 10 years and cost 200,000 lives. Spain finally granted the reforms, including the abolition of slavery, in 1886. The rebellion broke out again in 1895. It was caused in part by a financial panic in the United States that led to the repeal of a tariff preference for Cuban sugar. The colonial government could provide no remedy for sudden and severe unemployment in the island. The rebels again conducted a guerrilla war, and the Spanish authorities exacted the usual grisly reprisals. Cane fields and sugar mills were burned. American interests were not an objective, but inevitably there was destruction and loss of life. By then Cuban-American trade came to $100,000,000 a year, a very large sum at the time, and the holdings of American corporations were valued at $50,000,000. Thousands of Americans lived and worked there. William Randolph Hearst's New York *American* and Joseph Pulitzer's *World* began using atrocities in Cuba, real and invented, as circulation builders. President Grover Cleveland, a Democrat, ignoring editorial demands for war with Spain, ordered a naval patrol of the island to prevent armaments from getting to the insurgents.

President William McKinley, a Republican, who took office in 1897, was less forbearing. When riots broke out in Havana in December of that year, he dispatched the battleship *Maine* to protect American lives and property. On February 15, 1898, while the *Maine* lay at anchor off Havana, her back was broken by an explosion, and she sank with the loss of 260 lives. The Hearst press screamed that the Spanish forces had destroyed the *Maine* with a mine or torpedo, an accusation for which any proof was lacking. Madrid said that if it hadn't been an internal explosion aboard the ship, the rebels were unquestionably responsible. War fever cracked the thermometers in the United States. Spain rejected McKinley's demand for an armistice with the rebels and the appointment of the United States as mediator. McKinley then asked Congress for authority to use the armed forces to bring peace to Cuba. Congress approved and for good measure passed a resolution favoring Cuban independence. Spanish pride overmastered good sense, and on April 24, 1898, Spain declared war on the United States.

The conflict lasted only two and a half months. When it was over, half the Spanish navy lay at the bottom of Manila Bay and half on the bottom off Santiago de Cuba. Theodore Roosevelt left his post as Assistant Secretary of the Navy to organize a regiment of volunteer cavalry, the Rough Riders. Fighting as infantry in its only significant action, the regiment captured San Juan Hill outside Santiago. The press, desperate for a hero in a war that was an obvious mismatch, turned what was essentially a brisk skirmish into a titanic struggle on the order of Thermopylae or Waterloo.

The war cost Spain what remained of the overseas empire that had been conquered 400 years before. Cuba became a protectorate of the United States, and the Philippines, Puerto Rico, and Guam became possessions. Roosevelt, who had been elected governor of New York on the strength of his martial prowess, was chosen as McKinley's running mate in 1900. When McKinley was assassinated the next year, Roosevelt succeeded to the presidency.

The outcome of the Spanish-American War, in which all of the important engagements were fought at sea, appeared to confirm Mahan's theories. The importance to the United States of an isthmian canal was confirmed during every second of the 67 days it had taken the new battleship *Oregon* to steam 12,000 miles from San Francisco around Cape Horn to join the squadron that was waiting for the Spanish fleet to emerge from Santiago Bay. She got there, but only in the nick of time. Roosevelt had become a believer in Mahan, and in an isthmian canal, while serving in the Navy Department. In 1900, he had been one of the leaders of the opposition to a treaty between the United States and Britain concerning the canal. As David McCullough notes in his excellent study of the building of the canal, *The Path Between the Seas,* Britain gave up its right to joint possession and operation of a canal that had been envisioned by the treaty of 1850 in the new agreement. Britain was willing to regard Central America and the Caribbean, excluding its own possessions, as an American sphere of influence, and the time when the two countries might fight each other seemed past. Moreover, as the possessor of what were by far the largest empire, navy, and merchant fleet, Britain stood to gain greatly from the construction of the canal.

Roosevelt, who regarded American control as essential, applauded that section of the treaty, but he objected, strenuously, to the section that stated that the canal would be "free and open in time of war as in time of peace, to vessels of commerce and of war of all nations, on terms of entire equality." He pointed out that if the canal had been operating on that basis in 1898, the United States would have been obliged to permit Spanish warships to use it. Roosevelt's view prevailed, and the Senate rejected the agreement. A second version, with the offending sections deleted, was then negotiated, signed, and ratified.

There was general agreement that the canal should be built in Panama and that it should be a governmental rather than a private under-

55

taking. A railroad, which was essential to construction, already existed, and 10 or 20 percent of the excavation work had already been done by the French. Their costly machinery was still in place and was being well maintained. Price was the problem. The canal company was demanding $100,000,000 for its concession and equipment. The American negotiators were offering $40,000,000. To pay more, they said, would increase the cost of the Panama route to the point that Nicaragua would be preferable. The French, affecting outrage, said they had paid $20,000,000 to its American owners for the railroad alone and walked away from the table.

The American negotiators faced another vexing problem. Colombia refused to go beyond the terms of the original concession by yielding the full control envisioned by the treaty between Britain and the United States. The Americans, who were for once guarding public money as though it were their own, then began formal discussions with Nicaragua. It was a bluff, but neither the French, who knew that there were few potential customers for giant steam shovels and bucket conveyor systems in the Panama jungle, nor the Colombians could be certain. Muttering about Yankee piracy, the French finally accepted the $40,000,000. The Colombian Ambassador, after a protracted correspondence with Bogotá, signed a treaty in January, 1903, granting to the United States, in return for a payment of $10,000,000 and an annual rental of $250,000, control of a zone six miles wide across the isthmus for 100 years.

Roosevelt had decided that the canal was going to be his monument. Thus, his elation at having got it under way turned to a corresponding degree of rage when the Colombian government tried to renege on the deal. It said that the Ambassador had exceeded his authority and that in any case, the price was entirely inadequate. In August, 1903, the Colombian Senate unanimously rejected the treaty. The famous Roosevelt grin turned into an ominous scowl. He thought Colombia was trying to hold him up, and he may have been right. On the other hand, Colombia was just coming out of one of its civil wars, a three-year conflict in which 100,000 people were said to have died, and its government was probably more disorganized than usual.

Roosevelt was not inclined to improve the agreement, although it would have been both equitable and wise to do so. Nor did he try with sweet words to persuade Colombia to accept the original terms or to spread bribes where they would have done the most good. Instead, he decided to foment a revolution to detach Panama, which had always been a remote and restive province, from Colombia. By September, 1903, one of the three Panamanians who had been chosen to lead the fight for independence was in New York, getting his instructions from the man who had been chosen as the go-between. He was William Nelson Cromwell, a founder of Sullivan & Cromwell, a prominent Wall Street law firm; a power in the Republican party; and, not coincidentally, the French canal company's lawyer.

However, one of the Panamanians turned out to be a double agent. After a meeting with Secretary of State John Hay he told the Colombian Ambassador what was planned. The Ambassador alerted his government, which began gathering troops to send to Panama. Roosevelt, learning of this move, ordered warships to take up positions a couple of days' steaming from Colón on Panama's Atlantic coast and Balboa on the Pacific. Meanwhile, the loyal conspirators were aboard ship on their way back to Panama with the promise of recognition by the United States and a $100,000 bonus for themselves as soon as the rebellion began. On November 5, 1903, under the protective guns of the cruiser *Nashville*, the rioting started on schedule in Colón. The next day 400 marines were landed, ostensibly to protect American lives and property, and the independence of Panama was proclaimed.

Before leaving Washington, the Panamanian freedom fighters had been persuaded to appoint Philippe Bunau-Varilla, the French canal company's representative in the United States, as their interim diplomatic agent. Realizing belatedly that Reynard was guarding the henhouse, they sent cables revoking his authority. Bunau-Varilla chose to ignore them, and on November 18, he signed on behalf of Panama a treaty with the United States that was in all respects inferior to the one that Colombia had rejected. It widened the zone from six to 10 miles, gave the United States the right to take additional land, over all of which it would rule "as if it were the sovereign," and not for 100 years, but in perpetuity.

When the Panamanians learned of the provisions of the treaty, they threatened to reject it. In that case, Hay said, the United States would withdraw recognition, leaving them to face, in all likelihood, a Colombian firing squad. He was almost certainly bluffing; but the dazed Panamanians capitulated, and the treaty was approved. This was the chain of events on which Panama was later to base its argument that the United States was illegally occupying the Canal Zone.

Roosevelt was sure he had done splendidly, but he had to admit that some people disagreed. He asked his Attorney General, a corporation lawyer named Philander Knox, to erect a defense for his actions. "Oh, Mr. President," Knox is said to have replied, "do not let so great an achievement suffer from any taint of legality." On another occasion Roosevelt is said to have provided a lengthy justification to the Cabinet. He then asked his Secretary of War, Elihu Root, if he had adequately answered his critics. As quoted by McCullough, Root replied, "You certainly have, Mr. President. You have shown that you were accused of seduction and you have conclusively proved that you were guilty of rape."

These anecdotes received wide circulation. Liberal thinkers condemned Roosevelt's high-handedness, and the Senate hotly debated the treaty before ratifying it in February, 1904. The country, however, seemed inclined to laugh off the Panama affair or at least to decide that whatever wrongs Colombia had suffered were far outweighed by the value to the world of a great enterprise that otherwise might not have been built for many years, if at all. Three days after ratification, Bunau-Varilla resigned from the Panamanian diplomatic service and returned to France with a large commission in his pocket. Sullivan & Cromwell became the legal counsel for the republic of Panama and was retained by many concerns that did business in Latin America, among them the United Fruit Company. John Foster Dulles joined the firm in 1911 and was followed by his younger brother, Allen. In 1953, they became Secretary of State and Director of the Central Intelligence Agency, respectively, and not to the disadvantage of their former clients. In 1914, the canal was triumphantly opened. In 1921, the United States paid $25,000,000 to Colombia as conscience money. It was small enough recompense for what was, in some respects, the country's most valuable natural resource.

4
Send In the Marines

HAVING BECOME a property owner in Central America, Roosevelt soon found that he disapproved of his neighbors. It was one thing to chuckle over press accounts of their antics, but quite another to try to get to sleep when Señor El Salvador was accusing Señora Guatemala of infidelity at the top of his voice, Nicaragua and Honduras were drunkenly debating arcane points of international law with machetes, and Señorita Costa Rica was threatening to scratch Señorita Panama's eyes out. They were, moreover, supporting their bad habits by reckless borrowing. Every official in Central America, from president to village constable, had the same conception of public service and followed the same code of conduct. That was to steal as much as possible as quickly as possible. Bribery and extortion were the old reliables, but the commissions on foreign borrowings and kickbacks on whatever the money was used to buy came in larger amounts. The result was that irritable bankers, many of them from Europe, were arriving by warship all over the region to try to collect overdue loans.

The United States had already assumed the financial and political guardianship of Cuba, and in 1904, running for a full term in the White House, Roosevelt said he was willing to shoulder the same burden all over the hemisphere. His only desire, he said, was to see his neighbors "stable, orderly and prosperous." Soon afterward he made his message even clearer. "Brutal wrongdoing or an impotence which results in a general loosening of the ties of civilized society," he declared, "may finally require intervention by some civilized nation, and in the Western Hemisphere the United States cannot ignore this duty."

Roosevelt easily won the election, and in his annual message in 1904 he restated his theme, adding that the United States was merely fulfilling "the international duty which is necessarily involved in the assertion of the Monroe Doctrine.'' This declaration became known as the Roosevelt Corollary to the Monroe Doctrine. His position was by no means entirely self-serving. The region had been, after all, sunk in brutality and injustice and soaked in blood since the time of the *conquistadores*. However, the corollary had nothing much to do with the Monroe Doctrine. Despite Roosevelt's reference to the entire hemisphere, the corollary applied, in practice, only to the states of Central America and the Caribbean. Britain dominated the economies of the major nations of South America and continued to do so until the Second World War.

In its first application, in 1906, the corollary worked like a healing poultice. An exile army invaded Guatemala from El Salvador and Honduras. It was trying to overthrow Manuel Estrada Cabrera, a *caudillo* who had held the country in an iron grip for eight years. The fighting was unusually heavy, and casualties numbered in the thousands. With the agreement of Mexico and Costa Rica, Roosevelt sent a cruiser to Salvadoran waters. Representatives of the warring nations were invited aboard in no uncertain terms. They were told that they would remain afloat until they signed a truce. They came to an agreement in a single day—at least in part because the sea was rough and the delegates were not good sailors—and the slaughter ceased.

Soon afterward Roosevelt convened a Central American reconciliation conference in San José, Costa Rica. Nicaragua, which was being led by a *gringo*-hating *caudillo* named José Santos Zelaya, stayed home, but the accomplishments of the others more than made up for its absence. They pledged that they would no longer permit their territories to be used to foment rebellions in other countries, a practice in which they all had habitually indulged since the earliest days of independence. At the prompting of the United States, they established both a Central American Bureau to serve their common interests and a permanent tribunal to arbitrate disputes.

Central America enjoyed the blessings of peace for an entire year. Then Honduras invaded Nicaragua, accusing it of encouraging a rebellion. Although he had neither attended the conference nor signed the agreement, Zelaya took his case to the new tribunal. It ordered both sides to disarm along the border. Having won his case, Zelaya rejected the finding. Certain that Honduras would violate the agreement, he refused to pull back, and the war resumed. Nicaragua scored a quick knockout and then prepared to attack El Salvador, which it accused of having helped Honduras.

60

Roosevelt called another meeting, this time in Washington. He wanted to expose the Central Americans to democratic institutions. The change of scene seemed to help. The delegates put their earlier accomplishments to shame. They established a Central American Court of Justice with far greater power than the arbitration tribunal, solemnly promised to cease once and for all their interference in one another's affairs, and assigned to the Central American Bureau the task of promoting unification. Andrew Carnegie, the steel magnate and philanthropist, provided $100,000 to construct a building for the court in San José. In the first case to come before it, Zelaya accused El Salvador and Guatemala of plotting to overthrow the man he had put in power in Honduras. The court, again finding for him, ordered El Salvador and Guatemala to cease and desist. When they actually did so, Roosevelt announced that a new day had dawned in Central America.

The new day did not last long, however. When William Howard Taft entered the White House, Roosevelt's interventionist policy was stripped of its wisps of benevolence and bent to meaner uses. It was a period in which American interests, particularly in bananas, mining, and lumbering, were expanding rapidly. The Roosevelt Corollary was used solely to protect and promote them. Philander Knox, who had become Secretary of State, decided that the best way to stop European warships from collecting overdue loans was to refinance them in the United States, which could then use its own fleet to adjust any delinquencies. Critics denounced this policy as "dollar diplomacy" and "gunboat diplomacy," but it provided the basis on which the United States dealt with Central America and the Caribbean for the next 25 years.

Once again Zelaya of Nicaragua decided to be difficult. In 1909, he got a loan in London, exactly as though the United States had never spoken. Within a few months, and not by coincidence, he had a rebellion on his hands. Two Americans, captured while fighting with the rebels, were executed. The Taft administration used this event as a pretext for breaking relations. By then the rebels were penned up in Bluefields, on the Miskito Coast, surrounded by Zelaya's troops. Four hundred marines were landed from American warships to protect them from harm. From then on the rebels were generously supplied with weapons and money by American companies, and within a few weeks they controlled the country.

However, Zelaya's replacement turned out to be as irritating as Zelaya. In a rush of misguided patriotism, he refused to yield control of

Nicaragua's customs collections to American bankers. A second uprising was fomented, and a bookkeeper for an American mining company, one Adolfo Díaz, emerged as president. He agreed to everything, including a treaty that established an American protectorate. The Senate, with the Democrats in the ascendancy, rejected the treaty in 1911, but Díaz remained as president, and the influence of the United States remained paramount.

The thousand or so people who constituted Nicaraguan public opinion were outraged by the way the marines kept order. It was bad enough that the diplomats and bankers of the United States should deny them their right to a certain fiscal and commercial informality but far worse that the marines should deny them their time-honored right to slaughter one another without interference. Before long there were demonstrations and disorders and then local uprisings. Díaz, at Washington's insistence, dismissed Emiliano Chamorro, who led the opposition in the legislature, and the country rose in rebellion. Díaz asked, or was asked to ask, the United States for help in protecting life and property. Knox and Taft sent the marines back in—this time a full battalion of 800 men. One detachment landed at Corinto on the Pacific coast and, marching inland, occupied Managua and León, the Liberal stronghold. The other went ashore at Bluefields on the Atlantic coast. The Nicaraguans continued to fight among themselves, and the marines suffered casualties as they tried to separate the combatants. Washington increased the force to 2,700. Looking down the rifle barrels of those beefy, red-faced men, Emiliano Chamorro, the leader of the rebellion, permitted himself to be consoled by appointment as Ambassador to Washington. Then, with the United States supervising the election, Díaz was chosen as president.

In 1916, Chamorro and William Jennings Bryan, the prairie populist who was Woodrow Wilson's Secretary of State, signed the treaty that bears their names. The United States received the exclusive right to build a Nicaraguan canal, which was not worth much since the Panama Canal had opened two years earlier, the right to establish a naval base on the Gulf of Fonseca on the Pacific coast, and a lease on the Corn Islands in the Caribbean. Other sections of the treaty involving finances and rights of military intervention made Nicaragua not merely a protectorate but virtually a colony. The Senate approved the treaty only after the most offensive clauses had been removed.

Costa Rica and El Salvador went before the Central American Court of Justice to protest that the treaty violated their rights, respectively, to the San Juan River, which formed the boundary between Costa Rica and Nicaragua, and would be part of any canal, no matter how unlikely it was to be built, and in the Gulf of Fonseca, which El Salvador shared with Nicaragua. When the court that Theodore Roosevelt had founded decided in their favor, the United States chose to ignore the verdict. Nicaragua, with Washington's approval, withdrew from membership. The court's usefulness clearly had ended, and in 1918, at the end of the 10-year period for which it had been originally established, it quietly went out of business.

In 1920, the original five nations of Central America made yet another attempt to unite. They hoped to be able to proclaim federation in 1921, on the 100th anniversary of their independence from Spain. The chances are they would have been no more successful than in the past, but now that all of them, to one degree or another, were economic vassals, and the strategic importance of the region had been greatly increased by the opening of the canal, the United States no longer encouraged such efforts. The question of the Bryan-Chamorro Treaty and its bearing on Nicaragua's ability to become part of such a union arose at the unification conference. Nicaragua thereupon withdrew, but the other participants announced the formation of the Central American Federation. Washington made clear its displeasure by announcing that seven cruisers with marines aboard would be based in the Canal Zone if unification in fact took place. Having tweaked the eagle's beak and pulled a feather from its tail, the Central Americans dropped the subject of unification—as it turned out for good.

With the marines on duty in Nicaragua during most of the decade, the 1920's were generally peaceful and prosperous in Central America, at least for those in a position to prosper. The price of coffee remained high, and the opening of the canal reduced the cost of shipping it to the United States and to Europe from Pacific ports. Under the cold and watchful eye of American bankers, debts were paid. El Salvador, which had always been the most provident country in the region, found itself with a surplus in the treasury. The coffee barons lived in great splendor, collected chorus girls in Manhattan, tall blondes by preference, and became familiar figures at the baccarat tables of the Riviera. But no matter how big the profits were, the workers tended to make the same 15 cents a day, or whatever the figure happened to be that was just sufficient to keep them and their families from starving to death.

By then, another great agricultural industry, the growing of bananas, was flourishing in Central America. Unlike coffee, which was largely in the hands of local landowners, the banana industry had been established and was controlled by American capital. The United Fruit Company, which was by far the largest grower and shipper, was richer and more powerful than any of the countries in which it operated. In addition to millions of acres of land, it owned railroads, the best port facilities, a fleet of 100 ships, the commercial radio and cable system, and much else, and in three or four countries was by far the largest employer. Gratuities from United Fruit enriched generations of Central American politicians and military officers, and on the rare occasions when the company encountered an honest or merely cantankerous official, it could call on its good friends in Washington for help.

In 1928, as President-elect, Herbert Hoover visited Latin America. All he heard was complaints about gunboat diplomacy. When he took office, he let it be known that the Roosevelt Corollary was a dead letter. In 1931, he stated that the marines would leave Haiti, where they had been stationed most of the time for 15 years, by 1934. In January, 1933, a couple of months before yielding his office to Franklin Delano Roosevelt, he withdrew the marines from Nicaragua. Roosevelt went further. The Democrats had always opposed interventionism in principle, although Wilson, their only other President in the twentieth century, had practiced it as enthusiastically as any Republican. From then on, Roosevelt stated in his inaugural address, the United States would be "a good neighbor." The next year Roosevelt canceled the agreement of 1902 that permitted intervention in Cuba and, as Hoover had promised, withdrew the marines from Haiti. For the first time in years no American troops were stationed in the states of Central America or the Caribbean, with the exception of the naval base at Guantánamo Bay in Cuba, which has remained in American hands down to the present.

At the time the Good Neighbor Policy was announced, however, four of the Central American nations were being ruled by *caudillos* of unusual harshness—Jorge Ubico of Guatemala, Maximiliano Hernández Martínez of El Salvador, Tiburcio Carías Andino of Honduras, and Anastasio Somoza, who was running Nicaragua behind the scenes as commander of the National Guard. They persecuted the old Liberal and Conservative parties and found much to admire in Adolf Hitler and Benito Mussolini. The price of coffee and other exports had collapsed, and the hunger in the countryside expressed itself from time to time in uprisings that were, more often than not, simply an occasion for grabbing a merchant's corn and beans. Such manifestations of bolshevism were quickly suppressed and mercilessly punished, the most extreme example being the *matanza* in El Salvador in 1932. With the gradual improvement in the world economy, however, these outbreaks all but ceased.

In 1944, their weary subjects ousted Ubico and Martínez. Guatemala went so far as to have an honest election and choose as president an exiled university professor of liberal outlook named Juan José Arévalo. A new constitution was adopted, modeled on Mexico's. It provided for social benefits for the first time and gave labor the right to organize and strike. In 1950 Arévalo was succeeded by a protégé, Colonel Jacobo Arbenz Guzmán. In 1952, he expropriated 210,000 acres of idle land from the United Fruit Company for distribution to landless peasants. A few months later he seized another 177,000 acres. That left United Fruit with only 163,000 acres in Guatemala, although it still owned at least 1,000,000 acres elsewhere in Central America. Arbenz said he would pay about $3 an acre for the land. This was the valuation the company had put on it for tax purposes. United Fruit said that tax value was one thing and true value was another. Arbenz could have all the land he wanted for $75 an acre. When Arbenz said he preferred his own price, the company went to see its friends in Washington. United Fruit was old Boston money, Cabot and Lodge money, and when it complained, the Eisenhower administration listened.

At that, land reform alone might not have been enough to topple Arbenz. He could have said he had been forced to do it to stop the march of communism. Like Arévalo, Arbenz was a reformer rather than a radical. However, it is generally accepted that his wife, a Salvadoran, was a Communist sympathizer. She used her considerable influence over him to insinuate people who thought the same way into the government and the union leadership. They were inclined to be more interested in denouncing imperialism than in providing a better life for the poor. The rhetoric that went along with the expropriation was red-hot and pointlessly provocative.

In 1954, fearing American intervention, Guatemala tried to modernize its army. Unable to buy arms anywhere else, it purchased them in Czechoslovakia and thereby gave to Secretary of State John Foster Dulles, the old Sullivan & Cromwell partner, the pretext he needed to intervene. He turned the case over to his brother, Allen, the Director of the Central Intelligence Agency. Within months Arbenz had been ousted. His pliable successor returned the land to United Fruit and repealed an irritating law that permitted labor unions to exist. No one mentioned it, but the Roosevelt Corollary was back in force.

Latin American leaders pointed out that more such episodes were bound to occur again unless the United States provided significant economic and military aid. In the long run, they said, it would be cheaper than mounting covert operations. They also noted, more in sorrow than in anger, that the United States had spread tens of billions of dollars in aid all over Europe and Asia since the end of the Second World War as a roadblock against the march of communism, but they had received almost nothing. Washington kept saying the *dinero* would arrive *mañana,* but someone kept forgetting to put the check in the mail. In 1958, Vice President Richard M. Nixon was sent instead. As a goodwill tour it left much to be desired. He was pelted with rocks and bags of offal at almost every stop. His hosts apologized. What could they do? they said. It wasn't as though they hadn't been trying to warn the United States about the looming danger. Wily agitators, paid with Moscow gold, were having a certain success in leading the less intelligent and sophisticated of their people astray.

On January 1, 1959, Fidel Castro marched into Havana. He had sworn that, despite appearances, he was not a Communist, but that was when he was out in the Sierra Maestra and needed help. Within three months of his victory he had begun to glow pinkly, at least as far as the Dulles brothers were concerned, and within a year he had turned congested revolutionary red. A Communist tentacle was squirming and palpating only 90 miles from Key West. Allen Dulles was given the job of lopping it off, and United Fruit, International Nickel, and the other big American corporations began counting the days until they regained possession of the vast and highly profitable holdings that Castro had seized. While the CIA was recruiting and training the émigré army that would soon be making short work of the usurper, an aid program for Latin America was belatedly announced. The Inter-American Development Bank, with $350,000,000 in capital, was established. A total of $500,000,000 was earmarked for other assistance. A Central American Common Market was created for the stimulation of regional trade, as was an international coffee agreement to stabilize the market.

When John F. Kennedy entered the White House in January, 1961, he found that preparations for the Bay of Pigs invasion were far advanced. He decided to go ahead with it, but nervously. One of the things that concerned him more than the possibility of failure was the reaction in Latin America to the support that the United States was giving to the minions of the deposed dictator, Fulgencio Batista, who were spearheading the invasion. To balance whatever hard feelings might arise, Kennedy decided to enlarge greatly the Eisenhower aid program. The development bank and the rest were a step in the right direction, Kennedy's advisers acknowledged, but in their lack of scope they exemplified the blinkered, buggy-whip, cheese-paring mentality of the men around the amiable general.

It was in this expansive spirit, in March, 1961, two months after his inauguration and a month before the Cuban landing, that Kennedy announced the Alliance for Progress. Its primary aim, he said, was to increase per capita income in Latin America by a minimum of 2.5 percent a year for 10 years. It would build enough schools to provide at least six years of free education for all children, thereby eliminating illiteracy by 1970. Better food and health care would add five years to life expectancy in the same period. The alliance would also see to the building of factories, where the unemployed could find work, low-rent housing, where they could live, and a comprehensive list of other good things. Kennedy said that an annual capital investment of $10 billion, or $100 billion in all, would be required. That sounded like a lot of money, but the President pointed out that the Latin American nations had promised to raise 80 percent of it themselves. The United States would give or guarantee loans amounting to 60 percent of the remaining $20 billion, or $1.2 billion a year. Grants and low-interest loans from other governments and private investment would make up the balance.

In outlining his proposal, Kennedy stated, "Unless necessary social reforms, including land and tax reform, are freely made, unless we broaden the opportunity for all people, unless the great mass of Americans share in increasing prosperity, then our alliance, our revolution, our dream, and our freedom will fail."

Heads of state who, with one or two exceptions, would have disastrously lowered the moral and intellectual tone of Alcatraz if they had been confined there responded enthusiastically. Some of the more vivid members of this pantheon were Rafael Trujillo of the Dominican Republic, who amused himself with children, fed his enemies to the sharks, and was himself about to be assassinated by the CIA, an action that in a tiny way justified its existence; "Tacho" Somoza, who contented himself with owning no more than 25 or 30 percent of Nicaragua; "Papa Doc" Duvalier, who as the pope of the voodoo church was both the spiritual and temporal ruler of Haiti; and General Alfredo Stroessner of Paraguay, many of whose best friends were fugitive Nazis.

They and their colleagues, the usual run of thieves and cutthroats, took Kennedy's words to heart. How clear he made it, the handsome young *gringo* with the rich father, the beautiful wife, and all those gorgeous girl friends. They could see now that what they and their predecessors had been doing was wrong, wrong, *wrong*! Wiping the tears of repentance from their furrowed cheeks, they asked how soon they could start getting the money, which wasn't so much when you considered how many ways it had to be split.

It turned out to be even less than they had hoped for. Congress, with commendable skepticism as to how the money would be spent, never appropriated as much as Kennedy wanted. As Juan de Onís and Jerome Levinson note in their excellent study *The Alliance That Lost Its Way,* half of what it did provide went straight to American banks to pay off overdue loans. From the remainder had to be deducted the salaries and generous allowances of the hundreds of bureaucrats who arrived from Washington to administer the program. The enabling act, moreover, required that the pipes and pumps and engines and shingles for the model housing projects, the slum schools, and the sewage disposal plants all be bought in the United States. Kennedy had correctly emphasized the importance of land reform and a fairer tax structure, but Congress refused to make grants contingent on progress in these areas. Lobbying by multinational corporations also led it, in fact, to prohibit the use of alliance funds to pay for expropriated land or to provide guarantees for land reform bonds.

The Cuban invasion failed disastrously, of course, making the alliance more important than ever, but it had hardly gotten started when Kennedy was assassinated. The interest of his successor, Lyndon B. Johnson, did not extend very far beyond Latin Americans who voted in Texas. One thing he was wary of was the political danger of letting Communists gain another Caribbean foothold, so he didn't require much persuasion to dispatch 20,000 troops to the Dominican Republic in 1965 to confound a bolshevik plot that appears to have existed only in the fevered brains of Trujillo's old associates, the American corporations that owned large parts of the country, and the Pentagon. A month earlier, Johnson had taken the first blundering steps toward catastrophe by sending American combat troops to South Vietnam. Thereafter, there was less and less time to think about Latin America and less and less money for the Alliance for Progress.

Central America nonetheless remained tranquil for most of the 1960's. World prices for its exports, coffee in particular, were high. The CIA's covert operations kept Cuba on the defensive. The Central American Common Market was working well. Light industry grew rapidly in El Salvador and Guatemala, often as joint ventures with American or German concerns. Guatemala easily suppressed an uprising that was said to have been inspired and led by Communists. In Nicaragua a handful of rebels who called themselves Sandinistas in honor of Augusto César Sandino, who led the resistance to the United States' occupation 50 years earlier, were being relentlessly hunted by the National Guard. Christian Democratic parties gained strength in El Salvador, Guatemala, and Honduras, although the military continued to rule. Democracy flourished in Costa Rica under the leadership of José Figueres. In Panama, General Omar Torrijos took power as a comparatively enlightened *caudillo.*

The halcyon days ended in 1969. Commodity prices cracked, incomes dropped, and social unrest increased. El Salvador and Honduras fought a four-day war, the first in Central America in 60 years. It was a pointless conflict, and despite its brevity, it seriously damaged the economy of both nations and destroyed the Common Market. Problems that had been papered over began to emerge again all over Latin America. The right and the left alike put the blame on the United States. The right said the alliance had delivered less than it had promised. The left said it had turned out to be just another imperialist *gringo* scheme. The alliance's name in Spanish, *Alianza para Progreso,* lent itself to black humor. *Para,* for, is also the third person present of the verb *parar,* to stop. Thus, Alliance Stops Progress. End of *chiste,* joke.

Not long after he entered the White House, Richard M. Nixon asked Nelson Rockefeller, then the governor of New York, to make a swing through Latin America. In view of his own trip in 1958, Nixon was unlikely to have thought that he was doing his old rival in national politics a favor. However, Rockefeller undertook the mission with enthusiasm. No political figure was better qualified. Rockefeller could talk to the owners of Latin America on equal terms, and then some, and could do it in Spanish. He had spent the Second World War safely and pleasantly, dealing with Latin American affairs in the State Department.

Rockefeller also had a personal stake in the region. He owned an enormous ranch in Venezuela, and Creole Petroleum, which pumped most of Venezuela's oil, had been part of the family's Standard Oil monopoly.

Rockefeller avoided a lot of trouble by skipping Nixon's triumphal motorcades. In some countries he went so far as to keep his arrival secret. In others, his conferences took place in the VIP lounge at the airport. Even with these precautions, he heard a lot of booing. In his report to Nixon, Rockefeller said that the United States' "special relationship" with Latin America was being imperiled by neglect and by Communist penetration, which had begun to seduce labor unions, students, and even the Roman Catholic Church.

"Clearly," he stated, "the opinion in the United States that communism is no longer a serious factor in the Western Hemisphere is thoroughly wrong." For that reason, Rockefeller said, the training of Latin American "security forces," one of the less publicized benefactions of the Alliance for Progress, and the sale of military equipment to them should be increased. He pointed out that officers who attended courses in wiretapping, interrogation, and the like in the United States or even at the branch campus in the Panama Canal Zone could better counteract Marxist influence because of their exposure "to the fundamental achievements of the U.S. way of life."

Nixon accepted Rockefeller's report, presumably did with it what Eisenhower had done with his, and then turned his attention to those parts of the world that interested him more, which was almost anywhere else. The only notable exception to this presidential indifference was Chile, where imperialism had long been a sore point. Chile was no banana republic. It had a long history of democratic government; its population was mostly of European descent; its climate was temperate, with vineyards in the uplands and skiing in the mountains. Yet its copper, its most valuable natural resource, produced enormous profits only for Kennecott and Anaconda.

The friction was increased, as Seymour M. Hersh notes in his *The Price of Power: Kissinger in the Nixon White House,* by the fact that Nixon disliked Chile's president, Eduardo Frei. It wasn't that Frei was a dangerous leftist. He was, in fact, a Christian Democrat, a moderate conservative who had quietly accepted campaign money from American business. Indeed, Frei's sensitivity on this point led him to ask Rockefeller to omit Chile from his itinerary. Frei was no happier than most Chileans about *gringo* domination of their economy, but as a be-

70

liever in private enterprise and a friend of the United States he could do little beyond trying to persuade the copper companies to listen to reason. This they were not prepared to do.

The United States would have been happy to have Frei remain in office indefinitely, but the Chilean constitution prohibited consecutive terms. An election was scheduled in 1970, and it looked as though the winner were going to be Salvador Allende, a socialist who had pledged to restore the national patrimony by expropriating it if negotiations failed. (The national patrimony, it must be said, always looks a lot better after the investments have been made, the risks taken, and the profits are rolling in.)

Nixon and his National Security Adviser, Henry Kissinger, didn't like the sound of that. They feared, moreover, that Allende was only masquerading as a democratic socialist, and once in office, he would reveal his hideous Lenin-like visage. As they discussed the looming crisis, Chile, although usually a synonym for remoteness, assumed vast geopolitical importance. Only the Andes, mere foothills of 20,000 feet or so, stood between it and the fertile pampas of Argentina. It was a double-ended stiletto pointed north at the heart of Peru and Ecuador and south at Antarctica. It dominated the Cape Horn shipping route, and it would be a doughty skipper indeed who tried to run his brigantine through the Strait of Magellan under its hostile culverins.

The two masterminds decided that Allende's election had to be prevented by any means necessary. Kissinger came up with a bon mot for the occasion. "I don't see why we need to stand by and watch a country go communist due to the irresponsibility of its own people," he said. However, their efforts, largely restricted to secret subsidies to Allende's opponent, were inadequate. Allende won the election, but without a majority, throwing the election into the Congress. Fearing that he would win there, too, the CIA tried to arrange a military coup. General René Schneider, the chief of staff, refused to join the plot and was assassinated.

Allende won the runoff, took office, and, with the support of Congress, enacted the expropriation laws. Worse, he brought major sectors of the economy under state ownership. Britain and France could get away with socialization, but in Latin America it was strictly forbidden. Nixon and Kissinger, who were also taking a lot of kidding from the boys at Anaconda and ITT, which owned Chile's telephone system, redoubled their efforts. Finally, in September, 1973, they succeeded. Allende was overthrown and murdered. General Augusto

Pinochet, his successor, was a throwback to the *caudillos* of the 1930's who admired Hitler and Mussolini. Pinochet executed hundreds of leftists and imprisoned thousands. However, even he lacked the effrontery to give back the copper, although he paid the former owners generously for it.

With so much going on, it was scarcely surprising that Nixon and Kissinger failed to object to, or even, apparently, to notice, the outcome of the presidential election in El Salvador in February, 1972. The military government stole the victory from a Christian Democrat named José Napoleón Duarte. Nor was the resignation, in September, 1972, of the chairman of the Inter-American Committee for the Alliance for Progress, Carlos Sanz de Santamaría of Colombia, an occasion for comment. In fact, it didn't even make the papers until an official of Senator George McGovern's presidential campaign brought it up a couple of weeks later. Sanz said that the alliance was stagnating and would continue to do so until it accepted "a plurality of ideologies" in the hemisphere.

By then, in any case, the 10-year period in which the alliance was supposed to turn Latin America around had ended, and almost nothing had happened. The failure of a Kennedy program could not have distressed Nixon very much, but it was still no cause for cheering. The alliance was permitted to go quietly out of business, and its programs were transferred to the Agency for International Development.

There was no public postmortem, but the causes of the alliance's failure seemed clear enough. The plan was hastily drawn up by minor members of the White House staff, none of whom knew anything much about Latin America. The alliance's goals were far too ambitious. With one or two exceptions, the nations of Latin America had no intention of even trying to enact the domestic reforms it envisaged, and nothing much was done to mobilize the support of Congress or the American public. (James Reston, the distinguished columnist, once wrote that Americans would do anything for Latin America but read about it. It is an amusing apothegm, but only half-true. They won't do anything, either.) Finally, Kennedy's assassination left the alliance fatherless just as it was getting started. Whether he would have maintained his interest in Latin America is problematical. No President since Theodore Roosevelt has been able to do so, and Roosevelt's main interest was the Panama Canal rather than the dry land on either side of it.

* * *

For 450 years and more the Roman Catholic Church had preached to the wretched multitudes of Latin America the necessity of submission to temporal and spiritual authority, of patient acceptance of the inscrutability of God's plan, and of the certainty of reward or punishment in the hereafter. However, in 1968, in a speech in Bogotá, Pope Paul VI declared, "We wish to personify the Christ of a poor and hungry people." It was a revolutionary utterance and has continued to reverberate throughout the region.

Paul, who was making the first papal visit to Latin America, was inspired by the encyclicals of Pope John XXIII, the *Mater et Magistra* of 1961 and the *Pacem in Terris* of 1963, by the deliberations of the Second Vatican Council, from 1962 to 1965, and by his own *Populorum Progressio* of 1967. These documents eased the rigid doctrines and discipline of the church. Above all, the encyclicals said that mankind had the inalienable right to social justice this side of the hereafter.

When he spoke in Bogotá, the Pope was on his way to Medellín in the Colombian highlands to open a meeting of the Conference of Latin American Bishops. The prelates could agree that the church was in crisis in Latin America, but they differed as to its cause. The traditionalists said it was materialism and atheistic communism. The modernists said it was the church's passive acceptance of tyranny, injustice, and pervasive poverty. Whatever the reasons, the results were plain to see. Something like half the world's 700,000,000 Catholics lived in Latin America, but not a tenth of them ever set foot inside a church, except for a wedding or funeral. Poverty and piety no longer went hand in hand. A third of the children of God in Latin America were desperately poor, and another third were utterly destitute. They should have been praying night and day for help, but they weren't, at least not in church. The number and the quality of the men and women who entered holy orders had dropped to the point that foreign missionaries made up a third of the clergy. Many rural churches received only monthly or even yearly visits from a priest. In lands in which, 100 years earlier, Protestant worship had been forbidden, the evangelical sects of the United States were gaining millions of converts. Latin American Catholicism had become an irrelevancy, a whited sepulcher, shabby and corrupt, dominated by ignorant, narrow men who preached the evil of Luther, Voltaire, and Marx to bent old women in their moldering cathedrals and assiduously served the pretensions of grasping oligarchs and sawdust Caesars.

There were exceptions, of course—prelates and priests who confronted hostile governments and landowners on behalf of the helpless. Notable among them were Cardinals Aloisio Lorscheider and Paulo Evaristo Arns and Archbishop Dom Helder Cámara, all of Brazil, who had persuasively argued at the Vatican Council that Catholicism must once again become, as it had not been since its beginnings, a church of the poor.

With the momentum of the Vatican Council, with the support of the Pope, and with control of the conference machinery, the modernist prelates carried the rest of the conference along with them. It adopted reformist programs dealing with education, the organization of labor, and lay participation in church affairs. Influenced by the *Pacem in Terris,* it agreed to what was in some ways a Marxist critique of capitalism and imperialism and, inferentially, a defense of socialism. The conference documents provided the doctrinal framework for what became known as the Theology of Liberation.

One issue of the greatest importance, birth control, was omitted from the Medellín program. (The opposition of the hierarchy had also prevented its inclusion in the Alliance for Progress.) Although a Vatican study commission had voted overwhelmingly to remove, under certain circumstances, the church's prohibition against artificial means of contraception, Paul's encyclical *Humanae Vitae* had retained it. The decision, which the Pope acknowledged he had agonized over, was unhelpful to Latin America. Considerable economic progress had been made in the region during the 1960's, but it was wiped out by the soaring birthrate. At the same time, agriculture was being mechanized, forcing millions of *campesino* families off the land and into shantytowns that stretched for miles around the major cities. Populations were doubling every 20 years, with no remote prospect of jobs, schools, or even food or water. The projections for the year 2000 were horrifying.

With Allende disposed of and Castro lying low, Kissinger, who continued to serve in the administration of President Gerald R. Ford, was able in good conscience to turn his attention elsewhere, confident that history in Latin America would stand still until he had the chance to look again. However, by the early 1970's the golden years of social order were beginning to fade. Military dictators ruled in all but a couple of nations. Leftist subversion, which included wanting elections, was dealt with harshly. The *caudillos* knew that the United States wasn't going to object—not when it was helping train the counterinsurgency experts—but they failed to see the new spirit that animated their opponents.

In his inaugural address in 1977, Jimmy Carter said, "Our moral sense dictates a clear-cut preference for those societies which share with us an abiding respect for individual human rights." In his first speech to the United Nations, he said, "All the signatories of the U.N. charter have pledged themselves to observe and to respect basic human rights. Thus, no member of the United Nations can claim that mistreatment of its citizens is solely its own business."

American presidents had been saying the same things for years, but they were always talking about Russia, Eastern Europe, Vietnam, Cuba, and so on, not about Iran, South Africa, the Philippines, South Korea, and the dictatorships of Latin America. Certificates of honorary democracy had been granted to these countries and others in which human rights did not flourish. Some were allies of one sort or another. Others were strategically situated or, like China, had enemies in common with the United States.

Carter was persuaded that such distinctions were hypocritical and, in the long run, self-defeating. Communist prison cells and anti-Communist prison cells looked alike from the inside. The United States, he would have thought, had a moral duty to try to increase the total amount of freedom all over the world rather than in selected parts of it. The issue could even be argued in terms of narrow national self-interest. As allies, other democracies were likely to be more reliable than dictatorships. The problem was that aside from the United States, the British Commonwealth, Western Europe, and Japan, there weren't many countries in which people were permitted to assemble to damn the government and fewer still that gave them an honest chance to change it at the ballot box. Moreover, the countries that were most deficient in human rights, as in Latin America, were also the ones least likely to change their ways.

Undaunted, the eager young activists who joined the State Department's Human Rights Division sped from country to country, making their studies and issuing their condemnations. El Salvador, where another presidential election had been stolen from the Christian Democrats in 1977, and Guatemala, where the presidency had been stolen from the same party in 1976, as well as Argentina, Brazil, and Uruguay were among the first nations to be warned that aid would be suspended if they failed to make reforms. Predictably, they told the United

States to keep the aid, which didn't amount to a great deal, and they continued to impose public order as they always had.

The question of Nicaragua bedeviled Carter throughout his term of office. The country had been ruled by the Somoza family tyranny for more than 40 years. When it was finally overthrown in July, 1979, and Anastasio Somoza fled to Miami, Carter was blamed by conservatives for withholding the aid that might have saved one of the hemisphere's most dedicated anti-Communists and by liberals for having done too little to push Somoza out. The problem was that no one knew whether the leaders of the Sandinista National Liberation Front, who were Marxist-Leninists, would keep their pledge of democratic freedoms and economic pluralism when they took power. By the time Carter left office it had begun to look as though they would not.

The shock waves caused by Somoza's fall radiated most strongly in El Salvador. In October, 1979, young officers and civilians of centrist and moderately leftist sympathies ousted an unpopular military government. However, the country's oligarchy, supported by rightist officers, was able to prevent it from carrying out its program of reform. The guerrilla forces of the militant left thereupon launched an insurrection. As in Nicaragua, the Carter administration had difficulty in deciding which side it was on. Aid was suspended and restored and suspended in a not altogether successful effort to influence the Salvadoran government. In January, 1981, in Carter's final weeks in the White House, the guerrillas, armed at least in part with weapons smuggled to them from Nicaragua, began a "final offensive." Fearing that it might succeed, Carter restored military aid without conditions.

The one great success of the Carter administration in Latin America was the ratification of the Panama Canal Treaty and the passage of the enabling legislation over the intense opposition of the Republican right and strong elements of his own party. Something about the canal still incited merriment in North Americans. The service of S. I. Hayakawa, the famed semanticist, in the United States Senate might have passed unnoticed if it had not been for his oxymoron during the canal debate. "It's ours," he said. "We stole it fair and square." However, Ronald Reagan, whose boyish chest had swelled with pride when Teddy Roosevelt opened the canal, found its "give-away" no laughing matter. He led the opposition before it took place and campaigned for the presidency on the issue afterward.

The first Latin American Conference of Bishops since Medellín convened in Puebla, Mexico, in January, 1979. In the intervening 11 years the conservatives had regained control of the conference bureaucracy and agenda. In all but a few countries, conservative bishops decided on the composition of their national delegations. The highest-ranking churchman in El Salvador, Archbishop Oscar Arnulfo Romero of San Salvador, who was regarded by his colleagues as a dangerous radical, was not chosen. He attended the conference as the representative of a lay organization, but without official status.

John Paul II, who had been elevated to the papacy only three months before, made his first trip abroad to attend the meeting. His speech to the conference seemed to be an uncompromising rejection of the activism that was implicit in the Theology of Liberation. "You are not political or social teachers," the Pope declared bluntly. He condemned the portrayal of Jesus Christ "as a political figure, a revolutionary, the subversive Man From Nazareth."

But when his triumphal tour of Mexico took him to the poverty-stricken south, the section of the country that most closely resembled Central America, according to Penny Lernoux's *Cry of the People,* he discarded the speeches prepared for him by his conservative advisers. In Oaxaca, a state in which Indian languages are far more widely spoken than Spanish, he told an enormous audience, "You have a right to throw down the barriers of exploitation."

Addressing himself to the rich, he declared, "It is not right, it is not human, it is not Christian to maintain such clearly unjust situations. . . . If the church defends the legitimate right of private property, it teaches with equal clarity that there is always a social mortgage on such property, that the goods of the world were destined by God for the good of all. And if the common good so demands, there is no doubt that expropriation is the best measure."

In the years that followed, however, the Pope seemed to move steadily to the right. He apparently had decided that opposition to communism and the Theology of Liberation, which appeared to inspire revolution, were incompatible.

Although Ronald Reagan may have disappointed his staunchest supporters when he entered the White House in January, 1981, by not immediately sending an expeditionary force to recover the Panama Canal, he made it clear that he was not prepared to take a step backward anywhere else in Central America. He pledged to provide all necessary help to El Salvador and issued the first of many demands that Cuba and Nicaragua stop the shipments of weapons from the Soviet bloc to the guerrillas there. General Alexander M. Haig, Jr., his Secretary of State, worked himself into spasms of bellicosity. On one occasion he declared, "Cuban activity has reached a peak that is no longer acceptable in this hemisphere." If it continued, he said menacingly, "It would be dealt with at the source."

For Haig, tiny El Salvador assumed the same vital significance that Chile had in the early 1970's, when, as a mere colonel, he was Kissinger's flunky on the National Security Council. By fixedly staring at a map of the region tilted at a certain angle in bright sunlight, he could make himself believe that El Salvador was now the key piece in the Latin American jigsaw puzzle.

The Carter administration's military aid to El Salvador had included helicopters—strictly for transport, rather than machine-gunning purposes, it was said. Seventeen servicemen, instructors in flying and maintenance, arrived with them. Reagan quickly enlarged this training mission to 56 men, including 15 members of the Special Forces. The Pentagon emphasized that they would not be accompanying their students into battle. It suggested to the press that they thus might be more accurately described as "trainers," which had pleasant locker-room overtones, rather than as "advisers," which recalled the early stages of the involvement of the United States in South Vietnam.

In February, 1981, the State Department issued a White Paper, in effect a propaganda pamphlet, *Communist Interference in El Salvador*. It asserted that "over the past year the insurgency in El Salvador has been progressively transformed into another case of indirect armed aggression against a small Third World country by communist powers acting through Cuba."

What the theory of indirect armed aggression implied was that an insurrection in which any of the leaders were Communists of one sort or another would be deemed to be under Soviet control and that the United States reserved the right to oppose it with all the means at its command. The White Paper did not mention the Monroe Doctrine or its Roosevelt Corollary—scarcely anyone did—but it seemed clear enough that both remained in effect. Interventions had taken place in Latin America during four of the seven administrations since the Second World War. It could reasonably be assumed that the only reason Truman and Ford hadn't done anything was that there was nothing that needed to be done. In fact, the Carter administration was unique in having refrained from intervening in Nicaragua on the side of anti-communism.

5
The Smallest of All

IF I HEARD it once, I heard it 50 times—that the people of El Salvador were the smartest and most energetic to be found between the Panama Canal and the Rio Grande and possibly beyond. I always heard it from Salvadorans, of course, but that does not invalidate the proposition. Their theory is that to survive and prosper, small nations have to be shrewder than big ones. Since El Salvador is indubitably the smallest nation on the hemispheric mainland and, until a few years ago at any rate, had more than its share of wealth, the case is taken to be proved. (If this book is made into a movie, Herve Villechaize, Ricardo Montalban's diminutive sidekick on the television series *Fantasy Island,* is a natural to play El Salvador.)

As supporting evidence, Salvadorans point out that while their country has had its share of coups, rebellions, and wars, only once has it been saddled with the *caudillo* rule that has repeatedly been fastened on Guatemala, Nicaragua, and Honduras for decades at a time. It permitted foreigners to build and own its railroads and utilities for a while, but it never sold a foot of agricultural land to them. When it borrowed abroad, it did so with discretion and almost always paid its debts on time. As a result, it never suffered the indignity of having the United States marines as uninvited guests. In the 1950's and 1960's, when El Salvador went into light manufacturing, it began calling itself the Taiwan of Latin America, the one country where *mañana* really meant tomorrow.

The Salvadoran oligarchy says that if anything, its members have always been too smart and successful for their own good. It is an article of faith among them that the Kremlin cast a baleful eye on their tiny paradise as long ago as the 1920's. (The oligarchy is often referred to as *Los Catorce*, the 14 Families, a term that has the ring of history about it, but it appears to have first been used by *Time* magazine only in 1958. Many of them have intermarried through two or three generations, and their number is closer to 100 than it is to 14.)

In this interpretation, Stalin and his minions decided that the existence of El Salvador, where *campesinos* sang and danced their way through the coffee harvest, set at naught the teachings of Marx and Lenin. For that reason, they chose it as the place to stir up what the oligarchy describes as the hemisphere's first armed Communist uprising. After years of preparation it finally broke out in January, 1932. El Salvador found, in Hernández Martínez, a leader equal to the task, and he put down the rebellion with all necessary severity. But Communists have long memories, the oligarchs say, and they never stopped plotting against the country that had humiliated them. Almost 50 years later, aided by the misguided policies of the Carter administration and the treason of a few priests, they struck again.

A perhaps more objective account would note that after the collapse of coffee prices in 1929 the oligarchy used its control of the government and the banks to squeeze small landowners, who were overextended, and to add these lands, by foreclosure and purchase, to its already very large holdings. However, disagreements, largely petty and personal, within the oligarchy produced a field of five candidates in the election of 1931. The incumbent president, who had been insulted by the Quiñónez Meléndez family, which had put him in office, was so angry that he permitted an honest election. The extraordinary result was the victory of a Fabian socialist.

He was Arturo Araújo, a member of a landowning family. He had studied engineering in Switzerland and worked for a time in England, where his political conversion took place. Araújo's heart was in the right place, but he was a poor administrator and unable to summon up the ruthlessness to make himself obeyed in a part of the world in which laws and constitutions are not. This remains, as Duarte learned, a besetting handicap to reform.

The oligarchy, pulling itself together, prevented Araújo from accomplishing anything—most of all a land reform, on which his heart was set. The treasury was empty, and being unable to pay the army, he lost its support. In December, 1931, after only six months in office, he was ousted. His replacement was the vice-president, Hernández Martínez, who had been elected independently. A month after he had taken office, a peasant uprising began in the western part of the country. Among them were many of the country's 75,000 unassimilated Indians. Like Indians all over Latin America, and in much of the United States until recent times, they were the poorest of the poor. Whites and *mestizos* alike habitually referred to them as *chanchos,* or pigs.

The man who has gone down in history as the organizer and leader of the rebellion is Agustín Farabundo Martí. He gave the *hacienda* he inherited to his workers, fought briefly with Sandino in Nicaragua, and founded the Communist party of El Salvador. However, it has also been argued that the role of Martí and his handful of followers has been exaggerated by leftist historians and that it was the *cofradías,* the Indian brotherhoods, that brought about the uprising. In any event, Martí and his two closest associates, having been arrested with incriminating documents in their possession, were already in jail when the uprising began. They remained there until it was suppressed and the retaliation, which Salvadorans call *la matanza,* the slaughter, had begun. They were then taken out and shot.

As Thomas P. Anderson notes in *Matanza,* his study of the revolt and its aftermath, the rebellion spread from village to village like a train of powder. A mob of perhaps 1,000 barefoot, half-starved *campesinos,* most of them Indians, marched on Sonsonate, the nearest market town. A few carried firearms, but the rest had only their broad-bladed razor-sharp machetes. Some members of the small Sonsonate garrison mutinied. When the mob arrived, it overwhelmed the loyal troops. There were killings, and the town was looted. Villages lying between Sonsonate and San Salvador joined the uprising. Another mob formed and straggled toward the capital.

Hernández Martínez took command of the army—probably no more than 500 men and a few machine guns. He drove the rebels out of Santa Tecla, five miles west of San Salvador, and advanced quickly on Sonsonate. The *campesinos* dispersed to their villages and then into the mountains. Within a week the fighting had ended. The slaughter began and continued for more than a month. Landowners and their vassals roamed the western half of the country, killing as they went. Traditional Indian dress or language was taken as a mark of complicity, and the *matanza* is thought to have brought about the final dissolution of Indian society in El Salvador.

When the rebellion broke out, alarmist reports led the United States and Canada to dispatch warships to Salvadoran waters. Their captains had orders, according to Anderson, to land marines, if requested by Hernández Martínez, to protect foreign lives and property. By the time they arrived he was in a position to decline the offer with thanks. He said that the uprising had been crushed and 4,800 traitors "liqui-dated." In the absence of adequate records, Anderson estimates the total of the dead at 8,000 to 10,000. The right usually accepts Hernán-dez Martínez's figure, while the left favors the official Communist ver-sion of 30,000. The rebels, according to the government, killed 35 ci-vilians and 30 soldiers and police.

Hernández Martínez was now firmly in power—more firmly than the oligarchy might have wished. He suppressed political parties, ex-iled potential rivals, and ruled by decree. He discomfited the oligarchy by distributing token parcels of state-owned land to *campesinos* and by taking away their power to manipulate the currency. He indulged his eccentricities. These included spiritualism and a belief in reincarna-tion, which led to his being called *El Brujo,* the Witch.

It seemed that Hernández Martínez might rule for life, but in 1944, everyone had suddenly had enough of him. There were disorders that grew into a general strike. The armed forces ignored his orders. Her-nández Martínez went quietly, but only as far as Honduras, where he awaited a call to return. It never came. He bought a *hacienda* and lived quietly until 1966, when he was murdered by an employee. After the deposition of Hernández Martínez, his chief of police, Colonel Osmín Aguirre Salinas, one of the chief executioners of the *matanza,* briefly held the presidency. In 1981, he was shot dead by leftist assassins as he stood in front of his home with his grandchildren. Salvadorans have long memories.

A farcical election, won by a general, was staged in 1945. He was overthrown in 1948 by a coup of young officers. One of their number won the election in 1950. He imposed a harsh regime. It was over-turned by officers of a reformist outlook. They were ousted after only a year in power because, at the height of the postwar coffee boom, when growers were making fortunes every year, they decreed one day off a week with pay for the workers.

During the prosperity of the 1950's, the country's growing middle class became conscious of its lack of political power. The snubs of the oligarchs and the army were infuriating to physicians, lawyers, ac-countants, and engineers. As they saw it, the old system of exploitation and repression could not go on working indefinitely. If reforms were not made, there would eventually be a rebellion, and it was likely to be more successful than the one of 1932. The oligarchs could leave, but the middle class did not have bank accounts in New York and Zurich and mansions in Miami. The middle class found a vehicle of capitalist reform in the Christian Democratic party, which had already been successfully transplanted from West Germany and Italy to Venezuela, Colombia, and Chile.

In November, 1960, a couple of weeks after the election of John F. Kennedy as President, eight men founded the Christian Democratic party of El Salvador. One of them, José Napoleón Duarte, a civil engineer and contractor who was a graduate of Notre Dame University in Indiana, became its secretary-general. In its first public statement the party warned of the dangers of Communist penetration in the Caribbean, but it also demanded land reform, better schools and health care, and equitable taxation.

The Christian Democrats ran for office for the first time in 1962 and were wiped out. Two years later it was different. Duarte was elected mayor of San Salvador, and the party won 36 other mayoralties and 14 of the 52 seats in the Assembly, second only to the Party of National Conciliation, the PCN, which had so totally dominated politics since the overthrow of Hernández Martínez that it was known as the official party.

As mayor, Duarte transformed a largely ceremonial office into a full-time job. He put his social theories into practice by forming 60 Communitarian Action self-help organizations in the city's poorer districts. He installed streetlighting all over the city. San Salvador did not have independent borrowing power, so Duarte persuaded the central government to approve a loan of $6,000,000 from the Inter-American Development Bank to build new municipal markets. Lacking also the power to impose new taxes, he concentrated on collecting arrears that had been piling up for decades. In 1966, Duarte was reelected by a two-to-one majority, and in 1968, by three to one. In that year the Christian Democrats also elected the mayors of 79 cities and towns, including Santa Ana and San Vicente, the second and third largest cities in the country. They increased their representation in the Assembly to the point that the combined minority parties had more seats than the PCN.

As the Christian Democrats began preparing for the election of 1972, when Duarte, clearly the most popular man in the country, was to be the candidate, the 25-year period of peace and increasing prosperity to which the party owed much of its success was ending. Coffee, cotton, and sugar prices dropped for the second year in a row. The boom was

84

over. Worse, in 1969, El Salvador found itself, as a result of a rush of outraged patriotism to the brain, at war with Honduras.

To North Americans, the immediate cause of the conflict—the harassment of the Salvadoran national soccer team during a World Cup preliminary match in Tegucigalpa—would have seemed absurdly trivial. However, in most of the world, soccer is less a sport than a national passion. In Latin America, *fútbol* is less a passion than an obsession. Beyond that, Salvadoran rage had been fermenting for more than a year over an altogether more important matter. That was the expulsion of thousands of Salvadorans who were occupying vacant land in the border regions of Honduras. The Honduran government said it needed the land to distribute to its own landless peasants. Salvadorans thought otherwise. As they saw it, the Hondurans, who had more land than they knew what to do with, were bitterly jealous of the Salvadoran immigrants, whose intelligence, hard work, and thrift had caused desolate areas to bloom.

Diplomatic notes were exchanged. Demands for apologies and reparations were made and rejected. Salvadoran blood boiled, something that happens quickly in Latin America. The armed forces were mobilized. Two spearheads composed of a couple of dozen antique armored cars and light tanks and perhaps 1,500 men clanked across the border into Honduras. Four days of intermittent combat, in which most of the casualties were civilians, exhausted the military capabilities of both sides. Having satisfied national honor with a penetration into the Honduran wilderness of 20 miles at some points and having occupied a couple of towns, El Salvador was delighted to accept a cease-fire and a withdrawal arranged by the Organization of American States. Honduras, which had no prospect of ejecting the Salvadorans, agreed.

Salvadorans of every stripe had united behind the war. Duarte, the Christian Democrats, and the 60 Communitarian Action associations cheered as loudly as anyone else. Their enthusiasm for the war was in part genuine and in part a reply to accusations of leftist and pacifist inclinations. When the cheering stopped, El Salvador had a bill of tens of millions of dollars for its moment of glory. The Football War, as it was called, also wrecked, to El Salvador's great cost, the Central American Common Market. Honduras embargoed Salvadoran manufactures, for which it had been the biggest customer, and closed the Pan American Highway to Salvadoran shipments to Costa Rica and Panama.

The tiny Salvadoran Communist party, which had been lying low since the Cuban missile crisis, also supported the war, a decision that divided the party. In 1970, Salvador Cayetano Carpio, the secretary-general and a leader of the bakers' union, resigned in protest. He formed the Popular Forces of Liberation, the FPL, and went underground. It marked the beginning of the insurrection that by 1980 had become open warfare.

A month before the municipal and Assembly elections of 1970, the Christian Democrats convened an agrarian reform congress. Its guiding spirit was Enrique Álvarez, a member of an oligarchy family, who was Minister of Agriculture. To the consternation of the big landowners, Colonel Fidel Sánchez Hernández, the president of the republic, attended its sessions and did not publicly disagree with its conclusion that reform was imperative.

El Salvador was the smallest nation in Latin America, with an area of 8,260 square miles, about the same as New Jersey's, but since the 1950's its population had been increasing at the rate of about 3 percent a year. It was already by far the most densely populated country in Latin America—more densely populated, for that matter, than China or India, which have always been bywords for dense, teeming populations. El Salvador's population then stood at 4,200,000, and has since grown, despite the war, to 5,000,000 or more. New Jersey is also more densely populated than India, but unlike El Salvador, it is predominantly urban and suburban rather than agricultural.

El Salvador also ranked first in Latin America in its concentration of ownership of land and in its proportion of landless peasants. On the other hand, Salvadoran statistics may have been less inaccurate than those of other countries. In any case, 1 percent of the population owned 50 percent of the land, and the best land at that, and 2 percent owned 60 percent. Of the rural population, 35 percent had no land at all, either rented or owned, and worked as day laborers or not at all. Of those who owned or rented land, only 4 percent farmed more than 12 acres, the minimum for family self-sufficiency. Moreover, the population increase and the conversion of land used for corn and beans into pasture for beef cattle, sugar, and cotton for export were increasing the number of landless year by year. El Salvador's gross national product had been increasing at a rate of more than 5 percent a year during the 1960's, double the goal set by the Alliance for Progress, and income distribution had improved somewhat in the industrial sector of the economy, but in agriculture, in part because of the labor surplus, it had worsened.

Álvarez, who had given his *hacienda* to his workers to operate as a cooperative, urged the adoption of an expropriation law that would do the same with all of the country's big estates. Other delegates favored breaking them up into family plots. Sánchez Hernández and the National Assembly, under intense pressure from the oligarchy, rejected both proposals. Instead, the Assembly passed a law that set limits on the size of farms that benefited from public irrigation projects. It had almost no effect in reducing the size of landholdings.

The land reform congress did not help the Christian Democrats at the polls. Without Duarte, who had decided to prepare for the 1972 presidential election rather than to seek a fourth term as mayor, they barely managed to hold San Salvador. They lost 70 of their 79 municipalities and three of their 19 seats in the National Assembly. Overconfidence, the worsening economy, the prestige of the military in the afterglow of the Football War, and, in all likelihood, some irregularities in the counting of the vote all played a part in the defeat. However, the party was less downcast than it might have been, being certain that Duarte would lead a comeback two years hence.

In February, 1971, a member of El Salvador's richest and most socially prominent family was forced from his car and kidnapped near his mansion in Escalón. The victim was Ernesto Regalado Dueñas. The linked families—Dueñas was the maiden name of Ernesto's mother, which is customarily but not invariably appended to the father's surname—had vast landholdings and were thought to control as much as 15 or 20 percent of the nation's commerce. Their wealth was estimated at $500,000,000. Both the Regalado and Dueñas families had provided presidents of the republic. Ernesto's father was famous for his elaborate entertainments and more than once had chartered airliners to fly his guests to Spain or the south of France.

Ernesto was a full-time manager of his family's businesses. He lived a quietly opulent life with his wife, an American, and their children. The oligarchs were a largely unseen presence as far as the rest of the population was concerned. Their San Salvador residences often occupied entire large blocks surrounded by high stone walls or, in hilly Escalón or San Benito, stood so far above street level as to be invisible behind a screen of trees and shrubs.

The kidnappers demanded a ransom of $1,000,000. Eight days later, before it could be paid, Ernesto Regalado Dueñas's body was found. It was riddled with bullets and showed signs of torture. The kidnap-murder was the crime of the century in what was still a comparatively peaceful country. Scores of other abductions of members of the oligarchy, foreign businessmen, and diplomats followed over the next several years. Sometimes the victims turned up unharmed after the ransom had been paid, and sometimes they turned up dead or not at all.

There is no doubt that leftist groups committed almost all these kidnappings—in some cases they announced their responsibility—and that they used the ransom money to buy weapons for the armed insurrection to come. However, the abduction and murder of Ernesto Regalado Dueñas remain not only the first but also the most puzzling of these crimes. Several members of a radical group at the National University that had split off from the Christian Democrats were charged with the crime, but only one was arrested, and he was eventually acquitted.

Heading his defense was Rubén Zamora, who was then a member of the university faculty and now serves on the Diplomatic Commission of the Democratic Revolutionary Front-Farabundo Martí Front for National Liberation, the FDR-FMLN, the umbrella organization for the moderate and militant insurgents.

"It was astonishing," Zamora told me. "There was no evidence, and we got an honest judge and a courageous jury."

The Regalado Dueñas family was skeptical enough of the official version of events to hire former agents of the Federal Bureau of Investigation to look into the case. The dead man's younger brother, Raúl, published, under a pseudonym, a pamphlet, *The Regalado Case,* that implicated President Fidel Sánchez Hernández and General José Alberto Medrano, who commanded the expeditionary force in the war against Honduras. Ernesto, it was noted, had headed a committee that raised millions of dollars for new equipment for the armed forces. Much of the money had not been accounted for, and Ernesto was said to have accused the president and, possibly, Medrano of having stolen it. Raúl, who had a history of drug addiction, committed suicide not long afterward. His father died in 1974. The cause of death was given as a heart attack, but he was also said to have killed himself.

As the presidential election of 1972 approached, it was apparent that it would be in many respects a replay of 1931. The economy was weakening, putting the country's rigid political and social framework under tremendous stress. The Christian Democrats, as expected, nominated Duarte. On the theory that every vote helps they formed a coalition with two tiny parties of the left. These were the National Revolutionary Movement, the MNR, which was the equivalent of the Social Democrats of Europe, and the Democratic National Union, the UDN, the political vehicle of the Communist party. The UDN, because it was all but dormant, was still tolerated by the government. The MNR's Guillermo Ungo, the son of a founder of the Christian Democrats, became the vice-presidential candidate.

The political right was splintered, as it was in 1931—this time into three segments. One supported the PCN, the official party, which nominated Colonel Arturo Armando Molina. Another, composed mainly of coffee growers, backed Medrano. Yet another, so far to the right that it regarded the PCN as socialistic, backed a lawyer named José Rodríguez Porth. Ten years later Porth was generally thought to be the man who controlled D'Aubuisson's ARENA party from Miami.

Duarte waged an unusually vigorous campaign in every corner of the country, all 140 by 70 miles of it. He continued to do so even after an assassin, aiming at him, had killed his chauffeur. Duarte laid out the Communitarian program—economic planning, industrialization, assistance to small business, and democracy. He promised agrarian reform, an enforced minimum wage, the right to form unions, and better schools and health services. He made more than 600 speeches during the three-month campaign. He had worked hard to turn himself into the sort of orator that Salvadoran crowds liked to listen to—florid, emotional, and long-winded.

A Salvadoran who was then an admirer of Duarte but is no longer, told me, "He was not just a winner but also a charismatic figure. The women, especially, loved him. He was handsome and vigorous. He was always walking into the crowds, shaking hands and embracing the voters. None of the colonels ever did that sort of thing."

His opponents attacked Duarte, the Christian Democrats, and the coalition as Communists who took their orders from Fidel Castro. The PCN was unable to adjust to having serious opposition, and the other candidates were running for exercise. Molina, who had been Sánchez Hernández's secretary, visited the major cities and towns by helicopter, spent most of his evenings at home and his nights in his own bed, and left it to the party to get out the vote, pay for it, and count it.

* * *

The last chance that El Salvador may have had to transform itself more or less peacefully from a military-administered oligarchy into a functioning democracy came, and went, on that election day, February 20, 1972. The turnout was heavy all over the country, and no one now seriously disputes the fact that Duarte won. He did not, however, take office. The government, which controlled the election machinery, permitted the casting of tens of thousands of fraudulent ballots, mainly in the countryside. When the vote from San Salvador and the other major cities, which went overwhelmingly for Duarte, showed that these precautions had been inadequate, the government stopped announcing returns. The stuffed ballot boxes, or *tamales,* were brought to the headquarters of the Central Elections Commission in the capital. Enough creative recounting was done there to give the victory to Molina by a narrow margin.

Since none of the candidates had a majority, the decision was made by the vote of the National Assembly, which was controlled by the PCN. The Assembly convened three days later and, while the Christian Democratic members cried fraud, declared Molina the winner. Many of Duarte's colleagues demanded that he refuse to submit to so brazen a robbery. Some urged him to call a general strike. Others spoke of taking up arms. Duarte counseled patience and faith in the ultimate triumph of the democratic process.

The question was still being debated when, on March 25, Colonel Benjamín Mejía, an army officer of liberal reputation, attempted his own coup. As the commander of the Zapote Barracks, a walled compound that occupies a hill overlooking the Presidential Palace, he was in a strong tactical position. Mejía proclaimed himself the ruler of the country, peppered the palace and nearby areas with artillery fire, and arrested Sánchez Hernández, whose term did not expire until June 30.

Duarte, who had not known what was afoot, was implored to throw his support to Mejía. After several hours of soul-searching, he did so, at least to the extent of making a radio broadcast, in which he asked his listeners to strew nails on the highways to impede the movements of loyalist troops. By then convoys from outlying garrisons were already rolling into San Salvador, and the coup was quickly put down.

Sánchez Hernández vowed vengeance. Mejía had escaped his clutches, finding asylum with the Papal Nuncio and then receiving a safe-conduct to Costa Rica, so he seized the hapless Duarte, Ungo, and many of their supporters. Duarte was beaten while in custody. His nose and both cheekbones were broken. He was charged with treason, but instead of a trial or summary execution, he was deported to Guatemala. From there he made his way to Venezuela, where, under the protection of the Christian Democratic government, he spent the next seven and a half years as an exile.

Despite an official protest by the Christian Democrats, Washington took no official notice of the stolen election. Press coverage was uninformative. A wire service account of the election published in *The New York Times* described Duarte as "a leftist politician" and mentioned only in passing his charges of fraud. Mejía's failed coup rated only a couple of paragraphs.

Having been made aware of its utter powerlessness, the political center, ranging from the moderate left to the moderate right, fell into a long decline. If it were not for the unwillingness of mankind to abandon its favorite illusions, the center would have collapsed immediately. For the first time the radical left, whose influence had not previously extended very far beyond the campus of the National University, found recruits in the shantytowns, the factories, and the countryside.

New leaders emerged on the left, as intoxicated as the far right by bloody and uncompromising strategies. Many made their way to Cuba to study insurrection. Rival organizations to Carpio's FPL were established on the basis of differences over obscure points of Communist theology. From the beginning, the FPL followed the strategy of "Prolonged People's War" as enunciated by Mao Zedong and Ho Chi Minh. It required patient organization and indoctrination, the establishment of centers of strength in the countryside, the gaining of influence in unions, schools, and other organizations, and the development of secret support in the armed forces and the government. Only then, and only in situations in which success seemed assured, would hit-and-run raids, ambushes, and rapid retreats evolve into open warfare, first on the periphery and then, as the enemy became disorganized, at the center of his strength.

In 1971, the organization of militants at the National University, which called itself *El Grupo,* the Group, and which had been accused of the Regalado Dueñas kidnapping, transformed itself into the People's Revolutionary Army, the ERP in its Spanish acronym. Within a couple of years it split into two factions. One, led by Joaquín Villalobos, who still commands it, favored daring "insurrectionist" strokes at the heart of the government. The other, one of whose leaders was Roque Dalton, a poet and polemicist who had returned to El Salvador in 1973 from 13 years in exile in Cuba and Europe, favored the Carpio strategy.

The dispute simmered until 1975, when the Villalobos faction accused Dalton of being a spy for the CIA. Dalton and another man were murdered, reportedly by Villalobos himself. Dalton's literary works and his long residence in Cuba and Eastern Europe had made him, at home and abroad, the revolution's most glamorous figure. His murder by his own comrades was a considerable embarrassment. The Dalton faction then left the ERP to form the Armed Forces of National Resistance, or FARN. The total membership of the three groups was probably a couple of hundred, and none was able to gain any significant popular support until the government responded to their kidnappings and bombings with the indiscriminate use of counterterror.

In his first months in office, Molina made the ritual gestures of conciliation, decreeing a minimum agricultural wage of $1.10 a day, which landowners generally ignored, and establishing the Salvadoran Institute of Agrarian Transformation, ISTA, to carry out a widely publicized land reform. It turned out to be the sale of a few thousand acres of government-owned land..The suppression of the left was undertaken with more enthusiasm. Martial law was imposed. Hundreds of persons—far more, in all likelihood, than the membership of all the subversive groups combined—were imprisoned without trial. The National University, which was suspected, probably correctly, of being a hotbed of treason, was closed after a raid by the security forces in which 50 students were killed. As strikes and demonstrations became more frequent, so did the shooting of those taking part. The death squads of off-duty police and free-lance *pistoleros* were granted a year-round open season on leftist suspects.

Duarte was still in exile when the presidential election of 1977 rolled around. The Christian Democrats, disorganized and divided over the issue of whether to put up a candidate at all, finally selected an army officer who was not even a member of the party. He was Colonel Ernesto Claramount, who had commanded an armored battalion in the Football War. What recommended him, aside from a reformist outlook, was the fact that he could scarcely be accused of being a Communist. The PCN candidate was General Carlos Humberto Romero, who had been Molina's Minister of the Interior. (The Salvadoran constitution, like many others in Latin America, prohibits a president from serving consecutive terms. Unlike many other articles in that document, it has been observed without exception since 1945.)

The PCN rigged the election even more blatantly than it had in 1972. For some sections of the country, the official results list no figures at all. Claramount, unlike Duarte, at least did something. He and a couple of hundred of his followers occupied a church and remained there until his brother officers threatened to shoot his family. He gave up and went into exile in Costa Rica. Upon taking office, Romero didn't even go through the motions of acting conciliatory. Within months the repression had become so savage and so random that El Salvador received Amnesty International's lowest human rights rating and was condemned by the Organization of American States. The Carter administration warned Romero that arms sales would be cut off if he didn't start showing more concern for his citizens. Romero simply began buying in Europe.

Thanks to Romero's repression, the left began to attract supporters. They were formed into what became known as mass organizations, comprising groups of labor unionists, students, teachers, slum dwellers, peasants, and the like. Priests were prominent in their leadership. By the beginning of 1979, they were claiming a total membership of 100,000. The mass organizations provided the live bodies for demonstrations, strikes, and other shows of leftist strength, which also meant serving as sitting ducks for the security forces.

After the overthrow of the Somoza dynasty in Nicaragua in July, 1979, the Carter administration adopted a harder line toward El Salvador. By then, Romero was losing the support of the business community. Even some big landowners were wondering if it was wise to entrust their future to a government that seemed to make every problem worse. Even the army—in particular, junior officers who had not yet lost their youthful idealism—was unhappy with Romero.

In August, as Romero's fall began to seem imminent, the Christian Democrats and the nonviolent left, including the Communist party and elements of the mass organizations, formed a coalition called the Popular Forum. In October, a group of young officers asked Colonel Adolfo Arnoldo Majano, who was known as a moderate, and Colonel Jaime Abdul Gutiérrez to lead a coup. Romero submitted without a struggle and flew off to Miami. The two colonels invited three civilians to join them in forming a junta. Two of them, Guillermo Ungo, Duarte's running mate in 1972, and Román Mayorga, the rector of the Central American University, were leaders of the Popular Forum.

The junta retired or dismissed about 100 officers of the armed forces and the police who were thought to be connected with the extreme right and the death squads. Most of them were soon reinstated, but one who was not was Roberto D'Aubuisson, a major in army intelligence and a protégé of Medrano's. The junta also ordered the disbanding of ORDEN, which had been founded by Medrano in the early 1960's. The name, an acronym, formed the Spanish word for "order." Nominally a rural auxiliary police force, it also functioned as a subversive-hunting vigilante and extortion group.

A broad, progressive, and not entirely realistic social program was announced by the junta. With so much progress imminent, two of the guerrilla forces agreed to a 30-day truce. They broke it a few days later, when it became known that 300 political prisoners whose release had been promised had "disappeared" from their cells. It was presumed that they had been murdered by Romero's security forces, but few bodies were ever found. It also turned out that the junta, despite the membership of the two colonels, could not gain control of the armed forces or enact its program over the opposition of the oligarchy. The chief obstructionist was the Minister of Defense, Colonel José Guillermo García. In December, the junta dismissed him. García, supported by the commanders of the National Guard and the National Police, stayed in office.

In December, five Cabinet members, including Enrique Álvarez, the oligarch who was the Minister of Agriculture, resigned in protest. Salvador Samayoa, the Minister of Education, did so at a press conference. It ended when masked and armed guerrillas entered the room. Samayoa left with them, saying that the time for talk had passed. A few weeks later, Ungo and Mayorga said they, too, would quit if García did not step aside. García refused to budge, and on January 2, 1980, they, every other member of the Cabinet, most of the subcabinet, and several judges of the Supreme Court left the government.

It is generally accepted that the Carter administration, as it maintained, had nothing to do with the ouster of Romero beyond showing its displeasure with him. It also did little or nothing to help the junta in its test of strength with García. Majano and Gutiérrez named José Antonio Morales Ehrlich, who had succeeded Duarte as mayor of San Salvador, and Héctor Dada Hirezi, who had been Foreign Minister, as the new members of the junta. Both were Christian Democrats. Several other members of the party who had left the government with Ungo and Mayorga decided to give it another try. Among them were Mario Zamora, who resumed his post as Attorney General, and his younger brother, Rubén, the Minister of the Presidency, or liaison with other departments. Duarte, who had returned from exile after the overthrow of Romero, remained on the sidelines. He and the party leaders agreed that he would be the presidential candidate in an election that was expected to take place within a year.

On the same day that the new members of the junta were sworn in, the three guerrilla groups and the mass organizations set up a joint planning body called Political-Military Coordination. The Communist party, belatedly becoming militant, joined it. Shafik Handal, the leader of the party, soon became, with his connections in the Kremlin, one of its most important figures. (Handal is a member of a well-to-do merchant family of Lebanese Christian descent, one of many in Central America that began as peddlers. They are still collectively, and incorrectly, referred to as *turcos,* or Turks.)

In February, 1980, the coordinating group organized a protest march in the center of San Salvador. As usual, it was fired on by the police. The death toll was put at 20 to 50, depending on who was doing the counting, and the number of wounded as high as 250. Such events took place many times. The leftists created martyrs, and the police and troops had the pleasure of shooting down subversives who had nothing to shoot back with. Few nights passed in which the *escuadrones de muerte,* the death squads, did not claim at least five or 10 victims. In the first 10 weeks of 1980, according to the Salvadoran Human Rights Commission, 689 persons, all but a few of them leftists and almost none of them armed guerrillas, were killed.

Later in February, D'Aubuisson publicly denounced Mario Zamora, the Attorney General, as a secret member of the Communist party. In his efforts to find out what had happened to the 300 missing political prisoners, a subject about which D'Aubuisson may have known a thing or two, Zamora was learning how limited were the investigative powers of the country's chief legal officer. Two nights later, several men pushed their way into Zamora's home during a dinner party. They asked the men present to identify themselves. When Zamora did so, they shot him dead.

The police followed routine procedure in such cases—that is, they did nothing at all. Héctor Dada thereupon resigned from the junta. Rubén Zamora left the Cabinet and formed the Popular Christian Social

Movement, which split what remained of the Christian Democratic party. Washington was now gripped by the law of diplomatic gravity. That is, its determination to save El Salvador from communism increased in proportion to every occurrence that diminished its chance of doing so. The Carter administration decided that Duarte would have to come off the bench. In return, he demanded the immediate enactment of the reforms, agrarian reform foremost among them, that the military and the oligarchy had been blocking for years.

The American Embassy told García and the rest of the hard-line colonels that the acceptance of Duarte and his program was the price of continued aid. Even though the colonels may have suspected that Washington was bluffing, they chose Duarte, reasoning that the reducing of the power of the oligarchy could be made to work to their advantage. Thus, on March 6, 1980, immediately after Duarte had joined the junta, it issued three decrees. The banking system and the exporting of coffee, which were manipulated by the oligarchy for its own benefit, were nationalized. Most important, all *haciendas* of more than 500 hectares were expropriated and turned into cooperatives operated by their workers. (A hectare is 10,000 square meters, or 2.47 acres.) This was called Phase I of the land reform. In Phase II, for which no date was set, *haciendas* of between 100 and 500 hectares were to be expropriated. Phase III, which was enacted in April, 1980, gave to tenant farmers the right to buy the land they rented up to a maximum of seven hectares.

Because Luis Chávez y González, the archbishop of San Salvador, looked with favor on the reforms proposed at Medellín, they were not ignored so totally in El Salvador as they were in most others parts of Central America. But even with the archbishop's qualified blessings, only a few priests, almost all of them foreign missionaries and in particular the Jesuits, embraced the Theology of Liberation. As these activist priests saw it, the poor of the cities and the countryside were powerless to improve their lot because they were unorganized. Because the poor were inexperienced in forming organizations and making protests, the priests helped them. These activities brought them into contact, and often into collaboration, with the militant left. A community of interests was created. Priests began looking at the conflict in Marxist terms, as is easy to do in Latin America, where capitalists, imperialists, their lackeys, and the suffering masses portray themselves in vivid and unmistakable terms.

When Chávez retired in 1977, the year in which the presidency was stolen from Claramount, he was succeeded by his auxiliary bishop, Oscar Arnulfo Romero. Activist priests feared that the new archbishop, who had been known as a traditionalist, might oppose them. And so he might have, but three weeks after his elevation one of the most distinguished priests in his diocese, the Reverend Rutilio Grande, and two of his parishioners were murdered. Grande, a Jesuit, was the pastor of the church at Aguilares, about 25 miles north of the capital. He had made enemies there by helping to organize a successful strike at a sugar mill. After Grande's death, the other 54 Jesuits in El Salvador were warned that they would also be murdered if they remained. The threat was ignored.

Romero was outraged by Grande's murder. He closed church schools for three days. On the "ninth day" remembrance of Grande's death, all masses in the country were canceled except for his. Romero also informed President Molina that the church would not take part in official governmental activities until the circumstances of Grande's death were "clarified." They never were, and that July, despite pleas and threats, the archbishop refused to attend the inauguration of President Romero, to whom he was not related.

The archbishop's denunciations from the pulpit of government repression became more frequent and unsparing. The oligarchy and his fellow bishops, all but one of whom opposed him, complained to Rome of his "Communist" activities. Church inspectors, called apostolic visitors, arrived in San Salvador. The Papal Nuncio, speaking for the Pope, urged him to lower his voice. When he did not, he was summoned to Rome "for consultations."

In November, 1978, another priest was shot dead under circumstances that suggested that he had been accompanying a unit of the Popular Forces of Liberation, Carpio's group. Romero attended the funeral service. As he was leaving the church, he said, as quoted in the Reverend Plácido Erdozaín's *Archbishop Romero: Martyr of Salvador,* "When a dictatorship seriously violates human rights and attacks the common good of the nation, when it becomes unbearable and closes all channels of dialogue, of understanding, or rationality, when this happens, the church speaks of the legitimate right of insurrectional violence."

In March, 1980, not long after returning from the Puebla conference, Romero, in his Sunday homily in the Cathedral of San Salvador, declared, "I want to make a special appeal to soldiers, national guardsmen, and policemen: Brothers, each of you is one of us. We are the same people. The *campesinos* you kill are your own brothers and sisters. When you hear the words of a man telling you to kill, remember instead the words of God, 'Thou shalt not kill.' God's law must prevail. No soldier is obliged to obey an order contrary to the law of God. It is time that you come to your senses and obey your conscience rather than follow out a sinful command. The church, defender of the rights of God, the law of God, and the dignity of each human being, cannot remain silent in the presence of such abominations.''

Romero knew that the armed forces would see this exhortation for what it was—an incitement to mutiny. Two days later, while he was saying a memorial mass at the chapel of a hospital for cancer patients, a man with a rifle appeared at the doorway and killed him with a single shot.

Many foreign prelates attended the funeral. Among them was the president of the National Conference of Catholic Bishops, which had supported Romero. However, only one of the five Salvadoran bishops—Romero's protégé, Arturo Rivera y Damas—was present. Tens of thousands gathered in the square in front of the cathedral to listen to the service over loudspeakers. While it was in progress, shooting began from the surrounding buildings, and explosives were set off. Those closest to the church tried to force their way inside. In the crush, scores of persons were thrown down and trampled. Between 25 and 100 persons, depending, as usual, on the source of the estimate, were killed, either by shooting or in the melee.

The neobaroque cathedral where Romero preached and where he is interred is unfinished and likely to remain so. When construction was begun in the late 1950's, the hierarchy was counting on the generosity of the oligarchy, which then stood at a pinnacle of wealth and political power. However, for the rich of Latin America, more markedly than in most places, charity begins, and ends, at home. It is the poor who have always supported the church.

Within a few years, construction was slowing down for lack of money. By the early 1970's, it had come to a halt. At that point, Archbishop Chávez, filled with the spirit of Medellín, announced that whatever funds were available were from then on to be spent "on the Church rather than on churches."

And so the unfinished cathedral stands in the center of San Salvador, an ugly gray shell of reinforced concrete. It would no doubt look better if the scaffolding of iron pipe were removed, if it were sheathed, as planned, with limestone on the outside and marble within, if the window openings enclosed stained glass instead of translucent corrugated plastic, and if it were lighted by candelabra rather than fluorescent tubing. However, these cosmetic devices could not conceal the fact that the structure is too large for its site and so poorly proportioned that it seems to be both cramped and cavernous, inflated and oppressive. It has become a symbol of the end of the long "triumphalist" era in church history in Latin America.

The Central American University was founded by the Society of Jesus in 1965. Once again, the oligarchy looked the other way when the hat was being passed. Indeed, the university would not have been built at all without a long-term, low-interest loan from the Inter-American Development Bank.

The campus is set on a long hillside in the suburbs of the capital. It symbolizes the era of renewal of which Paul VI spoke as much as the cathedral does the past. Its buildings, which are constructed of unadorned concrete, are modest in scale and harmonious in design—simple geometrical elements linked by covered ramps and open cylindrical stairwells. Religion is a minor part of the curriculum, most of the teachers are laymen, and the great majority of its 5,000 students receive financial assistance. With the closing of the National University, it became the country's only major institution of higher education. There seems to be little political activity, let alone revolutionary agitation, on the campus, the Jesuits being more interested in keeping the university open than in using it to promote radical social theory or action.

On my first trip to El Salvador, in March, 1981, I spoke there with a Spanish Jesuit. He was a handsome man in his mid-forties, with a broad forehead, deep-set gray eyes, a straight, prominent nose, and a strong chin. When he spoke, it was with such measured and eloquent irony and fury that his words seemed like bolts of lightning and peals of thunder.

He recalled that the Jesuits were expelled from El Salvador in 1885 for agitating too vigorously against the seizures of church lands but were invited back in 1916 to establish a secondary school, the Colegio de San José.

"It was perhaps an error for us to do this since it turned out to be a school for the sons of the oligarchy," he said. "We liked too much in those days to sit at the tables of the rich. We were unable, in any case, to convert our pupils to true Christianity. Perhaps we could not do so because we had not been converted ourselves."

He paused to light another cigarette, and his hand shook. "After the Vatican Council and Medellín the church had second thoughts about itself," he said. "It recognized its faults and saw that its mission must be the promotion of faith and justice and that the two cannot be separated. First the people have to live, and only then be Christians. I am by birth and training a conservative, but in my 15 years in El Salvador I have been radicalized, not that I like that term. The dividing line, to me, is whether or not you have a human sensibility. I will tell you how anti-Communist I used to be. I *regretted* that the Bay of Pigs invasion did not succeed. I was *happy* when your marines landed in the Dominican Republic. It didn't even bother me when Allende 'committed suicide,' as your government said.

"Now I am humiliated to think of it," he said. "I admit I was wrong. And I will tell you something else. I wish the *gringos* to be beaten here! I will not call them *norteamericanos*! I will call them *gringos*! And I will tell you that the policy of the *gringo* Department of State is damned. *Maldito!* In Spanish this is a very strong word. The only stronger one would be to say that they are all sons of bitches! It is true that I favor the poor against the oligarchs. I am against violence, but even more against unjust violence. I talked yesterday to a nun in Chalatenango. She told me that seven guerrillas who surrendered under the amnesty were immediately taken out and shot. If the solution to this is Marxism, let it come, rather than what is here."

Even if it meant, I asked, the suppression of the church?

"Even that," he replied. "What is lost? Freedom of expression? Freedom to travel? Free enterprise? Who loses it? Not the *campesinos*!" He paused again, gazing at the ceiling through the smoke of his cigarette. "Not that I think this would happen," he said. "The strongest of the guerrilla groups are anti-Soviet. What I foresee for this country is an independent socialism like Poland's."

That conversation took place, of course, before the rise and fall of Solidarity and Lech Walesa.

In April, 1980, the moderate opposition in El Salvador formed the Democratic Revolutionary Front. Its chairman was Enrique Álvarez, the idealistic oligarch. Rubén Zamora's Popular Christian Social Movement became a charter member. At about the same time, D'Aubuisson formed the Broad Opposition Front, representing the extreme right. In May, he and 20 confederates were arrested by troops loyal to Majano and the junta at a *hacienda* outside San Salvador. Compromising documents were seized, and they were charged with plotting a coup. D'Aubuisson's high-ranking supporters blocked his prosecution, and he was quickly freed.

The next month, the guerrilla factions, whose number had increased from three to five with the addition of the Armed Forces of Liberation, which was affiliated with the Communist party, and the tiny Central American Revolutionary Workers party, headed by a student named Roberto Roca, formed the Unified Revolutionary Directorate and announced an alliance with Álvarez's Democratic Revolutionary Front. At that point, even collectively, the guerrillas were not an impressive force. Their combined strength was probably no more than 1,500. They were poorly armed and trained, and had done little actual fighting. Nonetheless, the directorate proclaimed the mountainous areas near the Honduran border in which they had set up their base camps as "the Free Territory of El Salvador."

The Salvadoran army at last knew where to look. Troops moved into the free territory, burning villages and shooting anything on two legs. In June, 1980, a Catholic missionary from Brooklyn, the Reverend Earl Gallagher, reported that 600 unarmed peasants, most of them women and children, had been killed as they fled across the Sumpul River into Honduras. The Salvadoran government at first denied the report but later conceded that 135 persons, whom it described as guerrillas and their auxiliaries, had been slain. Such massacres occurred many times in the next three years.

In August, the directorate called another general strike—there had been one in March—that tied up the country for two days. No sooner had it ended than the electrical workers struck, blacking out the country. The armed forces retaliated by occupying the campus of the National University and, according to the left, killing 20 students. The university, which had been permitted to reopen after the ouster of Romero, was closed again, and in late 1983, it had not reopened.

As the year went on, the number of dead rose to an average of 1,000 a month, a dreadful figure in a country of only 5,000,000. Perhaps 5 percent—government officials, members of the security forces, suspected informers, and the like—were victims of the left. Nonpolitical homicides may have constituted another 5 percent. The remaining 90 percent were almost unquestionably killed by the security forces, the death squads, and the military. Indeed, the occupations of the dead—peasants, students, teachers, union organizers, lay religious workers, land reform technicians, members of the mass organizations and their families—left no doubt of it.

In November, the leaders of the Democratic Revolutionary Front were meeting in the Jesuits' Colegio de San José when troops surrounded the building. Masked men in civilian clothing entered at gunpoint and abducted Álvarez and five others. Their mutilated bodies were found the next day. A group that called itself the Maximiliano Hernández Martínez Brigade, named, of course, for the leader of the *matanza,* said that it had been responsible.

Robert E. White, the United States Ambassador, called the murders "an unspeakable crime." So it was, but I later found myself wondering why these moderate leftists and even centrists, who could not have had the least doubt that their lives were always in peril, did not carry weapons or find trustworthy bodyguards. *Pistoleros* don't get paid enough in El Salvador—the standard salary is said to be $400 a month—to take serious risks. It may have something to do with fatalism, which runs deep in Latin America, and with having grown up hearing sermons on the glories of martyrdom.

Ungo was chosen as Álvarez's successor. He had been traveling in the United States and Europe on behalf of the front and was in New York at the time of the murders. He did not return to El Salvador but established the front's headquarters, with the permission of President José López Portillo, in Mexico City. Some of the front's surviving leaders, including Rubén Zamora, joined him there. Those who remained in El Salvador went underground. At about the same time the five guerrilla groups went through what turned out to be their last change of identity, naming themselves the Farabundo Martí Front for National Liberation, known as the FMLN, while retaining their individual identities and autonomy.

The first of all those thousands of murders to attract prolonged attention in the United States took place in December, 1980. Four American women, Catholic missionaries, were abducted as they drove from the international airport to San Salvador. Their bodies were found two days later in shallow graves. Their hands were bound, they had been shot at close range, and there were indications that they had been sexually abused. Two of the dead women, Sisters Ita Ford and Maura Clarke, were members of the Maryknoll order; one, Sister Dorothy

102

Kazel, was an Ursuline; and the fourth, Jean Donovan, was a lay worker.

All the circumstances suggested that the crime had been committed by the security forces or the death squads. Carter, who had been defeated by Ronald Reagan a month earlier, immediately embargoed "lethal" military supplies until the killers were arrested. He also sent agents of the Federal Bureau of Investigation to assist the police in whatever effort it might be making to find the killers.

A week after the murders, Duarte paid a quiet visit to Washington. On December 13, after his return, the junta announced that it had reconstituted itself. Duarte was now its president and El Salvador's chief executive, and Gutiérrez vice-president. Morales Ehrlich remained as the third member. Majano, the colonel who favored negotiations with the left, was dropped. "The government has been given to civilians," Duarte declared upon taking office. Not quite. It soon became clear that he still had no control over the armed forces—the only authority worth having during a rebellion.

A couple of weeks before Duarte's trip, D'Aubuisson had also quietly visited the United States. He met with his supporters among the oligarchy in Miami and then went on to Washington for conferences with members of the Reagan transition team and with members of the staff of his great patron, Senator Jesse Helms of North Carolina. Helms was a good man to know. He was the keeper of Reagan's conservative conscience and was about to become chairman of the Inter-American Affairs Subcommittee of the Senate Foreign Relations Committee. As it happened, D'Aubuisson had entered and left the United States illegally. Ambassador White had ordered the cancellation of his multiple-entry visa a couple of months earlier.

On January 2, 1981, two young land reform specialists from the Agency for International Development, Michael P. Hammer and Mark David Pearlman, were lunching with the head of the Institute of Agrarian Transformation, José Rodolfo Viera, in the coffee shop of the Sheraton Hotel. Two men drew pistols, shot the three men dead, and departed without haste by way of the kitchen. None of the many guards at the hotel pursued them.

After a week these matters had to be pushed aside. On January 10, leaders of the Farabundo Martí National Liberation Front held a press conference in Mexico City to announce that the "final offensive" had begun. One of them declared confidently, "I think Mr. Reagan will find an irreversible situation in El Salvador by the time he reaches the Presi-

103

dency." The rebels attacked, and Carter lifted his embargo. Helicopters, infantry weapons, and ammunition were rushed to El Salvador to match the arsenal that Washington said was being provided to the guerrillas by Communist nations. The attack began boldly. The guerrillas briefly held outlying areas of San Salvador and fought their way into several district towns. However, the general strike and the popular uprising they had called for did not occur. Within a few days, they had begun slipping back into the hills.

The Reagan administration took office as the fighting was dying away. It immediately said it was going to "draw the line" in El Salvador against what it described as "interventionist activity" by Cuba and the Soviet Union and sent in the 56 "instructors." Ambassador White, who had publicly criticized the Reagan transition team, the fellows who had entertained D'Aubuisson, for undercutting his efforts to bring about negotiations, was dismissed.

6
At Home with Duarte

THE INTERNATIONAL Press Club was established at the Camino Real Hotel in San Salvador in March, 1981, while I was staying there. To mark the occasion, the management of the hotel provided free drinks. It was an act of generosity so entirely without precedent in the hotel's history that the clock in the lobby stopped.

The party had been in progress for an hour or so when Duarte arrived unexpectedly. He was in an ebullient mood. The guerrillas were licking their wounds, the populace had shown its loyalty to the government, and the weapons and advisers needed to suppress the rebellion were arriving on every plane. For 40 minutes Duarte responded, forcefully but amiably, to questions. When he had finished and was sipping a scotch, I introduced myself, told him that I was writing a long article about El Salvador for *The New Yorker,* and asked for an appointment.

"How about now?" he said. "Come on home with me."

I asked if I might invite two colleagues, and he agreed. We left the hotel shortly after 9:00 P.M. in a convoy of three armored sedans and station wagons, escorted by four motorcycle police. The curfew had just fallen, and the moon-bathed streets were empty and silent. Good citizens sat behind locked doors and drawn curtains, watching dubbed American sitcoms or Mexican soap operas on television. In their shacks, the poor lay down on their mats in the darkness and prayed that they would live to see the light of the morning.

Duarte lived on a treelined street in Escalón. The house was concealed behind a 15-foot brick wall topped with barbed wire. It was illuminated by floodlights and guarded by soldiers. Duarte led us inside, introduced us to his wife, one of his daughters, and a couple of grandchildren, and then escorted us onto the patio. It was a pleasant and roomy dwelling, but only a humble shelter compared with the mansions of the oligarchs in the vicinity.

Little had been written about Duarte, at that time, and not much since. I asked him to start at the beginning of his life and go on from there.

"The beginning is that I was born in San Salvador in November, 1925," he said, sipping a scotch and Coke that his military aide had poured for him. "I was the second son. My father came from a little town in Chalatenango. He was apprenticed to a tailor and took tickets in a movie theatre at night. My mother was—how do you say it?—a *modiste*, a dressmaker. She was from Santa Ana in the western part of the country. They had come to San Salvador to make a better life for themselves. They met, and they got married. By the time I was born, my father had opened his own custom tailoring shop. It was right across the street from the Casino Salvadoreño, the best men's club in the city. Many of the members were his clients. They knew his suits were just as well made as any that they could have bought in London or New York.

"In 1928, my father was elected president of the San Salvador Society of Artisans," he went on. "It wasn't a union, but an association of craftsmen. The society was mainly social and philanthropic, but conditions were very bad in 1932, and the members decided to back Arturo Araújo in the presidential election that year. When Hernández Martínez took over, he arrested all of Araújo's leading supporters, including my father. They were in jail for weeks, hundreds of them. Every day the guards would lead out a group of prisoners and tell them they were going to be shot, but they would shoot only one or two and send the others back to their cells. After a couple of weeks of that, my father and the others who hadn't been shot were freed. He tried to reopen his tailor shop, but Hernández Martínez sent two policemen to stand at the door. Everyone was afraid to go in. My father lost his clientele. He had to start from zero again.

"What he did was, he and my mother began to make candies at a little stove in the kitchen," Duarte continued. "Hard candies, toffee, things like that. The wrappers had little sayings or mottoes on them. No one had done that before, and they sold very well. He was able to increase his capital little by little. He bought candy-making machinery and hired people to work for him."

The parents did well enough to send their three sons, Rolando, who

106

is a year and half older than José Napoleón, and Alejandro, to the Liceo Salvadoreño, which was run by the Brothers of the Holy Cross and was second in prestige in the city to the Jesuit school.

"I was a senior in 1944, when the people finally decided they wanted to get rid of Hernández Martínez," Duarte said. "Everyone went on strike, and we said we were going on strike, too. Our teachers warned us that if we did, we would be punished, but we went ahead anyhow. We marched in the demonstrations, and nothing happened to us. My father, though, stayed at home. He said he had had enough of politics.

"Our parents were very ambitious for us," Duarte continued. "My father always said, 'I want you to be big men, to excel.' He knew that if you wanted to be someone in our world, in El Salvador, you had to learn English and study abroad. He wanted us to learn something about American institutions and American business. The head of the *liceo* said he thought we could get scholarships at Notre Dame. Rolando went there in 1943. The next year so did I.

"I'll say this for Notre Dame—it taught me to have guts. Rolando and I didn't speak a word of English when we got there, so we had to study twice as hard. At the same time, I worked in the laundry. Later on I served in the cafeteria, and then I washed dishes. I got up at five A.M. and went to bed at midnight. I even tried out for the freshman football team. I had played soccer and basketball at the *liceo,* but not American football. One reason I wanted to go to Notre Dame was that the football team used to be in the newsreels we would see here. Anyhow, I went on the field, and they threw the ball to me. I caught it and ran about 20 meters, and then—boom!—I got hit by some great big guy."

He smacked his fist into his palm to illustrate his obliteration under one of the 220-pound tackles from the Pennsylvania coal region whom the Fighting Irish used to recruit.

"Boom!" he repeated, and laughed. "That was the end of my football."

At that, Duarte has the build of a football player or a brewery worker. He is about five feet 10 inches and 190 pounds, broad-shouldered and barrel-chested. He has acquired a bit of a belly, which may be why he wears a *guayabera,* a fancy short-sleeved shirt that is worn outside the trousers. His head is massive and set on a thick neck. His brown eyes are deep-set under upward-slanting eyebrows. He has a splendidly arched nose and a granitic chin with the hint of a cleft. His cheekbones are broad and high. The injuries that he suffered in 1972 have been corrected by plastic surgery. Duarte's hair is still thick and jet black, and his skin has the faintest coppery burnish. Almost every Salvadoran has at least a trace of Indian blood, and while, overall, Duarte's appearance is very Spanish, these details suggest that he probably does, too. His English is lightly accented and idiomatic, although he sometimes has to grope for *le mot juste*.

I mentioned that I had heard somewhere that his father had financed his entry into the candy business with a big prize in the national lottery.

"Not exactly," he replied. "He was already in the candy business and doing very well when he won the lottery. It was in 1944, the year I went away to Notre Dame. He won 40,000 colones [about $16,000]. He gave the ticket to his closest friend, José María Durán, and said, 'Here, go and collect the money for me. This is my new house.' Don José was also a poor boy from the country. He started as a carpenter and became a very successful contractor. He was also my father-in-law—he is dead now. When I got back from Notre Dame with my degree in civil engineering, I married his daughter Inés and went into business with him. His family lived next to us all the while I was growing up. I am two years older than she is, so I can honestly say I have known her all my life."

If the sons or cousins of the oligarchy had been engineers and contractors, Durán-Duarte, as the firm was called, would have been building chicken coops, but they weren't, so the firm had a chance to get major contracts, and it prospered. Among its projects, Duarte said, were the Central Bank, a five-story Art Deco structure; the Bloom Hospital, one of the few privately endowed charitable institutions in the country; and the unfinished cathedral.

Duarte was a joiner and a booster, and it was his community activities, which are by no means as frequently undertaken in Latin America as they are in the United States, that eventually led him into politics.

"I was in the Boy Scouts, and I am still a member of the international training committee," he said. "When I went in the Boy Scouts, I took an oath, and it made a great impression on me. I've always been interested since that time in service. I used to be active in the Red Cross and the Anti-Tuberculosis Society and even the volunteer firemen. I traveled all over Central America founding chapters of the Twenty-Thirty Club. It's like the Kiwanis and the Rotary, dedicated to service, but for men between 20 and 30.

"It was because I have always been a man of concepts and principles that I decided to enter politics. One day in 1960, I was invited by a friend of mine to attend a meeting of a group that discussed the social doctrines of the church that you could find in the encyclicals like Leo XIII's *Rerum Novarum*. I began comparing what was being said with what I believed and with what I saw around me. In this country, which then had a population of 3,000,000, fewer than 100,000 people had any privileges at all. There were fewer than 2,000 teachers in the entire country. From that time I decided to form a political force to look for a solution to the country's problems."

That force turned out to be the Christian Democratic party. Its model was the reformist capitalist parties of that name in Western Europe.

"You must realize that until then there were no political solutions, no real political parties in El Salvador, only coups d'état," Duarte said. "The Christian Democrats represented an electoral solution. All the political intellectuals said we were crazy, but we decided to take part in the elections of 1962 against the whole machinery of government. They got 450,000 votes, we got 37,000 . . . something like that. We didn't give up. We kept working and in 1964 tried again. We won 37 mayors' offices, including San Salvador, which I won by 500 votes.

"I did things for the people. I went to the electric company, which was then owned by Canadians. I told them I wanted streetlights, which we had in only a few parts of the city, for everyone. I showed them how we could pay for them from the taxes I was collecting. They said no. So I went to a friend of mine and asked him to build a factory to make the poles and fixtures. When the electric company saw what I was doing, it changed its mind. When the lights went into service, people went out in the streets to dance. It was like a fiesta. They danced all night. The lights completely changed the attitude of the people. After that, every city and all the little towns in the country were demanding streetlights, too.

"I wanted to build a central market building," he continued. "We had never had one. When the national government found out what I was going to do, they took it away from me and did it themselves, to try to get the credit for it. It was the same with the Communitarian Action organization. I went to the poor people. I listened to them. I tried to help. When the government saw how successful it was, they made it a part of the presidential office and stopped doing anything."

This program of decentralization of authority, the creation of neighborhood organizations able to carry out self-help projects, is the heart of the doctrine of communitarianism, which was evolved by a Chilean philosopher, Jaime Castillo. Duarte has published a book by that title. Another of its exponents is Luis Herrera Campíns, the president of Venezuela. In the United States, the town meeting and neighborly co-operation date back to the Pilgrim Fathers, but communitarianism was a revolutionary doctrine in Latin America, where bossism is far more pervasive, corrupt, and violent than it has ever been in the United States, and is based on family and personal loyalties. Since colonial days, it has been customary for a local political leader, or *cacique,* to agree to become the godfather of scores, perhaps hundreds, of children. Godfatherhood establishes a patron-client relationship that often continues for generations.

"The question is 'What is a community?' " Duarte went on, in explaining communitarianism. "A family is a community, but a town is just a vicinity unless the inhabitants are connected to each other in some way. If you provide the connections so that the people can join together in dealing with social problems, you have created a community. The idea is for them to do as much as they can and leave to the municipality only the services, such as garbage collection, and capital investments, like public markets or streetlighting, that they cannot do efficiently or because they are too expensive.

"I went over the books, and I found out that the Regalado Dueñas family, the richest family in the country, hadn't paid their garbage or water taxes in 30 years," Duarte said. "There were a lot of families like that. I went around and collected from them—sometimes I did it myself—and used the money for community action. When I presented them with the bills, they got very angry at me. They said, 'Mr. Duarte is going to suffer because he is *touching* us.'

"When I was running for my second term, Tomás Regalado [Ernesto's father] invited me to his house. I had never been there before. No one I knew had. Three or four of the richest men in the city were there. They gave me a big drink, and we talked for a while. Then Don Tomás asked me to come upstairs with him. He said he wanted to show me a painting, but what he wanted to do was to talk to me about how I could serve them—the oligarchs. How much did I want to resign and take a job with them? Whatever I needed they would give me. They would ask only one thing: that I drop out of politics. I said, 'Thank you for the offer, but no. . . .' I left the house and I never went back."

Speaking of the 1972 election, Duarte, between sips of another scotch, said, "We knew that the official party [the PCN] would try to cheat us, and they did, but they made a miscalculation. They had brought in polling experts, just like you have in the United States. The experts said that we would get about 200,000 votes, so they figured their cheating on that basis. They thought 300,000 would give them a great victory. But we got 324,000, and they had to stop counting the vote and go back to all the little towns and villages where they were in complete control. They still had only 316,000, so they just took 9,000 away from us and gave it to themselves. When my people found out what happened, they gathered in the streets. One word from me, and they would have burned down the city, but I told them, 'I believe in democracy. I don't believe in turmoil or violent solutions. You must be patient.' "

Duarte obviously didn't enjoy talking about Mejía's attempted coup. A shadow fell across his lively brown eyes. He was uncharacteristically evasive and, at some points, inexact in describing his role. The reason might have been that he now agreed that he should have acted more decisively.

"The police violated diplomatic privilege to arrest me," Duarte said. "They dragged me out of the house of a Venezuelan diplomat and took me to the central police headquarters with my hands handcuffed behind my back. I was blindfolded, and my mouth was covered with adhesive tape. They left me in the car for a while, and then they came back, one by one, no one saying a word, and began to beat me. They used their fists, blackjacks, brass knuckles, a pistol butt. I could feel the shape of whatever they were beating me with. They beat me unconscious in complete silence. Then they dragged me, still blindfolded, to a cell. When I came to, they began questioning me. They wanted to know how we got the money for the campaign. Was it supplied by the Communists? Because they had spent millions, they thought we had spent millions. I thought in the end they would kill me, but they threw me in a plane and flew me to Guatemala."

It was only after he got to Caracas that he was reunited with his wife and their younger children. He had plastic surgery for his facial injuries, and aside from a suggestion of bruises on his cheekbones and scars that are lost in the lines of his face, he bears no obvious marks of the beating. Most of the last joint of the three inner fingers of his left hand are missing. There is a persistent rumor that they were clipped off while he was in custody, although as a technique of torture it seemed far too subtle for the Salvadoran police. Duarte assured us that he had

111

lost them as the result of an accident at a construction site in the Venezuelan hinterland.

"In 1974, I was notified that I could return to El Salvador," he said. "When I arrived at the airport here, hundreds, maybe thousands of my friends were there to meet me. I returned to Caracas to help the family pack. Then I got another message from our embassy—I could not return after all. Why did they change their mind? Because they thought that by then I would be forgotten, but when they saw what happened at the airport, they knew I had not been.

"In the election of 1977, we decided to try a new formula to show the military we weren't against them," he said. "So we nominated Claramount for president and Morales Ehrlich for vice-president. Once again we knew the other side would try to rob us. This time I was not so naïve. If the United States government would say something, it might make a difference. I flew to Washington and met with Senator Kennedy and Vice-President Mondale. Neither one could give me much time. With Mondale it was 'Hello,' and then a photographer appeared."

Duarte's voice became distant and ironic, and he mimed the pushing together of the two men, the synthetic smiles, the handshake, and the sudden glare of the strobe light.

"After that, 'Good-bye.' I have the photograph still. I tried to arrange a meeting with the staff assistants of members of Congress. I am told they are very influential. The Republicans wouldn't talk to us at all. But we expected 20 or 30 Democrats at the meeting. We had . . . three! A lunch for newspaper people . . . five! We were trying to be heard; but nobody would listen, and the fraud this time was complete."

Duarte returned to Washington to protest the theft. He received a hearing before the House Foreign Affairs Committee, but for all the good it did him or the Christian Democrats he might just as well have spoken to the walls of his hotel room. In his testimony, Duarte pointed out the obvious—that nonintervention amounted to an endorsement of a corrupt and repressive government. "The United States, at this moment," he went on to say, "has an historic duty . . . [to] support those basic principles which form the basis of the so-called American way of life."

The first time that an American official got in touch with him, Duarte said, was in August or September, 1979, which was, not coincidentally, a month or two after the triumph of the Sandinistas in Nicaragua

112

and at a time when the Romero government in El Salvador was already shaky. He had a visit in Caracas, he said, from Viron P. Vaky, then the Assistant Secretary of State for Inter-American Affairs. Duarte said that Vaky discussed the likelihood of Romero's overthrow. (Vaky later told me he had no idea that anything in the way of a coup was being planned.) Duarte said he made clear his opposition, as a matter of principle, to coups d'état, and advanced a program of his own.

"I said I had a formula so that Romero would accept a dialogue and that the Christian Democrats would wait until the elections for the National Assembly in 1980. All parties would then enter the government, and we would prepare for a presidential election in 1982."

Duarte said that his plan was scuttled by the leftists, who were the dominant civilian element in the first junta, and by the church, particularly the Jesuits who were Archbishop Romero's most trusted advisers. Their objective, Duarte said, was to head off the possibility of compromise with the center, as exemplified by his segment of the Christian Democrats, and the moderate right. He charged that the first junta resigned after only three months in office to precipitate a crisis.

"I found documents explaining why they had done so," Duarte said, without describing them further. "They wanted to end pluralism, to break up all the democratic possibilities, and, by letting the military rule, which is what they thought would happen, to create a civilian-military confrontation. We [the Christian Democrats] didn't want that, so we accepted the challenge of trying to govern. Mr. Ungo has lost his mind. He's lost his democratic concepts. He will accept no alternatives. He refused an invitation from the Christian Democrats to remain in the government. The left has lost the people, but the war will have to go on until the people isolate both the far left and the far right."

Duarte rejected the opinion expressed by Ungo and other officials of the Democratic Revolutionary Front, many of whom were old friends of his, that his long exile had put him hopelessly out of touch with developments in El Salvador and that he preferred to ignore the fact that the Christian Democrats had split down the middle. In their view, vanity, which Duarte, like most men in public life, has an adequate supply of, had reacted with disappointment to produce a corrosive compound that had eaten away at his judgment.

"I'm carrying out political change; but I'm doing it intelligently, and it can't be done overnight," he said. "The army, as an institution, is willing to accept political solutions, but the others, the National Guard and the National Police, have been trained for 50 years to do it the other way, and it will take time to change them.''

Duarte said that he could already see a decline in the support that the *campesinos* were willing to give to the guerrillas. ''The difference was the land reform,'' he said. ''I spoke for it as long ago as when President Kennedy announced the Alliance for Progress. The political concept is simple—to take away the power of the *hacienda* owners and give it to the *campesinos*. Both the extreme right and the left tried to stop the land reform, but they failed, and if you look at the places where the guerrillas are strong now, the regions along the Honduran border, you will see that these are also the places where there were few *haciendas* to expropriate.''

He finished a drink and stopped his aide from pouring him another. ''There is no such thing as inevitability or historical determinism,'' he said, emphasizing his words by bringing down his fist and then stopping when he recalled the top of the table was made of glass. ''You can change the laws of history by having the right people in the right place doing the right thing. I think I was selected by my people to be president in 1972. Now I have a second chance. The situation is very different. I have more enemies, and much of the world is against me, but I think we will succeed.''

7
Applying Land Reform

THE LAND reform in which Duarte reposed so much hope was the most comprehensive and most rapid ever undertaken in Latin America. It was also the first to be attempted during an insurrection and over the opposition of both the landowners and the revolutionaries. Even at the best of times, the shock to an agricultural country like El Salvador would have been enormous. For Duarte to have insisted, as he did, on carrying it out under such adverse circumstances, and at the same time as the nationalization of the country's banks and its international coffee trade, may have seemed risky to the point of foolhardiness, but as Duarte told me, he and his fellow Christian Democrats saw no other possible course of action. All three basic changes in the country's economy had been cornerstones of the party's program since its founding, and their enactment was essential if the power of the oligarchy was to be broken.

The United States, moreover, had formed an attachment to land reform in the years following the Second World War. In occupied Japan and South Korea and on Taiwan after the retreat of the Nationalist Chinese government there in 1949, big estates were taken over and divided among landless peasants. The two main objectives, which were achieved, were to increase food production, its being supposed that farmers would work harder and more efficiently for themselves than for landlords, and to create a conservative and anti-Communist class of peasant proprietors.

Unfortunately, those successes have not been achieved anywhere else. Mexican politicians never cease praising the land reform that was begun in 1917, but somehow the oligarchy, public officials, present and former, and agribusiness keep right on owning all the best land. Results have been mixed in Peru and Bolivia. Honduras has, in the main, distributed unoccupied publicly owned land. Land reform was a central element in the "nation building" program in South Vietnam throughout the period of United States involvement. The Saigon government, which was dominated by property interests, kept promising to do something about it, but it was not until the early 1970's that it started promoting rather than impeding land reform, and by then the war was all but lost.

If Washington was not entirely enthusiastic about the Salvadoran land reform, it was because it was based on Communitarian principles. Instead of being divided into family farms, the big estates were to be turned into cooperatives that would evolve into model villages with schools, clinics, stores, and sports and cultural centers. Washington had reason to wonder whether the members of the cooperatives could be relied on to observe the anti-Communist faith when they were already practicing a form of socialism. Beyond that, it all sounded rather utopian. In the United States and other advanced countries farmers often formed cooperatives to market their crops, but cooperatives of growers had never worked very well.

The large estates of El Salvador, moreover, produced coffee, sugar, cotton, and beef cattle. Unlike the rice of Japan, South Korea, and Taiwan, which is consumed domestically, these were export crops. No matter how uplifting the system under which they were grown, they had to be produced at prices that were competitive with the rest of the world. The penalties for small errors of judgment or simple bad luck were very large, and no one denied that the Salvadoran oligarchs and their managers and agronomists had been highly efficient growers.

For Duarte and his colleagues, these considerations scarcely applied. Cooperatives had become an article of faith rather than of reason. By and large, they were city boys, with no firsthand experience of farming. In the same way, Washington preached the merits of the family farm, while watching them grow fewer year by year. The disagreement ended in compromise. El Salvador, it was decided, would have cooperatives *and* family farms, and Washington would provide financial and technical assistance for both.

In all, 326 *haciendas* of 500 hectares or more were taken under Phase I of the land reform. They totaled 223,806 hectares, or about 12 percent of the country's arable land. These figures should be taken as approximations. The Salvadoran Institute of Agrarian Transformation (ISTA) never gave out the same set twice.

Overnight in March, 1980, just as the coffee harvest was ending,

30,000 to 35,000 dazed *colonos,* the permanent work force of the *haciendas,* became the proprietors of big agribusinesses. Reports of the imminent expropriation had been circulating for a couple of weeks in San Salvador. Many owners had hastily stripped their properties of machinery, livestock, which was trucked to Guatemala and Honduras, and even fencing. Some would no doubt have taken the soil, too, if they could have found a place to put it. The *colonos,* it must be said, were not promising managerial timber. Most of them were illiterate and had spent their lives hearing their overseers tell them that they were being paid to work, not to think. Few of them had even the vaguest notions of what a cooperative might be.

ISTA sent the few agronomists and accountants it could hire into the countryside to assist the new cooperatives. In the way of bureaucracies, it set up training courses—not for the *colonos* but for young men from the cities. When they got down on the farm, most of them were, at best, useless and, at worst, a source of confusion and contention. On many of the expropriated *haciendas,* the foremen and the bookkeepers stayed on for lack of other employment. Few joined the cooperatives, which would have put them on a footing of equality with men who had formerly stood before them hat in hand and submitted meekly to their kicks and blows. Knowing that they were indispensable at least for the time being, they demanded, and got, the same salaries they had received from *el patrón.*

The land reform had been in effect for 12 months when I paid my first visit to ISTA headquarters in March, 1981. A bomb had been set off in front of the building a month earlier. There had been no serious injuries, but it was as though the staff could see the handwriting on the buckled aluminum panels of the façade and the broken windows. No one had volunteered to take the place of the murdered Viera as head of the agency. Leaderless, it had sunk into a profound lethargy.

The men who worked there were dim figures in tight-fitting suits. The women were plump, girdled, and manicured, their hair dyed and swirl-dried. They wore dresses in the screaming prints and colors that never go out of style in Latin America. They chatted among themselves in the gloom of blocked windows and inadequate fluorescent lighting, carried on lengthy telephone conversations, or stared at their hands, while piles of files gathered dust on their desks and on the floor.

Campesinos who had come up from the cooperatives squatted against the walls for hours, waiting for someone to take notice of them. Their seamed coppery faces, their worn clothing and battered straw sombreros made them appear to be alien figures among the flaccid clerks. On my visits to the farms, I had been told that the only thing that was more difficult than keeping the crows out of the corn was to push loan applications and other paper work through ISTA and the nationalized banks. Plantings were delayed and reduced for lack of credit to buy seed, fertilizer, and insecticides.

There were other problems, too. Officials and military officers had taken over cooperative lands and were farming them as though they were their own. In some cases, the army was demanding payoffs for protection against the guerrillas. The accounts of many cooperatives were muddled, and there had been unexplained shrinkages of cash and crops. Almost all the cooperatives were delinquent in repaying crop and mortgage loans. Scores of ISTA technicians and *colonos* who had become officials of their cooperatives had been murdered, most often by death squads but also occasionally by the guerrillas, who had their own reasons for opposing land reform.

Phase III of the land reform, the "Land to the Tiller" program, was also being administered by ISTA with the assistance of the American Institute for Free Labor Development, the federally funded agency of the AFL-CIO. Since the Salvadoran government hadn't wanted Phase III in the first place, ISTA was happy to discuss its problems. Duarte told me, in fact, that he had agreed to it only under heavy pressure and after receiving a promise that Congress would appropriate $10,000,000 to make a start on paying for the land that was to be taken. The money had not been forthcoming, however, and the program had languished from the start.

Another of the reasons for its lack of success, I was told, was the immense amount of paper work involved. Although a total of only 178,056 hectares came under Phase III, 45,000 hectares fewer than Phase I, it comprised something like 150,000 separate parcels. In the first 12 months the law was on the books, comparatively few claims were made and scarcely any were processed, and the situation had hardly improved a year later. Some *campesinos* who tried to claim their rented land had been murdered, and this had undoubtedly dampened the enthusiasm of the rest for the program. Other renters did not want to own what were, more often than not, marginal hillside plots as long as they thought there was the possibility of renting something better. The people at ISTA also pointed out that in at least one respect, Phase III was unjust. All rented land was subject to expropriation, and it didn't matter if the owner's total holding was five acres or 5,000. For a certain number of old peasants, the rents they collected on small farms were their only incomes.

The most important properties, both in total area and in productivity, were the Phase II lands, the 1,739 farms of 100 to 499 hectares. They amounted to 342,877 hectares, half again as much as the Phase I lands, and grew 80 to 85 percent of the coffee, 60 percent of the cotton, and 45 percent of the sugar. The fact that these properties remained in private hands was generally taken as an admission that the owners, many of whom had close connections with the military and were often persons of great influence in their districts, had the power to prevent their seizure.

Among the other matters that ISTA had not got around to in the first year of the reform, and had only begun to deal with by the end of the third, was paying for the expropriated lands. Payments, when they were finally made, would not be lavish. The price was established by the tax valuation of the land. In El Salvador, the owners make their own assessments, and they were always far below market value. The new owners of Phase III were to receive 30-year low-interest mortgages. The former owners were supposed to be paid in full when the properties were taken, but no one seemed to know what the total cost of the program would be or where the money would come from.

The Phase I lands were to be paid for with bonds of 20 to 30 years' maturity paying an annual interest of 6 percent. Given the instability of the Salvadoran government and an inflation rate many times as high, the bonds didn't qualify as a gilt-edged investment. All but a few of the many former owners refused to assent to the expropriation by accepting payment when it was eventually offered. Nor would they exercise their right under the law to retain 100 to 150 hectares, depending on the type of land, of each seized property.

Because only 35,000 *colono* families, scarcely a tenth of the rural population, became members of the cooperatives as a matter of right, ISTA encouraged them to admit 42,000 "semipermanent" employees on the same *haciendas* and their families. Some cooperatives were said to be doing so, but others were not. In any case, more than half the peasants who had been unable, for one reason or another, to buy or rent land before the reform still didn't have any. They remained as seasonal laborers, no longer under a system that at least seemed inevitable and unchangeable, but now, in some cases, working for employers who a year before had been scarcely better off than themselves.

Duarte described the land reform as "irreversible," and so it might

119

have been if the former owners and their families had been executed, or if the seizure of the land had been the result of laws passed by a government of unquestioned legitimacy and confirmed by the highest courts in the land, or if the country's armed forces were prepared to defend it to the death. However, the junta that enacted it had come to power after a coup, the loyalty of the military was uncertain, and the former owners were alive and well and living in their second and third homes in Florida or Guatemala.

It was conceivable, of course, that some of the oligarchs were content with their bonds, but given the strong emotions likely to be aroused by the loss of estates that in some cases had been in their families for more than a century, that were worth, in the aggregate, hundreds of millions of dollars, and that were extremely profitable, it seemed more likely that the owners would do almost anything to get them back.

"The *campesinos* won't say it," an American land reform consultant told me, "but they've got to be wondering whether one of these days *el patrón* isn't going to show up with the National Guard to take back his land and punish them for having dared to think it was theirs."

It was on my first visit to El Salvador that I happened to meet Juan Hernández, as I called him—the man who looked after the interests of an oligarchy family that had gone to live in Florida. He was good enough to permit me to accompany him on one of his regular visits to the family's major holding, a coffee *finca* 25 minutes or so west of San Salvador. We made the trip in a four-wheel-drive station wagon that had been fitted with bulletproof windows and armor plating.

While we were driving, Hernández mentioned that the size of the *finca* was about 800 hectares, all planted in the last 20 years at a cost of $1,000,000. I asked how the family had avoided expropriation.

"These people are very smart," he replied. "When President Molina first set up ISTA in 1975, they decided to play it safe—not that they thought anything was going to happen. They divided their lands up, at least on paper, among a lot of different family and corporate names. The only thing they lost, in fact, was a *hacienda* that adjoins it. Someone had made a mistake in surveying it, and it turned out to be slightly more than 500 hectares."

Hernández said that he thought the widely accepted belief that the oligarchs were to blame for the rebellion was incorrect. "Some of them walk around like they own the world, but the ones I know are decent people who work as hard as I do," he went on. "They get all the blame for the way the *campesinos* were treated, but the truth is that they usually treated them pretty well. It was the 500 or 600 smaller landowners who were trying to *become* oligarchs who really ripped them off."

That sounded like special pleading, but I came to the conclusion that he was essentially correct. There weren't many Salvadoran landowners who treated their workers really well, but the oligarchs didn't have to squeeze the last drop of sweat out of them, and sometimes they didn't.

I asked Hernández what sort of profit the *finca* returned.

"The rule of thumb is that if you own 100 hectares of coffee and you are an efficient grower, you ought to net $100,000 in a good year," he replied. "We're not making anything like that this year because coffee prices are way down. In fact, we're just about breaking even."

That meant, I said, a profit of $800,000, or 80 percent of the original investment, for the family. An American farmer would have to strike oil to make that kind of money. Why, I asked, couldn't the family he worked for and the other oligarchs take a little less and pay the workers a little more?

Hernández did some rapid calculating and shook his head. The way he figured it, he said, $400,000 a year, half the profit, divided among the *colonos* and the thousands of people who picked the coffee, worked out to about half a tortilla a day.

"It wouldn't make any real difference in the way they live," he said, "and the owners would not be able to create reserves for improvements and against bad years and so on."

The highway followed the *meseta,* the belt of fertile volcanic soil that runs roughly northeast and southwest through most of Central America. The fields on both sides of the highway were broad and flat. Although this was the dry season, irrigation kept pastureland emerald green for grazing cattle. The cane and corn fields were covered with brown stubble. Smoke rose from fires that were burning it off in preparation for the new crops. Here and there in the fields and along the road stood slender trees that bore flowers of palest pink to richest red. It was the *maquilishuat,* Hernández told me, the national flower, which blossoms before the coming of the rains.

About 15 miles from Santa Ana, he turned off the highway and followed a bumpy dirt road that rose and turned among the hills for three or four miles. Coffee bushes grew on both sides. The harvest had been completed a couple of months earlier. The dark green leaves had lost their luster and turned grayish, but already the small white flowers of the next crop had begun to appear.

The road ended at a cluster of yellow-painted one-story buildings. The manager, a scowling, potbellied man who wore a broad-brimmed straw hat and carried a .45-caliber revolver at his hip, and his assistant, taller and younger and carrying a machete in an elaborately tooled and fringed leather sheath, greeted us on the road and led us into the office. Hernández examined the ledgers, which showed, among other things, that the *colonos* were receiving $2 or $3 a day, plus meals for themselves and free rent.

From the office we walked to the clinic. It was presided over by a plump, ingratiating man in a soiled white coat who, Hernández told me, had paramedical training. No one was waiting for treatment, and he was taking his ease in the living quarters attached to it when we entered. There were bottles of aspirin, antacids, and other simple remedies, a sterilizer, bandages, and the like. Without being asked, he produced his records. The small number of names for the previous few weeks spoke well for the health of the *colonos* and their families. Next to the clinic stood the *finca*'s school. It wasn't in session, and from the appearance of the single classroom, it hadn't been in some time.

From there, we walked to the cookhouse. In the dim interior, wood fires blazed in two brick fireplaces eight feet square. They were covered by iron sheets on which tortillas baked and pots of beans bubbled. Two women were taking handfuls of the dough made of ground corn and quickly kneading and slapping them into shape. These were not the crisp and dainty tortillas served in Mexican restaurants, but chewy disks nearly half an inch thick and eight inches in diameter. Hernández said that each worker got three of them and a ladle of beans three times a day. It is the invariable *campesino* diet, sometimes flavored with hot chili pods and augmented occasionally, although not by the owner of the *finca,* by a bit of meat, an egg, or a piece of cheese.

The *colonos* and their families—two adults and four or five children or more—lived in a long one-story building. Each family had a room about 10 feet square. A plastic shower curtain stretched across the doorway provided a semblance of privacy. Much of the interior space was taken by a bedframe crossed with leather straps, on which mats were placed at night. Running parallel with the front of the building, separated from it by a walk and protected by a roof, were the waist-high charcoal stoves at which each family did its cooking. In the rear, arranged in the same way, were washtubs. The privies were built 50 feet down the hill and could have been located by odor alone on the darkest of nights. However, both the privies and the washtubs provided magnificent views of Lake Izalco, 1,000 feet below, which filled the crater of an extinct volcano with crystalline water.

Hernández, perhaps sensing my disapproval, said that these dwellings had been the first to be built on the *finca* and that the newer ones were better. We got back in the station wagon and went bumping down another road for a mile or so. Eight or 10 *ranchitos,* as they are called, stood in a clearing in the coffee fields. They were indeed larger, about 14 feet square, built of brick, with corrugated asbestos roofs and porches about six feet wide. As residences for agricultural labor go in El Salvador, they were not bad, but the furnishings were mean and sparse, and the atmosphere was one of hopelessness and squalor.

An old woman sat in front of one of the *ranchitos.* Her left ankle and leg were bandaged with rags halfway to the knee. She said she thought her ankle might be broken. Hernández asked her if she had been to see the paramedic. She hadn't, she said. She was unable to hobble to the clinic, and he, it seemed, did not make house calls. A younger woman sat in a hammock in front of another *ranchito.* At her side was a cradle improvised out of a basket. An infant lay in it, motionless. Its belly was bloated, and its limbs and face were so thin that the skin was translucent. Hernández asked what was wrong. "It is his stomach," the woman said. "The food does him no good." She said that she had taken the infant to a physician but that he had told her nothing could be done. Her voice was vague and monotonous, as though speaking taxed her energy unbearably.

"I don't think she took him at all," Hernández said when we had returned to the station wagon. "It may sound terrible to say, but having children die is so common that it's accepted. It's no big thing to these people."

We stopped to watch a crew of eight men placing white coffee beans in precise rows of three in immaculately prepared seedling beds. The beds were shaded by a thatch of straw that is kept wet throughout the day. The *cabo,* literally corporal, as a foreman is called, greeted us, but the men didn't look up or stop work for a moment. It was an example of the sort of labor discipline that hasn't been seen in the United States in a long time. Hernández later mentioned that older men were assigned to that sort of work because it was not physically demanding.

After a couple of months, he explained, the seedlings would be transplanted to nurseries and from there to the crop areas. It is a continuous process, involving something like 200,000 plants a year, since the yield of a coffee bush, which is how it is classified botanically, starts to decline after 10 or 12 years.

"It's very expensive to keep replacing like this," Hernández said, "but it's one of the ways you can tell a *finca* that's efficient from one that isn't. Most Salvadoran *fincas* are very efficient."

We pulled off the narrow road to let a cart with solid wooden wheels about four feet in diameter pass us. It was drawn by a pair of yoked oxen. A boy walked alongside them, goading them into motion with a sharply pointed stick. With the price of diesel fuel way up, Hernández said, many *fincas* had started using animals again.

The droning of cicadas filled the air, but in counterpoint the dull clang of metal on wood could be heard. Men with machetes were pruning the *pepetos,* the trees that stand among the coffee bushes to shade them from the direct rays of the sun. The men worked in pairs. Before cutting a limb, the man in the tree tied a line to it so that he could lower it to the man on the ground, thereby preventing damage to the coffee bushes. The limbs were then carried to the roadway, cut into lengths, and used for fuel in the cookhouses.

From there, we drove down into the valley to visit the expropriated *hacienda*. Hernández told me that the family had not removed the tractors and other equipment and had even left behind several thousand bags of shelled corn.

"We've been trying to get paid for it or to have the cooperative replace it over the next couple of years," he said. "The cooperative admits that it owes it to us, but ISTA won't let it pay us until it pays off its debt to ISTA.

At the *hacienda* office, Hernández greeted the manager and the bookkeeper, both of whom had worked for the family. As they were talking, the treasurer of the cooperative, a small dark-skinned man, arrived. He sat and listened quietly and respectfully, as though the change of ownership had never taken place.

I picked up some of the conversation, and Hernández filled me in on the rest as we were driving back to the *finca*. "They say they haven't got their loans from the government yet and that the work isn't going well. Everybody stops at 10:00 A.M. every day for a meeting. Nobody works hard. I'll give you an example. On the *finca* the workers have a quota for transplanting 100 bushes a day. The co-op also has some coffee, and the manager told me they were transplanting only 35 trees a day. The members of the cooperative are confused. Salvadorans don't know how to work together the way you have to do in a cooperative. What they really want is their own piece of land. The way it is now, nobody thinks he owns anything."

Wasn't it likely, I asked Hernández, that the complaints of the manager and the bookkeeper were as exaggerated as the success stories that I heard when I visited cooperatives under the auspices of ISTA?

"I don't know about the others, but these fellows are telling the truth," he replied. "I've been trying to help them out—we repaired their only tractor for them in our shop, and we're running water down to them when they get short. So I know what's going on, and I'm not trying to criticize them or tell you that the land reform is no good. They're doing the best they can, but they've really got problems."

A squad of eight national guardsmen were at the *finca* office when we returned. They all were in their late twenties or thirties, hard-looking, expressionless men who made the Salvadoran troops I had seen look like so many Boy Scouts. They wore high-crowned steel helmets which bore the national coat of arms in silver-colored metal, tight-fitting dark green tunics with brass buttons, riding breeches, and black leather puttees. Each carried an automatic rifle. The guard is a volunteer long-service outfit. Its members receive two or three times the pay of soldiers. Seeing them there, I asked Hernández if there were guerrillas in the vicinity.

"Hell, no," he replied. "There have been so many hijackings on the road that they are delivering the *finca* payroll for us from San Salvador. They're always around. During the picking season, when we've got 2,500 people here, we've got 10 guardsmen stationed on the *finca* and 30 on payday so the fights and the gambling and so on don't get out of hand."

It struck me, I said, as an odd sort of arrangement, using them as private guards.

"I suppose you're right," he said, "but that's the way it always has been."

Although he was at that time nominally subordinate to the ruling junta, Colonel José Guillermo García, the Minister of Defense, was generally thought to be the most powerful figure in the Salvadoran government, but he said it wasn't so when I went to see him.

"I meet with the junta at least once a month," he said, which, when you thought about it, wasn't very often. "I advise them on military policy, and I accept their guidance. On matters concerning politics I step aside completely. That is their department."

García was then 47, but he looked older. He was a pudgy, sallow, graying man with a prominent mole on his chin. His dark green field uniform was rumpled and fitted poorly, and his shoes could have used a shine. His manner was unassuming, and he lacked, to a marked degree, the panache that one expected of a senior officer in a Latin American army. If García's appearance suggested Sancho Panza rather than Don Quixote, it may have been because, like most of the officers in the Salvadoran army, he came from the lower reaches of the middle class. Sons of the oligarchy or the professional classes in El Salvador, or any other country in Latin America, for that matter, seldom choose the military as a career.

"I wanted to be a doctor, but my father, who was a government clerk, couldn't afford it," García said. "The only free education I could get after high school was at the military academy, so I took the examination. I was graduated first in my class in 1956, and I later attended the Mexican army staff college and had Special Forces training with your army in the Canal Zone."

Just as the officers of the Salvadoran army are lower-middle-class, the enlisted men are peasants. In those days, you could look far and wide for anyone in uniform from the cities. The army relies on what it calls conscription, but anywhere else it would be called press-ganging. When a recruiting squad descends on a village, any likely-looking youth who is unable to prove that he has a job—and sometimes even if he has one—finds himself in the back of a lorry, about to start two years of military service.

"It is an old tradition," García said when I brought up the subject. "It helps to integrate the *campesino* boys into society. They can learn to read and write, and they get a chance to save a little money. Anyhow, city boys do not want to interrupt their studies for military service."

Pulling back a curtain, García revealed a wall map with a plastic overlay which indicated the position of his troops, the suspected location of guerrilla strongholds, and the usual crosses and arrows in red and blue grease pencil showing areas where sweeps and search-and-destroy operations were being carried out. These, he said, were having "positive results," pushing the guerrillas deeper into their base area. More important, García said, gesturing with his pointer, was the fact that the 3,000 to 5,000 full-time guerrillas were losing the allegiance of the peasants because of their exactions of food, money, and manpower.

"The *campesinos* come to us and tell us where the guerrillas are hiding and where the planes are landing that are bringing arms from Cuba via Nicaragua and Costa Rica," he said. "I call it the radar of the people."

Like Richard Scammon's speech before the Chamber of Commerce, I had also heard that one in Vietnam.

García continued down memory lane by saying that it was only a lack of mobility that prevented his troops from wiping out the guerrillas. As he pointed out the operational areas of the army's five infantry brigades on his map, it was impossible, he said, to concentrate adequate forces for a crushing attack before the guerrillas dispersed because fighting might break out almost anywhere in the country. However, the 1,200-man rapid-reaction force that was being trained by the American advisers would help. It would have 10 Huey helicopters, able to carry 10 or 12 men each, and its own wheeled and tracked vehicles.

García shrugged off a reminder that these tactics had not been overwhelmingly successful in Vietnam.

"Your armed forces have analyzed the Vietnam problem and discovered the mistakes that were made," he said. "It is always that way. The art of war, to me, is like playing the guitar. The more one plays it, the more one realizes that one does not play it well. If Napoleon should happen to wake up, he would be happy to come over here, to El Salvador, to learn."

The markings on García's map were thick in the vicinity of Suchitoto, which is situated about 25 miles north of San Salvador, and I visited it a few days later. The guerrillas entered the town during the January offensive. Many buildings had been destroyed in the fighting.

Most of the inhabitants had fled after the guerrilla attack and had not returned. The layout of the town was typical of the region. The church and the town hall faced each other across the ends of a rectangular cobbled plaza. Shops and *cantinas* lined its long sides under colonnaded sidewalks.

Jeeps, trucks, and two armored cars were lined up in the plaza. A military headquarters had been established in the police station. The commander, Major Benjamín Ramos, said there had been light contact the day before in a village on the road to Aguilares—the town where the Reverend Rutilio Grande had been assassinated—and on the slopes of the Guazapa Volcano.

"My troops have been pushing up the slopes for many days now," he said. "We've killed 30 or 40 of them in the past three or four days, we've had 10 men killed ourselves, and we're still far from the top. The guerrillas are dug in so deep that air strikes are useless. They have mortars and rocket launchers, and I think they must have sniper rifles, too, because many of our casualties have been from single shots in the head or neck fired at long range. [The guerrillas were still there two and a half years later.]

"It's going to be a long war the way it's going," he said. "The guerrillas have the advantage of knowing the terrain like the palm of their hand. Some of them have been out there for more than a year. They have a good knowledge of small-unit tactics, but they waste a lot of ammunition. We send out loudspeaker trucks urging them to accept the amnesty and to remember that this might be their last night up there, that they might die tomorrow. So far, there haven't been any deserters, and we haven't taken any prisoners. My own troops are good, but many of them are very young and have had only two weeks of training. But that's all right. The best way to learn is in the field."

The soldiers lounged in the shade on the sidewalks, waiting for lunch. They were a uniform type—about five feet six inches or less and dark-skinned. They had the open, friendly faces of country boys, and some said they were as young as 15 and 16. Their United States army issue boots and combat fatigues showed signs of rough wear. Most carried M-16 automatic rifles, some of them so awkwardly or carelessly as to make one hope that the safeties were on. They replied to my questions with shrugs and brief noncommittal words, looking at one another for confirmation. The army? Not so bad. The fighting? Tough, but we're winning. Their officers? Okay. Food? Pretty good, plenty of it. Pans were banged across the square, where troops were lining up in front of a mess truck. A sergeant walked up to us, glaring, and the soldiers slung their rifles, put on their helmets, and ambled over for chow.

Bob Adams of the *St. Louis Post–Dispatch* and René Cárdenas, with whom I was traveling, decided to stop at La Bermuda, a *hacienda*, where 200 or 300 adults and perhaps 600 children were living. They were usually described as refugees, but they told us that they were suspected guerrilla sympathizers from nearby villages. The National Guard had moved them off their land and burned their homes.

La Bermuda was an odd choice for such a camp. It was a restored 17th-century house shaded by tall pines. The earliest arrivals were living in it. The rest had built huts of split bamboo and adobe, called *barenque*, thatched with banana leaves. Many had brought their livestock with them. A dozen cows and calves, a morose team of oxen, and a couple of draft horses were tethered just off the road. A sow, surrounded by a swarm of piglets, was tied to a log by a hind leg. Cockerels strutted, their combs as bright as the flag of revolution. There were many dogs, most of them so thin that when they were lying down, they looked as though they had been outlined in the dust with a stick.

While the women cooked the inevitable tortillas and beans, the men squatted on their heels or lay in hammocks, their eyes shaded by straw hats.

"Some of us had been going back to our fields early in the morning," one man said. "That was because the soldiers made us leave before we had gathered all our corn. One day the soldiers caught me. They forced me to lie down. One of them put his foot on my shoulders and poked me here with his rifle."

The old man, who was becoming agitated as he told the story, touched the back of his head. "He said he was going to kill me. Shoot me in the head. I said, 'Before you kill me, let me say three words.' The corporal said, 'Well, then, what is it?' I said, 'I have come back to my fields with the permission of the *jefe* of the camp.' So he let me go, but they told me not to come back again or they would surely kill me."

We had made the trip in a van of the Green Cross, which provided medical services of a sort at the camp. (The organization is a schismatic offshoot of the Salvadoran Red Cross, which didn't seem to be very active.) We had just returned to the highway when we were flagged down. A young man lay bleeding on the ground. The driver and his assistants jumped out, picked him up, and placed him on the bench seat in the rear of the van. His mother and brother also climbed in.

The injuries turned out not to be life-threatening. Long slashes in his scalp and in his right shoulder and arm bled freely, but no arteries had been severed. The young man said he was a *jornalero*, or day laborer, and his name was Jesús Villalobos. He was not, as we had assumed, a victim of the military or the guerrillas. As he told the story, its being a Sunday, he and a friend had spent the afternoon getting drunk together. They had quarreled, and Jesús had passed out. His friend had returned with his machete, El Salvador's Saturday Night and Sunday Afternoon Special, and began hacking away.

"Once a *campesino*, always a *campesino*," Cárdenas said. "Give a *campesino* three colones a day, and he'll spend two and a half on *aguardiente* [any hard liquor, usually moonshine, made from corn or sugarcane]. Give him five colones a day, and he'll spend four and a half. One year El Salvador made the *World Almanac* for having the world's highest murder rate. [The records I found put Mexico first, with El Salvador and Colombia fighting it out for runner-up.] Any kind of problem, and mostly it's money or women, and the *campesinos* start drinking and decide to settle it with their machetes."

The stereotype is at least partly true, and the result, as in the ghettos of the United States, where the life is paradisiacal in comparison, is a high frequency of out-of-wedlock births, paternal desertion, female abuse, alcoholism, and murder and other crimes.

We returned to La Bermuda a couple of days later to check on reports that the National Guard had taken 15 men from the camp. It was true, one of the young men of the Green Cross said. "They showed up yesterday with two men wearing masks," he said. "They pointed out the men. The guard took them away in their trucks with their thumbs tied behind their backs."

The Green Cross man pointed out the wives of several of the men. Their eyes were blank, their faces immobile, frozen in an expression of hopeless pain. It is a look that I had seen before among poor and powerless people who may have supposed that they had nothing more to lose and have found out that they were wrong.

"I think they are already dead," one of the women said, her eyes focused on the dust beneath her bare feet.

The United States Embassy in San Salvador stands as a memorial to the blighted hopes of the Alliance for Progress. It is a four-story cube with continuous-strip windows set between wide, inward-sloping spandrels of smoothly finished cream-colored concrete. When it was opened, it must have suggested nothing so much as the suburban headquarters of, say, a small pharmaceutical firm. More recently, it had taken on the appearance of a beleaguered fortress. Walls of concrete blocks had been erected behind the fence of black-painted iron pickets. Blast shields protected the entrances. Sandbagged emplacements manned by marines now stood on the four corners of the roof of the embassy, and guards were also stationed on the roofs of nearby buildings. The receptionist sat in a booth of bulletproof plastic. Although the windows were also supposed to be bulletproof, a shot fired from a passing car a week earlier had pierced the inch-thick glass and gouged a hole in the wall over the ambassador's desk.

The opinions I heard expressed there in March, 1981, were, if anything, even more bellicose and uncompromising than Haig's. The possibility of talks with the left, even the non-Marxist left of the Democratic Revolutionary Front, was absolutely ruled out.

"This war will end when one side stops fighting," said one senior official. "What will constitute victory is a very frightening question. The Jesuits—you have no idea how they are hated in this country—have said that tens of thousands have to be prepared to die. They may not be far wrong."

Guillermo Ungo, the head of the front, was nothing less than "a paid agent of the Cubans," the senior official said. "The Mexican position is 'You ought to let these guys have their revolution,' " he continued. "We think we have the right to oppose in any way a revolution that would create an armed and hostile camp near our shores. El Salvador would be dominated by Cuba, make no mistake about it, if the revolution succeeded."

In those days, optimism ruled. "The situation is much improved," the official said. "The left is not the political and military force it once was."

If this were so, I observed, it might have been because so many of its noncombatant supporters had already been slaughtered.

He said that I was exaggerating and leaned forward to impart what he called a "realistic" assessment of the civilian death toll, which was then estimated at 15,000 since the beginning of 1980.

"The way we see it, 25 percent of the killing was done by the right, and we deplore it and are trying to get it reduced," he said. "Twenty-five percent is sure as hell being done by the left, and don't let anyone try to kid you that it's not. The rest could be done by anyone. A lot of it is just Hatfield-McCoy stuff. [That was an allusion to the Salvadoran propensity for violence.] It only goes under the rubric of 'right' and 'left' because of the international implications."

8

Salvadoran Voices

BEFORE DAWN on April 7, 1981, in Soyapango, a poor district on the outskirts of San Salvador, the Treasury Police dragged 30 men, women, and children from their homes and murdered them. Most of the dead were killed where they stood. The bodies of the rest were found later that day at El Playón. It was an unusual occurrence in only one way: American television crews got to Soyapango before the bodies were removed. The film, which I saw in New York, had a powerful impact in the United States. A State Department source was quoted as saying that the Treasury Police were "out of control." (Their primary official duty is to stop the distilling and sale of untaxed *aguardiente*. It is a big business in a country where people are poor and try to get drunk as often as possible. When they were not hunting moonshiners, the Treasury Police were suspected of moonlighting on the death squads.)

On April 15, the State Department announced the arrest of two Salvadorans—one in Miami and the other in San Salvador—in connection with the murders of Viera, Hammer, and Pearlman, the land reform experts. One of them, Ricardo Sol Meza, a member of an oligarchy family, was one of the owners of the Sheraton Hotel, where the killings took place. The other, Hans Christ, who was of German extraction, was his brother-in-law, the owner of a meat-packing plant and a son of a former president of the Salvadoran Association of Industry.

It seemed not unlikely that this burst of activity was related to the fact that Congress was considering a bill, which became law, to require, as a condition for further military aid to El Salvador, presidential certification that progress was being made in the human rights department. If so, it came too late because on the same day, April 29, the bill was passed by the House Foreign Affairs Committee by a 29–7 vote.

On May 11, Colonel García stated that six low-ranking members of

132

the National Guard had been arrested on that same day, April 29, in connection with the murder of the four women missionaries. They had been on duty near the airport when the abductions took place.

By then, El Salvador was already the United States' third largest recipient of financial aid, behind Egypt and Israel. For the fiscal year that ended September 30, 1981, it received $143,000,000 in economic aid and $35,500,000 in military aid, and the aid has increased in each year since then. A report of the Agency for International Development estimated that the total within five years might well exceed $1 billion.

In June, the White House announced that it was working on a $350,000,000 program of economic and military aid for the nations of the Caribbean and Central America. Like the Alliance for Progress, its purpose was to checkmate Communist influence in the region by improving the standard of living under capitalism.

In the same month, the *Wall Street Journal* reported that the State Department analyst who had gathered and evaluated the source material for the White Paper on El Salvador had acknowledged, in the face of detailed criticism, that it might in fact have been "misleading" and "over-embellished." He said that there had also been outright errors and a good deal of "extrapolation," in which mountains of conclusions on the "indirect armed aggression" of the Communists were balanced on a couple of pebbles of real evidence.

President José López Portillo of Mexico, who had called the views set forth in the White Paper "an insult to the intelligence," arrived in Washington for two days of talks with Reagan. A spokesman for López Portillo quoted him as having told Reagan that the aid plan, which was being called the Caribbean Basin Initiative, should have no military aspect at all, that it should not be conceived of as a plan for fighting communism, and that no nation in the region—an obvious reference to Cuba and Nicaragua—should be excluded from it. Aside from that, López Portillo was said to like it. The same could not be said for the farm, manufacturing, and labor lobbies. They opposed the lowering of tariff barriers on sugar and other agricultural products and some manufactured goods. Liberal Democrats said the proposal was entirely inadequate. This sort of criticism was catching, especially in a deepening recession. The White House seemed to lose its enthusiasm for the program, and the Ninety-seventh Congress adjourned in December, 1982, without taking action on it.

Guillermo Ungo, the cheated candidate for the vice-presidency in

133

1972, member of the first junta, Social Democrat, and chairman of the Diplomatic Commission of the Democratic Revolutionary Front-Farabundo Martí National Liberation Front, frequently visited the United States from his headquarters in Mexico City and his home in Panama. Most of the members of the commission traveled constantly, seeking financial and moral support in Latin America, Europe, and the United States, lobbying at the United Nations and other international and regional bodies. On the other hand, Cayetano Carpio and other guerrilla leaders were said to spend much of their time in the field. Their travel was clandestine. They seldom talked to the non-Marxist press. And they did all the fighting.

I brought up this matter with Ungo during a conversation in New York. Why was he so certain, I asked, that the guerrillas would share power if they should eventually win?

"For more than a year and a half we have had a pluralistic alliance, which means pluralistic practice," he said. "We have to stick to the rules of democracy in order to achieve our aims. Besides, the difference between being a revolutionary and being a democrat in a situation is not so distinct. We have learned since 1972 that since we don't have democracy in El Salvador, we have to stick together to achieve our common goals. The people aren't fighting for this or that party. They're fighting because they want to change the structure—the oligarchical structure—and they want free elections, which they have never had. We have enunciated clearly a program that calls for a mixed economy—state property, social property, and private property. What we don't like is oligarchy property, which is mainly land. The land reform that they have in El Salvador is not a structural change in any real way because it has been stopped, because Phase II will never be enacted."

I mentioned that the non-Communists in Nicaragua had thought they had the same sort of agreement with the Sandinistas. He replied that El Salvador was different.

"In El Salvador there are many political forces, and in Nicaragua there is only one—the Sandinistas with their three tendencies that now have gotten together. This came about because the Conservative party, the nominally anti-Somoza party, played along with the Somoza system and legitimized it."

Ungo, who was then 50 years old, spoke in a small, dry, mildly irritated voice. He was a lawyer and did not seem well cast as one of the leaders, even nonviolent, of a rebellion. He lacked the strong presence and personality of a Duarte, a D'Aubuisson, or, from what I had heard, of a grizzled old Carpio. He is a pale man of medium height. His face is markedly triangular in shape. His hair had receded, he wore rimless glasses, and his mouth was small and fussy.

Ungo had said that Duarte's willingness to serve as president of the junta revealed a "personal obsession for power and primitive anticommunism.

"If he keeps playing politics more and more like Colonel García, he won't have much to do with any political settlement. It's up to him. He keeps saying that if he quit, he would be replaced by somebody worse than him. He's wrong. If he stepped out, things would be just the same, but clearer and more open. I don't see what's democratic about *this* government."

The Diplomatic Commission was represented in Washington by Rubén Zamora, the Minister of the Presidency in the first junta. At our first meeting, in July, 1981, I asked why the junta had quit so precipitously.

"An accumulation of things caused it," he said. "I knew about most of them. For example, every time we discussed our legislative program with Garciá and Vides Casanova [Colonel Eugenio Vides Casanova, the commander of the National Guard and Garciá's successor as Minister of Defense in 1983] and the other commanders, they would say, 'Excellent, but now we have to convince the other officers.' Majano and Gutiérrez and the young officers who supported them had very little influence in these matters. Then nothing would happen for weeks and weeks and weeks. Nothing *ever* happened!

"Early in December, we sent a memorandum to the military saying, 'This is not working.' The last straw came at a meeting with the military. We said, 'You can't go shooting at demonstrators. That is not the way democracy works.' Vides Casanova did most of the talking for the military. He told us, 'We are not going to stop. Those people are subversives. We have to defend the country. Don't forget that anytime we want to get rid of you we are going to do it.' "

Zamora also disputed Duarte's assertion that the intrigues of the left had kept him out of the first junta. "In fact, the Popular Forum suggested his name to Majano and the other officers," he said, "but Duarte, who was still in Venezuela, was trying to convince the Christian Democrats not to participate in the government and to call for immediate elections. Of course, he was going to be the candidate. It was crazy! There was no possibility! All that history of fraud! All that violence! Even the election register was totally inaccurate and out of date! The conditions for elections simply did not exist. We told Duarte this, and we said that we would try to stabilize the situation a little bit and *then* we would have elections. But when Duarte came back in November, he pushed his own line, and the struggle inside the party developed."

Zamora also said that the reports that Fidel Castro had pressured the guerrillas into undertaking the January offensive were incorrect. "There was no pressure from Cuba or anywhere else," he said. "We simply overestimated our strength in the cities. Six months was not enough time to build up an underground movement."

On the question of where the guerrillas' weapons came from, Zamora confirmed my theory that the Sandinista government, like other governments in similar circumstances, including the United States, took no *official* notice of the fact that arms were being smuggled into Nicaragua and out again by the guerrillas. He said that the Sandinistas said as much to Thomas O. Enders, the Assistant Secretary of State for Inter-American Affairs, when he visited Managua in the summer of 1981. They were also said to have informed him that they would not try to halt the traffic.

However, Zamora said that the importance of Nicaragua as a source of weapons had been greatly exaggerated. By far the larger part had been purchased, mainly with ransom money, on the international arms black market. I was inclined to believe him, and subsequent events suggested that he was telling the truth.

Zamora made a persuasive case for immediate negotiations. The war was stalemated, he said. The Salvadoran army, with the help of the United States, could not be defeated, but it could not wipe out the guerrillas. The only result of continued fighting , he said, would be further devastation and loss of life. Meanwhile, as in Nicaragua, the guerrillas would gain in influence at the expense of the moderate and non-Marxist elements with every month that they remained in the field. That, in the long run, Zamora said, would make good-faith negotiations impossible.

In New York I also spoke with Jorge Pinto, the editor-publisher of *El Independiente,* the only newspaper in El Salvador that supported the left, until it was bombed into silence in January, 1981. The first thing he told me was that Archbishop Romero was saying a memorial mass for his mother when he was assassinated.

Pinto's account of Mejía's attempted coup, which I had heard in many conflicting versions, had the ring of accuracy. "Although I didn't personally care for Duarte, I backed him in the election and gave prominent display in my newspaper to his allegations of fraud," he said. "When he refused to call out his supporters, he lost them. Everyone thought he was a coward. Mejía then came to see me. I had known him for a long time. He was a very unusual officer—very progressive. He even used to read poetry to his troops. Mejía decided to stage a coup, not for Duarte but for himself. After he had arrested Sánchez Hernández, the outgoing president, the young officers who were with Mejía said that he should shoot him, but he wouldn't do it because he was practically a pacifist. He wouldn't even permit rat poison to be used in the barracks.

"Mejía and the others made what you could call a tactical mistake," he continued. "They blew up the power plant, and then they found that they couldn't communicate with one another or with their friends in the countryside. When they saw that they were losing, they decided to try to get Duarte to help them. There was one radio station that was still broadcasting because it had its own generator. Duarte spoke over it, but it was so weak that I don't think anybody heard him. Mejía and the rest of them got away, but Duarte was captured. Sánchez Hernández was so angry that he was going to have Duarte shot. If it hadn't been for Hesburgh, the president of Notre Dame, he would have been."

Pinto knew little else about this hitherto unrecorded event. I called the Reverend Theodore M. Hesburgh, a distinguished public figure in his own right, fully expecting to hear that the story was mere rumor. Instead, I received confirmation of it.

"I got a call from Rolando Duarte at about 10:30 that night," he said. "I knew both brothers very well because they had sat together in the first class I ever taught at Notre Dame, in Christian morals, in 1945. Rolando told me what had happened and said that they were going to give Nappy a fair trial and shoot him at dawn. I immediately got in touch with the Papal Nuncio, who was in Guatemala City, with the Vatican, and with the presidents of Venezuela and Panama. The president of Venezuela, who was also a Christian Democrat, called the president of El Salvador. He said that his government would regard it as a very serious matter if anything happened to Duarte. I also sent a wire to Secretary of State Kissinger, but by the time he got back to me, Duarte was safely out of the country."

After his dismissal as ambassador, Robert White became a fellow of the Carnegie Endowment for International Peace in Washington and began writing and speaking in opposition to Reagan's policies. White, a stocky Boston Irishman with deep-set eyes, told me that the question he was asked most frequently was whether or not El Salvador might turn into another Vietnam.

"I used to say no, but now I'm not so sure," he said. "This administration can't come to grips with reality. It continues to blame Russia, Cuba, and Nicaragua when the real villains are injustice, hunger, and dictatorship. My thesis is that United States' policy toward Latin America since the Second World War has been guided by the fear of revolution. It's nonsense that Latin America is incapable of democracy. What they're not capable of is establishing it when the United States opposes it, and that's what we've been doing for years."

Early in August, 1981, a guerrilla force—a handful of intrepid men according to Radio Venceremos and uncounted hundreds according to the government—overran the village of Perquín in the northeastern corner of El Salvador. They drove out the small garrison, capturing several soldiers and members of the local self-defense force. Although 400 troops were stationed only 20 miles away at San Francisco Gotera, the army made no effort to retake Perquín for more than a week. When troops were finally ready for an assault, the guerrillas slipped away. The army said it had driven them out.

A week or so later, and probably not by coincidence, Mexico and France issued a joint declaration recognizing the Salvadoran guerrillas as "a representative political force." The two countries explained their action by saying that the conflict was "a potential threat to the stability and peace of the entire region." A Mexican official went on to say, "We're not intervening in El Salvador's affairs, we're just recognizing a liberation movement."

Washington said the action was "unhelpful" but noted that at least the declaration had recognized the guerrillas as "belligerents," which would have permitted them to establish diplomatic relations with the two countries. Indeed, the effect of the declaration was largely intangible.

When Duarte visited the White House in October, 1981, he received what the press described as a distinctly subdued welcome. Duarte said that he didn't want American troops or more advisers. What his army needed, he said, was field radios, helicopters, and trucks, and Reagan promised he would get them. Duarte also addressed the General Assembly of the United Nations. His reception there was not enthusiastic either. To the Communist bloc he was an enemy. To the Third World and even the Social Democratic governments of Europe he was a creature of the United States. To the *caudillo* governments of Latin America he was no better than a Communist.

In the same month, the guerrillas blew up the Puente de Oro, the Golden Bridge, which was built with a loan from the World Bank. It spanned the country's only important river, the Lempa, 30 miles east of San Salvador, and linked the capital with the eastern third of the country. The Ministry of Defense insisted that Cuban frogmen had carried out the operation.

The guerrillas were trying to bomb their way to victory at the time I returned to El Salvador in November, 1981. The ethnographic museum, a branch bank, and several office buildings were damaged. Electric transmission towers and telephone switching boxes were being blown up faster than they could be replaced. A couple of time bombs went off in moving cars, presumably as they were being carried to the places they were to be detonated. It happened one afternoon on a boulevard a mile or so from the Camino Real. I was riding in a cab about a quarter mile behind the car when the bomb exploded.

The blast scattered pieces of the car, a Volkswagen Beetle, the driver, and anyone who might have been with him over a diameter of 100 yards or more. No identifiable human parts remained, but bits of pinkish gray flesh and yellow fat speckled the pavement. There was one other victim—a youth on a bicycle. The car was passing him when the bomb went off. His dismembered and headless torso lay on the ground. A photographer threw up after making his shots. The crowd that gathered had stronger stomachs. Men, women, and children stared implacably at that poor blackened lump of flesh.

I had already had to scratch one name from the list of people I planned to interview. That was Colonel Benjamín Mejía, the leader of the attempted coup of 1972. He and his wife had been shot dead in July, almost certainly by the right. Under the circumstances, I hastened to arrange another talk with Duarte and to meet two other persons who might have trouble buying life insurance. They were D'Aubuisson, who was then emerging as the political hope of the extreme right, and Colonel Ernesto Claramount, the Christian Democratic candidate for the presidency in 1977.

Mario Redaelli arranged the interview with D'Aubuisson. It took place at Redaelli's residence in Escalón, from which they were still running their new party, the National Republican Alliance, or ARENA. D'Aubuisson spoke in Spanish. What I didn't get was filled in by Redaelli, who grew up in Los Angeles, and Bob Rivard, the Central American correspondent of the Dallas *Times-Herald*, who accompanied me.

D'Aubuisson, pale, hollow-cheeked, obviously of entirely European descent, talked and chain-smoked with furious calm, with the compressed energy of the spring that drives a hair trigger, or sets off a bomb. He wore a sports shirt, khaki trousers, and western boots. He and Redaelli carried pistols in the waistbands of their trousers—the 9-millimeter Browning, whose 14-shot clip makes it a favorite of people who miss, or kill, a lot.

"I don't defend the rich," he said. "I defend principles. First of all, the constitutional system. We believe in representative democracy in which the power is in the hands of the public. We believe in a free market and human rights. There are far more human rights violations today than there were under the military government. There are now no human rights for the private sector. The system that Duarte has put into effect promotes corruption, violence, and economic chaos."

D'Aubuisson's opinions were predictably those of a former officer who had studied revolution and counterrevolution, as he told us, in Taiwan, at the International Police School in Washington, at the School of the Americas in the Canal Zone, in Chile, and in Uruguay. But it was also possible to imagine his holding radically different opinions because, as I had learned elsewhere, he came from the most unstable sector of a society like El Salvador's, and so did Redaelli. Both men were poor relations of rich families. D'Aubuisson attended the military academy because the money was lacking for university tuition. Redaelli's father, an Italian immigrant, was connected with the D'Aglio family of oligarchs. He was a coffee buyer for them when he was killed in the uprising of 1932.

"With D'Aubuisson I think there's a kind of inferiority complex," a Salvadoran of conservative outlook told me. "Politics gives him a chance to go around with the oligarchy and maybe to get his hands on some of the millions that they are making available for ARENA."

* * *

Since returning from exile in Costa Rica, Colonel Ernesto Claramount had lived quietly and taken no further part in politics. He was
a forgotten figure. His home was smaller than any retired colonel's
ought to be. Claramount showed us to comfortable chairs in the
small and overfurnished drawing room. He introduced us to his
wife and to his daughter. Clearly the fierce defender of his honor,
the daughter sat on the sofa and made notes of our conversation.

René Cárdenas, who accompanied me, recalled that they had met 15
years before, when he was in the Special Forces and the colonel was
taking a communications course in the Canal Zone.

"Of course," said Claramount vaguely. "It was an excellent course,
very useful."

Claramount was a courtly and amiable *caballero* of the old school.
His gray suit was shabby, but it was well cut. He sat straight-backed and
spoke in a melodious Spanish. His hair was graying, but his skin was
clear. His eyes were direct, and his long nose was underlined by a flar-
ing cavalryman's mustache.

He was, indeed, a horseman, he said—a graduate of the Mexican
army's famed cavalry school, as a lieutenant the jumping champion
of Central America, and a polo player of renown during most of his
years in uniform. His maternal grandfather, he said, was the comte
de Rozeville, a French nobleman who accompanied the emperor
Maximilian to Mexico. After Maximilian's execution in 1867, he
went to El Salvador and bought land. He married a niece of General
Gerardo Barrios, who was elected president in 1860. His father,
Claramount went on, was General Antonio Claramount, who ran
unsuccessfully for the presidency three times. He was one of the
candidates who opposed Arturo Araújo in 1931. After the seizure of
power by Hernández Martínez, he spent eight years in exile. He
sought the presidency again in 1945, in the first election after the
caudillo's overthrow and, according to his son, was cheated of victory when the votes were counted.

"I was a little kid when your father was running," René said. "He
patted my head once."

Claramount smiled, lighted a long, thin cigar, and continued his nar-
ration. His own career reached its zenith, he said, when he commanded the spearhead armored battalion in the Football War. He
asked his daughter to get his photograph album. There he was, his
mustache still black, wearing also a short, square-cut beard, a black beret on his head, riding crop under his arm, standing with members of

his staff in front of a sign that identified the Honduran town of Nueva Ocotepeque, the farthest point of the Salvadoran advance.

"In 1972, I was approached by Colonel Molina to take part in his presidential campaign," he said. "I refused, saying that I could not legally do so while in the service. Molina became very angry, and in 1974, he put me on the inactive list. When the Christian Democrats asked me to run in 1977, I said yes. I had never been a Christian Democrat. Basically I was apolitical, but I was disturbed by the corruption in the armed forces and by their involvement in politics. I made one condition. That was that neither I nor any other candidate of the coalition would attack the armed forces. I knew that reforms were needed, but I did not want to hurt in any way the men I had served with."

His daughter lifted her head from her pad and nodded fiercely.

"Our poll showed that we were going to get 78 percent of the vote to 15 percent for the National Conciliation party, the official party that always was in power, but the results were quite different," he said with a fine note of irony in his voice. "At seven A.M., when the polls opened, our watchers said that many of the *urnos* [ballot boxes] were already full. Tens of thousands of dead persons voted. Some people voted five or 10 times. The election was over before it began."

When his formal protests to the elections commission were ignored, he called his supporters to a demonstration in the Plaza Libertad.

"The first day there were 30,000 of us," he said, his voice taking on a crisp military tone. "The second day there were 60,000, all demanding nullification of the vote. Most of them slept in the plaza that night. There were protests all over the country. On the Sunday a week after the elections, more than 100,000 people came to the plaza. Molina was pretty worried by now. He sent troops and police to break it up. They fired on the crowd. It caused a panic. When everyone was running, they fired again. By the time the crowd dispersed, there were 800 killed and wounded. They had to call out the *bomberos,* the firemen, to wash the blood off the pavement. [The official totals of six dead and 80 wounded are probably too low but closer to the actual figures.]

"At one-thirty A.M. on Monday, those of us who were left took refuge in the Rosario church to escape the tear gas, and there we stayed. We hadn't eaten or drunk anything all day, and our throats were very sore from the tear gas. At three-thirty A.M., several officers pushed their way into the church. Many of them were old friends of mine. They warned me that if I didn't surrender, they would massacre everyone in the church. I could tell that they meant it. My son was with me, and so was

Bishop Rivera y Damas. I wasn't worried about myself, but I could see that I didn't have any choice."

Claramount no longer spoke in that dispassionate military way. It was, he told us, the first time that anyone had asked him about it in many years.

"They told me I had to go with them to Santa Tecla [a suburban town]. Rivera y Damas and the president of the Red Cross insisted on going with me. There several senior officers put a document in front of me and told me to sign it. It said that I had left the church voluntarily. I told them I hadn't, and that I wouldn't sign it. They said that if I didn't, they would kill my entire family. So I signed it."

Claramount stared straight ahead. There were tears in his eyes. It had not been bandits or guerrillas who had done this to him, but brother officers, comrades-in-arms, lifelong companions.

"Then they brought my wife over. They asked us what country we wanted to go to, and I said Costa Rica. We had to spend nearly three years there before we were permitted to return."

Since then, he said, he had spent his time managing a *hacienda* of a couple of hundred acres owned by his wife in Chalatenango Province, north of the capital. "I enjoy it up there," he said. "We have cattle and horses, so I get a chance to do some riding. Mostly, though, I try to do a good job"—he smiled at his daughter—"so that I won't be fired."

Duarte received me on this occasion at the Presidential Palace.

My questions six months earlier had been largely biographical, I said. This time I wanted to deal with questions of government, both practical and theoretical. I asked, for example, if it was entirely realistic to rely on goodwill and democratic notions to prevail over the weapons and fanaticism of the right and the left.

Duarte leaned forward and placed the palms of his hands on his knees. "Simplistically speaking, you are absolutely correct," he said. "But Gandhi didn't need any guns. He presented his reasons, his analysis, and finally it prevailed. I have a theory that there is no revolution in any direction if the people don't want it. So I believe that the best weapon anyone can have is the will of the people."

For 450 years, I said, Latin American governments have specialized in frustrating the will of the people.

"You're too pragmatic," Duarte replied. "I'm idealistic. Christ came to the world, not to impose on the people, but to talk to them and to convince them. I will be satisfied if I help my people to understand that there is no solution in violence or in taking advantage of others."

I said that Mahatma Gandhi and Jesus Christ would have lasted about 15 minutes in El Salvador, that no president could hope to govern a country at war with an olive branch, and that in the long run his idealism might do more harm than good.

"I agree with you, and this is the conflict I have," he said. "It would have been easy for me not to accept any post in the government. All I had to do was to stay in Venezuela because, in the end, I knew they had to come to me. But to let my people kill each other until then was not an acceptable solution. So I had to return and accept a lot that I did not want to. For example, being the president without being elected. I'm an illegitimate man in power, and people make the mistake of wanting me to act as though I were the legitimate possessor of the power that I have."

I was saying that he had at least the retroactive legitimacy of having been elected to the presidency in 1972 when the sound of an explosion rattled the windows behind the drawn curtains. Duarte called one of his aides to find out what had happened. He called back to say that another segment of the telephone system had been blown up.

Replying to my point about his election in 1972, he said, "I agree with you, but that's sentimental, not realistic. When I took office, it was not because the *people* summoned me. I talked to the army to try to gain its cooperation. That meant a deal, a compromise, right at the start. An elected government can always do more."

Why didn't he use his influence in Washington, I asked, to gain control over the armed forces?

"That cannot be done because the high command does not necessarily control everything," he replied. "Right now I am trying to get García to extend *his* control downward. Meanwhile, we are trying to exercise our authority over anyone who is trying to undercut our policy. That was the mistake the first junta made. It wanted all or nothing at all, and when it didn't get what it wanted, it resigned. I could have threatened to do the same thing many times. It might have worked, but it also might have failed. I was unwilling to stake the future of the country on a gamble like that."

A photographer entered the office. Duarte stood up and motioned me to stand beside him. The photographer crouched, fired his strobe light once . . . twice . . . three times, and made his exit in the dying of

144

the dazzle. It put me in mind of Duarte's meeting with Mondale in 1977.

"One strategy is to *take* power by violence or negotiations," he began, tenting his fingers as he put his thoughts together. "The other is to *give* power. That is our [the Christian Democrats'] strategy. We want to give it to the people to dispose of as they see fit through elections. Now let's analyze the left. They have presented only one formula with three points. One, they want to impose their own concepts of government. Two, they want their militias to take military power. Three, they want to exercise a veto power over the government. That adds up to surrender. The left won't take part in elections because they know they will lose. Ungo will never get any votes."

It was not in Duarte's nature to be entirely unkind about anyone, but his expression and intonation betrayed disdain as he spoke the name of his former running mate. What was the outlook, I asked, for Central America as a whole?

"It's very weak," he replied. "We are all under attack from the totalitarians of the right and left. The United States never thought of us, gave us peanuts, never let us have an honest opportunity to make progress. You let Japan sell you cars, you let China sell you textiles, but we could sell you only raw materials. We could sell you green coffee, but not roasted coffee or instant coffee, raw sugar but not refined sugar. You put Coca-Cola on our tables, and now our people would rather drink Coke than eat a mango. Oil prices have made everything worse for us. A pound of coffee used to buy something, but now it takes 10 pounds. You give us your concepts of freedom and justice, but you don't give us the means to bring them into existence. The Communists have a strategy for Central America, for all of Latin America, but the United States doesn't have one.

"There is no justice in our countries. He who has the power has the rights. This is the basis of what I call the social indiscipline of El Salvador and the other countries. The continuation of this oppression over centuries has created a certain state of mind, of simplistic violence. Frustration turns into hate."

"Coffee-picking time is like a holiday," Juan Hernández said as we rolled down the highway to pay another visit to the *finca* he managed for an oligarchy family.

Oh, sure, I thought.

"It's so easy that a lot of men won't do it," he went on. "They call it women's work."

I doubted that, too.

"Whole families come to cut coffee," he said. "That's what they say in Spanish, *cortar,* but you use your fingers. You get a family picking, and they can make themselves some money."

"How much?" I asked.

"The rate is 11 colones for a 100-pound bag of berries," he said. "The foremen tell me that the adults are averaging 20 colones a day [$8 at the official conversion rate]. There are 2,500 people picking. We never have any trouble getting help—a lot of places do—because we keep our trees in good shape and they bear well."

When we reached one of the areas that was being picked, we got out of the car and circled through the coffee trees. I could see that it was indeed close to an ideal sort of harvest. The day was dry, sunny, and relatively cool; it was shady under the trees; there were no insects to speak of; and almost all the berries were within reach of the extended arm of an adult. Berries that grew higher were picked by children of 10 or 12, standing in the forks of limbs that could not bear a greater weight.

The berries are picked when they have turned from green to red. They grow in clusters but do not mature at the same time. It takes sharp eyes to distinguish colors in deep shade. The pickers place the berries in shallow baskets about 18 inches in diameter that are carried by straps around the waist and neck. When the basket is full, the picker empties it into a burlap bag that is watched over by a still younger child.

As Hernández ran his fingers through the bags, he raised the foreman's traditional cry, "Too many green berries." Showing me three or four in his open palm, he said, "There shouldn't be more than one percent green."

The day's work ended at about four-thirty, when the light began to fade. The workers carried their sacks to scales at the roadside. Hernández told me that an expert could pick 200 pounds of berries a day, which would produce 40 pounds of beans.

We walked along the line of hundreds of men, women, and children waiting to have their day's harvest weighed. It was indeed a cheerful scene. There was laughing and talking. Portable radios were playing. Vendors of ice cream and soft drinks cried their wares. Hernández called my attention to single men with two full sacks and to families of four with three or four.

"These yours?" Hernández asked a young fellow who was putting two sacks on the scales.

He smiled and nodded.

"Good picking," said Hernández.

"Pretty good," the man replied offhandedly.

As we turned away, I said, speaking only half-facetiously, that I had supposed that a humble picker would have whipped off his battered straw hat and held it in both hands when *el patrón* deigned to address him.

"Good pickers are very independent," he said. "They know that all the *fincas* are looking for men or women who work fast and don't put green berries in their sacks."

In El Salvador, the coffee harvest runs from late November through late March. During that time each of the *finca*'s 3,500,000 coffee bushes would be picked three times. The demand for seasonal labor, depending on how you look at it, is a blessing for providing most of the cash that a family needs to exist for the rest of the year or a curse for condemning a large part of the landless rural population to only intermittent employment for the other eight months or so.

The killings and disappearances had settled down to a fairly steady 1,000 a month by the end of 1981. The death squads did well to keep from slipping. By then, the obvious candidates for torture, murder, and disappearance had been attended to, had joined the guerrillas, or had fled the country, and even their relatives, friends, and acquaintances had been pretty well shot up.

The only reasonably reliable figures available on civilian casualties were compiled by the archdiocese's Socorro Jurídico, or legal aid society. It received no help from the government, and its own volunteer workers occasionally ended up in its thick ledgers of the dead and disappeared. René and I visited its offices in a prefabricated building behind the chancery.

Three women, mothers, as we learned, of young men who had disappeared, were giving their descriptions and photographs to young clerks, who would try to match them with descriptions and photographs already in their files. Copies of the photographs would be sent to *La Prensa* and *El Diario,* the two major newspapers, which printed several every day.

It was impossible simply to watch and listen discreetly. One woman, who was close to tears, showed us a high school graduation picture of her son. She said masked men had seized him two nights before in front of the family's home and thrown him into the back of a van.

"My husband and I were not at home," she said with a ring of self-accusation in her voice. "The neighbors told us when we got back. How could they do it! He was only 17. He had a job. He wasn't in politics at all."

A day or two later, Juan Vasquez of the *Los Angeles Times,* Ray Bonner of *The New York Times,* and I visited Perquín. The village, which had been captured by the guerrillas in August, had been off limits to the press since its reoccupation. Perquín lies in the mountains of the northeast corner of the country, about a three-hour drive from the capital.

In San Francisco Gotera, the military headquarters for the region, the colonel, who alone could sign our passes, warned us that the Perquín garrison could be supplied only by helicopter, that the road was probably mined, that the guerrillas were especially vicious, and that they would have us in the sights of their rifles from the moment we left town.

Five miles out of town, the highway became a pale concrete ribbon of silence that rose through whispering stands of pine. We passed settlements of eight or 10 huts, an occasional *cantina,* and frames on which the pine trunks were placed for sawing. Slowing at a hairpin bend, we saw a ditch about 18 inches deep and a foot wide neatly cut across the width of the road. On one side was a ravine, and on the other were a steep wall of rock and a shoulder barely wide enough for us to squeeze by. We dangled a white towel from one of the windows, drove slowly on, and at last reached the village.

Perquín was a gloomy, characterless, ramshackle place set in a bowl in the hills. Most of its population had fled. Mortars had dug a few craters in the cobbled plaza, and a couple of buildings had been blown up or burned, but there were no signs of the epic struggle that the government communiqués had described.

We found the commander of the army detachment, a commando lieutenant, lying on his cot in a darkened room, holding a compress against his eyes. He said that he had a bad case of pinkeye.

"It's quiet now," he said. "Only a little sniping from the hills. I have 30 men here, and there are 20 men of the National Guard. Before the guerrilla attack there were only 30 all told. There used to be 2,000 people living here, but now there are about 300. There is no electricity, and there is little food."

He put on a pair of sunglasses tinted almost black and led us on a tour of the town. "It's not what you would call a defensible position," he said, gesturing to the hills on three sides, "but my tour here is over in a month. I think it will stay quiet for that long. After all, there is no reason for the guerrillas to take Perquín again."

The lieutenant commanding the National Guard unit was also the acting mayor of the village. He was a big-bellied man in his forties. He needed a shave. A half-consumed bottle of Black Label scotch stood on his desk. His .45-caliber pistol lay beside it.

Seated in a corner of his office were two women. They wore vivid makeup, tawdry costume jewelry, and low-cut dresses. The lieutenant did not introduce them or himself. He had little to tell us about the tactical situation, and we soon made our farewells.

On the way back to our car, we asked the commando lieutenant if by chance a Salvadoran USO troupe was performing in Perquín.

"You mean the girls?" he said. "The guard brought them in by helicopter from San Miguel. They entertain, but only for money."

In December, 1981, the administration announced that Salvadoran troops would be trained in the United States. A month later, the theory that the war was stalemated lost currency. Striking before dawn, the guerrillas penetrated Ilopango Airport, just outside the capital, and destroyed most of the Salvadoran air force. The list comprised 12 Huey helicopters, eight small jet fighter-bombers, at least three propeller-driven transport planes, and four observation planes. The administration announced it would replace the losses and throw in some extras.

A Mexican magazine, *Por Esto,* published an interview with Cayetano Carpio, whom it called "the Ho Chi Minh of Latin America." Carpio said that it was his men who had blown up the Puente de Oro. He said that despite his age, which was 62, he spent most of his time in the field and that he had narrowly escaped capture in October by an army unit commanded by an American adviser. He said that the guerrillas' strength was growing but denied that they were getting arms from Cuba or Nicaragua.

"Many of our units continue fighting with battered rifles, with homemade weapons, with arms and ammunition taken from the troops of the tyranny, even with their fingernails," he said.

149

Mount Haig, El Salvador's sixth active volcano, began to erupt again, pouring out red-hot rhetorical lava and the black smoke of confusion. On February 2, he told the Senate Foreign Relations Committee that the United States and its allies would do "whatever is necessary" to prevent the overthrow of the Salvadoran government. He enlarged on this theme with his customary clarity.

"I am not about to lay out a litany [*sic*] of actions that may or may not take place," he said. "We are considering a whole range of options—political, economic and security—in response to Cuban intervention in this hemisphere. . . . I think the President has made it very clear that he has very strong reservations about such a step [the sending of American combat troops] except in extremis, but as a general response to your question, we have not ruled out anything, and we're not going to, a priori, in a very dynamic ongoing situation."

On March 13, "a senior administration official" said the United States would not fall into the "Vietnam trap" by trying to solve the Salvadoran problem only in that country. A week later, a spokesman asserted that Castro had ordered an increase in arms shipments to El Salvador at a meeting with guerrilla leaders three months earlier to give them the means to disrupt the elections, which now were drawing near. (As we have seen, aside from fighting in Usulután, the country was unusually quiet during that period.)

Rubén Zamora of the Diplomatic Commission of the Democratic Revolutionary Front-Farabundo Martí National Liberation Front laid out its position on negotiations, which he called "the only rational possibility to end the war," in an article in *The New York Times*. The conditions for free and fair elections were absent, he said. Thus, it would be "stupid and suicidal" for the guerrillas to lay down their arms to participate in them, as the United States demanded, especially when the war was going in their favor.

Talks could take place, he said, only if five conditions were met: Both the FDR and the FMLN would have to be permitted to take part; the negotiations had to deal with the underlying as well as the immediate causes of the rebellion; a cease-fire was not to be a precondition of the talks but a subject for discussion; witnesses from other governments had to be present; the Salvadoran people had to be kept objectively informed of the course of the negotiations. Zamora proposed "two fundamental and broad issues" as the agenda: the "new economic and political order" that would emerge and the integrating of the guerrillas into the armed forces. He stated that efforts to separate the FDR from the FMLN would fail. The two organizations supported the same program, he stated, which was "based on principles of truly democratic and pluralistic representation of different social and political groups, complete respect for the human rights of the population, the creation of a mixed economy and an international policy of national independence and nonalignment."

Returning from a visit to Nicaragua in late February, President López Portillo of Mexico announced that he had worked out a peace plan for El Salvador and a program to reduce tensions in Central America. As with the joint Mexican-French declaration, López Portillo was asserting, in effect, Mexico's legitimate interest in what was happening in its neighbors to the south. Venezuela was saying much the same thing. As it happened, the two nations balanced each other since Mexico was sympathetic to the FDR-FMLN and Venezuela to Duarte's Christian Democratic government. However, instead of welcoming a chance to disencumber itself of the problem, Washington ignored them, and continued to do so.

9
Panama and the Canal

ANCON HILL is a rounded knob of gray rock thatched with green that rises above the Pacific entrance to the Panama Canal. The flag of Panama was raised for the first time on the pole at its summit on October 1, 1979, the day on which the United States yielded authority over the Canal Zone, and has not been lowered since. It is a large flag, 12 or 15 feet long, at a guess, and correspondingly heavy. To prevent it from drooping, a rod extends from the pole through its upper edge. At night it is floodlighted.

The sight of the flag flying over what for 75 years was the Canal Zone in place of the Stars and Stripes was still tranquilizing Panamanians three years later. They seemed content to ignore the fact that to a degree, the old zone was sailing under false colors. Under the terms of the treaties signed in 1977, the canal itself and 12 military installations, totaling about 40 percent of the area of the zone, will remain under the control of the United States until 11:59:59 A.M., local time, on December 31, 1999. Even beyond that date the United States has the right to intervene to keep the canal operating in time of peace and to defend it in time of war.

For Panamanians, the moment of fulfillment is already starting to seem unendurably remote. Demands for the canal "now" are beginning to be heard. The one man who might have been able to silence the mutterings of discontent was killed in an airplane accident in July, 1981. He was Brigadier General Omar Torrijos, Panama's dictator for 12 years, a protean figure who could appear as a traditional *caudillo* to the international bankers who accepted his invitation to do business in Panama, as a protégé in green fatigue uniform, smoking a cigar, when he was Fidel Castro's guest in Havana, as a simple man of action, womanizer, and two-fisted drinker when he was with his fellow officers of the National Guard, as the gentle and generous godfather to the *campesinos* during his frequent trips into the countryside, or as a philosopher *manqué* during weekends he spent at his beach cottage with men of letters like Graham Greene and Gabriel García Márquez.

In the absence of any functioning system of representative democracy, Torrijos was probably as good a ruler as Panama or most other countries in Latin America could hope to have. To match the repression and corruption, which were, in any case, possibly less onerous than Panamanians were accustomed to, there was land reform, the building of schools and hospitals, and labor and social legislation. Torrijos created the 505-member National Assembly of Municipal Representatives in place of the corrupt and discredited National Assembly. It had no powers, but for the first time it gave ordinary people a sense of having at least a small voice in the affairs of the nation.

In the mid-1970's, Torrijos was perceived as moving to the right, losing interest in the poor, permitting his social programs to decay. Many persons in Panama told me that Torrijos's outlook hadn't changed but that he had decided to change his tactics to improve his chance of earning a permanent place in Latin American history by bringing the canal under Panamanian sovereignty. Complete success was never in the cards, given the implacable opposition of a large segment of American public opinion, led by Ronald Reagan, the voice of the far right. Under the circumstances, even getting the process started, something no Panamanian leader had been able to do in 40 years of trying, required political and diplomatic skills of a high order.

For 20 years after the opening of the canal in 1914, Panama nursed its grievances against the United States with no hope of redress. Its nationhood was a joke. It was more firmly a colony than it had ever been as a remote and virtually autonomous province of Colombia. What else could you say when American troops were free to enter its two largest cities at any time and for any reason, when the United States could take property outside the Canal Zone on the merest declaration of need, when the United Fruit Company ran its vast plantations as an independent corporate kingdom? As for any direct benefit that Panama derived from the canal, aside from the insultingly small subsidy of $250,000 a year, it might just as well have been in Nicaragua.

But what really made Panama's cup of gall and wormwood overflow was the racism enforced in the Canal Zone. Not that Panamanians weren't racists themselves, as Latin Americans remain, by and large, until this day, with whites at the top of the social pyramid and Indians and blacks at the bottom. Inside the Canal Zone, Panamanians, aside from a privileged few, were treated equally—as an inferior race, regardless of their color. They were restricted to unskilled jobs and even had to use separate lavatories and drinking fountains.

Panamanians traced their troubles to the iniquitous treaty of 1903, which had been negotiated on their behalf by Philippe Bunau-Varilla. He also designed the Panamanian flag, an uninspired quartering with red and blue stars, symbolizing the Liberal and Conservative parties, at the upper left and lower right. The flag is far better known than that of many larger countries since it is flown by thousands of merchant ships that are registered in Panama because it is cheap to do so.

Not until Franklin Delano Roosevelt proclaimed the Good Neighbor Policy was any consideration given to Panamanian demands for renegotiation of the treaty. In 1936, the United States renounced its protectorate over Panama, as it had done two years earlier with Cuba, agreed to take no more land, and increased the annual payment to $430,000, which merely compensated for the devaluation of the dollar in 1933.

Because of the canal's strategic importance and its vulnerability to attack and sabotage, the reforms were suspended during the Second World War. The United States established no fewer than 140 military installations in Panama outside the Canal Zone, stationed more than 100,000 men there, and sent military police patrols through the fetid alleys of Colón and Panama City, empowered to arrest Americans and Panamanians alike. Agitation for treaty revision began again after the war. Panama was going through a period of quick-changing comic opera governments. Washington was unenthusiastic and, in any case, was still trying to decide whether to resume work on a third set of locks that had been started in 1940. Congress and the White House listened to a parade of consultants and in the end did nothing. In 1955, while Panama was enjoying a brief period of relatively tranquil and honest government, the Eisenhower administration agreed to increase the annual payment to $1,930,000, to build a bridge for the Pan American Highway over the Pacific approaches to the canal, and to return, except for one air base, the territory outside the Canal Zone that had been taken during the war. Washington also agreed that Panamanians who performed the same work in the Canal Zone as Americans would receive the same pay. It was a concession of only symbolic importance since they didn't do the same work.

In 1956, Egypt nationalized the Suez Canal and soon showed that its citizens, despite dire predictions to the contrary, were fully capable of operating it. Panamanians began saying that if the Egyptians could do it, they could do it. In 1958, a mob invaded the Canal Zone and planted the Panamanian flag there. The demonstrators were expelled with minor casualties but were back again the following year. In 1960, Washington agreed to permit the display of the flag at one site in the zone as a symbol of its "titular sovereignty." Since the treaty of 1903 gave the United States the use of the zone in perpetuity "as if it were the sovereign," the term was meaningless.

The Kennedy administration, in the spirit of the Alliance for Progress, increased the number of places in the Canal Zone at which the Panamanian and American flags could be flown side by side. One of these was Balboa High School. In 1964, American students at the school, the children of Canal Zone employees, raised the American flag alone. Panamanian students then raised the Panamanian flag. A scuffle followed, in which the Panamanian flag was torn. *Caramba*! The riot that followed lasted for three days, claimed the lives of 24 Panamanians and three American soldiers, and caused millions of dollars in damage to American businesses in Panama City and Colón.

Panama broke diplomatic relations with the United States and demanded, rather than pleaded for, the return of the Canal Zone. Without a new treaty, some Panamanians suggested, it might be impossible to prevent acts of sabotage that would close the canal. President Johnson pointed out that the time might have arrived for the United States to build a new canal to accommodate the growing number of ships that were too large to pass through the Panama locks, and that if Panama didn't want it, there were other countries, including Nicaragua, that did. The two countries then got down to serious bargaining. In 1967, preliminary agreements were reached that resembled in most respects the treaties that were signed in 1977.

This development galvanized the Republican right, some of whom, including Reagan, were old enough to remember Teddy Roosevelt and "big stick" diplomacy. The 8,000 Americans who worked for the Panama Canal Company said that they were being betrayed. These Zonians, as they called themselves, were masters of self-delusion. The work was easy, pay was high, servants were cheap, and the privileges vast. However, they had persuaded themselves that they were selfless

155

patriots risking death and disease in the pestilential tropics. It was as though yellow fever and malaria had not been eradicated there and the air conditioner not invented.

Many Americans who weren't afflicted by Communist nightmares also opposed giving up the canal. Suez provided no analogy, they said. It had been built by a private company, made a lot of money, and, being a sea-level ditch, was comparatively easy to operate. The Panama Canal, on the other hand, was the property of the United States, it was not run to make a profit, and its harbors, locks, artificial lakes, dams, and powerhouses formed a complex and easily disrupted system. Beyond that, although conceived in fraud, it was a great monument to American energy and technical skill and symbolized the country's emergence as a world power.

The outcome of the 1968 presidential elections in the two countries brought negotiations to a halt. The winners were Richard M. Nixon, who was attentive to the wishes of the Republican right, and Arnulfo Arias, who was taking office for the third time. He was a member of a landed family, a Harvard-educated physician, a spellbinding orator, and a fiery populist. Arias's hatred of the *gringos* had turned him into an early admirer of Hitler and Mussolini.

Arias's first election had been in 1940, succeeding his older brother, Harmodio Arias. At a time when the United States was giving all assistance short of war to Great Britain, he issued decrees prohibiting the arming of merchant ships sailing under the Panamanian flag of convenience and forbidding the United States from building defenses for the canal on Panamanian soil. Washington, of course, ignored him.

Arias then turned his attention to the country's monetary system. The Panamanian balboa had always been a legal fiction. Under the terms of the treaty of 1903, its currency was the United States dollar. Panama issued no money of its own larger than a 50-cent piece, and its coins were the same size and weight as the corresponding American coins. Panamanians preferred it that way, so when Arias began printing his own money, his fellow citizens would accept it only at gunpoint. By then, Washington had come to the conclusion that Arias was no longer an amusing eccentric but a dangerous nuisance. In October, 1941, he was deposed. Instead of being shot, he was sent to Argentina. His currency was immediately withdrawn from circulation, and Panama is still using the American dollar.

Arias was permitted to return to Panama after the war. He lost a presidential election in 1948 and charged, probably correctly, that he had been cheated. He organized a rebellion, abandoned it, and was shuttled in and out of jail so often that a pleasant room was permanently reserved for him in the Panama City lockup. He took office a year and a half later after a series of events that defy brief explication but was deposed by the National Guard within 18 months. He ran again in 1964, again said he had been robbed, and again spent some time behind bars. In 1968, capitalizing on a wave of anti-American feeling, he scored a victory so overwhelming that the office could not again be denied him.

Having twice been ousted by the National Guard, Arias tried to prevent it from happening again. He ordered Torrijos, the commander, to go to El Salvador as military attaché, and put an old friend in command of the detachment at the Presidential Palace. The senior officers of the National Guard said that Arias had besmirched their honor. Eleven days after his inauguration, he was overthrown again and sent into exile, this time in Miami. He did not return until 1976. Well into his eighties by then, he divided his time between his coffee *finca* in western Panama and political intrigue in the capital. His zest for life having been restored by a young second wife and, according to gossip, a face-lift, he was said to be considering another run for the presidency in 1984.

A period of junta rule followed Arias's ouster, but after a year of maneuvering Torrijos emerged as the *caudillo*. He was only 39 years old, the son of rural schoolteachers. Improving living conditions in Panama and gaining control of the canal were his two goals. Torrijos encouraged unions and agricultural cooperatives. At the same time, to build up Washington's confidence in him, he locked up radical leftists, imposed censorship, and suppressed political parties. Torrijos also enacted a banking law that removed restrictions on the flow of currency and guaranteed low taxes and minimal regulation to foreign banks. He was creating, in effect, another flag of convenience. At the time of his death, 140 banks, including the biggest in the United States, conducted much of their Latin American business from Panama and provided thousands of jobs for college graduates, who became executive trainees instead of revolutionaries.

When President Nixon continued to ignore him, Torrijos changed his tactics. He let the Communists out of jail, established relationships with revolutionary leaders, including Fidel Castro, and began showing up in his trademark green fatigue uniform and bush hat at Third World and United Nations conclaves, mobilizing world opinion on Panama's right to the canal.

When Ford replaced Nixon, canal negotiations began again. In February, 1974, the two countries had again agreed in principle to a new treaty in which the key provision would be the establishment of a definite date on which United States possession of the canal would end. There were no indications of progress, and in 1976, Torrijos called out the students. They demonstrated noisily and pushed their way into the Canal Zone. Torrijos said that if they did it again, "I have only the alternative of crushing them or leading them, and I will not crush them."

Because Ford mildly favored the treaty, Reagan made it a major issue in his campaign for the Republican presidential nomination. As Walter LaFeber notes in his study *The Panama Canal: The Crisis in Historical Perspective,* Reagan talked a great deal of nonsense on the subject, at one point stating, with the same blithe disregard for indisputable fact that he was to show in the White House, that the Canal Zone was as much a part of the United States as Texas.

As it turned out, Jimmy Carter, the Democratic candidate, won the election. He held the view that sovereignty over the canal was less important than keeping it operating and defending it in time of war. Not long after he entered the White House, the two countries reached agreement on a treaty, and in September, 1977, it was signed.

The Senate ratification hearings were long and stormy. Only the support of the Joint Chiefs of Staff tipped the balance in Carter's favor. They pointed out the obvious—that the danger to the canal from local guerrillas was immeasurably greater than from any external enemy. A hundred thousand troops could not stop a handful of men from firing rockets or mortars from the jungle at transiting ships. The sinking or disabling of a single freighter could halt operations for weeks. The crippling of the machinery of one of the locks or of a powerhouse would be even easier. Beyond that, the United States was no longer likely to have to move its warships quickly from the Atlantic to the Pacific. In any case, all the aircraft carriers built in the previous 20 years were too large to pass through the canal. Nor was the canal any longer the lifeline of American maritime commerce. Only 13 percent of the cargoes bound from or to ports in the United States passed through it.

After adding nine generally unnecessary "reservations" to the treaty that had the effect of underlining continuing American rights, the Senate ratified it in March, 1978, by a 68–32 vote, only one more than the required two-thirds majority. The United States seemed for once to have dealt successfully with a potentially serious problem. Panama had the symbols of sovereignty, but not the substance of it until the end of the century, and even then it would be qualified.

To soothe Panama's disappointment, there was a new financial formula. Instead of a small flat payment, Panama was to receive 30 cents a ton on freight passing through the canal, a matter of $40,000,000 to $50,000,000 a year. The United States also agreed to provide $295,000,000 in low-interest loans over five years for internal development projects and $50,000,000 over 10 years for arms. Convinced that these were the best terms possible, Torrijos urged ratification. Opponents of the treaty said that it confirmed Panama's colonial status. The treaty was approved, but the "no" vote was close to 30 percent, and a residue of ill feeling remained.

The new legislation under which the canal would operate had to be initiated by the House of Representatives, specifically the Merchant Marine and Fisheries Committee. Its chairman, John M. Murphy, a Democrat from New York City, might have been expected to support the treaty since the maritime industry, which favored it, was influential in his district. However, Murphy had been a classmate of Anastasio Somoza the younger at the United States Military Academy. The two men were friends and, as became known later, partners in business ventures. Murphy held the canal legislation hostage to punish Torrijos, who was helping the Sandinistas, and to prevent Carter from abandoning Somoza. Since Torrijos had said that he planned to lead the Panamanian parade into the Canal Zone on October 1 under any circumstances, the situation was awkward.

Murphy had the support of Robert E. Bauman of Maryland, a ranking Republican member of the committee. As a result, months passed in parliamentary skirmishing and steam-boiler oratory. Only in July, when Somoza's fall was clearly a matter of days away, did Murphy release the bill from committee, thereby permitting the administration finally to cut itself loose from the Nicaraguan dictator. Not until September 27, 1979, four days before the treaty was to go into effect, did the House adopt the enabling legislation. However, it added provisions that, as Carter said, violated "the letter and the spirit" of the treaty. The Senate passed the amended bill. Carter had no choice but to sign it into law as soon as it reached his desk.

The legislation established the new Panama Canal Commission as an appropriated agency. Its predecessor, the Panama Canal Company, had been a federal corporation. That meant that instead of being able to set the tolls at a level adequate to operate and maintain the canal without reference to Congress, as the treaty negotiators had envisaged, the commission, under the new law, was required to turn in the money to the Treasury and then apply to Congress each year for an appropriation. It could easily become an annual festival of logrolling and hair-splitting interference.

It was not that Congress had to guard against Panamanian wiles. American control was complete. Five of the nine members of the commission were to be appointed by the President of the United States. The chairman would be, ex officio, the Assistant Secretary of the Army for Civil Works. Moreover, until 1990, the administrator, the senior operating official, would be an American and his deputy a Panamanian. After that, the positions would be reversed.

No American lost his job as a result of the treaty, and almost none, despite noisy threats, resigned in protest. The workers were replaced by Panamanians only as they retired. In the first two and a half years, their number was reduced from 2,200 only to 1,800, and they still held 63 of the 65 top jobs. Those who had worked for the Canal Zone government, which ceased to exist, were offered comparable employment on the military reservations.

Both Murphy and Bauman, coincidentally, later got in trouble with the law. Murphy was convicted of receiving a bribe in the Abscam case, which led to speculation that his assistance to Somoza had not been entirely a matter of friendship. Bauman, an unctuous pillar of rectitude, resigned from the House after being caught by the police *in flagrante delicto* in a YMCA lavatory.

Torrijos invited Graham Greene to accompany him to Washington for the treaty-signing ceremony. In an essay, "The Great Spectacular," published in the *New York Review of Books,* Greene described the occasion. He noted that Torrijos began his speech with the observation "The treaty is very satisfactory, vastly advantageous to the United States, and we must confess not so advantageous to Panama." Then he looked up, smiled, and added, to show he had been quoting, "Secretary of State Hay, 1903." He had accepted the treaty, he said, with pardonable hyperbole, "to save the lives of 40,000 young Panamanians," who otherwise might have been killed fighting for the canal.

In December, 1979, Torrijos, in response to a personal appeal from Carter, admitted the mortally ill shah of Iran to Panama. The shah occupied a pleasant but scarcely palatial villa on Contadora Island, a resort 50 miles offshore in the Pacific.

"It appealed to Torrijos's sense of drama," said a man who is knowledgeable about these events. "It was his chance for him to play a role on the world stage. He knew that Carter and David Rockefeller and the rest of the shah's friends would owe him a big favor, and he thought maybe he could persuade the shah to invest some money in Panama."

The shah soon became intensely bored with the limited pleasures available to him as a castaway. When the Iranian government sought an extradition order, he had an excellent excuse for leaving for Egypt, where President Anwar al-Sadat offered a refuge. He died soon afterward.

After the fall of Somoza, the enactment of the canal treaty, and the departure of the shah, all within a little more than six months, Torrijos seemed to lose interest in government. He spent more time at his beach cottage, and his Saturday night bouts with the scotch bottle began to take place two or three times a week. He still made his "patrols" around the country, kissing babies, and writing checks on the spot for a new well or a roof for a school. In his absence from the capital, the military, the politicians, and big business returned to their favorite pastimes, stealing and intriguing for power. Torrijos's labor, land, and welfare decrees were ignored as often as they were obeyed.

In July, 1981, the light plane in which he was flying struck a mountain in a rainstorm. Torrijos was killed. He had been quoted by Greene in another essay, "The Country with Five Frontiers," as saying that he preferred to use young pilots because they didn't know any better than to take risks. "Sometimes when I know my pilot will refuse to take me by some route because of the weather," he said, "I ask for a young one. . . ."

It had been eight months since Torrijos's death when I arrived in Panama, but the redistribution of power had not yet been completed. Aristedes Royo, the former Minister of Education who was appointed to the presidency by Torrijos in 1978, continued to go through the motions of governing, as I saw one Saturday, when I was invited to join a group of journalists who were accompanying him on an excursion into the countryside to the west of Panama City.

Most of the country's farming is done on the fertile plain 10 to 20 miles wide that runs to the Costa Rican border, and a third of the population of 1,800,000 lives there. Aside from the city of Colón on the Atlantic coast and Panama City and its environs, the country has fewer than 10 persons per square mile. The area between the canal and the Colombian border is still mostly trackless wilderness and swamp, as hostile as it was when Columbus first went ashore.

The villages that we passed on the Pan American Highway reflected Torrijos's concern for the welfare of the *campesinos*. Most of the *ranchitos* were built of brick, with windows or jalousies, and the many schools and clinics were well maintained. Billboards along the highway also kept Torrijos's memory green. They showed his head in silhouette and quoted his apothegms: "The True Enemies of Our People Are Hunger, Misery and Ignorance," "What I Wish for My Children I Wish for My Country," "On Your Feet or Dead, but Never on Your Knees." They were signed simply "Omar."

We stopped for the dedication of a feed mill and then pushed on to the main event of the day, the burning of the mortgage at a cooperative about 100 miles west of the capital. Turning off the highway north toward the mountains, we bounced over dirt roads across gradually rising country. In Panama, as in most other parts of Central America, it is in such areas of thin soil dependent on rainfall that peasant landholdings are to be found. The land of the broad plain is owned by oligarchical and corporate interests.

The headquarters of the cooperative, which was called Los Higos, the figs, was hung with bunting. Distinguished visitors sat under a marquee eating *barbacoa,* drinking beer and *aguardiente*, and dancing. As the presidential convoy of sedans arrived in a cloud of dust, the guitars and trumpets and drums were overpowered by a National Guard band that had been lurking in ambush. It struck up a march, cruelly out of tune, like every Latin American military ensemble I ever heard. If someone hadn't told me, I wouldn't have been able to pick Royo out of the group of men who stepped out of the cars. He was a nice-looking fellow of about 40, but Torrijos clearly hadn't chosen him for his dynamism. Apparently trying to emulate his patron, Royo wore a dark green safari suit of military cut. He remained, however, a pale academic. The only men in uniform present were a lieutenant colonel of the National Guard, the area commander, and his aide. They gazed at Royo with the agreeable smile of a tiger that is thinking about how good something will taste when it gets hungry enough to eat it.

The first speaker was the head of the cooperative, an old, bowlegged *campesino*. He heaped praise on Torrijos, who had made it all possible, and read from the account books, scarcely leaving out the sale of a dozen eggs, to show that the members were making more money than they ever had before. He introduced the head of the government's cooperatives program, who got down to the serious business of the day, which was an unsparing indictment of North American imperialism.

Royo rang the changes on a similar theme. He said he regretted that the tranquillity and prosperity of Los Higos did not obtain elsewhere in Central America. He noted with scorn Washington's criticism of Panama's support of the Sandinista government and of the FDR-FLMN in El Salvador. He was cheered when he recalled that Torrijos had declared that Panama would not permit foreigners to decide who its friends would be.

Royo then announced that he would dedicate the co-op's fishpond. With the notables following, he hiked a quarter mile down a long slope. The newly dug pond, perhaps 100 yards in diameter, looked more like a pig wallow or a mosquito hatchery than a fish farm. It was unshaded by trees or shrubs, and the water had the color and consistency of roast-beef gravy. A pickup truck had backed up to the margin of the pond. In the back was a tank of fish, each an inch or so long.

"You wouldn't believe it but they'll be ready to harvest in three months, *señor presidente,*" one of the officials of the cooperative said.

Torrijos would have roared, "*Magnífico,*" given the man a big embrace, and demanded to be invited back for the first fish dinner, but all that Royo could think to say was "*Muy interesante,*" very interesting. One of the men handed him a scoop full of squirming fry. With a smile, he pitched the fish into the water. A third of them immediately turned belly up, and most of the survivors struck out awkwardly for shore.

I asked one of the men on the truck what kind of fish these were that didn't seem to take to water.

"They are called tiliapa," he said. "Very good fish, but maybe some of them were a little sick from the ride."

Tiliapa, I later learned, are one of those miracle fish. They can tolerate high levels of mud and salt and low levels of oxygen that would quickly kill a sensitive and aristocratic trout, say, while single-mindedly converting the most noxious algae, bottom weeds, and other pond-scrapings into firm, delicious flesh, and all but rolling themselves in flour and jumping into the frying pan.

When Royo had finished consigning the symbolic fish to the shallows for the photographers, the reporters began peppering him with questions. Someone asked him if he expected to remain in office until the presidential elections, which Torrijos, not long before his death, had scheduled for 1984.

"*Naturalmente,*" he replied with a smile.

Why had Panama refused to send observers to the Salvadoran elections, which were then about six weeks away?

"Elections can be held only in a peaceful climate," he said, "and this can be brought about only by negotiations between the parties involved in the conflict. Unless the *frente* takes part, the elections can solve nothing. That is why Panama has joined Mexico and France in its effort to start the two sides talking."

Royo ducked several questions, including one I asked about the absence of American officials at the day's ceremonies. A union leader from Colón who had connections with the American Institute for Free Labor Development had told me at lunch that the fishpond program was being paid for by the United States, a fact that went unmentioned at the dedication.

About halfway back to the capital one of the Panamanian journalists called my attention to a sign that said "Aeropuerto de Río Hatos." A moment later, we crossed the runway, which ran at right angles to the highway.

"This was one of the airports that your country built during the Second World War," he said. "When you were supposed to turn over all the military posts outside the Canal Zone, you asked for permission to keep this one for 25 years more. The National Assembly rejected the proposal, but the president said, 'Okay, but after this we positively get it back,' and you said, 'Okay.' When the lease ran out in 1972, the air force said, 'Please let us have it for another 10 years.' Torrijos said, 'No, positively not. A deal is a deal.' So do you know what the air force did before they gave it back? They smashed everything—the air conditioners, the toilets, the windows. That's how you gave Río Hatos back to us."

It was growing dark by the time we crossed the long cantilever bridge, built during the Eisenhower administration, over the entrance to the canal. Below us, the great bulk of container ships and tankers waited in line behind the long breakwater to enter the Miraflores Locks.

The Panamanian tapped my arm again. "Before the treaty went into effect, who do you think patrolled this bridge?"

I said I didn't know, but I could guess.

"The Canal Zone police," he said. "It was the same on the trans-isthmian highway. How would you like that if *you* were a Panamanian?''

I said I wouldn't.

"That might be the least important thing in the treaty, but as far as Panamanians were concerned, it was the most important," he said. "If the cops stopped us now, at least there would be one *gringo* and one Panamanian. That was a transition for two and a half years, but now it's about over. Panama starts policing the zone all by itself on April first, and those Zonians are really worried about it.''

The thought appeared to delight him.

Homesick patriots could still find the Stars and Stripes flying over army, navy, air force, and marine bases in the old zone. The spreading troubles in Central America were transforming Southern Command, or Southcom, which for decades had been a pleasant military backwater, a posting better known for golf and boating than for hard-nosed soldiering, into another bastion of democracy.

The infantry brigade that was stationed there was spending a lot more time on alerts and humping through the jungle. The members of the Special Forces group were climbing aboard unmarked C-130's at dawn, and reconnaissance planes from Florida and California were shuttling in and out. It put some of Southcom's senior officers under an unaccustomed strain. Many of them had been assigned there by friends in the Pentagon as a kind of familiarization course for their retirement. Thus, when they spoke to me about "our mission" and "rolling back communism," it sounded like a dimly remembered revival of the Saigon Follies.

Although the Canal Zone no longer existed, the chain-link fence that separated it from the republic still stood. For one thing, it wasn't offensively high—only four or five feet. For another, the Panamanian canal employees who were moving into the houses being vacated by Zonians as they retired didn't object to it. The former zone still looked like a place where there is plenty of cheap labor to trim lawns, prune trees, sweep up trash, spray the bugs, and whitewash the rocks when all other forms of make-work fail. There is an almost palpable sense of cradle-to-grave security. Many families have been Zonians for three generations.

The canal commission occupies the offices of the old canal company —three-story brick structures that might form the campus of a small college in the Midwest. It was there that I went to call on Fernando Manfredo, Jr., the deputy administrator of the canal and the highest-ranking Panamanian involved in its operation. Like Royo, he was one of Torrijos's bright young men. The son of Italian immigrants, he was already a successful businessman of progressive outlook when he was chosen by Torrijos to serve in several high government posts, among them acting Minister of Foreign Affairs and Minister of Commerce and Industry.

"Torrijos was a friend, a good friend, and he is still a hero to me, with all his defects," Manfredo said. "His death created a vacuum, and I think it will take a year or so to measure the consequences. Inertia will rule for a while. Torrijos's great accomplishment was that he at least showed the people that he cared, especially the people in the countryside. No one had ever done anything for them, and he saw the situation as a time bomb, just ticking away. If he could not give them all prosperity, he could at least give them hope."

Manfredo noted that the civil liberties that Panamanians were enjoying were also related to the treaty. To secure the support of Robert Byrd of West Virginia and Howard Baker of Tennessee, the Democratic and Republican leaders of the Senate, respectively, Torrijos promised to permit political parties to function and to schedule elections.

"I could call it a fairly good treaty since it has demonstrably satisfied Panamanian aspirations, at least for now, and has permitted the canal to continue operating efficiently," Manfredo continued. "However, no treaty is so well written that it does not leave room for interpretation, and Congress has interpreted the treaty in a narrow way that is favorable to the United States rather than in accord with the spirit with which it was negotiated."

What Manfredo was saying politely was that Congress, in transforming the canal commission into an appropriated agency, did something as sly as Secretary of State John Hay's negotiating of the treaty of 1903 with a Frenchman whose authority had been revoked. Manfredo added that the administrator of the canal, Lieutenant General Dennis P. McAuliffe, who headed the Southern Command, the United States military headquarters in Panama, before retiring from the army, had stated that being required to go to Congress for funds every year made the planning of long-term capital projects more difficult.

(Ambler H. Moss, Jr., who was then the Ambassador to Panama and was one of the negotiators of the treaty, told me, "From 1953, the canal had functioned as a government corporation, and the negotiators had no idea that it would function in any other way.")

Much major maintenance and renovation work was long overdue, Manfredo said. The fact that there had been no serious breakdowns was extraordinary, he said, since the original bull wheels and gears, some of them 15 feet in diameter, by which the locks are operated are still in service after 500,000 transits.

From the end of the Second World War until the mid-1970's, traffic doubled to the canal's present capacity of 38 transits a day. This figure will increase to 44 transits when current projects are completed. One is the widening by dredging of the ship channel that crosses Gatun Lake. This 163-square-mile body of water, which makes up more than half of the canal's length, was created by damming the Chagres River. Another is the installation of high-intensity lighting that will make it possible for large ships to use the canal at night.

No significant increase beyond 44 transits seems possible, Manfredo said, without the widening of the Gaillard Cut, where the canal passes through the continental divide, and the construction of a third set of locks large enough to permit the canal to handle ships that have now outgrown it. However, the cost, $2 billion or more, is now regarded as prohibitive if the canal is to remain self-supporting through the collection of tolls.

A team of American and Japanese engineers were looking into the possibility of digging a sea-level canal 100 miles to the east of the present canal that would be large enough to handle everything afloat. The canal's importance to Japan has increased to such an extent that it has begun providing economic and social assistance to Panama, something it does not do lightly. Panama could use it. Its foreign debt was then more than $3 billion, rivaling Costa Rica's on a per capita basis.

The size of the canal's locks, which are 1,000 feet by 110 feet, limits the size of ships that can use the canal to 950 feet, or slightly more in a pinch, by 106 feet, with a maximum draft of 40 feet and a weight of 65,000 deadweight tons. By 1982, more than 2,000 of the total of 27,000 oceangoing freighters exceeded these "Panamax" dimensions, some by a factor of five or more in tonnage. These gigantic ships, mainly tankers, carry an enormously disproportionate share of total cargoes. The increasing use of boxcar-size containers for general cargo has also diverted shipping from the canal. Container cargo from Japan—electronic products, say—destined for the East Coast is now likely to be unloaded at a West Coast port for transshipment by rail.

167

Although the canal is still operating at close to capacity, a rapid increase in toll rates has begun to worry the commission, Manfredo said. From the beginning, the canal was required only to meet operating and maintenance expenses through tolls. The United States did not seek to recover construction costs of $387,000,000. For 60 years after the opening of the canal, the toll charge remained unchanged. It was 90 cents per 100 cubic feet of cargo space, called a net ton, for laden ships and 72 cents for empty ones. (The average toll in 1979 was $21,557.) Through the 1960's, the increase in the number of transits covered the steady rise in operating costs. In the early 1970's, however, inflation, which was reflected in the wages of the canal's unionized employees, coincided with a recession in world trade brought about by the first major increases in oil prices and caused a decline in the number of transits.

To keep the canal self-supporting, tolls had to be increased by 19.7 percent in 1974 and by 19.5 percent in 1976. In 1979, there was a further increase of 29.3 percent to cover payments to Panama under the treaty, which came to $54,000,000 in the first fiscal year. Yet another increase of 9.8 percent took effect in 1983 to offset the estimated annual loss of $45,000,000 in revenue that will result from the opening of an oil pipeline across western Panama. Alaskan oil carried by tankers that are too large to transit the canal is being pumped across the isthmus to tankers on the Atlantic side.

During the treaty negotiations, Torrijos pressed the United States to provide $1 billion to begin the enlargement and rehabilitation of the canal. He also sought full Panamanian control in considerably less than 20 years. His arguments were rejected, but from what I heard in Panama, neither issue can be regarded as having been definitely settled.

All these circumstances led many Panamanians to say that the United States had been sly not only in getting and keeping control of the canal but also in giving it up. What will be handed over in 1999, they say, will be a senile waterway more useful for raising tiliapa, the miracle fish, than for the passage of ships.

For all that, the canal still casts a spell. Like many other works of man, it has been called the Eighth Wonder of the World. I was not inclined to disagree. To watch a 900-foot tanker rise inexorably, in obedience to Archimedes' principle, in the Miraflores Locks without tipping over and then to see her proceed across Gatun Lake, richly blue, surrounded by rich green hills, a couple of hundred feet above the level of the sea, is to feel both disoriented and excited. The canal may be obsolescent, it may no longer be of immense strategic importance, but as I traveled its length and considered the grandeur of the achievement, I couldn't help sympathizing with those Americans who couldn't bear to part with it.

10

Don Pepe's Costa Rica

FOR 40 YEARS, the biography of José Figueres Ferrer has been pretty much the history of Costa Rica, and vice versa. Sent into exile in 1942 for the crime of publicly criticizing the government, he led the rebellion that overthrew it in 1948. As president of the republic, an office he held three times, Figueres enacted reforms that amazed Latin America. Figueres restored democracy, established the government agency that has conducted honest elections ever since, turned Costa Rica, for better or worse, into a welfare state, and, as if that weren't enough, abolished its army. Figueres didn't stop there. As the declared enemy of all dictators, he helped Fidel Castro topple the cruel and corrupt Batista regime, and his 30-year feud with the Somoza dynasty in Nicaragua ended in victory.

It is true that his hitherto unblemished reputation acquired some spots in later years. When he tried to rehabilitate Robert Vesco, the international swindler, by giving him a chance to invest part of the $224,000,000 he had stolen in Costa Rican enterprises, it turned out that a couple of them were owned by Figueres and his family. Costa Ricans didn't seem to mind particularly, but Figueres's admirers abroad were scandalized.

The cost of Figueres's social betterment schemes helped Costa Rica run up a foreign debt of more than $4 billion, the per capita world record, and far above any hope of repayment. National improvidence is no virtue, but for once in Latin American history, ordinary people benefited, and fortunate is the land, especially in that part of the world, whose history is written in red ink instead of blood.

I called Figueres as soon as I arrived in San José in the spring of 1982, and we arranged to meet a few days later. Interviews with bankers, ambassadors, and generals are apt to be duty calls, but a man who had the vision to turn Robert Vesco into a one-man Marshall Plan was someone I looked forward to meeting. Don Pepe's house turned out to be a pleasant dwelling, but by no means imposing, on a treelined street. (Even schoolchildren call Figueres Don Pepe. "Don" is a modest sort of honorific, and Pepe is the usual nickname for anyone named José. Somehow, it fits him perfectly. His diminutive stature and air of playful shrewdness also put me in mind of Walt Disney's famous Jiminy Cricket.) While I was waiting in his study, I had plenty of time to take in my surroundings, right down to reading the framed mementos on the wall. One of these was a translation into Spanish of Tennyson's "Ulysses":

Si mucho nos quitaron, mucho queda
Y aunque ya no tenemos el vigor
Que in los lejanos días tierra y ciela movieron,
Aquello que antes fuimos, aún lo somos. . . .

Tho' much is taken, much abides; and tho'
We are not now that strength which in old days
Moved earth and heaven; that which we are, we are. . . .

Don Pepe appeared at last. Figueres, who was then seventy-five years old, was about five feet three inches tall, weighed perhaps 125 pounds, and was getting a bit rickety with age. His face is deeply lined and exceptionally mobile—one might even say rubbery. His nose is a mighty appendage. When he smiles, his mouth curls up in a U that begins high in his cheeks. He called to the maid to bring coffee. It turned out to be excellent. Costa Rica is the only country in Central America in which you can count on being served good coffee. Elsewhere, I mentioned to Don Pepe, it's as difficult to find as fresh orange juice in Florida.

"The other countries export all the best beans," he said. "The people can't afford them. Here they can."

Referring to the poem, I said that his reliance on brains instead of brawn reminded me of Ulysses. He smiled his thanks. I added that I had heard he had been enticed by the Sirens a few times himself. At that, Don Pepe, who has twice been married and divorced and is reported still to have a connoisseur's appreciation of beautiful women, laughed and bounced up and down in his chair.

"An old friend gave me that on my 75th birthday," he said. "I don't like to be reminded, but it was all framed, and I had to put it up, or he would have wondered where it was when he came to see me."

Since I was familiar with only the broad outline of Figueres's career, I said I would be his Homer if, before we got to such dreary matters as the national debt, he would tell me about himself.

"I was born and grew up in Alajuela," he said, settling back and folding his hands in his lap. "My father was a physician who had emigrated from Spain with my mother. Both of them were Catalans, from Barcelona. In fact, I spoke Catalan before I spoke Spanish."

I later visited Alajuela. It is a pretty colonial town in the mountains about 20 miles east of the capital. Nonetheless, it is no Barcelona, and I asked Don Pepe why a physician, more or less guaranteed a good living, had left that beautiful and cosmopolitan city for poor and remote Costa Rica.

"They were adventurous and wanted a new beginning, but they came to Costa Rica by mistake," he said, laughing. "My mother used to tell me that when she got to San José, she looked around and asked my father, 'Where is the sea? I was told it was an island with the sea all around it.' She thought they were going to *Puerto Rico*!

"My father wanted me to be a doctor, too, of course," Don Pepe continued, "but you know the young—always in opposition. While I was going to high school, I decided to teach myself physics and engineering. I sent away for courses from the International Correspondence Schools. I think they are still in business today. By the time I graduated I was designing and building small hydroelectric plants for farms in our area. One of them was in use until a couple of years ago. As soon as I heard about radio, I said, 'That's for me.' I was one of the first radio hams in the country. I also taught myself economics and philosophy, but when the Depression came, I saw that the theories that I had been studying were all wrong, so I started again. The Depression was so cruel. The stores were full of merchandise, but no one had any money to buy anything. I took a trip to New York, and it was the same thing—even in rich New York. Men were holding out bowls for free soup.

"When I got back home, I started a small business, building radios that could receive broadcasts from the United States. I built a radio station for the newspaper *Prensa Libre*. I made a little money, and I bought a farm about an hour's drive east of San José. I named it La Lucha, the Struggle. For the next six years, I devoted myself to growing coffee, to agricultural research, and to reading. For six years, I read

172

the German philosophers—Kant, Schopenhauer, Hegel—and the 19th-century socialists—Owen and Fourier—by candlelight. I've been a utopian socialist since I was a boy, and reading H. G. Wells is what made me antimilitaristic.''

In 1942, events in Costa Rica turned Don Pepe away from his scholarly pursuits. To understand what was happening, it is necessary to look back briefly. Because Costa Rica possessed neither a large Indian population nor gold and silver, it was not settled until the end of the 16th century and became, almost uniquely in Latin America, a land of family farms, owned by Spanish peasants.

Such men, like the settlers of the Thirteen Colonies, were not submissive to royal or clerical authority. They never got into the habit of paying taxes, bribes, or tithes. Their remoteness from centers of authority, comparative poverty, and independent spirit made punishing them likely to be more trouble than it was worth. Costa Ricans have never been religious fanatics. After independence, they did not split up into clerical and anticlerical factions. Unlike the inhabitants of their sister republics, Costa Ricans avoided strife and cultivated their gardens.

In the 1830's, Costa Rica became the first country in Central America to grow coffee for export; in the 1880's, the first to build a railroad to the Atlantic coast and, at about the same time, the first to have a flourishing banana industry. Coffee led to an increase in the size of land-holdings and to the creation of an oligarchy, but it never became as rich or as politically powerful as those elsewhere in Central America. In those days, moreover, the population of the country was no more than 500,000. There was plenty of land available for coffee cultivation without stealing it from Indians and small farmers. Because there was no surplus of labor, the big growers had to pay decent wages to attract workers.

The oligarchs passed the presidency around among themselves—no one else cared very much about having it—but elections took place more or less regularly and honestly. Coups occurred from time to time, but armed rebellion almost never, and the country was never ruled by a *caudillo*. During the depression of the 1930's, Costa Rica responded to hard times not with a dictatorship, as was the case elsewhere in Central America, but by electing moderate reformers to the presidency. One of these, Rafael Calderón Guardia, who took office in 1940, enacted social security and labor laws. The big landowners raised the cry of communism. Calderón thereupon made their fears come true by

173

allying himself with the left, including the Communists, of whom there were probably fewer than 100, to protect his program.

It was at this point, Figueres said, that he decided that the time had come for action. "As soon as the Communists get into a government, you can kiss freedom and democracy good-bye," he said. "The violence was already beginning, and I knew that unless something was done, we were going to end up with a dictatorship of the left or the right.

"So one day I decided to go to San José," he continued. "I went directly to *Prensa Libre,* the biggest newspaper. I walked into the radio station I had built for them. I argued my way in front of the microphone and read a speech denouncing the government. I had been speaking for 30 minutes when the people at the station told me that the police were coming to arrest me. By then, Calderón was trying to take away the right to criticize. I told the audience what was going to happen. As the police came into the studio, I said, 'I want to summarize all this by saying that this government has got to go.' They arrested me, held me in jail for three or four days, and then sent me to El Salvador. I had been exiled."

Figueres went on to Mexico, where he attended classes at the university and embodied his political thinking in a slim volume of essays, *Palabras Gastadas,* which might be translated, he said, as "Worn-out Words."

"I got permission to return after Calderón left office in 1944," Figueres said. "I discovered to my astonishment that I was a political hero. I had sent copies of my book to a few friends, and they had had an edition printed without telling me. All of the opposition groups opened their doors to me. They wanted immediately to overthrow Teodoro Picado, the man that Calderón had picked to keep his seat warm for him until he could be reelected. They said Picado had been elected by fraud. It was probably true, but I told them, 'Let's try once more for honest elections in 1948, and if we don't get them, then we'll fight.' "

Figueres formed his own political party, the Social Democrats, but in the election he supported a candidate of the moderate right, a newspaper publisher named Otilio Ulate, against Calderón. The balloting was disorderly, and the outcome was disputed. The elections commission declared Ulate the victor, but the legislature, which was controlled by Calderón's party, voted to annul the result. Ulate and many of his supporters were arrested.

* * *

"That was it," Figueres said. "Some rich people gave me $100,000, and I went to Mexico and bought arms. But the same people who sold them to me tipped off the police, and they seized them. It was typical of the Mexicans. Now I had to look elsewhere. I knew that after Juan Bosch's rebellion against Trujillo in the Dominican Republic had failed, his weapons ended up in Cuba. Carlos Prío Socarrás, the president, wouldn't give me the arms directly, but he agreed to ship them to Guatemala. The president of Guatemala, Juan José Arévalo, was a democrat. I went to see him secretly. He said he wouldn't give me the guns. You know why? Because he said Costa Ricans would never fight. We were supposed to be too peace-loving. I said, 'Okay, I'll show you. We'll begin fighting with our teeth.' He said, 'If you do, you can have them.'

"I went back to Costa Rica, and from my farm, La Lucha, I issued a call to arms," he continued. "Men came from all over the country to join us. We had just a few weapons—hunting rifles and shotguns and revolvers—but we began attacking army posts and police stations. We went to the airport at San Isidro and hijacked two army DC-3's at gunpoint. All we had were student pilots for a night flight over the mountains to Guatemala. I never thought we would make it, but we did. When we landed in Guatemala City, I went to see Arévalo. I told him what we had done and said, 'Put us in jail if you want to. Otherwise, we're not leaving without the weapons.' Arévalo said, 'Okay, they're yours, take them.' There were maybe 600 all told. We loaded them into the planes and flew back to San Isidro."

Don Pepe pointed to two firearms mounted on the far wall. "Those were part of that shipment," he said. "Argentine copies of the submachine gun your army issued during World War Two—you called it the grease gun—and of a Mauser rifle that the German army used in World War One. They weren't very good, but they were good enough.

"When the word got around that we had weapons, men really began to pour into La Lucha. They had to come over the mountains because the army was watching the roads. Men even came from outside the country. Some of them had military experience. That was lucky for us because none of us knew how to give commands or order certain maneuvers and so on. When Somoza saw what was going on, he began to help the government forces. Even then he hated me more than the Communists. We asked Washington for help, but they wouldn't do

175

anything for us. They told us we were troublemakers. It didn't matter to them that we were fighting against Communists.''

Although Figueres did not minimize his own accomplishments and called the close ones in his own favor, he did not depart in any important way from the generally accepted version of these events. Whether Calderón was as closely tied to the Communists and as generally wicked as Figueres says is another matter.

"We fought a guerrilla war," he went on. "Six hundred of us against an army and a militia that numbered 6,000. We took Limón on the Atlantic coast by an airborne assault. We flew in with 64 men in our two DC-3's. Somebody on *Time* magazine called us the Caribbean Legion. We were supposed to have freedom fighters from all over the place. We didn't. Except for one man from Santo Domingo, we were all Costa Ricans, but we didn't mind what we were called, because dictators like Somoza began to tremble in fear of this powerful force of 64 men with old weapons.''

After six weeks of fighting, the government forces surrendered. The struggle cost an estimated 2,000 lives, by far the longest casualty list in the nation's history. Calderón fled to Nicaragua. With Somoza's help, he attempted an invasion that Don Pepe, at the head of his forces, easily repulsed.

Figueres became provisional president but promised to step aside for Ulate after 18 months. That was the length of time he thought would be needed to put the country back on the road to social progress untainted by communism. What is more, he did so. It was an act that appears to be without precedent in Latin American history, and for that alone Figueres deserves to have his name in lights from Tierra del Fuego to Tijuana.

Before leaving office, Figueres enacted more than 800 decrees that permanently altered the country's political and social framework. However, the one that has been most widely publicized, the abolition of the army, was of mainly symbolic importance. The army that was abolished numbered only 300 men, was poorly trained and equipped, was led by nonprofessional officers, and existed almost entirely for ceremonial purposes. Figueres combined it with the National Police and called the new body the Civil Guard. It presently numbers 7,000 men—far smaller, less heavily armed, and less expensive than the forces of other Central American nations. It is also staffed on patronage principles. Its membership changes every four years, impairing its efficiency but reducing the possibility of the rise of a military caste.

The Supreme Electoral Tribunal was created by Figueres to prevent a repetition of the events of 1948. The tribunal is an autonomous and nonpartisan agency headed by judges appointed by the Supreme Court. Its responsibilities go beyond the conducting of elections and the counting of votes to the supervision of campaign practices and even to the issuing of the national identity cards that are a requirement for voting. The tribunal has also turned election day into the country's most important civil holiday, a kind of festival of freedom, marked by parades, concerts, and other patriotic manifestations.

Figueres also outlawed the Communists' National Vanguard party. His own feelings aside, Figueres was shrewd enough to understand that in dealing with the United States he could get away with almost anything—even plotting against Somoza and Rafael Trujillo, the monstrous Dominican dictator, who derived their power from Washington—if he succeeded in presenting himself as an unyielding anti-Communist. In the years that followed, Costa Rica also demonstrated that communism had no enemy as powerful as a reasonably honest government and a decent standard of living. In any case, the Communist party is now entirely legal and is regarded by most Costa Ricans with amused affection. Indeed, Figueres has praised Manuel Mora, who has been its leader for close to 50 years, as "a Eurocommunist," meaning someone who believes in democratic principles as well as Marxism.

Figueres also nationalized the banks and established the first of what in time became 102 autonomous public corporations, patterned, all too loosely, on the Tennessee Valley Authority. The first of these were given responsibility for utilities, public housing, and other social programs. When these worked reasonably well, as such enterprises are likely to do when they are still being managed by their idealistic, honest, and energetic founders, others were established to run the export-import trade, the marketing of domestic agricultural products, even manufacturing and insurance. These were less efficiently run, and since they had been given independent borrowing power, they made their losses up with loans, both domestic and foreign.

In 1953, Figueres permitted himself to be nominated and elected to the presidency. The next year he found himself peripherally involved in the event that marked the end of the Good Neighbor Policy—the overthrow of the Arbenz government in Guatemala by the Central Intelligence Agency. Although he didn't advertise it at the time, Figueres now makes no secret of the fact that he was on friendly terms with Allen Dulles, the CIA director. He also says that he tried to persuade Arbenz to avoid confrontation and the United States not to throw him out.

"I still don't think Arbenz was a Communist," he said, "but he had a wife, a rich Salvadoran woman, who was. I told him, 'Don't try to destroy United Fruit; civilize it.' I told Dulles he could get what he wanted if everyone just put pressure on Arbenz. I still think I was right, but no one would listen to me."

Don Pepe seized the moment to increase the export tax on bananas and to gain greatly improved wages and benefits for the banana workers. That might have been enough at other times for United Fruit to announce noisily that it was pulling out of Costa Rica or to start giving money and arms to Figueres's political rivals. But since they were dealing with Don Pepe, Latin America's only creative anti-Communist, company executives could do nothing but curse him under their breath and pay up.

In January, 1955, Figueres had the pleasure of humiliating Anastasio Somoza again. For 10 years, Somoza's pleasure in owning a large part of Nicaragua had been diminished by Figueres's refusal to recognize him as Central America's *caudillo número uno* and the United States' viceroy in the region. Somoza's blood pressure rose dangerously every time Figueres denounced corrupt dictators. It came to the point that Somoza could scarcely bring himself to utter Figueres's name, referring to him only as *El Enano,* the Dwarf.

"Somoza once challenged me to a duel," Don Pepe said. "I told him there was no way I was going to do that. I told him, 'No one would shed a tear if I killed you, but what a loss to the world it would be if you killed me.' "

Era el colmo, it was the last straw, as far as Somoza was concerned, when, in 1954, Figueres gave sanctuary to an opposition group that had tried to assassinate him. In a fine Latin fury, he organized another invasion of Costa Rica. Somoza said that the force was composed of right-wing exiles from Costa Rica, and there may have been a few, but it is generally accepted that the great majority were members of the Nicaraguan National Guard, out of uniform and carrying false identification.

There is nothing like a foreign invasion to bring a country together, and Costa Ricans didn't like Nicaraguans very much to begin with. For one thing, Nicaragua continued to claim Guanacaste, Costa Rica's westernmost province, on the ground that the plebiscite by which it had changed allegiance in 1823 had been illegal. (Costa Rica, on its part, had an old border dispute with Panama.)

In any event, while the Organization of American States was condemning Nicaragua and offering military help to Costa Rica, and the United States was begging Somoza to come to his senses, Don Pepe, with no army to call on, rallied a volunteer force that rushed to the threatened border in a fleet of commandeered trucks. After a couple of sharp clashes the invaders were driven back into Nicaragua, and Figueres was a hero again.

By the time he completed his term, Figueres had become a minor international celebrity. His scrupulous adherence to the constitutional prohibition against the reelection of a president for eight years following the completion of his term and the fact that the opposition National Union party gained the presidency only enhanced his fame. Figueres was hailed as one of the few true democrats in Latin America, as a sworn enemy of dictatorships of the left as well as of the right, and as a faithful but not uncritical friend of the United States. He was buried under awards, citations, and honorary degrees.

Although out of office, Don Pepe was not out of power. He still controlled the National Liberation party. The party controlled the legislature, and the legislature had powers comparable to those of the United States Congress. Moreover, his friends tended to dominate the autonomous corporations that were becoming more powerful every year. Thus, while he had no official position, Figueres was not prevented from undertaking his next foreign policy initiative—the sending of help to Fidel Castro.

"In 1958, Castro and his handful of followers were fighting in the Sierra Maestra," Don Pepe said. "All they had were .22-caliber rifles. They were in terrible shape. After Herbert Matthews of *The New York Times* went to see Castro, he brought me a letter from him, pleading for help. I still have the letter. He swore he wasn't a Communist, and I believed him. I also knew that he was trying to overthrow Batista, who was one of the most corrupt dictators anywhere. I got arms and ammunition for him. I sent him his first radio. I got a plane and I got parachutes to make an airdrop. I saved his neck. A month and a half after he came to power, it was clear the direction he was going in. He invited me to Havana, and at a big rally there, in front of 100,000 people, I had a fight with him."

A disappointed Don Pepe watched Castro suppress all opposition and seemingly go out of his way to provoke the United States. "Finally I went to Allen Dulles and said, 'This SOB has got to be overthrown,' " Figueres said. "I begged him, though, not to use Batista people in the invasion force. Instead, they hardly used anyone else. It was a great mistake."

Don Pepe shook his head. "I didn't speak to Castro again until July, 1980, when both of us were in Managua for the first anniversary celebration of the overthrow of Somoza. A lot of people wanted us to shake hands. They said Castro would if I would. So, finally, I agreed. I said, 'Fidel, come to Costa Rica as my guest, and we'll discuss the direction you're going in,' but he said he didn't want to do that."

With Figueres on the sidelines, the National Liberation party was losing its following at the polls, so in 1970, he ran again and won easily. Not long after Don Pepe took office, a man named Clovis McAlpin turned up in San José, footsore and weary, a couple of jumps ahead of agents of the Federal Bureau of Investigation. McAlpin, a stock market swindler by profession, was under indictment for income tax evasion. When he said he wanted to invest a lot of money in Costa Rica and his lawyers pointed out that the crime of which he was accused was not covered by its extradition treaty with the United States, Figueres permitted him to stay.

McAlpin bought land and began promoting Costa Rica as a vacation and retirement paradise. For a man accustomed to selling underwater real estate and stock in nonexistent corporations, peddling dry land, much of which was, indeed, exactly as advertised, was a cinch. The climate *was* wonderful, the people *were* friendly, the country *was* peaceful, and the cost of living *was* low. The number of Americans who bought property or took vacations in Costa Rica rose quickly, and a land boom began.

In 1972, Robert Vesco, who was also on the lam, arrived. He explained to Don Pepe that he was a fugitive from justice in the same way that Jean Valjean had been. He said that, like Victor Hugo's hero, he had been traduced by powerful enemies. He thanked God for a country like Costa Rica and its wise and humane leader. He, his wife, and their children hoped, Vesco said, to start a new life in the Land of Eternal Spring and to make whatever small investments in its economy that his limited means permitted.

Vesco was referring to the $224,000,000 he had looted from the assets of Investors Overseas Service after he bought it in 1971. It was the biggest and most brazen scam in the checkered history of American finance. After fleeing to the Bahamas from the United States, Vesco was indicted for the theft and for making an illegal contribution of $250,000, possibly in hopes of buying a little leniency, to President Nixon's reelection campaign in 1972.

Asked how he had happened to meet Vesco, Don Pepe replied that it had been pure chance.

"My family has a business that is managed by one of my sons that makes the bags that coffee is shipped in," he said. "It badly needed $2,500,000 to buy new machinery. A loan was arranged from a bank in the Bahamas, and it turned out that Vesco controlled the bank. That was it."

But what of all the reports, I asked, that they had been introduced by McAlpin? Don Pepe gazed at the ceiling, trying to find a needle of trivia in the giant haystack of his career, and said, perhaps only to be polite, that in fact McAlpin might have been the go-between.

How could he, I asked, affecting the dismay of a paid-up member of the Good Government League, have stained his spotless toga by dealing with a man like Vesco?

"Costa Rica has always been an open-door country," he said. "I very much wanted investors, and Vesco said he was ready to invest at least $25,000,000 and probably much more. I thought the money should be invested in what I call the poor world. Besides, I didn't agree with the American law."

What about the $325,000, I asked, that turned up in Figueres's account in a New York bank?

"I've got nothing to hide," Don Pepe said. "If I did, I wouldn't have tried to hide it in a New York bank. If you're doing something illegal, you do it in a place where there are secrecy laws and numbered accounts. Part of that money was a donation from Vesco or one of his associates to the National Symphony Orchestra. I frankly don't remember what the rest of it was for, but it was something similar. After all, I've been handling much larger sums than that for Latin American revolutionaries and whatever for 35 years, and no one ever raised any questions. It doesn't matter in any case because I have already drawn

181

up my last will and testament and it provides that any assets I have will go to the state."

The pain and sorrow in Don Pepe's voice and expression caused by doubts as to his probity gradually changed to resignation and forgiveness. In fact, people I spoke to in San José agreed that Don Pepe may have slipped a bit in his dealings with Vesco but that on balance he was a model of fiscal deportment, and not merely by the standards of Latin America.

"It shows what a good reputation will do for you," said a Costa Rican banker. "Vesco knew that he would have been stripped clean any other place he went. They would have held him for ransom, for God's sake. Vesco wouldn't have come to Costa Rica at all if he hadn't figured he could trust Don Pepe."

The political opposition seized on the Vesco affair, of course. Criticism also came from the university, the press, and even Figueres's own party. Don Pepe chose to ignore it. He sponsored laws to make the investment of Vesco's money extremely easy and his extradition all but impossible. From time to time Washington said that it wanted Vesco back, but it seemed unlikely that President Gerald Ford was anxious to take the lid off Watergate by putting him on trial.

Having received a residence permit, Vesco made showy donations to Costa Rican charities, but aside from the loan to the Figueres enterprises and the purchase of a house in San José, a ranch in Guanacaste, and other real estate, Vesco seemed to keep his money in his pocket. He was reported to have backed a daily newspaper, *Excelsior,* as a voice for Figueres's National Liberation party, but he was never definitely connected with it. In any event, it didn't last long.

After 18 months of heavy losses, the putative owners of the newspaper announced that they were turning it over to its staff to run as a cooperative. After going over the books, the new owners ran a front-page story with the headline "They Defrauded Us." The paper, it turned out, had many debts and few assets, and the previous owners of record, who would have been liable for substantial severance pay under Costa Rican law, had disappeared.

As Don Pepe prepared to leave office for what has turned out to be the last time, the Vesco entanglement faded to insignificance in comparison with his accomplishments. Few nations anywhere, and certainly none in Latin America, have ever come close to making the progress that Costa Rica did during the years from 1948 to 1974. Every index—per capita income, literacy and education, infant mortality, longevity, housing, miles of paved road—showed dramatic improvements. Moreover, it was done without compulsion and with a level of graft that, by the standards of the region, was nonexistent. Amnesty International reported that Costa Rica was the only country in Latin America from which not even a single *allegation* of political murder, imprisonment, or other serious abuse of power had been received.

"When we won the war, 84 percent of the people of Costa Rica went barefoot," Don Pepe said. "Even in San José half the people had no shoes. Now they have . . . what? Two or three pairs of shoes each *and* socks."

I agreed that he had brought forth a miracle. How, I asked, had he done it?

He gazed at me for a long moment and folded his face into that beatific U-shaped smile. "That's easy," he replied. "By borrowing."

Don Pepe could not run for reelection in 1974, but his party's candidate, Daniel Oduber Quirós, won. It was the first time since the rebellion of 1948 that any party had held the presidency for consecutive terms. However, Oduber got only 43 percent of the vote, and he probably would have been badly beaten if the opposition ballots had not been split among four candidates. Costa Rica may not have been outraged about Vesco's residence, which had become the major campaign issue, but it clearly wasn't altogether pleased about it, either.

Even so, Oduber did not seem eager to free himself of a political liability. The likely reason emerged only several years later, when it became known that Vesco had put up most of the money for his campaign. The opposition brought legal actions against Vesco. A defrauded shareholder in Investors Overseas Service also filed suit. Vesco responded by applying for Costa Rican citizenship, and his son married a Costa Rican woman. In 1977, Oduber, no longer able to take the heat, politely asked Vesco to leave the country. Vesco didn't budge. He clung to Costa Rica like a limpet to a rock.

In the 1978 election the opposition, which had united behind a single candidate, Rodrigo Carazo, made Vesco the only issue. Carazo declared that Vesco had corrupted a nation and promised that his first official act would be to deport him. Vesco bought time on television to make a plea for compassion. Costa Ricans who were familiar with the career of Richard Nixon called it his "Checkers" speech. Carazo won a narrow victory, and four days before his inauguration Vesco quietly returned to the Bahamas.

No sooner had Vesco left than, coincidentally, the Costa Rican economy collapsed. The foreign debt, the most important measurement, had quadrupled from 1974 to 1978 to $800,000,000. During Carazo's administration, from 1978 to 1982, it quintupled to $4 billion. Being unable even to pay the interest, Costa Rica hired Lehman Brothers Kuhn Loeb, the New York investment firm, at a fee of $1,000,000, presumably paid in advance, to come up with a way of holding off its creditors.

In the beginning, these were such easy marks as the World Bank, Citibank, and Chase Manhattan. At the end, Costa Rica had been reduced to begging for a couple of million until next Tuesday at sinister financial institutions in places like Hong Kong and Beirut, where even a sovereign state gets half of what it borrows and repays the full amount at rates that would make a Mafia loan shark blush.

"It wasn't Carazo's fault as much as people said," said Don Pepe charitably. "Three things cost us $200,000,000 a year each. These were the decrease in coffee prices, the rise in oil prices, and the rise in interest rates. You read all these ads for the banks in the American papers. 'Give us your money and watch it grow with the power of compound interest. A hundred dollars doubles in five years.' Et cetera, et cetera. The only trouble is that for you to collect yours, somebody has to *pay* even more interest. That's where countries like Costa Rica get stuck."

(Carazo was filling out the last few months of his term before the inauguration of Luis Alberto Monge, a Figueres protégé. I found him seated in his office in the National Palace, which, uniquely in Central America, was guarded by only one man, and in civilian clothes at that. He asked me to convey his gratitude to Don Pepe for his kind remark. "It's too bad he didn't say that during the campaign," he added.)

It is also true that in Costa Rica the problem was compounded by a decline in productivity that ran along with the steady increase in public employment. Something like a quarter of the country's workers are on the payrolls of the government or the autonomous corporations. By general agreement, it is a terminal case of bureaucratic bloat. Permitting the autonomous corporations to borrow was recognized as an error. Bankers assured me that not until the country's credit rating hit the rocks at the end of 1980 did anyone take a close look at what the foreign debt of these agencies amounted to. It turned out to be far larger than anyone had imagined.

In any event, the attention of Figueres and his friends was focused elsewhere. The Sandinistas were on the march. Don Pepe went back into the arms-smuggling business and saw himself reborn when one of his sons went to fight with them. When the Sandinistas marched into Managua, Don Pepe hurried there to congratulate them in person. The Costa Rican government confiscated a vast ranch owned by Somoza.

"I've been disappointed by what has been happening in Nicaragua lately," Figueres said, "but to me it looks like the United States is doing all it can to drive the Sandinistas into the embrace of Cuba and the Soviet Union. You can say the Sandinistas are dictatorial and ask what's the difference between them and Somoza. Well, there *is* a difference. The Sandinistas at least have a core of idealism. The Somozas and the rest of the dictatorships of the right that I've dealt with are all alike. The only thing they're interested in is power and money."

Was the flame of his anticommunism, I asked, burning less brightly than it had in the past?

"Maybe that's so," he replied after a moment of thought. "They were the devils 40 years ago, but since then, I think, we have lost a little bit of our saintliness."

He paused and smiled again.

"I sometimes wish we had a few more Communists here in Costa Rica," he said. "Then we could call them a menace and get a little more aid money from Washington. In fact, if we cut down all our social services the way the bankers want us to, we really *will* have them in a couple of years."

II

Nicaragua and
the Somozas

In December, 1981, *The New York Times* quoted an unnamed official of the Reagan administration as saying that Nicaragua was "on the verge of becoming a Central American superpower." In the months that followed, Secretary of State Haig and others provided vivid descriptions of this tropical Sparta. Thousands of Cuban advisers, hardened veterans of Angola, were said to be creating a Nicaraguan army of 50,000, which would be by far the largest in Central America. Nicaraguan pilots were in Bulgaria, learning how to fly MIG jet fighters. Their delivery was expected momentarily. Weapons were said to be pouring in by way of Cuba from the Soviet Union, Eastern Europe, and even Vietnam. The emerging superpower was also accused of being the major source of weapons for the insurrectionists of El Salvador. Nicaragua was described as a menace to its neighbors and even a threat to the oil fields of Mexico.

With these allegations fresh in my mind, I was unprepared for what I saw on the taxi ride from the airport to my hotel in Managua. Most of the small factories and warehouses along the highway, which represented a large part of Nicaragua's industrial capacity, were destroyed or damaged during the final months of the rebellion of 1979. Set amid the rubble were long rows of knocked-together shacks in which most of the population of Managua has lived since the earthquake of 1972.

The view from my room at the Intercontinental Hotel did not fit in with the Fortress Nicaragua theory either. The earthquake destroyed the center of the capital, and 10 years later, it remained a vast vacant lot, covered by patchy grass that looked like a disease of the earth and quartered by two broad, empty boulevards. In the area between the hotel and Lake Managua, a mile or so to the west, and for a mile or more along its shore scarcely a dozen buildings stood. The lake, for that matter, is so intensely polluted that even tiliapa cannot survive in its waters.

The three-second shock, which came without warning at 12:22 A.M. on December 23, 1972, sent 50,000 buildings crashing down. At least 5,000 persons were killed, and as many as 300,000 were left homeless. What the world saw as a disaster, Anastasio Somoza Debayle, who had followed his father and his elder brother as the ruler of the family racket that was officially known as the Republic of Nicaragua, saw as a business opportunity. The National Guard, which Somoza commanded, stole the donations of food, medicine, and construction materials that were rushed from the United States and Europe and sold them for whatever the traffic would bear.

Foreign relief administrators and even the archbishop of Managua publicly confirmed what the press had reported. That was that the thefts were not isolated acts, which are common enough in such circumstances all over the world. They were systematic, they went on for months, and the proceeds ended up in the pockets of Somoza and his associates.

Although two-thirds of the population of the city had only temporary shelter, Somoza prohibited any rebuilding. Damaged structures were demolished rather than repaired. Exceptions were made only for the cathedral, which remains a roofless shell, with bushes growing through the floor, and the National Palace, which was less heavily damaged. Somoza pointed out that the center of the city was situated on three intersecting fault lines and had been destroyed by an earthquake in 1931 and severely damaged by another in 1967 and decreed that a new capital worthy of himself and his nation would rise several miles to the west. Not until the design had been completed would construction begin. Not coincidentally, Somoza, who was also the country's biggest businessman, monopolized sales of cement, structural steel, and roofing materials, and owned much of the land on which the capital was to rise.

But Nuevo Managua or Ciudad Somoza was not to be. Even as a consortium of Mexican architects and city planners made their surveys and their models, the Sandinista rebels, whose annihilation Somoza had been announcing every couple of years since the early 1960's, emerged again from their mountain hideouts. They struck at National

Guard outposts, robbed banks to buy arms, and faded back into the hills. In December, 1974, nine of them, wearing National Guard uniforms, broke into a diplomatic dinner party in Managua. They held hostage the 35 guests, who included the Foreign Minister and several members of the ruling family, until Somoza agreed to free 54 imprisoned rebels, to pay a ransom of $1,000,000, and to fly them all to Cuba.

Their safe departure galvanized the country. The Somozas had been publicly humiliated. It had never occurred to most Nicaraguans that such a thing could happen. Only the old folks could dimly remember a time when the family's boots had not been in their faces. Unlike some dictators, the Somozas had never achieved any sort of popularity, in part because they were all so obviously obsessed by money. After the earthquake, dislike hardened into hatred. The Somozas had convinced their subjects that they were invulnerable, but the Sandinista raid showed that they were not. From then on, the rebellion spread. Four and a half years of increasingly bloody fighting remained, but when Anastasio Somoza fled to Miami in July, 1979, and the Sandinistas marched into Managua in triumph, the entire country was marching with them.

The period of unity didn't last long. Most of the Sandinista leaders were Marxists of one sort or another. The people who joined the rebellion, by and large, were not. The Sandinistas promised to create the sort of society that everybody seems to want and hardly anyone gets— democratic socialism and a mixed economy—but they kept tight control of the government.

Within six months, businessmen said they were being harassed. A coffee planter who was organizing cooperatives was killed under mysterious circumstances. Hot words flew on both sides. Increasing numbers of Cubans arrived. The first contingents set up schools and clinics, but those who followed were military and security advisers. National elections were postponed until 1985. The United States cut off economic aid, ostensibly because of the arms shipments to El Salvador, and then began openly but inadequately to organize anti-Sandinista forces in the border regions of Honduras. Washington saw another Communist government emerging in the Western Hemisphere. The Sandinistas, for their part, saw a continuation of the American imperialism that had kept the Somozas in power.

The Somozas, minor backcountry landowners, became known to

188

history in the mid-19th century, when one of them was hanged as a horse thief. The next generation produced a member of the Nicaraguan Senate, an entirely respectable figure. His only son was Anastasio Somoza, the founder of the ruling dynasty and a throwback to his great-uncle.

In 1916, at the age of 19, Anastasio was sent to Philadelphia, where the family had relatives, to attend a business school. In those days, American bankers were running Nicaragua, a former clerk for an American company had been elevated to the presidency, and the marines were keeping order. With a knowledge of English and double-entry bookkeeping, a boy like Tacho, as he was called, could go far.

Somoza returned to Nicaragua in 1919. The next year he was married to the daughter of a surgeon whose family was a couple of rungs higher than the Somozas on the country's short social ladder. Somoza had supported himself in Philadelphia by selling used cars. Deciding that he had the gift of salesmanship, he established an automobile dealership in Managua. In his enthusiasm, Somoza overlooked one important point. Nicaragua had almost no roads.

Somoza heard that the Rockefeller Foundation was looking for an alert young man who spoke English. Its public health division was studying dysentery and other gastrointestinal diseases. An opening existed for a sanitary inspector. Somoza did not disdain honest toil, no matter how smelly. He took the job. Whatever the benefits to mankind, Somoza soon tired of taking samples from cesspits with a long-handled scoop. He turned next, according to widely accepted reports, to an occupation in which he thought he could really make some money, but this, too, ended in disappointment. Only the influence of his father-in-law, it is said, saved him from criminal prosecution for the counterfeiting of Nicaraguan currency.

His next big chance came in 1926. The countryside was aflame with rebellion. Somoza, thirsting for glory and the spoils of victory, joined the insurgents. Uprisings had been prevented since 1912 by the presence of the marines. In 1925, Washington, sensitive to charges of imperialism, withdrew them. Nicaraguans, prevented from murdering one another for political reasons for 14 long years, immediately began making up for lost time.

As it happened, Tacho did not even have to turn his coat since, as a matter of clan loyalty and regionalism, the Somozas were traditionally Liberals. He presented himself to José María Moncada, one of the scores of Liberal generalissimos, and was given command of a detachment. In his first engagement, Tacho was defeated and captured. He was released after promising to take no further part in hostilities. When it looked as though the Liberals were winning, Washington, which backed the Conservatives, sent back the marines.

In 1927, Henry L. Stimson, who was to become Hoover's Secretary of State and Roosevelt's Secretary of War, was sent to Nicaragua as a special envoy. Stimson proposed a peace plan to Moncada and the other Liberals. If they would lay down their arms, he said, the United States would guarantee their safety and would supervise an open and honest presidential election in 1928. It was during these discussions that Somoza was introduced to Stimson. The former salesman of used automobiles, inspector of privies, and suspected counterfeiter had by then, like hundreds of other Nicaraguans, conferred upon himself the rank of general. Stimson was delighted to meet a former public health expert for the Rockefeller Foundation who also spoke fluent English. He used Somoza as an interpreter on a couple of occasions and described him in his diary, according to Richard Millett's *Guardians of the Dynasty,* as "a very frank, friendly, likeable young Liberal."

With the marines holding them in check, all but one of the Liberal leaders accepted Stimson's proposal. The minority vote was cast by Augusto César Sandino, who had returned from Mexico to join the rebellion. Sandino denounced Moncada as a traitor, refused to surrender his weapons to the marines, as the agreement required, and led a band of 200 men to the jungle-covered mountains along the Honduran border to continue the struggle.

Moncada, who was duly elected president in 1928, the Conservative opposition, and the United States all agreed that Sandino was nothing more than a bandit. The reorganized National Guard, which was commanded by marine officers, was ordered to bring him in dead or alive. Sandino's forces struck first. They assaulted an outpost and were forced to retreat only when they were strafed and bombed by a squadron of marine planes.

Sandino's losses were heavy, and after that, he fought a guerrilla war. Each time he mounted an ambush or a night attack he issued another manifesto denouncing the men who had sold out the country. The world began to take notice of the doughty patriot who defied the might of the United States. Correspondents sought him out in his mountain hideout. Sandino was good copy. He was handsome and intense, he had a mordant sense of humor, and he dressed like a gentleman cowboy in a 10-gallon hat, hacking jacket, riding breeches, and boots, with a six-gun slung on his hip.

Sandino, the press learned, was the offspring of the classic colonial misalliance—the unsanctified union of a planter and an Indian girl. He had fled to Mexico in 1920 after being accused of wounding a man in a fight. He had worked in the oil fields of Tampico, studied the Mexican revolution, and read a bit of history. Although without military experience, he became, in the mountains, a brave and gifted leader of men.

When the National Guard failed to find Sandino, the task was given to the marines. Sandino thereupon ambushed a marine patrol blundering through the jungle, killing five men and wounding eight. President Coolidge was outraged. He sent reinforcements, bringing the total of marines in Nicaragua to 2,000. Still Sandino, with a force of perhaps 200, eluded them. He had become, worse than a menace, an international embarrassment.

Somoza, who had joined Moncada's staff, was soon dismissed. Bernard Diederich, in his study *Somoza, and the Legacy of U.S. Involvement in Central America,* says that there were reports that he was unable to account for $75,000 that had been entrusted to him to pay war damage claims. In any event, he was sent to San José as consul. He returned in 1931, when his wife's uncle, Juan Bautista Sacasa, a former vice-president, announced his presidential candidacy. Once again Americans supervised the balloting. Sacasa was elected, even though he was running on a platform of American withdrawal.

President Hoover agreed, and on January 1, 1933, the marines departed for the last time. Sandino let it be known that he wanted an honorable end to hostilities. The two causes of his insurrection, the American occupation and the Moncada presidency, no longer existed. A month later, he went to Managua under a flag of truce and negotiated an agreement that made him the governor of the western region of the country. By then, Sacasa had been persuaded to appoint Somoza as commander of the National Guard. Somoza, who could recognize a potential rival, opposed the agreement with Sandino. In February, 1934, Sandino returned to Managua at Sacasa's invitation. As Sandino and two of his aides were leaving a presidential dinner in their honor, they were seized by officers of the National Guard and murdered. Sandino's brother was killed on the same night.

As Sacasa's term drew to a close, Somoza began thinking of himself as presidential timber. However, a constitutional provision appeared to create an insuperable problem. It forbade persons who were related to hold the office within six months of each other, which, as a practical matter, prohibited successive terms.

Since the proclamation of the Good Neighbor Policy, the United States had stayed out of Latin American affairs. In 1936, a further step was taken. Washington said it would no longer withhold recognition from governments that came to power by extralegal means. As it happened, this statement fitted in perfectly with Somoza's plans. The Liberals and Conservatives took the extreme step of saying they would unite behind a presidential candidate to oppose him.

Behind a fog of threats, offers of compromise, and declarations of loyalty, Somoza prepared his coup. At the end of May, 1936, he struck. Within a week, Sacasa had been forced to resign and was on his way out of the country. Somoza, mindful of the constitutional restriction, placed a puppet in office and postponed the election until December. With the National Guard counting the vote, he won by 107,401 to 169.

On January 1, 1937, Somoza became president. The former counterfeiting suspect was now in charge of the treasury and everything else. As soon as he took the oath of office, he began to steal and never stopped. Behind the rifles of the National Guard he bought *haciendas* from political enemies at whatever price he chose to pay. His farmhands were placed on the government payroll. Nicaragua's public works program consisted of improving Somoza's properties and building roads to them. Millett quotes an American diplomat as estimating that Somoza, in his first three years in power, amassed a fortune of at least $3,000,000. It was an enormous amount in Depression dollars in a country with a population at that time of no more than 1,000,000. Whatever graft remained to be taken went to the National Guard.

On the other hand, Somoza's single-minded pursuit of money left him little time for tyranny. He suspended civil liberties, of course, and occasionally locked up or exiled a particularly annoying opponent, but he resorted to murder reluctantly and only when other methods of persuasion failed. There were exceptions, of course. In 1937, the last of Sandino's officers still making trouble was captured and executed. His head was sent to Somoza.

In 1939, Somoza revised the constitution to permit himself to serve a second term of eight years. Later that year, after having dropped endless hints to the American envoy, Somoza got an official invitation to visit Washington. He was greeted with elaborate ceremony. Everywhere he went, bands played and honor guards snapped to attention.

He and his wife slept in the best bedroom at the White House. Somoza would have been justified in thinking that he was very important to the United States. As Diederich points out, the Somozas were being used as stand-ins in a rehearsal for the visit of King George VI and Queen Elizabeth of Great Britain later that year. It was after that visit that Roosevelt, upon being questioned about his cordiality to Somoza, is said to have remarked, "He may be a son of a bitch, but he's *our* son of a bitch."

Somoza proved his loyalty by declaring war on the Axis powers two days after the United States. He immediately began seizing choice ranches owned by German citizens. The United States established a couple of bases on the coast and provided some new arms for the National Guard. Somoza enrolled his younger son, also named Anastasio and nicknamed Tachito, Little Tacho, in West Point.

In 1946, the elder Somoza let it be known that he was willing to go on shouldering the burden of the presidency, but the United States made it clear that it was time for a change. Reluctantly he submitted, at least to the extent of choosing his successor, Dr. Leonardo Argüello, who had been his opponent in 1936. It scarcely seemed to matter who was president, since Somoza kept command of the National Guard. However, as soon as Argüello took office he forgot whatever promises he must have made to Somoza. He transferred Tachito from command of the guard's best battalion and hinted that he intended to exile the father. That was recklessness, indeed. Twenty-five days after his inauguration, Argüello was ousted and an uncle of Somoza's was installed in his place.

Washington refused for a year to recognize the new president, but it was not prepared to do anything punitive. Later that year, Somoza swatted aside an attempted coup. Its leader, Emiliano Chamorro, was by then in his seventies, but he had been taking part in Conservative uprisings since the first decade of the century and apparently found the habits of a lifetime hard to break. In 1948, Somoza had his little run-in with Pepe Figueres, and in 1949, over Washington's objections, he resumed the presidency.

Somoza tried to improve relations with the United States by giving the political opposition a third of the seats in the legislature and by emphasizing his anticommunism. He had no Communists of his own to persecute, having already hunted them to extinction, so he began nosing them out elsewhere in the region. In 1954, he offered to lead his

National Guard into combat against Arbenz of Guatemala, but Washington declined with thanks.

Somoza regarded himself, with reason, as the bull's-eye in communism's hemispheric target. By then, his fortune was being estimated at more than $100,000,000. His holdings included *haciendas* totaling hundreds of thousands of acres, urban real estate, and Nicaragua's largest distillery. He took a commission on every important government contract. The success of his automobile agencies was guaranteed. The cars he sold were the kind of cars the government and a great many Nicaraguans decided were the kind to buy. There were even some roads on which they could be driven, although they all seemed to lead to a Somoza property.

Somoza was also a partner in the largest brewery, flour mill, bakery, ice cream company, and match factory. Much of what he and his relatives didn't own his lackeys did. He kept the peace with the old oligarchy families by letting them have what was left over. Somoza had a stranglehold on the Nicaraguan economy, but at least it kept out foreign imperialists. There wasn't much left in Nicaragua for them to own. The Nicaraguan people remained very poor, of course, but at least they could count on having enough food to last them a lifetime.

Somoza may have been sitting, if not on top of the world, at least on top of Nicaragua, but photographs from this period show only suspicion and irritation in his small eyes. His features seem not merely fleshy but inflated, flatulent, and liverish. Repletion had loosened his mouth and doubled his chin. In time his sons came to look just like dad.

In 1956, Somoza astonished no one by announcing he would again run for the presidency. He traveled to León, the center of Liberal strength, to accept the nomination. As he was greeting his supporters at a reception, a young man named Rigoberto López Pérez drew a revolver and shot him four times and was in turn shot dead by Somoza's bodyguards. López had a local reputation as a poet and a theoretical leftist and was thought to be a bit mad. Somoza, in a coma, was flown to the Canal Zone. The efforts of specialists sent by President Eisenhower were unavailing. Nine days later, he died, aged 60.

Somoza had chosen his elder son, Luis, as his successor as president, and had been preparing him with government posts of increasing importance. The younger, Tachito, the West Pointer, was to take command of the National Guard. Luis Somoza was a graduate of Louisiana

State University. His studies there seemed to have broadened him. Government in Louisiana was not notably more honest than in Nicaragua, but there was a tradition of sharing the loot, and Luis tried the same approach. He also announced that from then on, no president, including himself, could serve more than one term of six years.

There was a partial restoration of civil liberties, although an exception was made in the case of several persons who were suspected of complicity in the assassination. They were held without charges until 1960, when they were shot—according to the official account, while trying to escape. The country was not quiet for long. By the middle of 1958, Fidel Castro's insurrection was causing sympathetic vibrations. The irrepressible Pedro Joaquín Chamorro, the editor and publisher of *La Prensa,* the country's only independent newspaper, who had been held briefly after the assassination of Somoza, launched an invasion from Costa Rica. The National Guard quickly put it down and returned him to his cell.

Under the circumstances, the Somoza brothers were only too willing to have Nicaragua used as the major staging area for the Bay of Pigs invasion. Its failure helped them to persuade Washington that Nicaragua should become the front line of continental defense against communism.

At about the same time, three young men announced the formation of the Sandinista National Liberation Front. They were Carlos Fonseca Amador, who was 26 years old and was said to be the illegitimate son of an executive in the Somoza business empire; Silvio Mayorga, 25; and Tomás Borge, 30, whose father, a bookseller, was said to have fought with Sandino. Borge had joined a Communist cell while attending León University, and he and Fonseca had also been briefly jailed after Somoza's assassination.

The formation of revolutionary organizations by enthusiastic students occurred infrequently in Nicaragua. Somoza's secret police were efficient and ruthless. To improve their chances of survival, the three founded their organization in Honduras. The news of its establishment was not widely disseminated in Nicaragua. The only permissible political passions, aside from Somocismo, were fear and apathy. There was no help from the church, which was still in its preliberationist phase. Its advice to the faithful, in effect, was to render unto the Somozas whatever they wanted.

As he had promised, Luis Somoza did not seek a second term in

1963. He stepped aside in favor of an old family retainer named René Schick, whose serious drinking problem was a point in his favor. It was thought to make him incapable of the sort of double cross that Argüello had attempted in 1947, and he could usually be sobered up for state occasions. In any event, Tachito remained in command of the National Guard, assuring the Somozas of control.

The Sandinistas, meanwhile, had crossed the border into Nicaragua and established a base in the western mountains, where Sandino had evaded the marines for so many years. However, rebellion, which Castro had made seem so easy, turned out to be hard and dangerous work. The Sandinistas were tenderfeet. They got lost in the woods, suffered bites, stings, and fevers, messed up simple robberies, and found themselves unwelcome in the huts of frightened *campesinos*. The National Guard tracked their movements and swooped down on them. Fonseca was captured. To the astonishment of all, he survived to stand trial, probably because Luis Somoza wanted to show the world that the rule of law was supreme in Nicaragua. Fonseca was found guilty and given a long sentence, but it was commuted to exile. The Sandinistas were scattered and demoralized. Two years were to pass before they went into the field again.

Schick died in 1966. Another nonentity filled in for a year until Tachito could be elected president under the old six-month rule. The opposition united behind a candidate and waged an energetic campaign. A couple of weeks before the election, the opposition leaders realized belatedly that the National Guard would still be counting the votes. Unwilling to accept certain defeat, they fomented a rebellion. As usual, they forgot to plan it, and the guard put it down without the least difficulty, killing 40 persons and wounding 100. Pedro Joaquín Chamorro was jailed on a variety of charges, one of which should have been insurrectional incompetence.

Whatever his lack of popularity in Nicaragua may have been, Tachito Somoza more than made up for it in Washington. He had contributed to President Johnson's campaigns in 1960, when he unsuccessfully sought the Democratic nomination, and in 1964. At Johnson's request Somoza sent a battalion of the National Guard to the Dominican Republic in 1965. As Johnson became increasingly preoccupied with Vietnam, he was glad to accept Somoza's offer to act as a guardian of American interests in Central America.

By virtue of his West Point ring, his discreet assistance in anti-Castro operations, his preference for speaking English, and his noisily expressed admiration for all things American, Tachito was a welcome guest at the Pentagon and at Southern Command headquarters in the Canal Zone. He was rich in friends on Capitol Hill as well, foremost among them being his West Point classmate John Murphy, who was rising in seniority and influence in the House.

Luis Somoza had a fatal heart attack in 1967. After that, Tachito's power was undivided, as his father's had been, but he used it far less skillfully. Luis had run the business and political end of Nicaragua, Inc., a task that had required a certain degree of flexibility. Tachito had run the National Guard, which hadn't. Luis had not been averse, up to a point, to accommodation. Tachito, with his military background, demanded not only obedience but total subservience. Besides trying to show that he controlled the country more completely than his father had, Tachito was trying to outdo him as a moneymaker. To the family holdings he added a shrimp and seafood business, an export-import concern in Florida, stevedoring and warehousing ventures, the monopolies in cement and structural steel, and much else. He went into cattle ranching in a big way, which required the eviction of thousands of *campesino* families from their farms.

In "Doctor Jazz," Jelly Roll Morton sings, "The more I get, the more I want, it seems." It could have been the theme song for Somoza's television and radio stations or the slogan of his newspaper. The Somoza enterprises didn't publish annual reports, but knowledgeable people told me that despite total tax avoidance, interest-free government loans, and an absence of competition, their profits tended not to be large, and some of them actually managed to lose money.

"Tachito was greedy and aggressive, but he didn't know anything about business," said an American diplomat who used to be stationed in Managua. "He was always getting ripped off, or he would have some retired colonel trying to manage a factory. And he didn't leave enough for anyone else. That's why all the business people turned against him at the end. They weren't particularly interested in social justice or reform. Mostly they wanted to get rid of the unfair competition."

By then, Tachito was certain that he had at last wiped out the Sandinistas. Twenty of them, probably half their total strength, had been killed in a three-day battle with the National Guard near the Indian village of Pancasán. Silvio Mayorga, one of the founders, was among the dead. The Sandinistas say, retrospectively, that Pancasán marked a turning point in their struggle. Although they were defeated, they proved to themselves that they could stand and fight against the guard. In 1969, Fonseca was captured again, this time in Costa Rica during a bank robbery. His comrades hijacked an airliner, which they traded back to Figueres for a ticket to Havana for him. However, not until 1974 were they able to mount another offensive.

At this point, Somoza might have been wise to offer concessions to the legal opposition. He might even have built schools and hospitals, trying, in the absence of any charitable impulse, to buy goodwill. But no Somoza ever gave away a nickel, and even if he had been inclined toward conciliation, the election of Nixon to the presidency in 1968 would have banished the idea from his mind.

For the first time, Tachito could think of himself and a President of the United States as *compañeros*. Managua had been one of the few places where, thanks to the Somozas, Nixon had been cheered instead of booed on his vice-presidential swing through Latin America. In his book, Diederich cites reports that Somoza contributed as much as $1,000,000 to Nixon's campaign.

The next four years passed blissfully for Tachito. The Sandinistas were inactive, crops were good, prices were high, and to fill his cup to overflowing, Howard Hughes arrived in Managua in February, 1972, to discuss joint business ventures, one of which was the merger of Hughes AirWest with Lanica, the Nicaraguan national airline, which was, of course, owned by Somoza. Hughes and his entourage occupied the entire top floor of the Camino Real, of which Somoza was, naturally, a part owner. (While I was staying there, I went up to have a look at the rooms. They were just as small and ratty as those on the lower floors.) Hughes remained only three weeks but returned later in the year to sign the papers. He was at the Camino Real when the earthquake occurred. The next day, he departed by chartered jet, leaving Somoza to mourn a gigantic lost opportunity.

When Somoza started barking orders after the earthquake, he was forgetting that he was no longer president. He had given up the office six months earlier to a three-member junta that was to govern the country until 1974, when an election would permit Somoza to resume his hereditary title. As usual, he retained command of the guard.

The election went into the records as a great victory, but the entire Catholic hierarchy, protesting the blatant fraud, refused to take part in his inauguration. Pedro Joaquín Chamorro of *La Prensa* founded the

Democratic Liberation Union as a coalition of the growing number of nonviolent opposition groups.

With the election of Jimmy Carter in 1976, the scales tipped at last against Somoza. At first, the administration exerted pressure discreetly, but Somoza was not disposed to listen. He may have known that reform was impossible. The structure of the state that had been created over the previous 30 years was as rigid and as fragile as a pane of glass. Somoza could yield no share of his power without losing it all. Why should he run those risks, Somoza must have asked himself, when his opponents remained weak and disorganized?

Although there were no more than 500 Sandinistas, they were split into three factions that hated one another more than they hated Somoza. As in El Salvador, there were the insurrectionists, who had staged the raid on the dinner party and who thought that a sudden stroke could bring down the regime; the prolonged war group, which could almost not bear winning without fulfilling all sorts of ideological prerequisites; and those who thought the urban proletariat held the key to victory.

Fonseca and Borge came back from Costa Rica, where Figueres had given them refuge, to try to mediate these quarrels. In December, 1976, they were trapped by the National Guard. Fonseca was shot dead. Borge was captured and sentenced to 123 years in prison.

Although it was divided and leaderless, the Sandinista movement did not collapse. The National Guard devastated villages that were suspected of harboring them. From 1977 onward, by all accounts, a pall of smoke and the reek of blood hung over the western mountains and along the Costa Rican border. More often than not the guard was wrong, and every massacre brought recruits to the Sandinistas—men to whom ideology mattered less than revenge.

Meanwhile, Somoza had separated from his wife, who had gone to Miami, and was living openly with his mistress, Dinorah Sampson, a magnificent long-legged creature, all honey, cinnamon, and red-hot jalapeño pepper. She had come under Tachito's protection when she was only 17 and often appeared with him at functions at his fortified headquarters-residence adjoining the grounds of the Camino Real. In July, 1977, Somoza, out of shape and overexerting himself, suffered a heart attack. After recovering in Miami, he went on a diet, stopped drinking, and even began jogging.

Somoza's illness encouraged his opponents. The guerrillas went into action again. In Managua, a group of leftist intellectuals who called themselves *Los Doce,* the 12, tried to bridge the gap between the guerrillas and the bourgeoisie. In December, 1977, Pedro Joaquín Chamorro tried to gain support in Washington. Despite his years of opposition to Somoza with no taint of Marxism, he received little more than good wishes from the Carter administration.

A couple of weeks after his return, Chamorro was assassinated. Chamorro dead turned out to be far more successful than Chamorro alive had ever been. Tens of thousands of persons attended his funeral. It turned into an anti-Somoza protest, then a riot, and then a general strike. Almost all the owners of the struck businesses supported the strikers, even to the extent of keeping them on the payroll. The one exception, of course, was Somoza, Inc. The strike continued for two weeks. As it went on, the non-Communist coalition that Chamorro had only dreamed of began to take shape. It called itself the Broad Opposition Front. Over the next several months, it began to plan jointly with the Sandinistas. They, meanwhile, had composed, or at least papered over, their ideological differences.

In February, 1978, when the evidence of the National Guard's atrocities had become overwhelming, Washington cut off military aid. Somoza was only inconvenienced since Israel—acting independently, I was assured, rather than on behalf of the Pentagon—and Argentina sold him whatever he wanted.

"That was the wonderful irony," my diplomat friend said. "Somoza couldn't bring himself to spend the money. He bought rifles and other light weapons, which were comparatively cheap, but he had hardly any helicopters, jet fighters, or transport planes."

By then, the National Guard was no longer facing poorly armed and trained groups of 10 or 20 men, but well-equipped units 10 times as large. Costa Rica and Honduras permitted the Sandinistas to establish camps along the border. Torrijos gave money. Castro provided only moral support. Anything more than that, he said, was likely to anger the United States to the point that it would do more harm than good.

The Carter administration's freedom of action in Nicaragua was limited by the Panama Canal debate, but it was also curiously reluctant to do more than implore Somoza to resign. Somoza, judging the situation accurately, ducked, dodged, quibbled, and temporized for 18 months, feinting the administration into inactivity until the time was long past when it could have influenced events in any important way.

The tempo of the fighting and of the terrorism increased throughout

1978. In August, the Sandinistas struck at the very heart of Somoza's power. A force of 24 men, wearing National Guard uniforms, seized the National Palace and held more than 1,000 persons, including many members of the legislature, as hostages. After three days of negotiations, the government agreed to pay a ransom of $500,000, to free 58 political prisoners, including Tomás Borge, and to give them and the raiders safe passage to Panama. The leader of the attack, who called himself Comandante Cero, Commander Zero, became a national hero. He was soon identified as Edén Pastora, a businessman and one of a growing number of non-Communists who were joining the Sandinistas.

Before Somoza recovered his balance, the Sandinistas gave the orders for coordinated attacks that they hoped would develop into a general uprising. They struck at León, the country's second-largest city, at Estelí, Matagalpa, Masaya, and Chinandega. With the help of thousands of boys and young men, many of whom fought with target rifles, knives, and flaming bottles of gasoline, they held León for several days and Estelí for two weeks.

The fall of 1978 was also a season of mediation attempts led by the United States—of windy meetings of the Organization of American States, of condemnations of Somoza's violations of human rights, and of attempts to persuade him to permit a plebiscite on his continuation in office.

Somoza preferred to keep fighting, or, rather, to have the National Guard keep fighting, and to hope that the Sandinistas would resume their quarreling or have a falling-out with the rest of the Broad Opposition Front or that the Soviet Union would commit some outrage elsewhere in the world that would restore his standing in Washington. In late December, Somoza definitively rejected an internationally supervised plebiscite. Carter responded, in February, 1979, by formally ending military aid, which until then had been only suspended.

Later that month, the guerrillas formed the National Directorate, with three members, one from each "tendency," as the ideological groups were called. They again took Estelí and held it for six days. During the ensuing months, the initiative passed to the insurgents, and they could claim the active or passive support of almost the entire population. The guerrillas seldom inflicted heavy casualties on the National Guard. It fought tenaciously, but continuous skirmishing exhausted the men and wore out their equipment, which Somoza only grudgingly replaced. The guard's performance had less to do, in any case, with its devotion to Somoza than with the lack of an alternative. Its members feared, and with good reason, that the best they could hope for was quick execution if they surrendered.

In May, 1979, when a Sandinista force of several hundred men crossed the border from Costa Rica, Mexico became the first nation in the hemisphere to break relations with the Somoza government. Secretary of State Cyrus Vance recommended the formation of a "transitional government of national reconciliation" drawn from all segments of Nicaraguan society and the formation of a peace-keeping force drawn from members of the Organization of American States. By then, however, few people in Latin America were even pretending to listen to what Washington had to say.

In June, another general strike took place. The Sandinistas named the five persons who would make up the ruling junta when Somoza was beaten. They were Alfonso Robelo, who had been as successful in business as anyone not named Somoza could be; Violeta Barrios de Chamorro, the widow of the murdered newspaper publisher; Sergio Ramírez, poet, professor, and one of *Los Doce*; Moisés Hassán, the country's only nuclear physicist and head of the United People's Movement, which organized students and the urban poor; and Daniel Ortega, the only Sandinista, a leader of its most successful faction, the insurrectionists.

In late June, the Organization of American States, by a 17–2 vote, called for "the immediate and definitive replacement" of the Somoza government. The United States voted with the majority. In early July, Washington finally sent a special envoy to Costa Rica to confer with the Sandinista leaders. He tried, absurdly, to persuade them to add two "moderates"—that is, members of Somoza's political apparatus—to the junta, and to keep the National Guard in existence.

Illnesses that could be treated only in Miami struck down one after another of Somoza's officials. He finally forbade the granting of exit visas without his consent. Somoza, in uniform and wearing the five stars of a generalissimo, directed military operations from his command post adjacent to the hotel. He complained to journalists about the treachery and stupidity of the United States. He said that he would never abandon his men, "like the shah of Iran," and that he was prepared "to fight to the death." However, his courage was coming out of a vodka bottle, and his mood swung from megalomania to paranoia and back again.

When the National Guard was unable to push the Sandinistas out of the industrial strip between the airport and what had been the center of Managua, he ordered such of his planes as were still flying to bomb the area flat. The operation was not completed because the air force ran out of bombs. When his staff reported that other munitions were also running low, Somoza decided that the time had come to leave. Calling the Congress into session shortly after midnight on July 17 at the hotel, he resigned in favor of the speaker of the lower house, Francisco Urcuyo. At 5:00 A.M., before the news could spread, he flew off to Miami. The next night, Urcuyo also took the Miami shuttle. After 43 years of misrule, the Somoza era had ended. After 17 years of dreaming and planning, organizing and fighting, the Sandinista era had begun.

12

The Sandinistas
Take Power

THE SANDINISTAS marched into the empty center of Managua on July 19, 1979, and formally installed the ruling junta and the Cabinet. The first order of business was to go over the books. The auditors reported that, aside from $3,500,000 that had somehow been overlooked by Somoza and his friends, the treasury was empty, and the foreign debt totaled $1.8 billion. Much of it had been run up during the last years of Somoza's rule, and nearly half of it was due in 1980. The Government of National Reconstruction, as it was called, promised to pay it off eventually. Its creditors, delighted to have the debts acknowledged at all, granted an extension. One obligation the new government refused to honor. That was $5,000,000 due to Israel and Argentina for armaments purchased by Somoza.

The property of the Somoza family was confiscated. It turned out that its members owned about a quarter of the country's farm and pastureland. Somoza had not found a way to take his real estate with him, but he had done the next best thing, by mortgaging it to the hilt to banks he controlled, converting the cordobas into harder currencies, and adding the proceeds to his foreign bank accounts. The sum that the Somozas had sent abroad in more than four decades of single-minded theft could only be estimated, but no one put the figure at less than many hundreds of millions of dollars. In one fully documented arms purchase, the total amount of $160,000,000 included a "commission" of $28,000,000 to one of Somoza's sons. In Miami, Somoza insisted that his net worth had never been more than $100,000,000 and that $80,000,000 of that had been lost. No one bothered to ask how he had accumulated even that much.

The seizure of the holdings of Somoza and his supporters permitted the new government to begin to create a mixed economy with little immediate inconvenience to the many large property owners and businessmen who had supported the rebellion. The hundreds of thousands of acres of land that became the property of the state were transformed into cooperative, collective farms and small private holdings. Banking, insurance, the export-import trade, and the few foreign-owned enterprises were nationalized. Owners not associated with Somoza got pledges of compensation.

The United States quickly recognized the new government. It in turn established diplomatic relations with Cuba, the Soviet Union and its satellites, and even Libya. Nicaragua said its foreign policy would be neutrality, nonalignment, and independence. If Washington could accept the fact that Nicaragua's days as an American outpost were over, relations could be cordial. The more countries Nicaragua had relations with, of course, the more that it could ask for economic aid, which was badly needed. The National Guard's carefree use of artillery and the air force's heavy thumb on the bomb button had caused enormous damage. Factories, sugar mills, cotton gins, and tens of thousands of dwellings had been destroyed. One of the few places, in fact, that escaped extensive damage was the center of Managua.

The Carter administration thawed out $40,000,000 in aid that had been frozen during Somoza's last year in power and asked Congress to appropriate $75,000,000 more. Venezuela and Mexico provided oil at 30 percent below the world price and on easy credit, as they had been doing elsewhere in Central America. Libya extended a low-interest loan of $100,000,000. Scores of other nations, including the Soviet Union, contributed cash, food, or both. Cuba, still dependent on Russian generosity itself, sent 1,500 teachers, physicians, nurses, engineers, as well as military and security advisers—200 by its count and 2,000 by Washington's.

During its first months in office, the new government seemed miraculously to have repealed the laws of political chemistry. A ruling junta, whose members included a millionaire and a Marxist, worked happily together. The 18-member Cabinet was just as diverse and, moreover, included three Catholic priests, one of whom, Miguel D'Escoto, was the Foreign Minister. Instead of a legislature chosen by district, there was a 33-member Council of State, whose members were elected by organizations of peasants and proletarians, the clergy, teachers, private enterprise, and the old political parties.

The real power, however, was in the hands of the nine-member directorate of the Sandinista Front of National Liberation. Many of these *comandantes,* who were mostly in their twenties and thirties, also held Cabinet posts. However, in the first euphoric months of victory it was easy for the rest of the nation to forget that they owned the rifles and, in the event of serious disagreement, would call the shots.

In the days following the surrender, many members of the National Guard were executed, usually by the armed mob that called itself a militia rather than by the Sandinistas. That, however, was the end of the bloodletting. Castro publicly told the *comandantes* that his execution of hundreds of members of the Cuban secret police, informers, and war criminals, while justified, had been too costly in terms of international goodwill. He urged them to show restraint, and they did so.

The government said that 6,310 persons were brought before revolutionary tribunals on charges of murder, torture, informing, and the like. Most of the defendants were members of the National Guard or civilian officials of the lower ranks, their superiors having departed in good time. Some were confronted with irrefutable evidence from captured files. The proceedings often took only an hour or two, and the opportunity to present a defense and to call witnesses was limited. By the time the trials ceased, in February, 1981, 4,331 of the defendants had received sentences ranging from one to 30 years. Amnesty International, which had criticized Somoza's denial of human rights, stated that many convictions appeared to have been based on "association"—that is, the fact of service in the guard—rather than on specific evidence of crimes.

But after the property of the Somocistas had been confiscated, the guilty punished and the valorous rewarded, the government had to face the fact that little more than glorious memories now united its many elements. The Sandinistas were still divided. The Prolonged People's War Tendency and the Proletarian Tendency were inclined to forget the pledges of democracy and a mixed economy that had been made in the heat of combat. The Insurrectionist Tendency, whose members were called Terceristas, a term that derived from the word for "third," favored gradualism and accommodation. The Terceristas had done most of the fighting, mainly because they had not required combat volunteers to sign a Marxist loyalty oath. At first their viewpoint prevailed, but they gradually had to give ground to the other factions. In December, 1979, the Terceristas agreed to changes in the Cabinet that made it pinker, and in April, 1980, to the enlargement of the

Council of State to 47 members. The new seats went to representatives of the mass organizations, which were controlled by the other factions. Robelo, the millionaire who spoke for the Superior Council of the Private Sector, the equivalent of a Chamber of Commerce, and the Social Democratic party, and Violeta Barrios de Chamorro, who was in poor health, resigned from the junta in protest.

In Washington, the Democratic leadership in Congress announced that the $75,000,000 aid bill would be defeated if the new junta members were less moderate than Robelo and Chamorro. By then, the Sandinistas had coalesced from three camps to two. These were known as the pragmatists, led by Daniel Ortega, a junta member, and the ideologues, led by Borge, who was the Minister of the Interior. When it came to aid money, pragmatism won out. Arturo Cruz, the former director of the Central Bank, and Rafael Córdova of the Somoza-era Conservative party, received the appointments, and the aid bill passed.

The non-Marxists, encouraged by these developments, began pressing the Sandinistas to set a date for elections. The Sandinistas did not enjoy being reminded of promises that they did not wish, or perhaps did not intend, to keep. Advocating elections was seen as the mark of the counterrevolutionary, or *contra,* as opposed to a *compa,* which was short for *compañero,* or comrade. The mass organizations were inspired to hold indignation meetings against the *contras,* to strike their businesses, and to occupy their farms and factories.

In September, Somoza was back in the news for the last time. From Miami, at the suggestion of the Carter administration, he had gone to the Bahamas and had then accepted an invitation from General Alfredo Stroessner to spend his sunset years in Paraguay. Somoza, the faithful Dinorah Sampson at his side, bought a villa in Asunción, the capital, and a ranch. One morning, as he was being driven to a business appointment, his car was blasted by machine guns and two rockets. Somoza, his driver, and a bodyguard were instantly killed. The Nicaraguan government said it had "nothing to do directly" with the killing. Several months later, the Mexican weekly *Por Esto* reported authoritatively that the murders had been carried out by two Argentinian revolutionaries, one of whom, Hugo Alfredo Irurzún, known as Capitán Santiago, had fought with the Sandinistas.

When Secretary of State Haig began warning Nicaragua to stop helping the Salvadoran rebels, the Sandinistas replied that they had the right and, indeed, the duty to help, since the Salvadoran *compas* had helped them. As it happened, they added, the Salvadorans had not asked for more than moral support, and that was all that they had provided. A year or so later, the Nicaraguan government more or less acknowledged that the odd rifle, pistol, and box of ammunition used in the Salvadoran offensive of January, 1981, might have passed through Nicaragua, but without its official knowledge.

In February, Arturo Cruz resigned from the junta. He said that he no longer wanted to be the arbitrator of the increasingly bitter quarrels between the Sandinistas and the opposition. He accepted an appointment as Ambassador to Washington, where he could seek political asylum by stepping outdoors. The junta was reduced to three members, and Daniel Ortega, whose brother Humberto was the Minister of Defense, became its leader with the title of coordinator.

In April, the last $15,000,000 of the $75,000,000 in aid that Carter had thawed was refrozen, and the Reagan administration announced that there would be no more assistance until Nicaragua stopped helping the Salvadoran rebels. Nicaraguan "freedom fighters" began training in the Everglades. Journalists who visited the camp found a couple of dozen fellows, wearing uniforms still stiff and shiny from a surplus store or costume company, drilling listlessly under the supervision of a man known as *La Bombilla,* the Light Bulb, who was a figure of fun in the Cuban émigré community. In Honduras, more seriously, 600 Nicaraguans, many of whom were former members of the National Guard, set up camps near the frontier and began raiding across the border.

In Managua, in May, 1981, President José López Portillo stated that Mexico would defend "the cause of Nicaragua as her own." He added, "Amid falsehood and sophistry, we have reached the extreme in which the campaign against Nicaragua is carried out in the name of democracy. It is no small paradox that the destruction of a democratic regime is proposed in order to save it from future risks or that an attempt is made to create a chain of peripheral dictatorships to maintain the welfare of the central democracies."

Robelo, the former junta member, said that the five opposition parties, all of which were small and weak, refused to give up. "We're going to participate even though we have been deceived before because we have to exhaust all hopes of correcting the process," he told *The New York Times* in June. Many of his colleagues disagreed and quietly got exit visas and flew to Miami.

In July, Edén Pastora, Comandante Cero, the hero of the National

Palace attack, resigned his largely ceremonial post as Vice-minister of Defense and flew to Panama. The three members of the junta pleaded with him on television to return. Pastora said that he had acted to protest the increasing influence of Russian and Cuban political and military advisers.

In August, Thomas O. Enders, the new Assistant Secretary of State for Inter-American Affairs, paid his first visit to Managua. Two weeks later, Lawrence A. Pezzullo, who had been the American Ambassador since June, 1979, and was liked and trusted by both the Sandinistas and the opposition, was ordered home. Pezzullo, a specialist in Latin America, did not receive another assignment, and the next year, at the age of 56, he retired.

In October, the board of directors of the Superior Council of Private Enterprise, or COSEP, addressed an open letter to the junta. It noted the comment of Humberto Ortega, the Minister of Defense, that COSEP members would be "hanged from lampposts" in the event of a foreign invasion and accused the Sandinistas of preparing "a new genocide in Nicaragua." The letter went on to say:

It is worthless to proclaim a mixed economy when you continue to confiscate businesses. There is no freedom of the press if you keep closing down the media; and there is no pluralism or trade unionism if you continue persecuting political parties and labor unions. Those whom you call reactionaries are not against the people of Nicaragua; they are only opposed to the Marxist-Leninist project you are perpetrating behind the people's back.

When the letter appeared in *La Prensa,* the Chamorro paper and the last independent voice in the country, four members of the board of COSEP were arrested. Three of them, including the president, Enrique Dreyfus, who had been a supporter of the rebellion, were quickly tried, found guilty, and sentenced to seven months in jail. To balance the scales of justice, four leaders of the old-line Communist party, who had publicly accused the government of "turning the revolution over to the imperialists," were sentenced to three years each. *La Prensa,* which had been suspended five times in the previous three months, was threatened with permanent closure.

From the shantytowns in which most of the population of Managua still lived emerged *las turbas,* the mobs, organized and led by the Sandinista Defense Committees, to which neighborhood bullies and busybodies gravitated. They surrounded the homes and offices of opposition politicians, trade union leaders, even the archbishop, and shrieked insults and threats, breaking windows, destroying cars, and covering the walls with graffiti.

President Luis Herrera Campíns of Venezuela, during a visit to Washington, insisted that a pluralistic society could survive in Nicaragua. Instead of making threats, he said, the United States ought to be strengthening what remained of Nicaragua's democratic opposition by resuming economic support. It was an opinion that should have been taken seriously. Venezuela had a Christian Democratic government that, by Latin American standards, was honest and responsive, was anti-Communist, and generally sided with the United States.

In February, 1982, López Portillo told the directorate, making sure that the information reached the press, that the price of Mexico's continued support was the freeing of COSEP officials and the encouragement, rather than the harassment, of the private sector. The four men were quickly released, although the Communists, for whom Cuba and Russia did not speak up, remained in jail. López Portillo made an offer, which was ignored by Washington, to serve as mediator.

Instead, the State Department, assisted by the CIA, argued that Nicaragua's military buildup was "far in excess of what was normally required purely for defensive purposes." In a revised estimate, the Sandinistas were said to be creating an army of 25,000 to 30,000, the largest in Central America, and a militia of 50,000. The press was shown aerial photographs of new airstrips, military camps, tank parks, and soccer fields. The soccer fields, it was said, proved the presence of large numbers of Soviet bloc advisers, since Nicaraguan youths still preferred baseball.

A few days later, Haig was able to announce that the Salvadoran army had captured and was shipping to the United States for public display a Nicaraguan soldier who was ready to expose his country's aid to the Salvadoran guerrillas. When the young man, Orlando José Tardencilla Espinosa, who was only 19, was presented to a group of correspondents at the State Department, he recanted every significant statement he was said to have made. Instead, he said that he had gone to El Salvador as an individual volunteer and that he had never seen any other foreigners fighting with the guerrillas. His false confession, he said, had been made after he had been in custody for more than a year, and then only to save himself from execution.

In Managua, where I happened to be when Tardencilla confounded the *gringos,* the Reverend Miguel D'Escoto, the Foreign Minister, called a press conference. With the youth's mother seated at his side, weeping softly, he demanded that he be restored to the bosom of his family. I saw D'Escoto again the following morning by appointment. By then the State Department had agreed to let Tardencilla go home.

D'Escoto told me that Nicaragua's reliance on Cuba and the Soviet bloc had been exaggerated. "We are a small country in the process of a profound transformation of society, and this is the basis of our political options," he said. "Our Sandinista pattern, or model, is a unique process. We reject the following of other models. Each nation has its own identity. You can't transplant revolution. Overdependence on one country or on a group of like-minded countries may put them in a position of pushing us into doing what's good for them but not necessarily good for us."

D'Escoto is plump and pale. His expression is untroubled, even unctuous. He wears spectacles, and he constantly smokes Benson & Hedges cigarettes. His comments had been polished, at a guess, by frequent use at international forums, in his briefings of the delegations that stream into Nicaragua, and in many interviews. His position as a priest of the Catholic Foreign Mission Society of America, or Maryknoll, made him particularly effective in explaining to skeptical non-Communists the Sandinistas' devotion to pluralism and democratic socialism. On the other hand, D'Escoto and two other priests continued to serve in the Cabinet in defiance of Archbishop Miguel Obando y Bravo's order to resign. The archbishop then suspended them from the saying of mass, and they had ignored that ruling as well.

D'Escoto said that, as a protest against the Somozas, he had not set foot in Nicaragua for 30 years prior to the Sandinista victory. For 10 of those years, he had been the director of Maryknoll's communications department. During the later stages of the rebellion, he worked with the Broad Opposition Front in Costa Rica.

"People ask us why we trust Mexico and distrust the United States so much," he said. "The answer is simple—the historical record. Knowing the United States' attitude toward revolutions, we have good reason to keep our guard up. My message to President Reagan is a very simple one: Please understand that there is no reason to fear the Nicaraguan revolution. The cause of freedom is served every time people are able to shake off the yoke of exploitation and repression. Please do not try to push every movement of this type into the shape of East-West conflict.''

In view of his forthright stand on repression, I asked him to explain the imprisonment of Dreyfus and the other COSEP officials.

''In putting the blame on the government for poor economic conditions they were lying,'' D'Escoto said. ''The truth is that although more than 70 percent of our factories were damaged or destroyed by the National Guard, the United Nations' Economic Commission on Latin America reported that we were one of only two countries whose gross national product rose between 1980 and 1981.''

I then asked about the postponing of national elections until 1985.

''Since there have never been free and honest elections in Nicaragua, our first task was to gain some credibility for the process by holding a variety of other elections—municipal, union, the Council of State, and so on,'' he replied, tenting his fingers and gazing, as he often did, over my head. ''Democracy can't be decreed; it must be built step by step. When we first came to power, the opposition did not want immediate elections. They feared there would be a Sandinista sweep because of the enthusiasm of the moment, and even now they are not asking for immediate elections.''

Alfonso Robelo, the former member of the ruling junta and leader of the National Democratic Movement, smiled when I told him what D'Escoto had said.

''It's true,'' he said. ''No definite date was ever set for elections. The Sandinistas said, 'As soon as possible,' and we assumed that would be two or three years. I suppose we were naïve. How can they talk about pluralism when they won't let us hold political rallies, when they keep us off television and use mobs to try to intimidate us? They think they're being generous because they let us move around freely, hold small indoor meetings, permit us a weekly radio program and access to *La Prensa*. They call it pluralism because they permit the Christian Democrat and Liberal parties to operate, but both of them are their puppets.

''Discussions of the law governing elections and political parties have come to a standstill,'' he said. ''There still isn't any registration plan. The Sandinistas say that the requirements of national defense come first, but the truth of the matter is that the Sandinistas don't want elections at all.''

We were seated in deep leather armchairs in the drawing room of

Robelo's residence, a large and opulent neocolonial house in the hills above Managua. The mob had already visited Robelo on a couple of occasions. What remained of his domestic staff had done their best to scrub its artwork and slogans off the white exterior walls, but traces remained, like a whispered warning. Robelo was living there alone. His wife, I was told, had defected to the Sandinistas. The reason was artistic rather than political. She had always thought of herself as a poet, but the opinion was not widely shared until the Sandinistas published her verses in one of their magazines. Their sensitivity to art won her allegiance, and a young revolutionary was said to have won her heart.

"I was ready to give away as much as was necessary to permit me to live in social peace," Robelo said as a maid in a pink uniform served coffee. "For example, I was in favor of nationalizing the banking system, although I was a director and shareholder of one of the largest of the banks. When I was a member of the junta, I never had any problems with the Sandinistas on economic and social issues, only on politics. That's why I resigned. I didn't want to. Being on the junta was fun. Everything was open to you. But when they enlarged the Council of State, it was the last straw. It originally was 33 seats with the Sandinista National Liberation Front controlling about 13 of them. Now they control all but 11 or 12 of the 47."

Robelo said that the opposition, rather than the Sandinistas, was turning out to be the victims of Washington's bellicosity.

"Whenever a foreign government attacks, or threatens to attack, another, you can expect a very strong nationalistic reaction," he said. "No Nicaraguan, including myself, likes the idea of being threatened by a superpower. Even now I would have to fight with the Sandinistas if the United States openly intervened. So I have to say that Reagan's policy is definitely strengthening the Sandinistas.

"The Sandinistas have turned out to be tremendously inefficient administrators," he went on. "They have lost popular support. If you leave us alone, this opposition will have a chance to grow, and if Edén Pastora should return to lead us, it could produce a situation, as with Somoza, in which foreign help would be needed and accepted. I would like to be here to meet him, but the way things are going now, I doubt that I will still be in the country a year from now."

La Prensa had come to symbolize reasoned opposition to the Sandinista government. I had a conversation with Pedro Joaquín Chamorro, who had succeeded his murdered father as its editor. The paper's plant on the airport highway had been burned on Somoza's orders during the final months of the rebellion. Since then, it has been edited and printed in what was formerly a newsprint storehouse at the rear of the gutted building. Pedro Joaquín had irritated the Sandinistas as much as his father did Somoza. As a result, the paper was frequently suspended, its contents were censored, it was visited by the mob. It had also been attacked as subversive by Managua's two other dailies, *La Barricada* and *El Nuevo Diario,* both of which reflect the Sandinista outlook. There may be an element of professional and familial jealousy as well. The editor of *La Barricada* was Carlos Chamorro, Pedro Joaquín's younger brother, and the editor of *El Nuevo Diario* was their uncle, Javier Chamorro. Despite these handicaps, *La Prensa*'s circulation of 40,000 or so was two or three times the combined circulation of the other two.

"The funny thing is that Carlos and I had the identical education—El Colegio Centro America here, which is run by the Jesuits, and then McGill University in Montreal—and he turned out to be a Marxist and I didn't," Pedro Joaquín told me. He was a slim, handsome and mannerly man of 30. Even so, he managed to look and sound like a journalist.

"Uncle Javier was the most capitalistic member of our family until the revolution," he went on. "Opportunism might have played a part in his conversion, but it's not the whole story. His sight is badly impaired, and you could say that he can't see what's going on right under his nose. I'm married and have a family, and so does Carlos. We usually see each other at my mother's house, and since *Barricada* is a morning paper and we're an afternoon paper, we don't meet too often. When we do, we try to keep the peace for her sake."

The Chamorro family has owned *La Prensa* since 1928, he said. The plant was destroyed in the earthquakes of 1931 and 1972, was harassed throughout the Somoza era, and once was shut down for three years.

"I first went to work on the paper while I was still in school, sweeping floors during my vacations," Pedro Joaquín said. "After college, I started full time in the business department. I also took news photographs. From 1974 to 1977, we were under very tight censorship. It was a period in which corruption in the government increased astonishingly, partly because it could not be reported in the press. There were tremendous kickbacks on government purchases and the buying up for resale of highway and housing sites. A lot of people around Somoza got rich very fast.

214

"When Somoza realized that he was going to lose the war and that his murder of my father was one of the main reasons everyone turned against him, he sent his men out here in the middle of the fighting with orders to burn the building to the ground, but with all the confusion they only damaged it badly. I only began writing and editing in 1979, and I found out that I liked it, and I think I do fairly well at it. We are not precensored now, but the Sandinistas and their Cuban advisers look at every issue with a microscope. We are trying to avoid suppression, but still using as much as we can of the margin of freedom that is left to us."

He said that Washington's policies were narrowing the margin, and he mentioned the press briefing on military preparations in Nicaragua, which had taken place only a week or so before, as an example. "I'm angry at the U.S. about those pictures, the aerial photographs," he said. "They don't prove what they were intended to prove—that the Sandinistas are helping the Salvadoran guerrillas. Our military buildup, which I oppose, is another matter."

The atmosphere at *La Barricada,* which I visited next, was markedly different. It was as though the Students for a Democratic Society had managed to take over their hometown daily and were running it with a dedication to ideology so intense it made the windows rattle. The guards, receptionists, and secretaries addressed me condescendingly as *compañero.* The staff was predominantly young and white. Nicaragua was no different in that respect from the less progressive parts of Central America, or, for that matter, Castro's Cuba. Skin color was still a generally accurate index of status. Some members of the *Barricada* staff wore fatigue uniforms, and others designer jeans and polo shirts. A few young women even wore pretty dresses and jewelry.

Carlos, who was 25, resembled his brother. He was pleasant but a bit remote. Frequent glances at his wristwatch, interruptions on the telephone, and the perusal of galley proofs indicated that he was a busy man.

"I joined *La Prensa* as a reporter after my father's death," he said. "At the same time, I was working underground for the Sandinista National Liberation Front. My family was aware of what I was doing, but not the extent of it. I was not a *combatiente,* but I was often under fire. Most of my work was what I would call educational, propagandistic, and logistical."

215

He made a face when I mentioned his brother's comment about the same education's producing such different results.

"I'm not a Marxist, and neither is the government, despite what Pedro thinks, but it's true that I think that Marxism can be a useful analytical tool," he said. "I'm not sure what I would call myself. I don't like labels in general. In any case, the education we received was not as similar as Pedro thinks. There was five years between us at school. When I went there, the Jesuits at the *colegio* were being influenced by the Theology of Liberation, and I left there with a strong feeling of social consciousness. On the other hand, McGill had become a lot more conservative."

Carlos's ideas, as they emerged, had the sharp, straight edges preferred by the young and militant. He was untroubled by doubts, and while it may have been true, as he said, that he regarded Marxism only as a useful tool, he did not seem to be using any others. He laughed when I said as much, and I asked him if he didn't suffer a qualm or two when *La Prensa* was suspended.

"I believe in freedom of ideas and opinions, although I believe that *La Prensa* is destructive rather than constructive and not very genuine in its criticism," he replied. "I also wish that *La Prensa* was more nationalistic and tried to separate itself more from the most aggressive aspects of North American foreign policy. But that is not the reason it gets suspended. It is because *La Prensa* distorts the facts."

When I asked for an example, Carlos Chamorro thought for a moment. "It always calls the counterrevolutionaries that are attacking our borders armed opposition groups, putting them at the same level as the political groups in this country," he said.

The mood at the American Embassy in Managua was gloomy. Most of the staff had been there during Pezzullo's tour of duty, and the ones I talked with said that his conciliatory but by no means supine approach had been working. Since his recall eight months earlier, the embassy had been largely frozen into inactivity under a chargé d'affaires. The new Ambassador, Anthony C. E. Quainton, was due to arrive within a few days. Quainton, who previously headed the State Department's Office for Combating Terrorism, was regarded as a true believer in the Haig-Enders policy of overawing the Sandinistas.

One of the attachés I spoke with, who, under the rules, must remain nameless, said he thought that the policy would fail.

"The moderate *comandantes* know in the long run that they haven't

216

got anyone else to sell their bananas, their coffee, and their sugar to,"
he said. "Russia isn't going to carry them indefinitely. Castro himself
warned them publicly of that. It's already spending much more than it
wants to on Cuba. They also know that the average Nicaraguan still
prefers the United States to Russia or Cuba. What we haven't taken into
consideration sufficiently is that *all* of the *comandantes* fought for
years to get rid of Somoza. To expect them to start loving capitalism
and the United States immediately is to expect far too much. We
should have been a great deal more patient. Pezzullo used to talk to
them like a Dutch uncle, and it was effective. But when he left, we lost
most of our influence.

"Last October, when we had that naval exercise off the Honduran
coast with an attack transport with 500 marines aboard, we lost it all,"
he went on. "All that we're doing with these tactics is to help the hard-
line Marxist-Leninists. More and more business and professional people decide they don't have any future here. That lets the Sandinistas
say that they need Cuban doctors because 180 Nicaraguan doctors emigrated in the first six months of 1981. I don't know about that, but I *do*
know that my dentist, who was the best in Managua, went to Miami for
good a couple of months ago."

Another embassy official said that he thought that Haig's bombast
was a smoke screen that was meant to hide the lack of any coherent
Latin American policy.

"Basically, it doesn't have much to do with the region," he said.
"The harsh words are supposed to make the folks at home feel good.
The administration is most afraid of being blamed for the 'loss' of Nicaragua and Central America, but I don't know what we can do about it
short of invasion. I have the feeling sometimes that our advice from
here isn't just rejected but not even considered. Information comes
from the top down instead of vice versa. For example, Washington
keeps talking about the flow of weapons from Nicaragua to El Salvador. There's no doubt that the traffic exists, but, as near as we can tell,
it's not very large."

As it happened, Bianca Jagger was in Managua while I was there. The
most famous living Nicaraguan had been taking a sympathetic interest
in the problems of her native land. The Sandinistas, confident that they
could lay to rest allegations that they were abusing the Miskito Indians,
flew her to the coast and gave permission for the press to accompany
her.

We set out from the hotel before dawn. Our old and rattling DC-3 landed at the airstrip of a gold-mining settlement called Bonanza, about 200 miles northwest of Managua. Julio Rocha, the Deputy Minister for Atlantic Affairs, briefed us on the government's scheme to resettle the Miskitos at a distance of 50 miles or so from the Coco River, the border between Honduras and Nicaragua. He admitted that the government shared the blame for the turmoil in Miskitia by being, in effect, too wonderful.

"We tried to move too fast to correct illiteracy and disease, and we were misunderstood," he said. "Now we are trying to correct things, but the United States believes it is in its interest to continue to make trouble for all of us."

What the government had failed to grasp, he said, was how little the Miskitos had in common with the rest of Nicaragua's population, from whom they were separated by 100 miles of jungle that is traversed by only a couple of very bad roads. Britain held an informal protectorate over 400 miles of the coastline, extending from Trujillo in Honduras to the Costa Rican border from 1687, when the governor of Jamaica crowned a "king" of Miskitia, until 1860, when it yielded to Washington's demands for withdrawal. Only in 1894 did Nicaragua establish a military and political presence there, but Miskito life went on as before. The Indians lived in their settlements of thatched huts built on stilts along the rivers and lagoons, fishing, growing corn and beans in jungle clearings, and working, as occasion and inclination offered, for the foreign companies that cut the region's vast stands of timber. Like so many Huckleberry Finns, the Miskitos gave a low priority to money, hygiene, and education. They preferred to be ignored by the government, to which they occasionally had to pay a little tax money, and to spend their time in drinking, dancing, and lovemaking.

Many, perhaps most, of the estimated 150,000 Miskitos and smaller associated tribes are actually of mingled descent. The blood of *conquistadores,* buccaneers, black migrants from the West Indies, and Chinese merchants flows in their veins. This genetic jambalaya has produced many women of cheerfully sensual beauty—Dinorah Sampson, Tachito Somoza's mistress, for one. In addition to their own language, which is itself a patois, they speak English rather than Spanish. The Miskitos are Moravian Protestant—the sect's missionaries went to the coast at the invitation of the Miskito king in the mid-19th century—and strongly anti-Catholic and anti-Nicaraguan.

The Miskitos happily watched Spanish-speaking Catholics kill one another during the countless uprisings of the 19th and early 20th centuries. When the marines landed, the Miskitos gave them a friendly greeting because they spoke English and were unaccompanied by priests. The Miskitos continued their policy of nonalignment during the Sandinista rebellion. Although disappointed in the Miskitos, the new government decided that their failure to join the uprising was the result of stunted social and political development. The answer was schools, conducted partly in Spanish, clinics, better roads, and a heaping tablespoon of ideology twice a day, sweetened by higher prices for their fish and shrimp.

The Miskitos were happy to take the money, but they decided that they already had all the civilization they could stand. They went to the new schools about as often as they had gone to the old ones and refused to have their revolutionary consciousnesses raised. The Sandinistas' worries about an American landing on the Caribbean coast made them doubly impatient with the refractory Miskitos. Before long they had stopped making suggestions and begun issuing orders. When the orders were not obeyed, they imposed punishments.

As befit descendants of the corsairs of the Caribbean, the Miskitos did not supinely submit. By September, 1980, they were calling strikes, rioting, and even attacking army and police outposts. The mass organization that the Sandinistas had established was taken over by the Miskito opposition. It was led by a young man named Steadman Fagoth Müller, who had attended the University of Managua and fought with the Sandinistas. Fagoth, who was of mixed German and Miskito ancestry, demanded more autonomy than the government was prepared to grant.

In February, 1981, after four Sandinista soldiers had been murdered, he and the other leaders of the opposition were arrested on charges of trying to set up a separatist government. Fagoth was released after a couple of months on his promise to go to Europe for graduate study. Instead, after visiting Washington, he turned up in Miskito villages in Honduras, proclaiming a war of liberation.

By the beginning of 1982, something like 5,000 Miskitos had fled to Honduras. Armed Miskitos attacked Sandinista border posts along the Coco River while bands of *contras* struck farther inland. Both groups were getting weapons, money, and training from the CIA, a fact that was self-evident but was not acknowledged for 12 months. The Sandinistas responded by forcibly removing Miskitos from the border region and resettling them, under guard, 50 miles and more to the east.

Fagoth accused the government of slaughtering hundreds of Miskitos who resisted and letting hundreds of others die of starvation and disease. Haig offered in evidence a photograph from a French magazine that purported to show piles of Miskito dead. It turned out to be a picture of non-Miskito Nicaraguans who had been killed by the National Guard a couple of years earlier.

Journalists were welcomed to hear the horror stories in person at Miskito refugee camps in Honduras. It was to counter this propaganda barrage that the Nicaraguan government permitted the presumably not unsympathetic Jagger expedition to go to Miskitia. The possibility of visiting the Coco River itself had been held out to us, and we raised the point energetically with Rocha, who regretted that mumble-mumble-mumble made it impossible.

Rocha's presentation was numbingly complete. He had charts that showed the characteristics of the soil in the areas to which the Miskitos had been moved, lists of foodstuffs that were being provided for them until they could harvest their first crops, a survey of their family status, education and health, and even architectural renderings of the model villages that would one day be erected for them.

"Life for the Miskitos along the Coco River was subsistence agriculture combined with low-level technology and low productivity," Rocha said. "They were scattered along the 280-kilometer length of the river, so that it was extremely difficult to bring the services of the revolution to them. Another hazard was the yearly floods on the lower river, which drove them out of their homes and caused epidemics and widespread hunger."

The briefing finally completed, Rocha said our transport awaited us and led us to two pickup trucks unequipped with roof, seats, or even pillows. Bianca refused the comfortable seat next to the driver to which she was entitled. Like a good soldier, she climbed in the back with the rest of us. Ten minutes after we set out, bouncing downhill from the mine on a rutted gravel road, it began to rain heavily, which at least laid the dust that had been blowing in our faces.

The rain stopped, and a blazing sun came out. The road ran through cutover jungle. The feeling was timelessly African rather than hectically Latin American. Thatched huts stood alone or in clusters every mile or so. On the banks of swiftly flowing streams, women beat their washing against the rocks. White and gray herons stood in shallow pools, spearing fish with their knitting-needle bills. High in the sky, vultures dozed on pillows of cloud.

Rocha had excused the simplicity of our transportation by saying that it was only a short trip to the camp. Indeed, it took only an hour and a half. Over the entrance, there was a sign in the Miskito language. It said, *War Lakat Aip Aswankaisa Rebolusan Karnica,* meaning, we were told, "Work That Unites Us Is a Revolutionary Force." That didn't sound too good for the Miskitos.

No one on the staff that greeted us was a Miskito. The only heavy work was being done by Nicaraguan soldiers. They were cutting trees with power saws to enlarge the campsite and dragging the trunks away behind a bulldozer. The din was appalling, and there was a kind of shadeless, arid, dusty comfortlessness and rootlessness that defines all refugee camps, regardless of ideology.

There were, we were told, 300 Miskitos in the camp. Almost all of them were women, children, and old folks. They looked blank when we asked, through interpreters, where their husbands and fathers were. They had probably fled across the Coco River. It must have been a difficult transition for a people who, in happier times, had been able to dive off the front porch for a prebreakfast swim.

Until their model homes were built, the residents of the camp were bunking together in three long sheds roofed with plastic sheeting that smelled liked baked rubber under the tropical sun. They complained about the accommodations, the food, and their forced removal with a vehemence that suggested that, whatever their other sins, the Sandinistas had not yet tried to beat them down.

Circling the camp with a colleague, we came upon a group of Miskitos weaving palm thatch. One of the men jumped up and extended his hand to one of my colleagues, who, to show his sympathy, shook it firmly. The Miskito chatted away in a mixture of Spanish, English, and Miskito, not making a lot of sense in any of them. All I definitely established was that his name was Isaac and that he had no nose and only one ear. The last joints of several fingers were missing, and the others were knotted up.

"What do you suppose is wrong with him?" he asked as we walked away.

"I'm no doctor, but it looks like a virulent case of mountain leprosy or coastal syphilis," I said. "You shouldn't have shaken hands with him."

"You mean you can catch it?"

"More than likely."

He rushed off to the dispensary, and I was continuing my circuit of the camp when word was passed that if we wanted to return to Managua that night, we would have to leave Bonanza before darkness fell. We hurried to the trucks, the drivers stepped on the gas, and we got to the airstrip just as the pearl-and-rose tropical twilight was a fading line in the west. The last one through the door of the plane was Bianca. She had been buying soft drinks for everyone. The revolution hadn't stopped for food or drink that day, and we gave her three cheers.

The Cubans were an invisible presence in Nicaragua. Their embassy and compound had a high wall around it. Their vehicles and uniforms were no different from the Sandinistas', and only an expert could have caught differences in Spanish accent. If they were drilling Nicaraguan troops, as seemed likely, they were doing it in places that were prohibited to *gringo* journalists.

Thus, when a report circulated that they were present in great numbers around the town of Estelí, Bernard Diederich of *Time,* Dick O'Mara, the foreign editor of the Baltimore *Sun,* Stanley Meisler of the Los Angeles *Times,* and I drove there. That the Nicaraguan army should be concentrating there seemed reasonable. Estelí is on the Pan American Highway about 100 miles northwest of Managua and 75 miles or so from the Honduran border. During the rebellion, the Sandinistas occupied it and lost it twice, so it was not without symbolic importance as well.

We found Estelí, far from being an armed camp, dozing in the brilliant sun of the highlands. None of the idlers in the plaza had heard of any Cubans in the vicinity, and the only uniformed men to be seen were a couple of police and firemen. The town still bore the marks of the fighting. The façade of the cathedral was pocked with holes. Many of them were evenly spaced, indicating that they had been made by bullets from a traversing machine gun. Several badly damaged buildings remained unrepaired, and there were gaps in the lines of residences. Accounts of one of the battles for the town said that 800 persons had been killed, but the extent of the damage suggested that this was a considerable exaggeration.

On the way back, we stopped to watch a baseball game—the CIA had been right about that, at any rate. Near the diamond was a hospital, built, according to the cornerstone, by the Seventh-day Adventists and

222

manned since the revolution, we learned, by Cubans. We asked the guard if we could talk to one of the doctors. He returned with a blond young woman wearing a long white jacket over her dress and with a stethoscope around her neck. Irritation was written all over her face. Gazing down at us with professional and ideological hauteur, she declined to answer any questions or, indeed, even to give me a couple of aspirin for a headache.

The one Sandinista *comandante* I asked to meet was Tomás Borge, the only surviving founder of the movement. He had lived for nearly two decades as guerrilla leader, fugitive, exile, and, for seven of those years, a prisoner, tortured, half-starved, and never knowing if the next hour or day would be his last. Now he himself was the Minister of the Interior, in charge of the police, the security forces, and the prisons.

He was usually accessible to the press, but the raids of the Somocistas across the border and the noisy threats of the United States made unusual demands on his time. Not until just before my departure was the interview, with me and Diederich, whom I had included in my application, arranged.

Borge bears a resemblance to Torrijos of Panama. He is stocky, he projects energy, his brown eyes are direct, his graying hair is cut short, and he carries himself like a soldier. Borge is only in his middle forties, but he is 10 years older or more than most of his colleagues. He is given to irony, to mockery of himself and others. After seven years in Somoza's dungeons, he is thought to be less prone to revolutionary enthusiasm than the other Sandinista leaders and, for the same reason, less likely to yield on matters he thinks important.

"We have weapons," he said, referring to the State Department briefing. "We do not deny this. The United States is threatening us, they threaten to attack us, and then they get mad because we are arming ourselves. This is incredible! They discover this when they take the liberty of flying over to photograph our country. It is as though I went into your house to take pictures while you are making love to your wife and then I get mad because you get mad. That is what Mr. Reagan and his government do.

"Why will the United States attack us? Why do they threaten us? Because they say we are going to be totalitarian. Not because we *are* totalitarian. Not because we have ended democracy, but because we are *going* to. Because we are *going* to enter the Soviet orbit. Because we are *going* to establish a Marxist-Leninist regime. I must say that I think it is wonderful that your government knows so many things that are *going* to happen."

He glanced at papers on his desk—a theatrical pause—and continued. "The United States also threatens us because they say we are sending weapons to the Salvadoran guerrillas. We have said that, well, if arms for El Salvador go through Nicaragua, show us where. Why don't they order their puppets in Central America to join us in patrols of the border? We are willing to patrol the Honduran border jointly, because if the weapons go through Nicaragua, they must go through Honduras.

"I don't dismiss the possibility of weapons' going through here from other countries. We sympathize with the Salvadoran guerrillas, and we have solidarity with their movement. That is one thing, but I wish the know-it-all experts of the CIA would tell where the weapons are that we are supposed to be sending to them. It has been reported that weapons go from the United States to the *frente* in El Salvador, from Panama, from Europe. In our war we bought weapons from the U.S., and we also got them through Mexico, Guatemala, El Salvador, and Honduras."

Borge laughed as he said that, and then his expression became serious. "I think that conflicts must be resolved through negotiation. We want to avoid war with its inevitable terrible costs, but let's be clear that we do not flee from danger and confrontation. We harbor historic distrust of the United States, but these things can be diminished to some extent on the negotiating table. Hell, I don't see why it's so difficult to negotiate with us. It is so easy for you to negotiate with Pinochet in Chile and Stroessner in Paraguay. But with us you find it hard to negotiate, even though we were the ones who took the initiative. The real trouble is that the United States is not used to negotiating with Nicaragua but to imposing its views, and that came to an end on July 19, 1979."

As is inevitable in interviews, certain questions did not get asked and others did not get answered, and other answers struck me as less than altogether candid. For example, Borge's denial that he was a Marxist when everything else he said made it appear that way. "You must realize that the world is changing," he said. "The seas are agitated, but revolutionaries have made rafts that never sink. When idiots who know nothing of history finally learn that revolutions cannot be sunk, then, perhaps, the bases of coexistence might arise."

13
In Bananaland

THE TERM "banana republic" has been applied to all the nations of Central America, but among them Honduras is surely preeminent. It grows the most bananas, it has yielded most amiably to the economic embrace of Uncle Sam, and its statesmen have comported themselves, more often than not, with a dignity, probity, and concern for the public good that recalls Ben Blue, in baggy pants, tight checked jacket, and undersize derby, doing "Floogle Street" at the old Minsky's burlesque house.

Take, for example, General Policarpo Paz García, whose presidential term ended in 1982. Paz was a well-known connoisseur of old whiskey and young women. On one occasion, I was told, when he had celebrated for two weeks straight, his colleagues, concerned by his neglect of pressing matters of state, took the extreme step of removing his clothing and locking him in his bedroom at the Presidential Palace.

After a refreshing nap, Paz knotted sheets together, lowered himself to the ground, and scaled the fence around the palace. Shoeless and in his underwear, he hailed a cab and ordered the driver to take him to his favorite brothel. There he celebrated his freedom with the most comely of the maidens until his bodyguards, knowing where to look, recaptured him and led him home.

Honduras's difficulty in taking itself seriously may derive from the fact that the banana is essentially comic. Pompous people, at least in comic strips and old movies, are always slipping on them, sailing wildly through the air, and landing on their silk hats. The unmistakably phallic shape of the banana also conduces to levity. "To have a banana," signifying a sexual encounter, was a catchphrase in the England of 50 or 60 years ago. Nowadays "bananas," as in the Woody Allen film of that title, signifies a cheerful, unfocused lunacy.

225

Even the old United Fruit Company, a Boston concern of puritanical respectability, fell victim on at least one occasion to sexual banana-mania. In *An American Company,* Thomas P. McCann recalls an advertisement that it placed in equally respectable national magazines in the 1950's. The illustration showed a banana with a tape measure alongside it. The copy stated, more or less, that smaller bananas were okay as far as they went but that no banana less than eight inches long and a full three inches in diameter could bear the Chiquita trademark.

The banana remained only a fantasy of delight in the United States until 1870, when Lorenzo D. Baker, master of the schooner *Telegraph* out of Wellfleet on Cape Cod, calling at Kingston, Jamaica, bought several stems of green bananas. As a very rich man many years later he recalled that it was an impulse purchase. At a price of 25 cents for each stem weighing at least 50 pounds, he figured he had little to lose. Baker arrived in Boston before the bananas rotted, the major hazard of the trade, and sold them at a profit of 1,000 percent.

For several years, Baker continued to pick up bananas in Jamaica as occasion offered. He finally decided that the banana had a future. He persuaded 10 acquaintances to put up $2,000 each, and they founded the Boston Fruit Company. By 1890, it had several schooners plying the Jamaica run. The market for bananas, like the market for coffee, seemed infinitely expandable.

At about the same time that Baker made his historic voyage, an American railroad builder named Henry Meiggs received a contract from the Costa Rican government to build a line, the first in Central America, from San José to Limón on the Caribbean. Although only about 75 miles in length, it had to traverse mountains, swamps, ravines, rushing streams, and deep jungles. The engineering difficulties were compounded by financial problems, and it was not until 1890 that the railroad was opened for its entire length.

To provide traffic for the railroad, Meiggs's nephews, Minor Cooper Keith and Henry Meiggs Keith, who were supervising construction, planted bananas on a small part of the 800,000 acres along the right-of-way that the government had awarded to them and to their uncle. They formed the Tropical Trading and Transport Company, sent their bananas to market in New Orleans by steamer, and prospered.

It was a period of cartelization in the United States. In 1899, Boston Fruit, Tropical Trading, and several smaller concerns were amalgamated, under the benevolent gaze of J. P. Morgan, into the United Fruit

Company. United Fruit issued millions of dollars' worth of stock and used the proceeds to buy, clear, and drain more than 1,000,000 acres on both coasts of Central America.

For 50 years thereafter, the fruit company, as it was called on Wall Street, or *El Pulpo,* the Octopus, as it came to be known among those not receiving its benefactions in the countries in which it established itself, was far richer and more powerful than all the governments of Central America combined. Rebellious *caudillos* soon learned that United Fruit and the United States were one and indivisible. Theodore Roosevelt, the great trustbuster, showed no desire to interfere with the operations of a company that maintained economic and social stability on both coasts in the vicinity of the Panama Canal. Presidents of both parties who followed him, Republicans with greater enthusiasm, saw the benefit of letting United Fruit rationalize banana production and politics in its own way.

Not that the company always did. It was the loser, at least temporarily, in one of the most celebrated and picaresque of Bananaland adventures. The central figure was Samuel Zemurray, who, as a young immigrant from Russia, went into the banana business in a small way in Mobile, Alabama, at the turn of the century. As described by Charles David Kepner, Jr., and Jay Henry Soothill in *The Banana Empire,* Zemurray negotiated a contract with the fruit company to buy bananas in imminent danger of becoming overripe at the wharf, leaving the impression that he intended to use them to make alcohol. Zemurray found a loophole in the agreement and started peddling the bananas to stores to which they could be shipped overnight. His price undercut the fruit company's but left him an ample margin of profit.

The company worked out a compromise. In return for the voiding of the contract, it went into partnership with Zemurray, putting up 60 percent of the money needed to return a derelict banana plantation near Cuyamel in Honduras to production. In 1907, the company sold its share of the enterprise to him. Zemurray had scarcely got going on his own when war broke out between Honduras and Nicaragua. The plantation was near the border, and before long drunken soldiers were drifting through, firing their rifles and frightening the workers.

The forces of José Santos Zelaya, the Nicaraguan *caudillo* and *gringo* hater, overthrew the Honduran *caudillo,* Policarpo Bonilla, and sent him into exile. His successor, at Zelaya's suggestion, immediately began making things as difficult as possible for the plantation owners. Zemurray's position was more precarious than the fruit company's. He was also more aware of the danger, since he managed his plantation himself. United Fruit's senior executives and directors seldom traveled far from their Boston headquarters. In 1910, with Zelaya at his most irritating, Zemurray conferred with Bonilla in New Orleans. Bonilla acknowledged that he would like to be president again, and would be suitably grateful to anyone who helped him achieve his ambition.

Zemurray thereupon bought a small steamer and put several cases of arms and ammunition aboard. He hired a platoon of professional gunmen led by one Lee Christmas, a former locomotive engineer who styled himself "general" and was beloved by the editors of the Sunday supplements of the time as an intrepid soldier of fortune. Washington, learning of the plot, tried to stop it. It did not disagree with Zemurray's objective but apparently believed that the overthrowing of governments ought to be left to the marines.

Trailed by hard-faced men with marshal's badges, Zemurray and Bonilla repaired to the Crescent City's most luxurious brothel, ordered caviar and champagne, and gave every indication that they were going to spend the night in debauchery. While the agents watched the front door, Zemurray and Bonilla slipped out the back way, joined Christmas and his adjutant, Guy "Machine Gun" Molony, and their men aboard the ship, and made for Honduras. With local help, the invaders quickly returned Bonilla to the presidency. One of his first acts was to grant Zemurray vast concessions. United Fruit, which had presumably assisted quietly in the restoration, received the Sula Valley lands that 70 years later were the center of what remained of its holdings in the country.

The marines made a brief appearance in Honduras in 1911. After that, the banana growers were free of government interference. United Fruit continued to be the dominant force in the industry, but as the world market continued to expand, the company's share dropped to about two-thirds of it. Zemurray's Cozumel Fruit Company and Standard Fruit, a New Orleans concern, were the other major growers.

Zemurray, who still spent most of his time in Honduras, soon established himself as the most efficient grower and marketer. From 1920 to 1928, his share of the market rose from 3,000,000 to 9,000,000 stems annually. Most of the increase came at the expense of United Fruit, and it decided to buy him out. Zemurray was happy to sell. He had been in the business for more than 30 years by then, and he wanted to devote his remaining years to philanthropy, travel, study, and the enjoyment of his wealth. In December, 1929, a few months after the stock market crash, Zemurray sold his holdings, which comprised 250,000 acres of land, a sugar mill, 16 ships, and 145 miles of railroad, for United Fruit stock worth $32,000,000.

Three years later, however Zemurray was no longer so rich. United Fruit's shares had lost 90 percent of their value. Zemurray, who was by far the largest individual stockholder, presented his ideas for turning the company around at a meeting of the board of directors. He was tall, commanding, beautifully tailored, and still a long way from the poorhouse. However, he was also a Russian Jew who in his youth on the wharves of Mobile had been known as Sam the Banana Man when the blueblooded directors were prepping at St. Paul's and Groton and calling one another Chip and Pudge. When Zemurray finished speaking, the chairman, a Boston banker, said, according to McCann, "Unfortunately, Mr. Zemurray, I can't understand a word you say."

Zemurray left the meeting without further comment. He quietly began to collect proxies from other dissatisfied shareholders and soon had enough to take control of the company. He returned to a meeting of the directors a few months later, dropped the proxies on the table, and reportedly said, "You gentlemen have been fucking up this business long enough. Now I'm going to straighten it out."

No one knew more about bananas than Sam the Banana Man. When the world economy began to improve, United Fruit was ready to move forward again. The 20 years of Zemurray's leadership marked the apex of its fortunes. At a time when virtually all Central America was ruled by *caudillos,* it had found a *caudillo* of its own, and he ruled a domain that extended from Cuba to Colombia. It comprised more than 1,700,000 acres, 82,000 employees, 1,000 miles of railroad, 100 oceangoing vessels, entire port complexes, and a cable and telegraph division. The steamship line was called the Great White Fleet in the company's advertising. Its unofficial slogan was "Every banana a guest, every passenger a pest."

In 1950, Zemurray, past 70 and suffering from Parkinson's disease, retired, and the company slipped back into the control of the people he had thrown out 18 years earlier. In 1953, threatened with an expropriation in Guatemala, it could think of nothing better to do than to beg its friends in the Eisenhower administration for help. More efficient growers, particularly in Ecuador, were cutting its share of the banana market from two-thirds to one-half or less, and it was slow to diversify into other products. Fidel Castro, whose father had been a United Fruit foreman, took special pleasure in confiscating the company's holdings, mostly sugar lands, after he had come to power.

In 1968, the fruit company was staggering along, its treasury full but the price of its stock depressed, when a shoestring conglomerator named Eli Black, who operated out of a two-room office in New York, began buying up its shares with borrowed money. Within a year, he had taken over the company. He paid a total of $540,000,000, which analysts reckoned was $200,000,000 more than it was worth. However, the package of shares in the successor enterprise, United Brands, debentures and notes with which he paid the shareholders made United Fruit's watered stock of 70 years earlier look like pure gold.

Black, a small, pale, nervous-looking man, had been an Orthodox rabbi before turning to finance. Beginning with a tiny company that made bottle caps, he had used credit to take over other concerns, the largest of which was John Morrell, the meat-packing house. With the proud old company in his hands, Black undertook the laborious task of turning it around. In 1968, it had posted a profit of $33,000,000. In 1970, with Black at the helm, it lost $2,000,000. The next year it lost $24,000,000, and the panic was on. Black began selling its most profitable subsidiaries to raise cash, but nothing worked. By 1974, the annual loss in what had been, even in the Depression, a loss-proof business, had increased to $70,000,000, and Black had been reduced to mortgaging his home to pay his bills. He had overlooked the fact that while he knew a good deal about structuring deals and borrowing money, he knew nothing about the growing, shipping, and marketing of tropical fruits.

With the whale about to go belly up, the sharks began to gather. Seven Central and South American countries formed a banana cartel and imposed a $1 export tax on each 40-pound box. Fearing that the public did not regard bananas as a necessity of the same sort as petroleum, Black's agents in Switzerland paid a bribe of $1,250,000 to Abraham Bennatón Ramos, Honduras's Minister of the Economy. Honduras thereupon settled for a 25-cent tax, breaking the cartel before it got started.

Bribing Central American officials, or submitting to extortion, which may have been the case here, was also a skill that Black did not possess. The Securities and Exchange Commission quickly learned of the payment and began an investigation. Black knew that he now faced disgrace and prison as well as bankruptcy. One morning in February, 1975, he broke a sealed window in his office in the Pan Am Building in New York City and jumped to his death.

United Brands passed into different hands. If they were not so strong as Zemurray's, they at least had fewer thumbs than Chip's and Pudge's and were less slippery than Eli Black's. After a difficult two or three years, the company began making money again. In Honduras the president was overthrown in a coup, possibly because he and Bennatón had failed to cut their colleagues in on the loot. Although the crime was discovered, the money was not paid back.

Eduardo Aragón, who was in charge of United Brands' operations in the region, told me that his domain was considerably smaller than it was in the old days. The company operated only in Panama, Costa Rica, and Honduras, he said, and owned a total of only 100,000 acres, all in Costa Rica and Honduras. It sold its lands in Panama to the government and leased them back. The company was still the largest private employer in all three countries, but the total number of workers declined from more than 100,000 in the mid-1950's to 30,000 in 1983.

In Honduras the company reduced its landholdings from 400,000 to 30,000 acres, mainly in the Sula Valley on the Atlantic coast, and its work force to 10,000. The Honduran government, Aragón said, expropriated 100,000 acres in the late 1970's without objection by the company. Other holdings were sold or abandoned to the jungle. In all three countries, the company sold tens of thousands of acres on easy terms to small banana producers, many of whom were former employees, and provided technical assistance.

"We're as much a marketing company as we are a growing company," Aragón said. "It's also a different company than it was when I started with it 35 years ago. I'll give you just one example. In those days, all of the executives, white-collar workers, and skilled blue-collar workers, right down to the locomotive engineers on the railroad, were *gringos*. Now there are a grand total of six in the whole division, plus some research scientists."

A few days later, I flew to San Pedro Sula, the country's second city. From there I was driven to the company's field headquarters, where I was greeted by Roberto Turnbull, one of the senior managers. We visited the company's laboratories, where seed selection generation after banana generation had at last produced a plant only 10 to 12 feet high, a little more than half the usual height. They were, he said, far less likely to be blown down by hurricanes and were easier to harvest.

We looked in on a couple of classes at one of the company's elementary schools. The building was Spartan by American standards and could have used a coat of paint, but the students were attentive and, by the standards of the region, well dressed and well fed, and the teacher looked as though she liked what she was doing. High school students were transported free to nearby towns, Turnbull said. We then stopped at a nursery school in a new building. The fee, he said, was only a couple of dollars a month.

"I'll give Black credit for one thing," Turnbull said. "He did a lot to improve social services, if that's what you call them. He put in the nursery schools so that mothers with young children could keep on working if they wanted to, psychological counseling, financial advice, you name it."

We then drove through a housing area. First came one-story barracks buildings that Turnbull said dated back to the 1920's and 1930's and were no longer occupied. Then there were two-story, two-family dwellings that dated from the 1940's and 1950's, some of which were still in use. They were built on stilts six feet off the ground and had steeply pitched roofs. It is a sensible design in an area where the rains are torrential, flooding is common, and snakes, scorpions, and tarantulas proliferate.

Finally, we took a look at a development of the 1960's and 1970's. These were one-family stucco cottages with tile roofs, porches, screened jalousie windows, and, as Turnbull pointed out, running water and indoor plumbing. Most of the plots on which they stood were planted with fruit trees and flowering shrubs. The houses were small—600 or 700 square feet, at a guess. Many owners had added a room, and a few a second floor. The houses struck me, all in all, as the equal of many houses occupied by blue-collar families or retired couples in Florida.

The concrete roads came to an end, and we bounced along a gravel lane bordered by deep ditches and a glossy green wall of banana plants. Above them, every 100 feet or so, rotating sprinklers sprayed pinwheels of water that the sun turned into the fragments of rainbows. We stopped and walked into the fields. The banana plants arched over our heads, and the broad leaves created deep shadows, even at midday. The ground was spongy underfoot, and the air was dank. The banana, Turnbull said, was actually an enormous herb that bore one stem of bananas, and only once. "You start with a shoot, and a year later, give or take a couple of months, you're ready to harvest," he went on. "At night, when it's quiet, you can hear them growing, and that's no joke."

Each stem of bananas was wrapped in Pliofilm to keep off insects. It hung like a chandelier. The bending trunk was braced with wire to keep it from splitting. The plants were spaced about 15 feet apart. Ducking and pushing the thick, limp leaves out of our way, we came to what Turnbull was looking for—a harvesting crew.

One man, using a 10-foot pole with a flat blade mounted on the end, slashed the thick stem, causing it to bend without breaking. The second man positioned himself under the stem of bananas, which sagged to a height of six or seven feet. The first man made another cut, and the stem settled gently on a thick pad on the second man's shoulder. He trotted to an overhead conveyor system that ran between every 10 rows of plants. A third man took the stem off the second man's shoulder, hooked it to the conveyor, and started it rolling toward the packing sheds.

While this was happening, the first man had finished cutting down the banana plant and had hurried on to the next one. It looked like a scene from *Modern Times*. Everything was taking place at double time. Turnbull said that the men were paid by the stem. Each man on the crew could make $15 a day, an excellent rate of pay in Honduras, if they all kept hustling.

"The rate is set in bargaining between the company and the union, and it's not a company union," he said. "The contract also covers working conditions. For example, the conveyors are placed where they are because the contract limits the distance that bananas can be carried to 100 feet."

Over lunch, I asked Turnbull to tell me something about Zemurray, whom he had known well in his youth.

"Well, he used to call everyone sport," he replied. "He liked to be down here, out in the fields, looking over everything that was happening. He always said he loved the Hondurans, and I think it was the truth. If I were Zemurray, I wouldn't be eating chicken, I'd be eating iguana stew. It was his favorite dish. He always used to be saying to the cooks here, 'When are you going to make me some iguana stew?' "

To my astonishment, everyone I spoke with in Tegucigalpa, including the leftists, agreed that United Brands had become, in the term beloved by boosters everywhere, a corporate good citizen. I had come to doubt by then that the old United Fruit Company was ever so wicked as it had been painted, or, it might be said, as it had painted itself. In those days, after all, a reputation for sweating labor, squeezing competitors, and subverting governments tended to assure stockholders that their interests were being safeguarded.

By the standards of the times, even in the United States, United Fruit seems to have been no worse than big business in general, and by the standards of Central America, it was a great deal better. Leftist writers, who tend to dominate this field of inquiry, accuse the company and its major rival, Standard Fruit, of acquiring for almost nothing vast tracts of the most fertile land in the region. What they forget to say is that the land was empty and profitless swamp and jungle until millions of dollars were spent in draining and clearing it, and that, unlike the mining and timber interests, the fruit companies improved the land rather than ravaged it. These commentators also point out how little the banana companies paid in taxes but neglect to add that, by immemorial custom in Latin America, such payments had to be made to the private purses of those in power.

United Fruit merely wanted to grow bananas and make money without interference. If the nations in which it operated understood this, all was well. If not, as in Guatemala in 1954, an event that will be discussed in the next chapter, the company could be merciless.

But for decades on end before that, the company was an unseen presence. Its plantations were remote from the capitals and the settled areas. For many years, the company had to recruit most of its workers in the West Indies, few Central Americans being willing to work in the steamy coastal plain.

Labor discipline was harsh on the company's plantations, as it was also in the United States in the years before the legislative enactments of Franklin D. Roosevelt's first term, but it was a great deal less harsh than on the *haciendas* of the region.

More important, in a region in which agricultural employment has always been largely seasonal, the fruit company's workers had year-round employment and cash wages that were considerably higher than they could have earned elsewhere and, by local standards, good housing. The free company infirmaries and elementary schools were grossly inadequate when compared with the Mayo Clinic and Andover, say, but few other Hondurans ever saw a physician or got a chance to learn to read and write.

For all that, no one would have called the wage rates generous, and even if they had been, the arrogance and racism of the *gringos* who ran the company right down to the foreman level would have created discontent. From the 1940's onward, the company was a frequent object of labor agitation. In 1954, when a union thought to be Communist-dominated was making headway, Washington, which was unwilling to intervene as it had in Guatemala, persuaded the company to permit its workers to be organized by a union affiliated with the American Institute for Free Labor Development, or AFILD. Since then, the workers have had a union, which, if not highly militant, gained many of the improvements in working conditions, wage rates, and fringe benefits that have been described.

Through the mid-1960's, United Fruit's profits were certainly very large by American standards, but modest by those of Latin America, where businesses are said to expect an annual return of at least 35 percent on equity. Moreover, the banana business was risky. Besides hurricanes, there were revolutions that could not always be prevented and sometimes interfered with production, and the possibility of a new blight that would destroy the banana fields always existed.

While the company's public benefactions were small, it did more in Central America than any other business or individual I heard of. During Zemurray's years of leadership, it built and endowed an agricultural institute in Honduras and created a splendid botanical garden, which I visited, near Tela, on the Atlantic coast. Among Zemurray's personal philanthropies was the endowment of a center for Latin American studies at Tulane University in New Orleans.

No one doubts that the company and Standard Fruit, too, did many things that were all too common practices of big business everywhere during the first third or half of the century—destroying competition, giving bribes, and fixing prices. What it also did, however, was to bring a fruit that had been an exotic luxury to market at remarkably low prices. In New York City, for example, bananas still sell, more often than not, for less than apples from the Hudson Valley.

The top banana at the American Embassy in Tegucigalpa when I visited there was John Negroponte. I had known him in Saigon in 1967. He then worked for a section of the Agency for International Development that was thought to be a front for the CIA. From there he had gone from success to success, mainly in the Far East and Europe. His assignment in Honduras, where he had arrived a few months previ-

235

ously, made him, at the age of 42, the youngest Ambassador in the Foreign Service.

The status of the embassy was raised at the same time. Under Negroponte's predecessor, Jack Binns, it had been fourth class, the State Department's lowest classification, which requires the Ambassador to polish the car and mow his own lawn. Binns, like many other Central American specialists, was sent into retirement by Haig as an inveterate and unrepentant North-Souther. On Negroponte's arrival, the embassy was promoted to second-class status, and the staff was enlarged to 40 persons. Negroponte was tall, social, and rich, although not so tall and probably not so rich as was his superior at the State Department, Thomas O. Enders, but that was not the only reason for the upgrading.

Honduras had suddenly been promoted from banana republic to anti-Communist bulwark. It was no empty honor. Being a bulwark brought immediate financial rewards. Aid was increased to $41,000,000 a year. (The only nations in the hemisphere that got more were El Salvador and Jamaica.) Military assistance would shoot up to $11,000,000. And those were only the hors d'oeuvres. In the fall of 1981, Honduras was offered a $200,000,000 loan, most of which was to go to the private sector. Although its foreign debt was already $1.7 billion and it stood on the brink of bankruptcy, the terms of the loan were so easy that to refuse it would have been a crime against the state.

The quid pro quo was that Honduras start living up to its new responsibilities. It could begin by electing a physician and rancher named Roberto Suazo Córdova to the presidency that November. That way, Washington could herald the country's return to civilian and democratic government while the armed forces continued to run things. The proposal was quickly accepted. Some officials may have thought it wiser to keep out of their neighbors' quarrels, but American aid and American loans stick to the fingers. They can solve all problems and make all dreams come true.

For the rest of the country, the need was also great. The per capita annual income of its 2,700,000 people was said to be less than $400. In the hemisphere, only Haiti's was lower. Such statistics are not entirely reliable in countries like Honduras. Even so, it was clear enough that although no one starves in Honduras, the *campesinos,* except for those fortunate enough to be employed by the fruit companies, live close to the margin. This poverty has less to do with the grinding oppression of an oligarchy than with geography. In Central America, the most fertile land lies on the Pacific side of the continental divide, but except for a narrow corridor, Honduras is situated on the other side.

Although Honduras's agricultural prospects are poor, it is perfect as a barrier against revolution. Nicaragua lies to the east, El Salvador to the south, and Guatemala to the west. Most of whatever arms were being sent from Nicaragua to the Salvadoran rebels were almost certainly smuggled across Honduras's Pacific corridor or were carried by small boat across the Gulf of Fonseca. Honduras was already playing host, reluctantly, to 40,000 refugees from the three countries.

In establishing Honduras as a bulwark, the United States could build on a long period of friendly relations. Hondurans, by and large, did not seem to be bothered by the economic domination of the United States. They went right on liking and admiring *gringos*. The people I spoke with advanced various reasons for this phenomenon—a mysterious natural affinity between the two nations, the excellent record of the fruit companies in recent years, and the accomplishments of a large and unusually efficient Peace Corps mission.

So Suazo was duly elected, the loan was approved, and Abraham Bennatón Ramos, who had picked up the $1,250,000 bribe from United Brands in Switzerland and was the confidant of the country's richest family, the Facussés, returned to government service as an adviser to the president.

Close to 100 American military advisers were sent to Honduras—nearly twice the number assigned to El Salvador. The ragtag Honduran army got new equipment, and the air force got new planes and helicopters. American and Honduran units held joint exercises along the Atlantic coast that were probably meant to start the Sandinistas shaking in their boots. Destroyers and frigates of the United States Navy cruised the Gulf of Fonseca, hoping to lock their radar onto arms smugglers. The Honduran armed forces cooperated with Guatemalan and Salvadoran troops in antiguerrilla operations in the border regions.

Honduras became the staging area for operations against Nicaragua that were organized and paid for by the United States and carried out by freedom fighters who a few years before had been members of Somoza's National Guard. The Central Intelligence Agency hired advisers from Argentina for them, although it was hard to think of anything having to do with murder and torture that the Somocistas didn't already know. When Argentina, enraged by Washington's modest assistance to Britain during the Falklands war, withdrew them, it seemed unlikely to delay or advance the march to Managua.

* * *

In one of his more imaginative moments, Haig declared that the threat of an invasion by Nicaragua was the reason Honduras needed more arms. What he was expressing, of course, was a hope. Any sort of border crossing by the Sandinistas, even if it was only a lorry driver's taking a wrong turn, would provide a pretext for the United States, by invoking treaty obligations, to send in combat forces.

It was for precisely that reason that the diplomats, businessmen, academics, and politicians of the center and the left I spoke with agreed that invasion was the remotest of possibilities and that the dangers to Honduras in becoming a bulwark outweighed any likely advantages. They thought it far more likely that the border raids of the Somocistas would increase anti-American sentiment in Honduras, especially among students, and that revolutionary activity would inevitably follow, with or without Sandinista encouragement. Despite its poverty, Honduras remained generally tranquil, but discontent existed. It focused on a once promising land reform that had ended because of the opposition of the big ranchers. Now, they said, it was a rebellion waiting to happen.

14
The Guatemalan Puzzle

"FIRST, THERE is the silence and then the initial demand. It is usually set absurdly high—$10,000,000, say. The victim's family or employer say they can't possibly pay that much. They can pay only $1,000,000. That's a mistake. It's what the kidnappers want. A floor has been established. From then on, the bargaining will *begin* at that level."

The speaker was an Englishman, a former officer in the British army whom I will identify at his request only as the captain. He was retained by Lloyd's, the London insurance exchange, as a specialist in what is known in the trade as "K and R," which stands for kidnap and ransom. If someone on whom Lloyd's has written such coverage is abducted, it is the captain's job to get the victim back as quickly and cheaply as possible. Such coverage sells itself, but it doesn't come cheap. The captain said that $1,000,000 in coverage for a businessman from the United States or Europe would cost about $500 a day.

It was November, 1981, and we were sitting in a quiet corner of a hotel cocktail lounge in Guatemala City. Although his work took him all over the world, he had been spending much of his time in Guatemala City recently, he said, because it had replaced Rome and Milan as the kidnap capital of the world.

"There have been simply dozens of big kidnappings here in the past couple of years and God knows how many small ones," he said. "Only a very few become known to the police or get into the newspapers, but very big money is involved. The average ransom in the cases I have worked on here, and there have been several, was $2,000,000. That may sound like a great deal, but it was a great deal less than the kidnappers originally wanted.

"Everyone has gone into kidnapping," he continued. "Since they all pretend to be someone else, it can get a bit tricky. One never can be sure whether one is dealing with professional criminals, amateurs, groups associated with the radical right or left, or even members of the police or the government security services.

"Persons who are taken by professional criminals are generally the most fortunate—comparatively speaking, of course. Their assets and those of their relations may be rather badly dented, but if the ransom is paid, they are almost certain to be returned. Actually, the professionals try to take good care of their victims. They know that the quickest way to ruin the business is to fail to carry out their part of the bargain. On the other hand, if they are convinced that the family is holding out, refusing to pay what it is able to, they can be rather rough on the poor chap and may very likely end up just dropping him in a hole in the ground somewhere and covering him up."

The captain stopped speaking as a couple was shown to a table perhaps 10 feet away. He let his eyes slide over them and then picked up his account in a voice not much louder than a murmur. It was a time when Guatemala City stank of terror. There was no curfew, but by 9:00 P.M. the streets were empty. Kidnappings, murders, and disappearances were nightly occurrences. A presidential election campaign, which is generally a time of greater than usual violence in Latin America, was just beginning. The guerrillas of the Poor People's Army were striking at outlying towns and villages and, from time to time, in the capital itself.

"One thing that is absolutely essential in a kidnapping is not to let the police become involved," the captain said. "For one thing, they may have done the job themselves. Or they may be protecting the gang that did it. Or they may be more interested in getting their hands on the ransom money than in getting the victim back. At best, they will bugger up the case and get the victim killed through sheer bloody incompetence. That, I am sure, is what happened with Clifford Bevans, the Goodyear executive. In fact, I can't recall a case the police ever handled efficiently.

"One professional gang did two kidnappings in Guatemala last year and got a ransom of $5,000,000 in each case," he said. "On the other hand, each was well planned, required the services of several men, and the victim had to be kept in custody for six months in one case and three in the other. Both were returned safely, according to the agreement. But you don't have to be a millionaire to get kidnapped in Guatemala. Shopkeepers are routinely abducted for a ransom of $500 or $1,000.

"I suppose it seems odd to use the word," he went on, "but some kidnapping gangs are less scrupulous than others. There have been cases where a gang squeezed out every bit of money possible from a victim's family and then, instead of freeing him, said, 'Thanks for the first installment.' I know of another case in which a gang got the ransom that had been agreed to and then sold the man to another gang. Of course, the very worst bastards are the ones who take the money, kill their prisoner, and don't even have the decency to tell his, or her, family what's been done."

The captain looked up quickly as the waiter approached and then settled back. He had chosen, not by chance, I suppose, a table at which he faced the entrance.

"I also consult on anti-kidnapping security," he said. "It's the usual thing, mostly—changing travel routes, having reliable bodyguards, and so on. If money is no object, I recommend Israelis, former paratroopers, or commandos for choice. The trouble with the local chaps is that you never know whose side they are on."

Being a Christian Democrat in Guatemala at that time was as dangerous as being rich. Comparatively few were kidnapped. Mostly, they were shot down wherever they happened to be. If they were abducted, it was only to be murdered in some quiet place. So perilous had the situation become that Vinicio Cerezo, the head of the party, and Luis Martínez Montt, his chief assistant, had been forced to suspend their belief in nonviolence. They both were armed when I went to see them.

"We had no choice," Cerezo said. "Since 1978, we have had 150 of our party leaders killed, including at least 20 mayors. This year there have been 175 to 200 political killings a month. We think we have a Christian duty to defend our lives. However, after an attempt was made to kill me in February, I sent my wife and our four children to Washington. It wasn't fair to expose them to the danger."

The assassination attempt took place outside the modest house in a run-down section of the capital where we were speaking. It belongs to Cerezo's father, who was one of the founders of the party. Masked men opened fire on the son as he got out of his car and walked to the front door. He and his bodyguards shot back, and the attackers fled. The security police were almost certainly responsible. A car abandoned at the scene was traced to one of its units. The official explanation was that the car had been left there a day or two earlier after a mechanical breakdown.

Uniquely among such events in Guatemala, an arrest was made. Cerezo was charged with the murder of a passerby who was killed in the fusillade and spent several days in jail. He was freed, alive and unharmed, to his amazement, after it had been established that the man had been killed by a bullet from a .45-caliber pistol, the standard weapon used by the police, and that Cerezo and his bodyguard carried 9-millimeter automatics.

"I don't have to tell you that no one tried to match the bullet to any of the guns carried by the men who were assigned to that car," Martínez said.

The attempt on Cerezo's life, they agreed, was meant to deprive their party of its most popular and energetic leader before the presidential election. Cerezo was only 33, too young to seek the office himself, but he would be an eloquent spokesman for the centrist coalition that the Christian Democrats were trying to put together. They were ready, Cerezo said, to have it headed by the representative of one of the other parties.

"We think this is an election in which we really have a chance," Cerezo said. "We're absolutely sure that the people are looking for a new road. We are so confident, in fact, that we refused the offer of a coalition with the official party because we decided that it would make no significant changes. We also are certain that if the official party steals *this* election, then Guatemala will be Communist-dominated before the next one."

It was generally acknowledged that the elections in 1974 and 1978 were decided by fraud in favor of the Popular Democratic Front, or FDP, the so-called official party. It is the electoral vehicle of the military, business, and some landowners and, needless to say, is neither popular nor democratic. In 1974, the victim of the fraud was the Christian Democratic coalition, the candidate of which was General Efraín Ríos Montt.

At the time of my visit General Ríos Montt was living as obscurely as Colonel Claramount in San Salvador, retired from the army, no longer active politically, and serving as the principal of an evangelical church school. At that, he was more fortunate than his running mate, Alberto Fuentes Mohr, a Social Democrat and a former Foreign Minister, who was assassinated in 1979.

In 1978, the defrauded candidate was Mario Sandoval Alarcón, who had previously been vice-president. He was the candidate of the right-ist National Liberation Movement, or MLN, and a reactionary of such ferocity that one was disinclined to shed any tears for him. Sandoval was once again a candidate for the presidency on a platform that resembled D'Aubuisson's in El Salvador. He was promising to suppress the guerrillas even if it meant burning every village and slaughtering every Indian in the country.

Sandoval could no longer speak comfortably, his cancerous larynx having been removed a couple of years earlier. He was able to croak orders to his staff, but his wife generally read his speeches, and he did not give interviews. I arranged, therefore, to talk to his vice-presidential candidate, Leonel Sisniega Otero, who, I was assured, held identical opinions, and was, if anything, more ferocious. Our meeting took place at his mansion on the outskirts of the capital.

A young, pretty maid in a pink uniform led me to the drawing room. It held many examples of ecclesiastical art, painted panels and the like, that must have dated from the 17th and 18th centuries and many *objets d'art*. One in particular caught my notice. It was a vanity table done in the elaborate style of the Second Empire that stood in an anteroom. Flanking the mirror were two candleholders on long pivoting arms. What was most striking about it was that it and its low-backed chair appeared to be made entirely of silver.

Sisniega walked in scowling, smiled briefly as he took my hand, and then resumed his look of furious dissatisfaction. He was a stocky man, baldish, with a clipped mustache. His eyes were small and suspicious, and I could see that the bloom of red in his plump cheeks had been caused by the bottle rather than by regular exercise.

As we shook hands, I congratulated him on the beauty of his possessions. He said that the vanity table, which was indeed made of silver finer than sterling, had passed down to him through his mother, who was a granddaughter of Justo Rufino Barrios, the Guatemalan *caudillo* from 1871 to 1885. He then pointed out a photograph, framed in silver, of course, of a young man in military uniform.

"My son," he said. "At this moment, he is leading an infantry company in Quiché in antiguerrilla operations."

He was, I said, the first rich man I had met in Central America who did not appear to believe that it was solely the duty of other people to defend his property. Speaking of that, I asked why he was unwilling to permit the armed forces, of whose anticommunism there could be no doubt, to continue governing the country.

"Lucas is a good man, a brave man, an admirable man, and so is Guevara," he said, speaking of the president, General Romeo Lucas García, and General Aníbal Guevara Rodríguez, who had been nominated by the official party to succeed him. "But the ministers of the government are corrupt good-for-nothings. Public works are really private works. The peripheral highway, the dams, the oil are nothing but bottomless pits of graft for them. We will wipe out corruption and Communists both when we come to power."

Was it true, I asked, that Sandoval had said that Guatemala's population was far too high and that "Communists" should be killed not by the hundreds but by the tens of thousands?

"Mario didn't say that 7,000,000 was too many people," he replied. "Just that it was too many for the army to guard. We favor the establishment of an anti-Communist militia of 50,000 to help with that."

Wanting to see him erupt again, I asked his opinion of Cerezo and the Christian Democrats.

"They are just like the Christian Democrats under Allende," he replied, beginning to glower. "They are merely a different type of Communist."

Sisniega's face had gone so dark with rage that I thought he might have a stroke. At that moment, fortunately, the maid arrived with coffee in a silver pot on a silver tray. She poured it and served it as carefully as a robot, never daring to gaze at her master. As soon as she had left the room, Sisniega got going on the servant problem.

"The truth is that our people are very lazy," he said, his face again darkening dangerously and his eyes bulging like a frog's. "We have four people who work here—two in the kitchen and two to dust and clean. In your country you would have someone in two or three days a week. Here they start at 7:00 A.M. and work all day long and"—he jumped up, strode to the table on which his son's photograph was displayed, and ran his finger along the mellow antique mahogany—"it's dusty! Always dusty! Three men work outside. What do they do all day? Yet everyone dares to talk about 'rights' instead of obligations."

Sisniega shook his head in disbelief, but his face returned to its normal putty color. I went on to ask him about the significance of a figure of Jesus that was displayed behind glass at the MLN headquarters.

"That is the Christ of Esquipulas," he replied. "Esquipulas is the town where [Colonel Carlos] Castillo Armas and his army entered Guatemala from Honduras in 1954. He stopped to pray before the figure of the Savior in the church there for success as he began his march to the capital. He said that the Christ of Esquipulas would be the captain general of our souls. When his mission was crowned with success, the figure became an object of special veneration to him and to those who fought with him and who keep alive his ideals today in the Movimiento Liberación Nacional."

Sisniega's face softened and relaxed as he recalled the glory days of his youth. "Others say they are against communism, but they don't prove it," he said. "I fought against communism in 1954 while others did nothing."

In 1977, when the Carter administration gave the Guatemalan government the choice of continuing to receive military assistance or continuing to violate human rights so spectacularly, Guatemala had no trouble deciding in favor of murder, torture, and disappearance. It rejected American arms before Carter could cut them off and, like Nicaragua and El Salvador, began buying them from Israel, South Africa, Argentina, and elsewhere.

Its being an inflexible rule of international relations that the warmth of any country's welcome to American journalists is in direct proportion to the megatonnage of the weapons that the United States is supplying, I found myself unable to gain access to President Lucas or any other senior official. I was snarled at frequently, found myself the object of calculatedly sinister looks, and was, I think, followed on occasion. Nonetheless, I managed to speak briefly with General Guevara, the official party's presidential candidate.

The occasion was a press conference at the headquarters of the party, the Popular Democratic Front. It was a curious event, inasmuch as Guevara scarcely opened his mouth. He sat on the platform, his thick fingers folded together in his lap, his small eyes glazed with boredom, suspicion, and incomprehension.

After each question, Guevara would nod and then incline his head to his vice-presidential candidate, Ramiro Ponce Monroy, a former mayor of Guatemala City, who answered it.

Guevara had resigned as Minister of Defense to accept the nomination. His brother was chief of staff of the army. Like Lucas, the incumbent, Guevara had the reputation of being less than bright except where his bank balance was concerned.

I had arranged to speak privately with him after the press conference. However, several Guatemalan reporters crowded in to listen. The general sat behind a desk, just as inert as he had been on the plat-

245

form. He was a thickset man of medium height. He was only 54, but looked much older. His cheeks were pouchy, his mouth loose, his expression vacant.

Given the scores of people being killed every week, I asked if he could regard criticism of Guatemala's human rights record as entirely unjustified. He blinked and paused. I got the feeling that questions like that took a long time to work their way through the worn-out wiring inside his head and that the answers were formulated a letter at a time.

"I think your country is very hard on us," he replied. "You don't criticize England for what's happening in Northern Ireland. People over there are starving to death. [He seemed to have confused the situation with the famine of the 1840's.] It's more painful for a man to die of starvation than it is by shooting."

Guatemala's modern era began in 1944, when General Jorge Ubico was deposed by the same sort of spontaneous rebellion that ousted Hernández Martínez in the same year in El Salvador. In 1945, Guatemala had its first honest election. The winner, with more than 90 percent of the vote, was Juan José Arévalo, a professor of philosophy who had returned from 10 years in exile in Argentina after Ubico's fall.

Arévalo pushed bills through the Assembly legalizing labor unions, establishing a minimum wage and a social security system, and improving education and public health. Although Arévalo called his program spiritual socialism, he did not interfere with private enterprise beyond requiring it to pay taxes and decent wages. The closest he came to land reform was a law passed in 1949, requiring the owners of *haciendas* to rent unused land to peasants who wanted to farm it. He kept Communists in check, going so far as to close their center of studies.

The oligarchy, foreign business, notably United Fruit, and the military and political figures who had prospered under Ubico began plotting to restore the traditional Guatemalan way of life. Many coups were attempted, but the philosophy professor also turned out to be an effective politician and a decisive leader. To protect himself against the army, Arévalo took some of its weapons and armed his supporters, notably the railway workers. Guatemala made remarkable progress during Arévalo's administration, but the new constitution prohibited consecutive terms for the president, so in the election of 1950, he withdrew in favor of his Minister of Defense, Colonel Jacobo Arbenz. The opposition candidate, Miguel Ydígoras Fuentes, had been a member of Ubico's Cabinet.

It was a rough campaign, but for a change it was the rightist candidate who went into hiding. Arbenz won easily in what was acknowledged to be an honest vote. He was only 36 years old when he took office. He lacked Arévalo's brains and sophistication and, as noted, his wife, a Salvadoran, was a Communist sympathizer. Under her patronage, leftists flourished in the ministries and the unions. They were less interested, perhaps, in carrying out the programs that Arévalo had set up than they were in expanding their power.

In 1953, Guatemala adopted a land reform law, providing for the expropriation of uncultivated land and its sale on easy terms to landless peasants in parcels no larger than 42.5 acres. United Fruit was the country's largest landowner. It held 550,000 acres, of which only 75,000 were planted. The decree required it to surrender 210,000 acres. The government proposed to pay $628,000, the assessed value of the land, in long-term bonds. Another 177,000 acres were subsequently taken in the same way.

The company argued that the land was worth 20 times the assessed valuation, but Arbenz replied that the company had set the value itself to keep real estate taxes low. The company also stated that it needed the unused land as a reserve, since its plantations might be devastated at any time by blight, pests, or natural catastrophes. That was, of course, a possibility, but the real reason, as McCann points out in *An American Company,* was that the company wanted to keep it out of the hands of competitors.

United Fruit would certainly have fought the expropriation, no matter how it was carried out, but the actions of the leftists in the government made it easier for the company to justify its position. These ideologues were less interested in actually putting peasants on the land than they were in a noisy confrontation with *El Pulpo.* Arbenz later hinted, as Stephen Schlesinger and Stephen Kinzer point out in their *Bitter Fruit: The Untold Story of the American Coup in Guatemala,* that he had been willing to compromise, but by then the company was seeking its remedies in Washington.

If the company was being picked on, it was understandable. It had used its power in Guatemala more nakedly and selfishly than anywhere else it did business. Its railroad ran from coast to coast and served the capital and the major cities, but the company used it, in combination with its ownership of the major shipping line, port facilities, and communications, to choke off competition and to manipulate freight rates in its favor.

When Stalin died in March, 1953, an extravagant tribute was paid to him in the Guatemalan Assembly. It was another pointlessly provocative act, unless it was connected with a shopping trip that the Arbenz government made at about the same time. The rightist opposition was becoming more active and more violent, native oligarchs liking the land reform even less than did United Fruit. Unable to buy arms from the United States or in all likelihood from its allies, Arbenz sent agents behind the Iron Curtain to get them.

The purchase was made in Czechoslovakia. The CIA was aware of it and tracked the ship that was carrying the consignment most of the way across the Atlantic, lost it, and then found it again just as it was docking at Puerto Barrios in May. Agency operatives attacked the train that was carrying the arms to the capital, killing a couple of Guatemalan soldiers, but failed to stop it. They could have saved themselves the trouble. The weapons turned out to be obsolescent junk, more suitable for mounting over the fireplace than taking into the field.

In August, the National Security Council decided that, after 21 years, the Good Neighbor Policy had lapsed and that the Arbenz government was to be overthrown. The task strained the brains of the CIA's covert operations branch for nearly a year and cost countless tens of millions of dollars. The CIA interviewed several candidates before choosing Carlos Castillo Armas to lead the rebellion. He was a former colonel whose military career had ended in 1950, when he organized an unsuccessful uprising against Arévalo. Castillo was a small man with a nervous manner, a long nose, an unassertive chin, and a Chaplin mustache.

Arbenz reportedly turned down a big bribe to leave quietly, but many of his old comrades in the army accepted the CIA's bounty. When Castillo Armas crossed the border, they ignored Arbenz's call to arms, either staying in their barracks or going out to greet the conqueror. In July, 1954, the new *caudillo,* his small head wobbling under his gold-braided cap, rode into Guatemala City in unopposed triumph.

The sudden collapse took Arbenz and his supporters by surprise. Hundreds had to seek asylum in foreign embassies. According to Schlesinger and Kinzer, John Foster Dulles tried for weeks to persuade Castillo Armas to drag them out and try them for treason. Failing that, he urged that safe-conduct be granted only if they agreed to expose their true loyalties by going directly to Moscow. Much as Castillo Armas might have liked to do so, he refused. The right of asylum was too well established in international law and too useful in Latin America to insurrectionists of all political persuasions to be violated.

Arbenz, his wife, and their daughter, who had found refuge in the Mexican Embassy, flew to Mexico City. From there, they traveled to Switzerland. He was told he could reside there only if he renounced his Guatemalan citizenship. He refused, and a long period of wandering began. Arbenz and his family went on to France, where they were shadowed ostentatiously by the police, to Prague and Moscow, to Uruguay, and, after Castro's triumph, to Cuba. Arbenz ended up back in Mexico City. He had been drinking heavily since his overthrow, and in 1971, he died by drowning in his bathtub. His widow returned to her family in El Salvador, and there her enthusiasm for communism faded away.

Castillo Armas was not disappointing those who had had faith in him. The vote was taken from the 75 percent of the electorate that was illiterate. The peasants were thrown off most of the 1,500,000 acres they had received from the Arbenz government. United Fruit got its holdings back. Unions were prohibited, and several organizers at the company's plantations were murdered. The chief of internal security during the Ubico dictatorship got his job back. Communists, who were more or less defined as anyone to the left of Castillo Armas, were proscribed. Subversive books were burned.

As it happened, United Fruit was not long able to use and enjoy its Guatemalan properties. Soon after Arbenz's overthrow the Justice Department brought an antitrust suit against the company. The case had been begun during the Truman administration and had continued to simmer after the Republicans had come to power. In 1957, United Fruit signed a consent decree and began selling off its properties, including the railroad, in Guatemala to competitors like Del Monte and to native growers. It even gave land to the peasants. By the early 1960's, it retained only a few minor businesses in Guatemala. By 1980, there was nothing at all.

Castillo Armas was assassinated in 1957. The motive for the crime appeared to be personal or monetary rather than ideological. His successor, who was supported by the United States, was General Miguel Ydígoras Fuentes. He also turned out to be a reliable friend, permitting the CIA to set up training camps for the Bay of Pigs invasion force and to use Puerto Barrios as its main port of embarkation. An uprising by a group of army officers in November, 1960, protesting Guatemalan participation in the plan, was suppressed when Washington sent an aircraft carrier to the Atlantic coast. Two young lieutenants, Luis Turcios Lima and Marco Aurelio Yon Sosa, refused to surrender. They joined forces with leftists who had been living underground or were slipping back into the country and raised a rebellion.

The Alliance for Progress provided funds for what was euphemistically called internal security, so it was simple for President Kennedy to send military advisers and equipment, including bombing planes, to the Guatemalan armed forces. The bombers were particularly useful for destroying in complete safety "Communist strongholds," which were defined as villages that were destroyed by bombs. Within a year the insurrection had been put down.

In 1962, Arévalo, who had been living in exile in Mexico, announced that he wanted to return to Guatemala to run for the presidency. Ydígoras, to the consternation of his supporters, gave his permission. When Ydígoras refused to rescind his invitation to Arévalo, his Minister of Defense, Colonel Enrique Peralta Azurdia, again with the approval of the United States, threw him out and assumed the presidency. Arévalo, meanwhile, had secretly entered the country. At a clandestine press conference, he declared that he was there to stay. Finding himself a hunted man and considering the alternatives, however, he soon changed his mind and departed again.

Mario Méndez Montenegro, the centrist civilian candidate in the election of 1966, and, in effect, a stand-in for the absent Arévalo, was found shot dead in his home a couple of months before the voting. The official verdict was suicide, but whoever heard of a political candidate killing himself? His brother, Julio César Méndez Montenegro, agreed to stand in his place. He was elected, and even permitted to take office.

By then, the guerrillas had reorganized—in Zacapa Province, about midway between the Atlantic coast and the capital. The army ignored Méndez in deciding how to fight them. Colonel Carlos Arana Osorio, who was known for his strong stomach, was put in command of the rebellious province. The United States sent $10,000,000 worth of military equipment and a detachment of Special Forces troops that trained Arana's men and went into the field with them. Reports reached the capital of village after village being wiped out. Turcios was killed late in 1966, and Yon Sosa vanished.

The army also carried out its counterinsurgency campaign in the cities. Leftists, liberals, and centrists and their families were murdered by the thousands. For two years, the slaughter continued, ruthlessly and remorselessly. The guerrillas struck back as they could, with ambushes in the countryside and terrorism in the cities. In 1968, two senior American military advisers, one of whom was thought to have worked out Arana's counterinsurgency tactics, were murdered. The American Ambassador, John Gordon Mein, was taken from his car in a kidnapping attempt. When he resisted, he was shot dead. By 1970, however, the uprising had been crushed. The officer corps selected Arana, the Butcher of Zacapa, as he was called, as its presidential candidate that year, and a grateful nation elected him.

Despite the turmoil of the preceding 15 years, the Guatemalan economy had grown rapidly. Foreign investors, believing that the United States was in effect guaranteeing that the country would not be permitted to go Communist or even to slide very far toward the center, opened factories and built handsome office towers in Guatemala City. Profits were high, and little trickled down past the ownership and management level. A docile and, not infrequently, terrorized labor force did not dare strike and was extremely cautious about even asking for a raise.

The election of 1974 established the military succession and the ascendancy of the Popular Democratic Front as the official party. The winner was Ríos Montt, the candidate of a centrist coalition, but it was General Kjell Eugenio Laugerud García, the candidate of the front, who took office. (Like Arbenz and many other officers, Laugerud had an immigrant father, from Norway in his case, who married a Guatemalan woman.) Ríos Montt went off to comfortable exile in Madrid as the military attaché.

In December, 1976, Amnesty International said that more than 20,000 persons had been murdered or had disappeared in the previous 10 years. All but a handful were victims of the death squads and the military. In 1977, President Carter announced that Guatemala's military aid would be reduced because of its gross abuses of human rights.

Another presidential election was held on schedule in 1978. By then, as in El Salvador, the Christian Democrats and the other centrist parties had become disorganized, thousands of their activists having been murdered or forced to leave the country. Unions of urban workers and *campesinos,* which remained in existence despite the terrible dangers, boycotted the election. In the days before the balloting, there were strikes and demonstrations throughout the country.

The winner of the three-way contest was generally acknowledged to be Sandoval Alarcón, the fanatical anti-Communist. The army cheated him as thoroughly as it had Ríos Montt in 1974 and installed its candidate, General Romeo Lucas García.

Reacting to the fall of Somoza in July, 1979, a new organization, the Secret Anti-Communist Army, began cutting down "subversives." The law faculty of the San Carlos University was almost destroyed. In June, 27 labor leaders were abducted, never to be seen again. Students, priests, lay religious workers all were murdered by scores and hundreds and finally, in that one year, by the thousands. Francisco Villagrán Kramer, the vice-president, resigned in protest and joined thousands of Guatemalans in exile.

As the center and the non-Communist left were being destroyed, the guerrillas were proliferating and subdividing into antagonistic groups —exactly as in El Salvador. By late 1980, in addition to the Guerrilla Army of the Poor, or EGP, there were the Revolutionary Organization of the People in Arms, or ORPA in its Spanish acronym, the Rebel Armed Forces, or FAR, and the Guatemalan Workers party, the PGT.

Little was known about the size of these organizations or the identity of their leaders, but their strategy was self-evident. That was to try to win the support of the Indians, who formed at least a bare majority of the population. Without their support, no revolution was likely to succeed; with it, one could scarcely fail.

It was easy for young militants to dream of leading those small, dark, implacable men, machetes at their waist, automatic rifles on their shoulders; to see them silently surrounding garrison after garrison, an enormous surge of them at last coming out of the mountains and the remote valleys, engulfing the cities, wreaking revenge on the Ladino exploiters, hoisting the red flag from Ubico's brooding National Palace. But the hard fact was that one thing the Indians had learned in the long centuries of their subjugation was that Ladinos, the whites, were not to be trusted. So the Indians had turned back into themselves, their families, and their clans. They left their villages in the mountains, to cut the Ladinos' sugar and pick their cotton and coffee on fertile valley land that had once been theirs, only because they needed the money to survive for the rest of the year.

It was to these remote villages that the guerrillas went. They gathered the Indians together, called them brothers, lectured them on the wickedness of the government, and urged them to join in the fight for freedom. The Indians listened silently and pretended, as they always did, that they understood nothing.

252

Then the soldiers would arrive. The very fact that the guerrillas had entered the village and spoken to the inhabitants could be construed as treason, even if the villagers had had no choice but to listen to these armed men. And so there would be punishments. How far the killing, raping, pillaging, and burning would go depended on the commander's mood. After that the Indians might start making choices, however reluctantly, among Ladinos. One side killed; the other side offered arms to kill with.

The guerrilla attacks that were reported in the Guatemala City papers were almost always small-scale operations in distant and inaccessible villages, but one day while I was there, an account appeared of an assault by a force of at least 200 guerrillas on Sololá, the capital of the department of the same name, about 100 miles west of Guatemala City. The governor of the department, the deputy police chief, and several soldiers and police were reported to have been killed. The day after the story appeared, Roderico López, who served as my interpreter and driver, and I set out for Sololá, which sounds like a singing exercise, on the Pan American Highway.

For the first 60 miles or so, it was a pleasant drive on a smooth and well-graded concrete road that winds through upland valleys and between the forested mountains. Then, rounding a bend, Roderico had to brake suddenly. Large pines had been cut on the side of a steep hill and allowed to drop across the highway. Roderico drove onto the shoulder, and we went on. There were other trees lying on the road, and, here and there, burned cars and broken glass. Traffic had been light for many miles, but now there was almost none. Continuing slowly past another fallen tree, I saw two men, Indians, at a guess, wearing worn shirts and trousers. They were nestled in the branches, as though asleep. However, blood was oozing through their thick black hair. They were dead.

Five miles farther on we saw first a column of smoke, rising rapidly, then 15 or 20 troops standing at the side of the highway. I asked Roderico to stop, and we walked up a rise to the village. Huts and market stalls were burning. Aside from the soldiers, the place, which was called Chupol, was deserted. I asked two young lieutenants, who said their names were Jerónimo Alonzo and Francisco del Cid, why the village was being burned. They called over a soldier and told him to show us what he had in a sack he was carrying. He produced three mines—

olive drab metal disks about the size of Frisbees. They had been found in the village, the lieutenants said.

I examined one of the mines. It bore no markings, but I thought I couldn't go wrong by saying, *"Cubano."*

The two lieutenants nodded and led me to the other evidence of guerrilla activity they had discovered. These were two pits about three feet in diameter and five feet deep. At the bottom of each was a length of log into which had been placed six or eight wooden stakes that had been sharpened to a pencil point and dipped in excrement. (In Vietnam, they were called punji stakes.) The pits had been covered by a straw mat over which earth was brushed.

"One of our soldiers fell into it," said one of the lieutenants, reconstructing the accident with gestures. "One of the spikes went right through his leg."

"There are many terrorists up in the hills," said the other. "We come, they go. We go, they come."

I mentioned that what looked like a couple of them were lying on the highway not very far away.

They exchanged glances. "Another company is patrolling in that area," one of them said.

Their amiability was decreasing by the moment, so I wished them good luck, and Roderico and I got back into his rump-sprung and bald-tired 1970 Plymouth and continued on our way. We turned off the highway onto a roughly paved secondary road that darted through a narrow valley planted in corn, apples, and vegetables. Indian children stood at the side of the road, selling apples and peaches, straw baskets, bunches of marigolds. Indians, singly or in groups, walked along the road. Some were returning from the market in Sololá. Others were going, carrying kindling and charcoal or nets full of corn on their backs.

The Indians, ruddy, wrinkled, round-headed, are small people. Few of the men stand higher than five feet six inches, and most of the women barely reach five feet. The women and girls wore embroidered blouses and long skirts woven of intricately checked or striped fabric in blues, reds, and greens, which identify their tribe and clan as distinctively as a Scotsman's tartan. Ribbons were twisted into the braids that hung down their backs. Some of the men wore kilts or trousers of the same fabrics.

Sololá is probably no uglier or dirtier than most provincial towns in Central America. It just seems that way because its setting is so magnificent. Spread out 500 feet below was the broad blue mirror of Lake Atitlán. On the far shore, three volcanoes rose 5,000 feet above the lake. But Sololá scarcely glances at this panorama. What should be a promenade is the ugly concrete market. The narrow cobbled streets are not in the least picturesque. The central plaza is small and scruffy, with no view of the lake. At its center are a garden and a bandstand. Flowers can't wait to bloom in that soil, with that sunshine and air, but the garden seemed to have been defeated by sheer malevolence, and the bandstand was in a state of terminal decay. Men, most of them old, at least a few of them with that air of boneless repose that suggests a hangover is being slept off, occupied the benches around the plaza.

Roderico and I got our shoes shined and asked the *limpiabotas* about the attack.

"They came in two vans," said one of the boys. "They shot at the police headquarters and the town hall and the bank. Then they came here to the plaza. They had a loudspeaker. They said that they were the Guerrilla Army of the Poor. They threw down little sheets of paper with writing on them. No one picked them up because we thought the police would kill us if we did. When they went away, the police made us pick them all up and give them to them."

The boys, who couldn't have been more than 10 years old, directed us to the police station and the town hall. The windows of both buildings had been shot out, and the walls had been pitted by bullets. A policeman with a bandaged hand was standing near by. I asked him if he had been wounded in the attack.

"Not exactly," he said. "I cut my hand on a piece of glass while I was crawling on the cobblestones."

The only honest cop in Central America more or less confirmed the shoeshine boys' account. The guerrillas, perhaps 15 in all, attacked their objectives more or less simultaneously. The deputy police chief was shot dead at his desk. The governor, who was an army colonel, was killed when he walked into the street to find out what was happening.

He said that press reports that the guerrillas had been armed with rocket launchers and grenades were incorrect.

"They had only rifles, but they were *automatic* rifles," he said. "All we had were our revolvers and a few old carbines from your army that fire one shot at a time. They outnumbered us, and they had the advantage of surprise."

After he turned away, Roderico whispered, "The kids and the other people say that the cops and the soldiers all ran away when the guerrillas came. Now they all think that they're shit.''

The afternoon was wearing on, and neither of us wanted to be on the highway after dusk. The fire was out at Chupol, but the fallen trees still blocked the road, and the bodies were still lying there. A couple of miles farther along, we saw a small pickup truck, loaded with household goods, standing abandoned on our side of the highway. A hundred yards or so beyond the truck, a small red sedan—a Toyota, I think—stood in the middle of the road, facing away from us. Both doors were open. Behind each of them crouched a man in civilian clothes with an automatic rifle. A third man stood at the far side of the highway.

"What should I do?" asked Roderico, taking his foot off the gas.

"Unless they tell us to stop, keep going," I said.

As we drew abreast of the sedan, both of us scrunched down a little in the musty upholstery. It took only 10 or 15 seconds for us to draw out of range, and those moments passed very slowly indeed. Back in Guatemala City, I also asked several acquaintances who the armed men might have been. Some said police; others, guerrillas and police. I wondered what had become of the people in the truck.

15
The Day of the Dead

ON ALL SAINTS' DAY, which is celebrated in most of Latin America as the Day of the Dead, I was invited by friends to visit Santiago Sacatepéquez, a village of Cakchiquel Indians in the mountains 25 miles south of Guatemala City. The Cakchiquels are one of 20 linguistic groups in the country, all of which are part of the Maya nation. Many Indian villages mark the day by flying kites over their cemeteries, and the kites of Santiago Sacatepéquez are among the largest and the most beautiful. Many Ladinos, after visiting their own family graves, drive out to watch the flying of the kites.

It was both a solemn and an amiable occasion. Indians sold food, drink, and souvenirs. A bar was set up in a tent, selling half-pint bottles of *aguardiente.* The cemetery covered most of a hillside. Well-to-do families had mausoleums at the top of the hill. They were painted pale blue or pink or light green, and they bore names like Yacute, Itzol, and Sactic. Lesser families had ordinary graves on the lower slopes. The large number of small graves reflected the infant mortality rate. Marigold petals stripped from the flower, each a pointillist's spot of vibrating color, covered the tops of the mausoleums and outlined the graves in tones of yellow and orange. Their light, peppery scent hung in the air, blending with the odor of the loamy earth.

The visitors remained at the top of the hill. They smiled and whispered among themselves and did not stare. The Indians, squatting around the graves, did not so much ignore them as to seem to will themselves to be unaware of their presence. Some drank and ate, speaking softly to one another, watching their young children at play and smiling and ruffling their hair when they approached. Others remained silent and motionless, seeming to see nothing.

The kites swooped and fluttered in the strong breeze, and streamers

257

of cloud raced past them in the steel blue sky. There were 20 or 30 of them, mostly box kites. Some were 10 or 12 feet tall. The paper that covered them was a patchwork of vivid color. Bits of mirror and shiny metal glittered in their tails. Straining, laughing crews of three or four men held the lines, sometimes tripping or falling or getting entangled with other crews, following the kites where the wind led them.

Every hour or so, from 8:00 A.M. to 3:00 P.M., a jet fighter took off from the Guatemala City airport. Each carried two bombs that I estimated to be 250-pounders under its wings. I could see them plainly from my hotel room. The newspapers never mentioned bombing raids against the guerrillas, so I asked a military spokesman about the mission of the planes.

"It is only for practice," he said, his eyes fixed on the ceiling of his office. "They are dropped in the sea."

At the Israeli Embassy, I asked Shmuel Mirom, the second secretary, two questions. Were Israeli advisers secretly working with the Guatemalan armed forces, as I had heard, and why, in view of the American arms embargo, did his country sell its famous Galil automatic rifles and other weapons to Guatemala?

Mirom denied the presence of advisers. As for the weapons, he said, "We would rather sell them toys, I assure you, but it is weapons that they want to buy, and we have to keep making weapons to remain an efficient source of supply for our own army."

Guatemalans are famous in Central America for their scathing wit. General Lucas, the president, who was thought to be rather dim, was the butt of several I heard. One went like this:

Lucas is getting his shoes shined when the boy begins telling him the latest Lucas joke.

"Young man," he says indignantly, "*I* am General Lucas."

"That's okay," the boy replies. "I'll tell it slowly."

Guatemala has always been a violent country at every level. Two young men who worked for the Bank of America in Guatemala City told me that lending money was a more delicate business than in the United States.

"Say a loan is delinquent," one said. "You have to dun the borrower. In New York, he at least promises to pay, even if he doesn't intend to. Here, he may tell you that if you don't quit bothering him, he's going to kill you—and he means it."

In Antigua, Guatemala's colonial capital, while I was taking a total-immersion Spanish course—I nearly drowned—I stayed at a pension that was owned by an American and his Guatemalan wife. I was introduced to one of her sisters, who was married to a retired colonel in the army. Speaking of the rebellious Indians one evening, the sister said, "I really don't see what they're unhappy about. They've got such beautiful views up there in the mountains."

The annual international trade fair was held in Guatemala City while I was there. The exhibition halls stand in the city's main park, admission is a few centavos, and thousands of ordinary Guatemalans feast their eyes on heavy machinery, cars and trucks, and consumer goods of all sorts. Guatemala's Indian heritage was also on display. There were Indian musicians, singers, and dancers and exhibits of Indian carving, weaving, and pottery. In all these, the level of artistry and craftsmanship is declining as manufactured goods replace them.

The feature of the afternoon's entertainment was a sky dance, performed by a troupe of five Quiché Indians. They were from Chichicastenango, a colonial town in the mountains. The army had turned the surrounding countryside into a killing ground in its pursuit of the guerrillas. The five men wore tribal dress, short jackets, knee-length trousers of black cloth embroidered in red, blue, green, and yellow, and intricately patterned headcloths. As a marimba orchestra struck up, they quickly climbed a pole, which was stepped like the mast of an old sailing ship, and rose, at a guess, to a height of 75 feet. At the top, with the end of the mast as its hub, a spoked wheel about 12 feet in diameter was set horizontally. The structure resembled the gibbets depicted in certain chilling paintings of Pieter Breughel.

One of the men started the wheel moving slowly, while the other four crept out to positions on the rim. Each of them inserted a foot into a loop at the end of a rope. Heads downward, backs arched, they dropped off the wheel and began to turn in a descending spiral. The ropes payed out of a drum at the center of the wheel. As the wheel spun more rapidly, centrifugal force pushed the men outward from the mast. Arms extended, muscles rigid, they swung slowly downward. The marimba music was soothingly monotonous, doubling back, repeating itself. The marimba is an Indian instrument, a xylophone with

259

resonators made of gourds beneath the wooden bars. Even when the tune is sprightly, its sound has overtones of melancholy.

The dancers reached the ground in a final cascade of notes and thrust themselves upright. At that moment, one of those jets with the bombs under its wings rose above the trees and headed for the mountains.

A missionary priest spoke to me about the Indians. "I spent many years in the Cuchumatanes Mountains near the Mexican border," he said. "It was five or 10 hours by Jeep, on muleback, or on foot, depending on the condition of the trails, from the nearest road. Only a minority of the Indians in these villages were Catholics, and even they retained much of their old religion. The rest held fast to the Mayan beliefs.

"They have two central concepts—time and nature," he went on. "Not time ticking away, but time as a living being. There are 20 time spirits that pass the world on to the next day. The cross has a place in their religion, but it has nothing to do with Christianity. It is directed to their four main spirits—the sun, the rain gods, the god of maize, and the moon, goddess of fertility."

The priest, who asked me not to identify him further, was a man in his fifties. He had spent his adult life in Central America.

"I became good friends with the Mayan high priest in one of the villages I served in, and it struck me that Christian and Mayan revelation could become one revelation. The Maya have a beautiful creation story. They say that God tried to make man out of mud, and failed; then out of wood, and failed; and, finally, out of corn, and He succeeded. They speak of their children and their wives and parents and their neighbors as all being parts of their bodies. So when we say, 'We are the body of Christ,' they know what we are talking about.

"Thirty years ago the church gave the sacraments," he said. "Period. The change came with the realization that there was much more than that to being a Christian. It was also part of being an American, wanting to do something. So we provided health services, classes in agriculture, taught them to read and write. Some of the leaders were given a course in reading the Guatemalan constitution, and it caused them to ask questions."

Now the Indians, he said, Christian and non-Christian alike, were being slaughtered. Not for being Communists, for none of them were, or for aiding the guerrillas, because few Indians trusted them any more than they did the army. They were being shot down, bombed, burned, because that was what the Ladinos had always done to keep them in bondage.

As the priest cited the massacres and the land thefts, I asked why he had kept silent.

"I often ask myself if we're doing the right thing," he replied. "It is a terrible choice. If we publicly condemned the government's actions, we might be killed, which doesn't frighten us so much, or be expelled from the country, which does, because then the Indians would be left without even the small measure of protection and help that we can provide. I have decided on silence, but only because I don't think that my words would mean anything in the United States." Then, with an upwelling of anguish, he said, "This is a second Holocaust. How can Israel, of all countries, sell arms to this government?"

Freedom of religion did not, of course, exist in Latin America under the Spanish crown. Such Protestants as were discovered could be burned at the stake. Orthodox Christians, Jews, Moslems, and Hindus stayed away. In most of the new nations, religious freedom didn't exist for 150 years after independence either. People had their choice of clericalism, which meant bending the knee to priest and bishop, or anticlericalism, which meant, in extreme cases, lynching them and burning their churches.

In the past 25 years, however, Protestantism—at least its fundamentalist branches—has been growing rapidly. Among them are the Mormons, Jehovah's Witnesses, Assemblies of God, and Southern Baptists. The mainstream Protestant denominations have generally allied themselves with the Catholic reformers and have done little proselytizing. By some estimates, fundamentalism has already won over 10 to 20 percent of the population of Central America. In fact, there are probably already more fundamentalist than Catholic congregations in Central America, although they tend to be smaller. It is possible that in any given week, at least as many Protestants as Catholics go to church. For one thing, the churches are more accessible. Villages of 200 or 300 population are likely to have at least one fundamentalist church, while the shortage of Catholic clergy grows worse year by year.

The fundamentalist missionaries, well supported by the folks at home, gather their flocks in the same way they do in the United States. They open churches, and often schools and clinics, too; they provide

261

lively music and preaching, and they advertise, mainly on radio and television. They band together to present guest stars—traveling evangelicals like Billy Graham or regional personalities who attract audiences of tens of thousands. Disdaining the years of study that are required of Catholic priests, the fundamentalist sects can create a native clergy in a matter of months.

Two events were crucial in the rise of Protestantism. These were the establishment of a Marxist-Leninist state in Cuba and the emergence of the Theology of Liberation. Both threatened the established order in a way that fundamental Protestantism did not. *Caudillos* and oligarchs alike welcomed their strong anticommunism and their emphasis on personal rather than social reform. In many ways, in fact, the Protestant fundamentalists and the reforming wing, at least, of the Catholic Church have changed places.

In no country in Latin America have the evangelicals been busier than in Guatemala. The climate is good in the *meseta*, living costs are low, and there are all those fallen-away Catholics and millions of heathen Indians, who are no less attractive to the evangelical clergy than they were to the Dominicans and Franciscans 450 years ago.

In Guatemala City, I spoke with the Reverend Ted Lindwall, the principal of a Baptist seminary on the outskirts of the capital. He was a tall, impressive-looking man in his mid-forties, with a resonant voice and piercing blue eyes. His hair was cut and blow-dried in the style of television preachers in the United States.

"The anti-Protestant attitude is still very strong," he said. "On the other hand, I think that many Catholics are beginning to realize that secularism is a greater enemy than Protestantism. In fact, many Catholics admire the biblical direction and fidelity to the faith of Protestants. There has been much copying by Catholics, especially of the Pentecostals' ecstatic religion, speaking in tongues, and so on, and with the full approval of the hierarchy.

"Most Protestants remain skeptical of what the liberal Catholics are doing," he went on. "They say, 'The Catholics sing our songs, and they have Scripture readings just as we do, but I don't see much difference in their lives.' I must say that I tend to agree. These developments have made Catholicism more vibrant, but the Catholics are not yet Christ-centered, and the Bible is still subsidiary to the institutions of the churches."

I asked Lindwall how Protestants, any more than Catholics, could ignore the injustice and brutality they saw on every side.

"In any society where power is in the hands of unredeemed men you're going to have abuses," he replied. "What would a missionary in Cuba say? My philosophy, and I think it is widely reflected, is that we can't expect much of any government until society itself becomes more basically Christian. I feel I can do much more to help Guatemala in trying to extend the real relationship of its people with Christ than in any other way. I don't think God has abandoned these countries. I think that He has his own instruments and that His plan is to raise men who truly believe in Him to power."

Six months later, when General Efraín Ríos Montt, an evangelical Christian, seized power, Lindwall might have been excused for thinking that he possessed the gift of prophecy.

It is easy to dislike the fundamentalist missionaries. They tend to be political and religious bigots. Their theology is narrow and simplistic. Some of them, according to information presented in Penny Lernoux's *Cry of the People* and elsewhere, have acted as informants for the CIA.

On balance, however, I think they do more good than harm. Going beyond their schools and clinics, they are showing hundreds of thousands of ordinary people in Guatemala and elsewhere in Central and Latin America how to organize themselves into congregations whose members are taught to help one another, spiritually and financially. Men are expected to take part in church work, which has always been a female monopoly in the traditional Catholic churches. Marital fidelity and the decent treatment of wives and children are demanded. Thrift is encouraged, and worldly success applauded. The prohibition of alcohol is a blessing in countries in which it is seldom drunk in moderation and is consumed most heavily by those who can least afford it.

On March 7, 1982, Guatemala voted. General Guevara, the military candidate, was declared the winner. Both Sandoval and Alejandro Maldonado Aguirre, the candidates, respectively, of the far right and the centrist coalition that included the Christian Democrats, said they had been defrauded. On March 16, Guevara's victory, with a reported 35 percent of the vote, was confirmed by the Guatemalan Congress. However, his inauguration never took place. On March 23, five days before the Salvadoran elections, a coup organized by junior army officers deposed President Lucas and replaced him by a three-member military junta headed by, of all people, Ríos Montt, the candidate of the Christian Democratic coalition in 1974. Ríos Montt was a member of a small evangelical sect, the Church of the Word. It was the first time, as far as anyone could determine, that an acknowledged Protestant had become a chief of state in Latin America.

The coup began in midmorning, when tanks and armored cars surrounded the Presidential Palace. At noon, its leaders ordered commercial radio stations to broadcast an appeal to Ríos Montt to come to their headquarters across the central square from the palace. At 4:00 P.M., Lucas yielded. He, his brother, Guevara, and their closest associates were put under house arrest.

That night, Ríos Montt spoke on television. "Eight years ago they cheated the people," he declared. "Four years ago they cheated the people. Just a few days ago they cheated the people again. We don't want any more political opportunists. We don't want the same faces." To the guerrillas and the death squads of the right, he said, "Lay down your arms. There will be no more dead bodies on the roadsides. We will execute by firing squad whoever goes against the law."

In concluding his address, Ríos Montt, his voice a trumpet of righteousness, declared, "I have confidence in my God, my master and my king, that He will guide me, because only He can grant or take away power."

Ten days later, when I arrived in Guatemala City from San Salvador, the capital still seemed drunk with happiness. The murders, kidnappings, and disappearances had all but ceased. The reason, clearly, was that many senior police and security officials had been arrested, and the Judicial Police, which was thought to provide the manpower for the death squads, had been abolished.

The American Embassy swore that it hadn't had anything to do with the coup and hadn't even had the faintest idea that it was coming. "I was supposed to meet with Guevara at 11:00 A.M. on the day of the coup," a senior official told me. "I got a call from him at 10:45. He said something was up and he had to cancel the appointment. 'None of our military units are responding to our phone calls,' he said. When we heard that the palace had been surrounded, we sent the defense attaché down to look into the situation. That led to the early reports that we were somehow involved."

A knowledgeable Guatemalan explained the circumstances that led up to the coup. "Everyone knew that President Lucas and his brother were stealing the country blind," he said. "The captains and lieutenants were out in the field for months at a time. A lot of them didn't like what they had to do to begin with, and they didn't even have decent radios and good light weapons, let alone helicopters. They knew that the money to buy them was going into the pockets of the colonels and generals, and there are a lot of them. In an army of 16,000 men, something like that, there are 900 officers, and maybe 250 of them are generals and colonels."

The junior officers chose Ríos Montt as their leader, he said, because of his reputation for honesty and his broad military experience. He had served as chief of staff of the army and commandant of the military college. Among the leaders of the coup were many officers who had admired him when they were cadets. Ríos Montt's familiarity with civilian politics was of less importance, I was assured, and may have even been a drawback.

"That's why the young officers wouldn't go for Sandoval or Sisniega," he said. "They simply don't trust civilians."

Sisniega looked grouchier than he had on my previous visit. When I asked him if he was disappointed not to be in the government, he said he preferred to serve as an informal adviser rather than to tie himself down in a secondary post.

"It's only for a little while," he said. "The military won't let Ríos Montt stay in power indefinitely. Then they will have to go to a civilian president because they won't be able to decide which one of them should have it."

But what about Ríos Montt's condemnation, I asked, of corrupt civilian politicians?

"He can't be talking about us [the National Liberation Movement] or the Christian Democrats either," he said bitterly. "We've been out of power for so long we haven't had a chance to be corrupt."

Sisniega had assured me, naturally, that his party had won the election, but when I went to see Luis Martínez Montt of the Christian Democrats—Vinicio Cerezo, the young head of the party, was in the United States, visiting his wife and children—he assured me that *his* party had won.

"I'll tell you what Mario Sandoval said after the election," Martínez recalled. "He said, 'I don't know whether we won or the Christian Democrats won, but I know that Guevara *didn't* win.'"

Martínez was full of praise for the planning and execution of the coup. "It was really remarkable," he said. "Not a shot was fired, not a drop of blood was shed. A lieutenant and four enlisted men seized the military academy and arrested the commandant. 'You can't do this,' he said. 'We're doing it,' the lieutenant said.

265

"The funny thing is that I don't think it was corruption or having to be out in the mountains that pissed off the junior officers," he went on. "It was that there were so many senior officers on active duty that the army had just created a new rank, senior captain, and that meant it would take four years longer for them to get promoted to major. I'll tell you something else you didn't know. One of the men who has been locked up is the inspector general of prisons. Too many of his guests disappeared."

"All we can do is hope," he said when I asked him if he thought Ríos Montt would hold elections. "Until now there has been absolute darkness. Now there's a small ray of light. If anyone can start the democratic process in Guatemala, Ríos Montt can."

That Sunday I walked over to the Church of the Word. It was situated not far from my hotel in the pleasantest section of the city. However, having been established only three or four years ago, it was still housed in a big tent, large enough to accommodate 700 worshipers. The tent, gaily striped in green and yellow, stands in the forecourt of the building that houses the sect's school. I arrived well before the start of services, and Francisco Bianchi, the administrator of the church, told me what had taken place there on the day of the coup.

"It was a Tuesday morning," he said. "That is the day on which parent-teacher meetings are held. As academic director of the school and of the Sunday Bible school, Efraín was present. At about 11:15 we started hearing that a coup was taking place. Then a parent, arriving for her appointment, said, 'Efraín, they're calling for you on the radio.' We turned on our radio and heard the announcement. Efraín then called the elders together and asked our advice. We prayed together and decided to see what developed.

"At about 1:00 P.M. an officer who was taking part in the coup, a Major Sánchez, telephoned. He told Efraín, 'We need your counsel.' 'What sort of counsel?' Efraín asked him. 'We want to talk to you,' the major said. 'It's very important that we get together.' So we prayed again, six of us, and Efraín decided that he should go. He wanted to do it quietly, so we borrowed a Volkswagen van with tinted glass windows from a member of the church. Another elder and I went with him. You know what happened after that.

"The funny thing was that last September the Christian Democrats asked Efraín to be their presidential candidate again," he added. "We spent three days in fasting and praying, and we decided that it was not the time. On the first day, we were playing volleyball and Efraín sprained his knee. He had to have a cast put on it. When he came back, one of us said, 'I think it's pretty obvious that the Lord doesn't want you to run.' ''

"Efraín still worships with us, of course," he said. "I expect him here today. He also remains active in our church in the home program—the meetings we have in members' homes on Tuesday nights—but we have had to replace him as the school administrator."

A few minutes later, there was a stir, and Ríos Montt and his wife, María Teresa, accompanied by a couple of discreet bodyguards, entered the tent. Ríos Montt, who was 55 years old, was a wiry man of medium height. His eyes reflected sharp intelligence. He had a seamed face and a prominent nose. His full head of hair was still raven black, but his mustache had turned silver.

He and his wife took their seats quietly, and the hymn singing continued without interruption. Although it was Palm Sunday, the only palms in evidence were growing outside the tent. There was no holy communion, no prayer book, and nothing that could be described as a liturgy. Not even a hymnal. The words were projected on a screen.

Five officials from the mother temple, Gospel Outreach, in Eureka, California, were present that day. James Durkin, the founder of the movement, preached the sermon. He discussed Joseph's dream and then said, "Another miracle has taken place. God has raised up a leader of his nation, a man who heard the teaching here, and who said, 'I know how to give orders, but that is not enough. Now I want to learn how to serve as Jesus served.' ''

When the service ended, Ríos Montt quickly departed, ignoring the journalists who were present. Durkin, who remained to answer questions, said that he was a former minister of the Assemblies of God, a Pentecostalist sect. Gospel Outreach grew out of a Christian community that he founded near Eureka in 1970. It was called the Lighthouse Ranch.

"We first came down to Guatemala in 1976, bringing relief supplies after the earthquake," he said. "And the church just sort of took shape."

Escuintla, of which Mario Ríos Montt, a younger brother of the general, is the bishop, is a market town about 50 miles south of the capital. It is dominated by an early 19th-century cathedral that is badly in need of repair. There is a long, deep crack across the façade that was caused by the earthquake of 1976. Drunks lie on the cool stone in the shade of the cathedral and pick themselves up to urinate against it. The scarred old center door was surrounded by beggars—a legless man, a macrocephalic boy, a couple of girls, scarcely more than children themselves, carrying babies, and many old women dressed in black. Just inside the door, an old Indian played a wooden flute, and another banged a small drum to no discernible rhythm. Dusty pink gauze hung in festoons over the center aisle. Birds nested under the roof. The votive figures—the crucified Christ, the Virgin in glory, nameless missionary saints in brown robes—seemed dusty, even behind glass, and somehow unlooked-at.

The bishop was at his residence, a half mile from the cathedral. Like his brother, Mario Ríos Montt had come to resemble some archetype of his calling. He was mild-mannered and looked rather harried.

"I am sorry, but I can give you only 30 minutes," he said. "I must conduct a service at the cathedral. You have seen it?" He shrugged. "It is very difficult. I have only four priests in my diocese—for 500,000 Catholics. There are probably five times that many Protestant missionaries."

I asked Bishop Ríos Montt to tell us something about his family.

"Of course," he said. "We are from Huehuetenango [pronounced way-way-ten-ango] in the western part of the country. There were 13 children, 10 of whom survived infancy. My father began working when he was seven years old, became a clerk in a store, and then got a job in public works. He is dead, but our mother is still alive and well at the age of 75. She was always a great example to us. Sometimes she had to feed the entire family for 25 centavos a day, but she made sure that we were all able to attend school.

"One brother, Julio, was murdered in 1974, very cruelly and under mysterious circumstances," he went on. "It was the year that my brother the general was running for the presidency. Julio was working in his campaign, and we think that may have had something to do with his death. Efraín and I have not been very close. With his being a general and me a bishop, we thought it was unwise. I didn't want my priests to think I might be taking orders from a military man, and vice versa. He did not consult me on his conversion, but we remain respectful of each other's views.

"I happened to be in Guatemala City when the coup took place," he said. "I was less surprised than I was worried. That wasn't any bouquet of flowers that they handed him. I have seen him only once since then.

I was a member of a delegation of bishops that met with him last week, and I must say his greeting to us was much warmer than we ever received from his two predecessors. We carried a letter with us, and the opinions he expressed were very close to those that were contained in the letter. He said he wished the church well, and I believed him—but he is not the only person in the government.''

The junta held its first formal press conference while I was in the capital. It took place in one of the highly decorated reception salons of the Presidential Palace. Ríos Montt's two colleagues on the junta were present, but he did all the talking, presenting what he called the 14 points that would animate his government.

The 14 points summarized everything that had been missing from Guatemalan government and society since the arrival of the *conquistadores*. The first was "To make the citizenry feel that the authorities are at the service of the people and not the people at the service of the authorities." The second and third were "To seek the reconciliation of all Guatemalans and a peace and security based on an absolute respect for human rights." Others provided for the creation of honest electoral and judicial systems and the elimination of official corruption. The 11th was the most radical. It called for improving the standard of living of the populace so as to diminish the existing "contradictions"—a term frequently used by Marxists.

When the press conference was over, I introduced myself and asked a couple of questions of my own. Did he, I asked, have any plans for land reform?

"The matter is under study," he said. "It is nothing that we can rush into. What we are certain of is that it takes more than bullets to end a rebellion."

Would he, I asked, try to improve relations with the United States?

"Absolutely," he replied. "No country in the world can fight against the United States."

16

Weekend in Belize

WHEN I ARRIVED in Belize, it was immediately apparent that while I was still in Central America, geographically speaking, I had passed, in every other way, from darkness into light. Belize had been fully independent for six months, and any truly Central American government would already have been rent into savagely conflicting factions, spreading death and destruction across the land.

But no one was murdered or disappeared in Belize, no one was in rebellion, and refugees from El Salvador and Haiti were finding it a garden of peace and security. The only reminder of the dangerous world that lay beyond its borders was the presence, at the request of the Belizean government, of a British military force of 1,800 men. Its function was to guard the country against an invasion by Guatemala, which had claimed the territory as its own for 150 years.

Belize is the northernmost extension, in effect, of the Miskito Coast—the region that was colonized and ruled, de facto, by Britain long before the nations of Central America achieved independence. The first settlers on the coast supported themselves by cutting logwood, the name that was given for no reason other than that it was exported in the form of logs, to the *Haematoxylon campechianum,* a tree that produced an excellent black dye for woolens. The Spanish tried many times to regain their lost territory. The final attempt, as Narda Dobson noted in her *A History of Belize,* was made in 1798. A Spanish fleet was driven off by a much smaller British force, assisted by the settlers, who mounted cannon on logwood rafts.

In 1862, Britain, after failing to reach an agreement with Guatemala as to its status, formally annexed the territory. Guatemala later rejected British proposals that the question of sovereignty be decided by the International Court of Justice. In the years following the Second World

War, a Belizean independence movement appeared. Its leader was a former Catholic seminarian named George Price. The People's United Party, which he founded, won control of the colonial legislature in 1957. In 1964, when British Honduras became a self-governing colony, Price was elected Prime Minister. He still held that office in September, 1981, when Belize became independent.

Six months earlier, Britain, Guatemala, and Belize initialed the draft of a treaty. In return for recognition of Belize, Guatemala was to receive rights of transit across Belizean territory to both Guatemalan and Belizean ports, the use of two offshore islets, and the joint construction of a road and a pipeline from the newly discovered oil fields of the Petén region, which Belize cuts off from direct access to the coast.

No sooner had the draft agreement been signed than rightist politicians in Guatemala began denouncing it as an indelible stain on the national honor. The Lucas government began raising objections. In Belize, where no one wanted to become part of Guatemala, there was a day of strikes and rioting.

Belize became independent on schedule, but Price asked Britain to keep its forces there until the dispute with Guatemala was finally settled. When I arrived, the force had been brought to a heightened state of readiness, and a British naval squadron lay offshore. It seemed not out of the question that Ríos Montt, despite his statements to the contrary, might try to emulate Argentina, which had just seized the Falklands.

Not that Belize is a great prize. It is slightly larger than El Salvador but has a population of only 150,000, a third of whom live in Belize City and its environs. Its Caribbean coast is mostly mangrove swamp, cut off from access to the sea for other than small vessels by the longest barrier reef this side of Australia.

Belizeans are not, by and large, agriculturally inclined. The sugar plantations and mills are owned by British concerns, and the citrus groves and what remains of the timber industry by Americans. Most of the country's food is grown by some 5,000 bearded, black-suited German-speaking Mennonites. They migrated from Mexico in the 1950's, purchased 25,000 acres of scrub and jungle for $5 an acre, and set to work. In return, they received a blanket exemption from military service and the payment of social security taxes, which violate the precepts of their pacifistic and self-reliant religion. The Mennonites, who live in three communities, do not mingle with the rest of the population and take no part in politics.

The potential of Belize, such as it is, is stunted by the lack of roads, ports, and processing facilities. Aside from the highway that links Belize City with Belmopan, the capital, which lies 50 miles in the interior, out of the path of hurricanes, the country has few hard-surface roads. The coastal settlements are linked only by boat.

Belmopan must be the least visible national capital in the world. The population is officially given as 4,500, but when I visited there, about 4,400 were in hiding. Only a couple of government buildings have been opened, and instead of houses and shops, there are signs saying where they will stand. Government employees who are assigned to work in Belmopan commute from Belize City each day. When the offices are closed, as they were during my visit, it is deserted.

In a humanitarian gesture that also will help populate the countryside between Belmopan and the Guatemalan border, which lies only 40 miles away, the government granted 50-acre farm sites to several hundred Salvadoran refugees. The United States and the United Nations have provided financial support. To balance the arrival of these Spanish speakers, an approximately equal number of black French-speaking Haitians were also being admitted. They are expected to adopt English rather than Spanish as their second language and to identify themselves with the black and Creole segments of the population. ("Creole" is the term used in Belize to describe mixtures of races other than *mestizo*.)

The present population is divided equally between English and Spanish speakers, 40 percent each, with the remainder fluent in both or, in the case of a small number of unassimilated Indians deep in the interior, neither. There has been little friction between the two major groups. However, the Creoles, who have been politically dominant, are fearful that the tide is turning against them. Not only are Spanish speakers arriving, but Creoles are steadily departing, many of them as legal and illegal immigrants to the United States.

Price, who is well known for his piety, began celebrating Holy Week early and thus declined to be interviewed. He was averse even to exchanging a few amiable words, as I found when I approached him as he was leaving Good Friday services at the cathedral. Price glared at me as I introduced myself and strode away without a word. His bodyguards, burly young fellows in whom the bachelor prime minister is said to take an avuncular interest, shooed me away.

Price was 62 years old when Belize gained its independence, but he looks much younger. He is tall and slim and dresses carefully, even when he is wearing only a sports shirt and slacks. He is a member of a well-established Creole family, and the Scottish blood of which he often speaks with pride can be seen in his features. As prime minister, he receives $8,000 a year, and although he is said to have some private means, he tries to live within his salary. His residence, the house in which he grew up, is a ramshackle two-story frame structure in the center of the city. Since few of the houses in Belize have been painted recently, Price has also let his crack and peel.

Belize City, aside from a couple of blocks of offices and warehouses, has a rather endearing Catfish Row appearance. Open storm sewers run down the sides of the streets, and the residents store their drinking water in large wood or concrete vats in their yards. The city is built on either side of Haulover Creek, which is perhaps 100 feet wide and was flowing swiftly when I was there. A few miles above the city, the water is as clear as gin, and youngsters dive from the trees that shade it, keeping a wary eye out for alligators and fresh-water sharks.

Price has dominated Belize's politics for so long that, as one journalist told me, "He knows damned near every voter in the country by name." He is affable in public, except to me, but a bit remote, as befits the father of his country. His opponents call him self-important and vindictive and too much under the influence of the Jesuits, who ran the seminary he attended. An American Jesuit is the country's only Catholic bishop. Price's faults, whatever they may be, vanish in comparison with his political virtues. His opposition, although excluded from patronage in the time-honored democratic way, is not harassed. Even they acknowledge that Price is honest and hardworking. His government, by the standards of the region, is a dream of probity. Elsewhere in Central America, for example, only the people who own the judges go to court. Belizeans, confident that no one can put his thumb on the scales of justice and enjoying the British ambiance of wigs and gowns, are notoriously litigious. Price himself was suing a local scandal sheet for libel when I was there, and everyone assumed that the judgment would be on the merits of the case.

In the absence of revolutionary movements and civic outrages, the gossip in Belize is largely restricted to such scandals as the arrest of a Mennonite, a pillar of his church, on a charge of growing marijuana for export, and the crowning of two queens of the independence festival, one of each sex.

* * *

273

The Belize Defense Force was being trained by the United States in Panama. That probably meant it would turn out to be poorly led and disciplined, mired in paper work, and badly tailored. The British contingent, as I saw when I went out to its headquarters at the airport, displayed the same panache that I had observed in Ulster and Hong Kong and in such lost bastions of empire as British Guiana, Singapore, and Fiji.

A captain of the Royal Marines led me around the compound, pointing out the four Harrier "jump jets," which were to prove so useful in the reconquest of the Falklands, in revetments under camouflage netting, and antiaircraft guns and missiles. A couple of young soldiers wearing khaki shorts, short-sleeved shirts, and berets with cockades walked past.

"They're the Royal Irish Rangers," the captain said. "There's a battalion assigned here. We rotate them in and out every six months or so. The chaps like it in the winter, not so much in the summer."

He led me into an office, dimmed the lights, and turned on a slide projector. An outline map of Belize appeared on the screen.

"It's all quiet right now, but you never know what may happen," he said. "Guatemala's official maps don't show any national boundary, and the Guates keep calling Belize their twenty-third department. Anyhow, there's a company of the Royal Irish on the border, supported by armored cars, spread out around the highway. [He pointed the position out on the slide.] There are a couple of platoons in the north around Orange Walk, but most of the force is down in the south, in the mountains along the Guates' Atlantic corridor. We've got another company of the Royal Irish and a company of Gurkhas."

It was even money, I suggested, that the Gurkhas, those fierce little men from Nepal, could beat the entire Guatemalan army.

"They could certainly give them a damned good thwacking," said the captain, "although I hope it doesn't come to that. Anyhow, they're very much at home down there, and they get along very well with the Maya. After all, they're distant cousins."

17
Mexican Masquerade

FOR 300 YEARS of colonial rule, the viceroyalty of New Spain, with its capital at Mexico City, had authority over the captaincy general of Guatemala, which encompassed all of the provinces of Central America except Panama. It might have been supposed that this domination would continue after independence, but Mexico's brief invasion and attempted annexation of Guatemala and El Salvador in 1822 had no sequel. The viceregal authority had been, in any case, largely theoretical. No one was anxious to make tours of inspection that required traveling hundreds of miles by muleback across mountain, jungle, and swamp. These difficulties multiplied after independence. The royal fleet was no longer available, and the *camino real* fell into disrepair.

More important, coups and rebellions were no less frequent in Mexico in its first 25 years of independence than they were in the nations of Central America. Then, in 1845, came the disaster of the war with the United States, which cost Mexico half of its national territory. As soon as it recovered from the amputation, its leaders fell to fighting again. By 1858, there were two governments, one Liberal and anticlerical, the other Conservative. The Liberals' leader was Benito Juárez, an Indian from Oaxaca. He had been educated for the priesthood, but his dream of a just and honest government led him into politics. In 1860, his army recaptured Mexico City, from which he had been ousted three years earlier.

With an empty treasury, Juárez had no choice but to suspend the payment of interest on Mexico's foreign debt. It was the excuse that the European powers, which favored the Conservatives, had been waiting for. In 1862, British, French, and Spanish troops, forming a joint collection force, landed at Veracruz. Meanwhile, Conservative leaders had persuaded Napoleon III that the imposition of a European

prince would tranquilize Mexico, and he persuaded a Hapsburg prince-
ling, Maximilian, to accept the throne. When Britain and Spain learned
that their troops would be helping realize Napoleon III's dreams of imperial glory, they withdrew them. Napoleon III sent reinforcements to
take their place. This French army defeated Juárez's exhausted and
badly equipped troops and drove him out of the capital once again.
Juárez retreated to the Texas border. The town where he made his
headquarters now bears his name, Ciudad Juárez. He appealed to the
United States, which had recognized his government, for assistance,
but President Lincoln also had a war on his hands.

Maximilian, meanwhile, was turning out to be a Liberal in disguise.
He confirmed Juárez's reforms and denounced his own supporters for
their corruption and rapacity. Speaking of the army, the clergy, and the
judiciary, he wrote, "They live for money alone." Juárez, rejecting
Maximilian's offers of conciliation, carried on his struggle. With the
end of the Civil War, the United States made its displeasure known in
Paris. Napoleon III, seeing nothing but trouble ahead, withdrew his
troops. Maximilian, however, refused to leave his throne. Taking personal command of what remained of his army, he met Juárez's forces at
Querétaro, north of the capital. Maximilian was defeated and captured.
The implacable Juárez ordered his execution.

An uneasy peace continued until Juárez's death in 1872. Four years
later, Porfirio Díaz, one of his generals, ousted Juárez's chosen successor and proclaimed himself president. Díaz presented himself as a reformer. His slogan was "Effective suffrage and no reelection." After
the completion of his first term, he withdrew in favor of a complaisant
underling. He returned to power in 1884, however, and, under the
same slogan, ruled without interruption until 1911.

Díaz was a *mestizo*, born, like Juárez, in Oaxaca, but his policies
could scarcely have been more different. He permitted the great landowners to enlarge their already enormous estates, mainly at the expense of the Indians, who lost the best of what remained of their communal lands. His supporters received enormous grants at knockdown
prices. There were *haciendas* of 1,000 square miles, sweating tens of
thousands of peons, but 99 percent of the population didn't own
enough land to be buried in.

Díaz also opened Mexico to foreign investment. American and British capital flooded into the country. Textile mills and railroads were
built. The gold, silver, and copper mines were reopened. In 1900, Díaz

granted the first foreign oil concession. In 1904, the first major strike was made, in the Tampico region on the Gulf of Mexico. Exports of coffee, sugar, and cotton doubled and doubled again. For the first time, the peso became a hard currency. Mexican bonds were gilt-edged investments.

In the cities, Díaz's police and, in the countryside, his *rurales,* a mounted paramilitary force, imposed iron discipline and summary justice. Mexico's wealth increased enormously during the Díaz years, but the real wages of Mexican workers dropped by 25 percent or more. In 1910, when he announced that he would run for the presidency yet again, a rebellion broke out. Francisco Madero, an opposition leader who was living in Texas, crossed the Rio Grande and gathered a motley army. Peons and Indians, miners and factory workers joined him by the tens of thousands. They fought with the fury and fatalism of men who have nothing to lose.

Within a year, Díaz had fled to Paris, and Madero was installed as president. It was not the end of a dark period, but the beginning of 15 years of warfare, massacre, and destruction that took the lives of 10 to 15 percent of Mexico's population. From the beginning, Madero was victimized, as democrats in Latin America always have been, by his lack of ruthlessness. After only 15 months in power, he was deposed by one of his generals, Victoriano Huerta, who had been, before changing sides, one of Díaz's most savage commanders. Huerta imprisoned Madero and his vice-president. A few weeks later, while still in custody, they were murdered.

As it became clear that Huerta saw himself as another Díaz, new rebellions broke out. Francisco "Pancho" Villa and Venustiano Carranza raised armies in the north, and Emiliano Zapata and Álvaro Obregón did so in the south. In February, 1914, President Woodrow Wilson recognized the rebels as belligerents, permitting them to buy arms legally in the United States. Britain, which dominated the expanding oil industry, and Germany, which had important commercial interests, supported Huerta.

By April, Wilson had American warships cruising off Veracruz and Tampico. Learning that a German merchant ship carrying arms for Huerta was about to dock, Wilson ordered the seizure of the Veracruz customs house. Huerta withdrew his troops, but the cadets at the naval academy and hundreds of volunteers remained to oppose the landing of the marines. The American ships bombarded the city. Fighting went on for 12 hours, and before Veracruz fell, 126 Mexicans and 19 Americans had been killed. Even Carranza, one of the rebel leaders Wilson meant to help, was outraged by the violation of Mexican sovereignty.

Wilson's adventure ended untidily. The arms were landed 100 miles down the coast. Meanwhile, as the rebels advanced on Mexico City, Huerta resigned and went into exile aboard a German cruiser. Like Díaz, he did not depart empty-handed. According to Friedrich Katz's *The Secret War in Mexico,* the ship's skipper reported to Berlin that Huerta had chests of gold, currency, and securities and that his wife and daughters were loaded with diamonds.

Carranza emerged as president and immediately halted the distribution of *hacienda* lands to the peasants. Zapata and Villa turned against him. They captured Mexico City but had a falling-out, and Carranza returned in triumph. His troops pursued Zapata south and Villa north to Chihuahua, his native state. Villa was defeated there, the United States having permitted Carranza's army to cross the border to attack him from the rear.

By way of retaliation, in 1916, Villa led the remnant of his cavalry into New Mexico. He shot up the hamlet of Columbus, New Mexico, killing two or three persons. Without asking leave of Carranza, Wilson dispatched troops to Mexico to bring Villa to justice. The troops fruitlessly beat their way through the desert until they were withdrawn in February, 1917.

In 1917, during a brief pause in the fighting, Carranza was persuaded to call a constitutional convention. It adopted a document that would have brought a new dawn of freedom and justice to the ravaged country if Carranza or anyone else had observed it. Zapata kept on fighting for *tierra y libertad*. Carranza put a price on his head, and, in 1919, Zapata was betrayed by one of his men and murdered.

Carranza's turn came the following year. He was deposed by his ablest general, Álvaro Obregón. Carranza followed tradition by loading all the gold in the treasury aboard a special train and headed for Veracruz and exile. In another time-honored tradition, a trusted associate betrayed him. The train was attacked by persons unknown. Carranza fled into the hills but was hunted down and murdered. The gold was not recovered.

With the accession of Obregón, the fighting died away. Villa, the last of the rebel leaders, made his peace and accepted a large ranch in Durango from a grateful government. Villa kept his promise to stay out of politics, but unfortunately for him, he remained highly popular, and in 1923, he, too, was murdered.

Obregón's peace was short-lived. One provision of the constitution of 1917 that was observed was the disestablishment of the Catholic Church, which had slavishly supported Díaz. Its lands, endowments, the churches themselves became the property of the state. The church was forbidden to operate schools. The number of ordinations was limited. Foreign priests were expelled. Anticlerical officials went even further by persecuting priests and desecrating churches.

In 1926, the Vatican retaliated by placing Mexico under an interdict. No services could be held, no masses offered, no baptisms, no last rites or funerals. When the government refused to yield, the priests called the faithful to rebellion. They called themselves *cristeros,* and there were many pious women in their ranks. They were unarmed and unorganized, but they prayed for a miracle that did not occur. What followed was less the suppression of an uprising than the massacre of thousands. Scores of priests were killed or executed. Six bishops were exiled. Obregón had just been elected to a second, nonconsecutive term in 1928 when he was murdered by a *cristero.* The interdict was lifted in 1929, and an uneasy peace was restored.

Since then, Mexico has been peaceful. Not coincidentally, during this period, it has been governed by a single party. Its name has changed a couple of times—it is now known as the Institutional Revolutionary party, or PRI—but its dedication to stability has not. Only the Communist party of the Soviet Union has held power longer. Since the advent of the PRI, no president has served more than the one term prescribed by the constitution, only one has served less than a full term, and there have been no significant uprisings or attempted coups. No other country in Latin America, and few in the world, can say the same.

During this long period of peace and comparative prosperity, however, Mexico has had only one president who can be described as distinguished. He was Lázaro Cárdenas, who ruled from 1934 to 1940. Cárdenas set up his own New Deal, and most of Mexico's social legislation dates from his administration. What he may be best remembered for, however, was his expropriation of the oil industry. The date on which he signed the decree is a national holiday.

For more than 35 years, Mexicans had angrily watched British interests, which controlled 60 percent of the production and refining, and American interests, which owned almost all the rest, pocket enormous profits. In 1921, for example, while Mexico was being torn to pieces

279

by revolution, it produced 193,000,000 barrels of oil, a quarter of the world total. Given the uncertainties of the times, the oil companies exploited their concessions as rapidly as possible, and the waste was enormous. Production declined throughout the 1920's. The companies saw no reason to prospect for new fields in Mexico when cheap oil from Texas, Oklahoma, and the Middle East was readily available. By 1932, Mexican production had fallen to 33,000,000 barrels, most of which was being consumed domestically.

In 1936, the oil workers, with Cárdenas's encouragement, formed a union. It demanded a large increase in wages that the companies said they could not afford. Cárdenas had secured company documents that showed that their profits on Mexican oil were several times higher than in the United States. An arbitrator found for the union. The companies appealed to the Mexican Supreme Court, lost again, but still refused to grant the increase.

In 1938, the union, backed by the president, called a strike, and on the same day, Cárdenas nationalized the industry as Petróleos Mexicanos, or PEMEX. Because Cárdenas promised to pay fair compensation, Roosevelt was deaf to the pleas of the companies, to which, in any case, he owed nothing politically. Britain, whose companies, primarily the Shell group, had suffered the greater loss, found itself unable to act alone.

To the professed astonishment of the dispossessed owners, PEMEX successfully operated the fields, refineries, and terminals. However, its oil was boycotted, and equipment manufacturers refused to sell to it. Only with the start of the Second World War did Mexico cease to be a petroleum pariah, and not until the 1960's was agreement reached with the British interests and final payment made.

State ownership of oil has become, along with the land reform, the iron collar put on the Catholic Church, and the constitution of 1917, the foundation stone on which the myth of a "revolutionary" Mexico has been erected. The reality seems to be that the country has been either marking time or marching in the opposite direction since Cárdenas left office.

Land reform and the limits placed on ownership of irrigated land became a dead letter. Token distributions were made from time to time, but by the late 1970's even these had all but ceased. Official statistics are incomplete and unreliable, I was told by specialists in the field, but it does not appear that more than 10 or 15 percent of the land that made up the great *haciendas* in 1910 was given to the peasants, as either family parcels or communal *ejidos,* and what they got was the poorest and driest.

Moreover, nowhere in Latin America is the gap between rich and poor wider. The top 10 percent of the population gets 40 percent of the income, and the top 1 percent probably gets half of that. The bottom 40 percent receives 10 percent and lives a life no better than the poor of Guatemala or El Salvador.

The constitution of 1917, providing for a representative government, free elections, the separation of powers, checks and balances, an independent judiciary, a free press, and a great many other good things, remains the national charter. Orators never tire of hailing it as a work of sublime genius, ignoring the fact that it has no bearing on the way the country is governed by the Institutional Revolutionary party.

There is nothing revolutionary about the PRI. It sustains itself by patronage and graft, electoral fraud, nepotism, the co-optation of opposition leaders, and, no more frequently than is absolutely necessary, intimidation and murder. The party's back rooms are darker and smokier than any others. Its presidential candidates are chosen in a secrecy so complete that only a few people even know how it is done. The best guess is that the incumbent president, either acting alone or, more likely, in consultation with former presidents and senior party officials, makes the selection.

In recent times, the president has been a bureaucrat like López Portillo or his successor, Miguel de la Madrid, who had spent his entire career in government, usually in the ministries of the Interior or Finance. Some presidents seem to move a little to the left, like Luis Echeverría Álvarez, or to the right, like his successor, López Portillo, who left office at the end of 1982, but in fact, they scarcely move at all.

Despite what the constitution may say, each one rules for six years with scarcely less power than Porfirio Díaz had. The only function of the legislature is to applaud the president's acts. The nation's judges are the party's faithful servants. The free press is printed on paper it can buy only by government allotment. Many of its publishers, editors, and reporters receive government payments. To enhance the illusion of democracy while splintering the anti-PRI vote, the government also subsidizes opposition candidates. For the same reason, 25 percent of the seats in the lower house of the Congress are reserved for them.

These disagreeable facts tended to be overlooked during the long period of peace and relative prosperity that continued until the mid-1970's. Production increased by at least 5 percent a year, and often more, keeping well ahead of the 3.5 percent annual growth of the population. Investment by American concerns, notably automobile makers, increased rapidly and totaled $8 billion by the end of the decade. The new professional, managerial, and technical class tended to believe that the only alternative to the PRI was a return to chaos.

By 1977, however, the economy was stagnating, export prices were down, inflation up, and the peso had just been devalued by 40 percent. López Portillo, who had just taken office, announced that Mexico's troubles would soon be over. PEMEX, stimulated by the soaring price of oil, had found enormous new fields on the Gulf Coast. Mexico's proved reserves of oil soared from 3.5 billion barrels to at least 50 billion—a figure surpassed only by Saudi Arabia, the Soviet Union, Kuwait, and Iran. Each barrel was worth at least $35 at the time, or a total of $1.75 *trillion.* Probable reserves were estimated at another 25 billion barrels.

As López Portillo described the coming paradise of high technology, prosperity, and social justice, the entire nation could have been excused for thinking that it had won the *gran premio* in the national lottery. The president, whose father was a senior official of PEMEX, was well aware that Mexico had derived no profit from its first oil boom. He pledged himself to abjure the reckless spending of the sheikhs or the shah and to safeguard the national patrimony.

"We have to make use of our oil in order to develop the rest of our economy—bearing in mind always that oil is a nonrenewable resource," López Portillo stated. "The right use of our oil will enable us to solve the basic problem of the country, which is unemployment, by the turn of the century."

The *técnicos,* the best minds in Mexico, drew up plans for refineries, pipelines, ports, fleets of tankers, and petrochemical plants that would be necessary to exploit the discoveries. Mexico's external debt was already $12 billion, which was large enough to worry the World Bank. Even so, the biggest commercial banks in the United States, Europe, and Japan, anxious to lend, or recycle, as they said, the tens of billions of dollars in deposits they had received from the Middle East, offered whatever sums Mexico needed on easy terms. American oil companies were begging to buy all the oil and gas that Mexico could spare.

What a rapturous moment for López Portillo! Until then, Mexican presidents had always been painfully aware that the United States was far more important to Mexico than Mexico was to the United States. Mexico sold 65 percent of its exports, mainly agricultural, to the United States, while the United States sold only about 3 percent of its exports to Mexico. The money sent home by Mexican workers in the United States totaled $3 billion a year, and American tourists spent close to $1 billion a year in Mexico. Without these sums, the deficit in Mexico's balance of payments could not have been tolerated and the rate of unemployment, especially in the northern regions, might have become socially dangerous.

Now, for the first time in its history, Mexico had something that the United States needed badly and did not seem likely to take by force. This unfamiliar situation tended to make the leaders of both countries irritable and led, inevitably, to misunderstandings. In 1977, the Carter administration vetoed a long-term gas sale because it thought that the price was too high. López Portillo had thought he had a firm deal and he did not conceal his anger. He limited total oil exports to 1,500,000 barrels a day, and decreed that no more than half could be sold to the United States, no matter how great the thirst. When President Carter made a placatory visit to Mexico in February, 1979, López Portillo lectured him publicly. "Among permanent, not casual, neighbors," he stated, "surprise moves and sudden deceit or abuse are poisonous fruit that sooner or later have a reverse effect."

Carter tried, it seemed, to lighten the atmosphere. He made a jocular reference to "Montezuma's Revenge," the diarrhea that often afflicts American tourists in Mexico who eat unwashed fruit and vegetables, thereby intensifying López Portillo's anger. The State Department, I was told on excellent authority, had made a point of cautioning Carter against using the expression, which Mexicans regard as profoundly insulting. That he did so was not necessarily an indication of a defective memory. He and López Portillo were reported to have developed an instant mutual antipathy.

Mexico's cordial relations with the Soviet Union and Cuba are part of a foreign policy in which Machiavelli could have taken pride. By refusing to follow the lead of the United States in branding Cuba a hemispheric outlaw, Mexico reasserted its rather tattered revolutionary tradition and gained the sympathy of Third World leaders and leftist intellectuals. Few readers of Communist or socialist publications, for example, are likely to be aware of Mexico's income distribution figures.

In return for this support, Fidel Castro appears to have agreed to do nothing to stimulate real revolution in Mexico. Cuban comment was muted when, in 1968, the security forces shot dead perhaps 100 persons and wounded hundreds at a leftist demonstration in Mexico City.

Although the government had obligingly created a pantheon of martyrs, no one worshiped at their shrine. The Communist party of Mexico remains so weak that it is entirely legal. It provides no leadership, or even encouragement, for the *campesinos* and Indians who from time to time try to occupy idle land or defend themselves against the illegal seizure of their own holdings.

Although the United States grumbles about the aid and comfort that Mexico gives to the enemy, my conversations in Mexico City and elsewhere suggest that Washington is not altogether displeased.

"The last thing in the world we want," a diplomat told me, "are Communist guerrillas in the Sierra Maestra or the shantytowns of Mexico City and Monterrey bombing Ford and General Motors assembly lines or slipping across the border into East Los Angeles, San Antonio, and the Imperial Valley. If Mexico can keep Castro out with words, how bad can that be?"

The reluctance of successive American presidents to deal decisively with the question of illegal immigration from Mexico has been at least in part an expression of gratitude for the subtle way in which Mexico, while seeming to embrace Cuba and the Soviet Union, has put a hammerlock on their activities there. Those who appreciate it most are the American manufacturers and food processors whose Mexican operations are enormously profitable.

In January, 1979, Mexico wildly welcomed Pope John Paul II. Because of the country's official anticlericalism, no senior government officials appeared in public with him, and López Portillo received him only in private. (Mexican presidents invert the custom of American presidents by never being seen in church.) It was also reported at the time that on the Pope's Mexican visa the space for "occupation" was left blank.

Throughout the rest of the year, López Portillo signified his intention of increasing Mexican influence in Central America. In May, Fidel Castro, as though to balance the Pope, paid his first visit to Mexico since coming to power, and the same month, Mexico became the first country in the region to sever relations with the Somoza government.

In the summer of 1980, López Portillo visited Cuba, Nicaragua, Panama, Costa Rica, Venezuela, and Brazil. He agreed to provide PEMEX crews and equipment to help Castro look for oil. In January, 1981, López Portillo permitted the Salvadoran insurgents to establish a headquarters in Mexico City. In June, he conferred with President Reagan in Washington and made his comment that the State Department's White

Paper on El Salvador was "an insult to the intelligence." In August, Mexico and France's Socialist government issued the joint declaration that gave the Salvadoran insurgents the status of "a representative political force." It was the first display of French concern for the region since Maximilian's execution. Not entirely by coincidence, perhaps, France had just received a daily ration of 100,000 barrels of Mexican oil.

While López Portillo was making the world aware that Mexico was now a regional power to be reckoned with, the oil famine that had made it all possible was turning into a glut. His advisers warned him that price reductions were inevitable. They told him that Mexico was facing a disastrous inflation and urged him to cut back on his grandiose development plans, to reduce foreign borrowing, and gradually to devalue the peso. It was supported by the Banco de Mexico at a rate of 26 to the dollar, thereby subsidizing the foreign investments of the Mexican rich.

López Portillo, who had based his administration on the creation of 1,000,000 jobs a year, the minimum he regarded as necessary to meet the needs of the expanding population and to preserve social peace, refused to contract the economy or even to permit PEMEX to cut its export prices to match the competition. As a result, Mexico's customers, including France, began canceling their contracts and buying elsewhere. In June, Jorge Díaz Serrano, the head of PEMEX, took the only step possible. Without asking the president's permission, he cut prices $4 a barrel. Although he was an old crony, López Portillo immediately dismissed him, but it proved impossible to go back to the old prices. The loss of revenue to Mexico was something like $3 billion a year.

In September, López Portillo announced that De la Madrid, the Minister of Planning and the Budget, would be the PRI's candidate for president in 1982. De la Madrid, a *técnico* with a degree in public administration from Harvard, was known as an economic conservative. In his acceptance speech, he gave a greater emphasis than usual to the problem of corruption. The chairman of the party resigned in protest.

In October, López Portillo presided at a 22-nation conference that was meant to symbolize Mexico's, and his, new eminence. It was described as "a North-South summit meeting," and it proposed to explore the means by which wealth might be transferred from rich to poor countries. The conference was held in Cancún, the resort on the Yucatán Peninsula. Among those present was Reagan, who was meeting López Portillo for the fourth time that year. Reagan agreed to attend on condition that Castro not be present. Aside from demonstrating that he was more desirable than Castro, Reagan's presence probably had more to do with oil and gas than with any sympathy for the purpose of the conference, which, aside from having engorged López Portillo's ego, seemed to have accomplished absolutely nothing.

One of the people I spoke with in Mexico City was an economist who was attached to a research institute. He was a native of another Latin American country and thus spoke with a degree of detachment. Because he regarded himself as a guest in Mexico, he asked me not to identify him.

"One of the great problems of Mexico, and of the rest of Latin America, is that its citizens have no sense of any duty they owe to the state," he began by saying. "Mexicans are very individualistic and very anarchic. The only reason that the political system, with all its flaws, works here is that it gives enough hope to enough people. I think I can also say that I think I see the beginnings of a sense of responsibility and accountability.

"There is very little doubt that almost everyone else who works for the government, PEMEX, the National Railroad, and other state enterprises has to kick back a percentage of his salary to the PRI and work for it at election time. In return, the clerks and police and even the garbage men get a license to commit extortion, and the people above them get their share. No business at any town hall in Mexico can be completed in less than 10 years unless you take care of the clerk.

"Police chiefs probably do the best of all," he went on. "They get their percentage from the cops who stop motorists and simply say, 'Give me 50 pesos, or I'll give you a ticket for going through that red light.' Needless to say, it doesn't matter whether you went through the light or not. The *jefes* get big money from the brothels and the gambling halls and the dope dealers and so on."

If these allegations seem to be laid on with a broad brush, it should be said that they are accepted as facts of life by all Mexicans over the age of six—a subject of bitter jokes rather than outrage. I asked the economist if he could estimate what the graft added up to in a year.

"It's impossible," he said. "There are never any real investigations because the criminal justice system is entirely corrupt and the political opposition never gets into power. You can only guess, but there are a lot of clues. A state governor suddenly is spending his weekends at a 10,000-acre ranch; a mayor's wife shows off her new diamond and emerald necklace—things like that. It certainly totals billions of dollars a year. Graft at least doubles, even triples the cost of public projects. Sometimes *all* the money is stolen, and the project never gets started."

In the 20 years prior to 1982, Mexico's population doubled to 70,000,000. Although the birthrate appears to be dropping from its peak of 3.5 percent a year to 2.8 percent, it will double again, or come close, by the year 2000. Mexico is already importing wheat and corn. Domestic harvests can no doubt be increased, but not to the point of meeting half of the country's food needs, and it seems unlikely that export revenues will be adequate, considering the enormous sums it already owes abroad, to make up the deficiency.

In Mexico, as elsewhere, the rate of population increase is highest among the poorest sectors of the population. With no means of making a living in their native villages, *campesinos* by the millions make their way to the cities. The population of Mexico City and its environs is growing far more rapidly than that of the nation as a whole. It stood in 1982 at 17,000,000, was increasing at the rate of 750,000 a year, and, if not checked, was expected to reach 32,000,000 at the turn of the century.

These new inhabitants find shelter where they can. For most of them, it is a hut in one of the *ciudades perdidas*, or lost cities, as they are called, that form a crust of misery around the capital. The largest of these is Nezahuacoyotl, "Place of the Coyotes" in Aztec, a municipality of 10 square miles that adjoins Mexico City on the east and has a population estimated, incredibly, at 4,000,000.

Neza, as it is called, has arisen on garbage dumps—flattened and compacted and covered with a few inches of earth. Under the garbage lies the bed of Lake Texcoco. It is one of several lakes that protected and beautified Tenochtitlán, the capital of the Aztecs. Nowadays only three remain. Every day hundreds of loads of garbage are dumped on Texcoco's banks. It has become a shallow, reeking, weed-choked sump perhaps a half mile across.

On its perimeter, Neza vibrates with Latin energy, but within, hidden by a façade of small shops and houses, lies the dreadful reality. Lining its deeply rutted, unpaved alleys, too narrow for a car, were huts of adobe brick or gray cinder block, scarcely larger than horse stalls. They made the meanest rural *ranchito* seem like a mansion. Even the radios and the shouting and crying of the children were muted. The

287

light of a gray, windy day faded in the swirling, stinking dust and the smoke of cooking fires.

My driver-interpreter and I spoke with a copper-skinned woman washing clothes in a green plastic bucket. She said that a man in the city owned her house and many others. Every week, she said, the landlord came to collect the rent. I could not find the amount in my notes, but I recall thinking that it was very high.

We walked a long way through those soul-chilling alleys and then drove to the eastern edge of the city. There was plenty of room for growth—a desolate plain that extended two or three miles to a line of low hills. We passed a 35,000-seat concrete stadium. A sign identified it as the home of the Neza Coyotes soccer team. Two school buildings stood nearby. They appeared to be new. Youngsters were playing outside. What was strange, as we saw when we walked over to them, was that the site had not been prepared at all. There were no trees, no grass, no driveway, no walks, not even a hard-surfaced schoolyard. The students were playing amid outcroppings of the garbage beneath.

We found the principal in a small office. She was a woman of 40 with a plump, carefully made-up face and a mass of dyed blond and heavily lacquered hair. She stared at us unpleasantly. It was the look that I got from every public employee I encountered in Mexico.

"You should have arranged this visit with the Ministry of Education," she said. "It is forbidden to enter the schools or talk to the students without its approval."

"*No le bace,*" I said. "It doesn't matter."

We headed back to my hotel in the Zona Rosa on a four-lane highway that ran along Neza's northern edge. On the other side lay low pyramids of garbage that extended a half mile or so to the lake. Real estate development had already begun, the garbage flattened and covered, hundreds of those same dun and gray kennels built. We drove down an unpaved lane to the last line of huts. Parked there was a red station wagon with the emblem of the PRI on the door. A burly man sat behind the wheel, talking to a young woman through the rolled-down window.

At my suggestion, my interpreter explained that I was looking into the PRI's grass-roots organization.

"I'm not with the PRI," the man said, ignoring my extended hand. "I'm a teacher. I'm talking to this woman about her kid's grades."

He snarled something that I did not understand. At the same time, I saw a holstered revolver that lay on the seat beside him. My companion turned, took me by the arm, and began walking rapidly away.

"He said for us to get the hell out of here," he whispered.

I looked over my shoulder as my companion turned the car around and caught a death-ray scowl right between the eyes.

A couple of miles farther on, we saw a crowd of several hundred collected on the median strip, which was about 150 feet wide and served as the right-of-way for the tall T-shaped towers of an electrical transmission line. We heard amplified music and saw signs and banners. The largest of these proclaimed that Neza was welcoming the governor of the state of Mexico. (The state, of which Neza is a part, encircles Mexico City. The capital is an entity like Washington, D.C., and is called the Federal District.)

The occasion, we learned after we had stopped once again, was the dedication by the governor of a soccer field, a scoreboard, and a shed for changing clothes that had been built on the stony and grassless median and the presentation of a plan for the reclamation of Lake Texcoco and the transformation of Neza into a garden suburb. Maps, architectural renderings, and ground plans were displayed on easels. Speaker after speaker told the crowd that these good things would come to pass only if the entire PRI ticket were overwhelmingly victorious in the forthcoming municipal elections.

Every 20 minutes or so, an excited voice interrupted the mournful music of a dusty mariachi band to announce that the governor would arrive momentarily. Upon hearing that, the members of the labor, cultural, and youth groups that formed the welcoming committee would raise their banners and straighten their ranks.

The junior soccer team, which would soon be cutting its knees on the stony field, had a banner. So did Neza's labor unions and social clubs. The largest and most artistic of them, embroidered in gold thread on green silk, was held aloft by three weather-beaten women. It said *Unión de Neza de Recolectores de Desperdicios.* These women were scavengers who roved the refuse ocean, looking for bottles, metal, rags—anything that could be sold. It was Neza's only industry, and I learned that the union members, almost all of them women, monopolized it.

"You should see what happens when someone who doesn't belong to the union tries to go out there," said a man, pointing to the dumps across the highway.

When an hour had passed without the governor's arrival, the crowd began to disperse. The union members and the other delegations re-

289

mained where they were, although they began to slump and grumble. The young soccer players kicked a ball around. The women of the scavengers' union leaned their banner against one of the goals of the soccer field.

While we were waiting, we crossed the road to watch some of the scavengers at work. Five or six women were waiting for each garbage truck. Before it finished dumping, they began raking through the refuse. Their sharp eyes and hard work would have made their fortune in any town dump in the United States, but Neza was slim pickings. One of the women, speaking over her shoulder, said that even rich women sold everything they could to the junk men who regularly made their rounds of the city. "Even bones, even bottles," the woman said. Archaeologists won't learn much about present-day Mexico City from its middens.

By then, the odor of the dump was becoming overpowering, and we returned to the *fiesta*. As the afternoon went on, the sky became grayer. A wind blew from the mountains that encircle the city, and the thin air at an altitude of 7,300 feet made it seem colder. What was left of the crowd was passing around bottles of tequila and mezcal to take off the chill. Tractor-trailers roared by, belching black smoke. Jet planes took off from the airport five miles down the highway and climbed slowly over the lake. The music was still playing at top volume. Garbage in the dump was burning. It was all noise, smoke, dust, desolation. Worse could be imagined—plague, famine, disaster, war— but on an ordinary day in a nation at peace, Neza was a vision of hell itself. And so at last we left without seeing the governor.

That night, while I was dining in a restaurant in an office tower on the Reforma, I felt strange tremors in my legs, and the room seemed to sway.

"Montezuma's Revenge and then some," I said to myself. I wondered what virulent pathogens I had breathed in that afternoon. Then I heard a babble of conversation and the word *terremoto*, earthquake. Earthquakes are frequent in Mexico, but it was my first. Diners headed for the exit, and I followed on unsteady legs. The door was as far as we got. The maître d'hôtel and two busboys stood there, refusing to allow anyone to leave who had not paid the check. By then, the swaying had stopped, and we returned meekly to our tables.

It was a heavy quake, 7.2 on the Richter scale, but the epicenter was placed in the mountains a couple of hundred miles to the southwest.

Several villages were reported to have been destroyed and a number of persons killed.

The figures for 1981 showed that Mexico's foreign earnings had fallen short of expectations, not by $3 billion, which was the midyear estimate, but by $6 billion. At the same time, the public debt held abroad had increased by $15 billion to $49 billion, and the private debt by nearly a third to $15 billion. Mexico, quite suddenly, ranked right up there with Brazil as the most indebted nation in the world. Capital flight had increased as oil revenues declined, while expenditures abroad had continued unchecked. As a result, the Banco de Mexico, the central bank, was exhausting its dollar reserves.

Reports of pressure on the peso had been circulating for months. On February 5, 1982, López Portillo made a speech, swearing to defend the peso *como un perro,* like a dog. Two weeks later, he agreed to a devaluation of 30 percent. The president also slowed PEMEX's rate of investment and implored his countrymen to keep their funds at home. This statement was taken as a last-chance warning. Capital flight turned into capital panic. By the end of the month, the peso had fallen to 45 to the dollar. Price controls were placed on 5,000 commonly used items and foodstuffs, stimulating the natural urge to hoard and profiteer.

López Portillo continued to make foreign visits and to issue statements supporting the Sandinistas, offering his services as a mediator in Central America, and saying that he was certain that Castro was ready to talk to the United States. However, the attention he received declined as Mexico's foreign debt increased. In April, 1982, with the news that inflation in January had been 5.7 percent, an annual compounded rate of 75 percent, the extent of the disaster became clear. In 1981, a rate of 30 percent was considered worrisome. A decrease in economic growth in 1982 from the 7 percent that had been the average for the previous four years to half that or less was forecast, making unlikely the creation of any new jobs at all. Foreign debt, public and private, had increased to $68 billion. Oil revenues were projected at $14 billion for the year, $6 billion less than the long-range estimates. The shortfall was money that Mexico could have used to service its debt. Capital flight, put at $8 billion for 1981, which was bad enough, was estimated at $2 billion to $4 billion in the first six *weeks* of 1982.

In the same month, these statistical abstractions received another dimension. The Alfa Group, Mexico's largest employer outside the government, announced that it was unable to meet its foreign obligations, which totaled $2 billion. The group, a privately held conglomerate whose products ranged from steel and cement to plastics and beer, had expanded rapidly and, some would say, recklessly, on borrowed money. Its sales were already declining in a contracting economy when the peso was devalued. Thus, its foreign debt and the cost of goods purchased abroad doubled overnight.

In July, De la Madrid was elected president. If ever there was an election in which the voters might have been tempted to throw the rascals out, this one was it, but the PRI turned out its usual 75 percent majority, or so the official results stated. De la Madrid would not take office until December 1, however, and in the interim, by custom, he would make no public appearances and issue no statements. López Portillo was forced to go on trying to deal with the most serious economic crisis in Mexico's history, which included a great many crises indeed, as the lamest of lame ducks. The government kept saying that the situation was improving, but in August, it had to admit that its foreign currency reserves were once again exhausted. It again devalued the peso, this time to 75 to the dollar, and set up a two-tier exchange system. The government continued to support the peso at 49.5 to the dollar for the importation of necessities. Everything else had to be paid for at the free-market rate, which immediately rose to 95 and then as high as 120.

Once again, the foreign bankers flew into Mexico City. These were not the genial fellows who had pressed the money on Mexico, but the somber specialists in delinquent accounts that the banks call workout men because one question they keep asking is: "How can we work this out?" It is put more delicately, of course, to senior officials of a sovereign state than it is, say, to an overextended garment manufacturer, but the import is the same. If you want to stay in business, do what we say.

The workout men said their banks would wait, would defer all principal payments for 90 days and stretch out repayment schedules, as Mexico asked, but there were conditions. They wanted austerity. That meant a tighter budget, fewer subsidies, such as food for the masses, and higher domestic gasoline prices, the imposition of strict foreign-exchange controls. Currency flight, as the workout men saw it, was nothing less than a device to put Mexico's assets beyond their reach. And, finally, they demanded that PEMEX, which was not a member of the Organization of Petroleum Exporting Countries, drop López

Portillo's export limit of 1,500,000 barrels a day and to try to sell as much as it could at the best price it could get.

Thus it was that three years after imposing strict limits on sales to the United States, López Portillo had to beg it to buy more. The Reagan administration agreed to increase purchases for the strategic oil reserve from 50,000 to 190,000 barrels a day and to pay $1 billion in advance. Not that Mexico ever saw much of the money. A New York banker who was involved in the workout told me that it was divided among Mexico's biggest American creditors.

Far from safeguarding the national patrimony, López Portillo had helped create a situation in which Mexico would be spending its entire income from foreign oil sales, and more, to pay its high-interest debt. The situation was explosive, and the workout men had to proceed cautiously. Owe a bank $1,000, the saying goes, and it owns you; owe it $1,000,000 and you own it. Meaning that the bank can't afford to write off all or part of its loan by putting you into bankruptcy.

In Mexico alone, for example, Citibank of New York had $3.3 billion at risk, Bank of America $2.5 billion, and Chase Manhattan $1.7 billion. The loss of such sums would put them out of business. The Mexican left was already advocating the repudiation of all or part of the foreign debt. It was not inconceivable that López Portillo might attempt to retrieve his reputation by pulling down the pillars of international finance in the name of freeing the Mexican people from economic serfdom. Thus, at the same time that they were squeezing him, the banks had to raise the specter of the red banner of revolution flying over Mexico City as well as New York, London, and Tokyo, and if that happened, the bankers kept saying, the foreign investments of López Portillo and his friends wouldn't be worth very much.

At about the same time, the Mexican government made public, with indignant denials, a State Department briefing paper that had come by unexplained means into its possession. The paper suggested that Mexico's financial troubles were likely to make its foreign policy "less adventuresome" and "less critical of ours." The reference was clearly to Central America and Cuba, and, in fact, it seemed to reflect what was happening.

In September, López Portillo astonished the financial community by nationalizing his country's 59 commercial banks. (The fact that he could issue the decree on his own authority demonstrated the enormous power possessed by the president of Mexico.) He also decreed that the $12 billion held in dollar accounts in Mexican banks, whether by Mexicans or by foreigners, could be withdrawn only in pesos at a rate of 69.5 to the dollar. Since the peso had by then gone to 140 on the free market, he was depriving these depositors of half of the value of their money.

In a rambling and emotional four-hour speech, almost in tears at times, with the government official who was reputed to be his mistress standing at his side, López Portillo charged that the banks were run by economic traitors who, despite his pleas, had speculated against the peso and aided and abetted the flight of capital. He said that Mexicans had banked $12 billion abroad and invested $25 billion in real estate in the United States alone.

"I can affirm," he declared, "that in recent years, a group of Mexicans, led, counseled, and supported by private banks, have taken more money out of the country than all of the empires that have exploited us since the beginning of our history."

He said that the looting had ended and that he would take steps, which were unspecified, to get the dollars back from abroad, that Mexico would survive the crisis, that it would honor its international commitments, and that the owners of the banks would be compensated. Some bankers reflexively objected to what looked like an example of leaping, rather than creeping, socialism, but the Bank of America, with $2.5 billion on its mind, seemed to speak for the majority when it described the expropriation as "a positive step."

But why had López Portillo, contrary to all custom, taken an action of such magnitude during his final three months in office? Two reasons were suggested. One was that he was trying to make the banks the scapegoats. They had, no doubt, done exactly what he accused them of, but their actions had been legal until the month before. The other reason advanced was that López Portillo hoped that his seizure of the banks would earn a place for him in Mexican history alongside Cárdenas, who had expropriated the railroads and the oil industry. It is doubtful that it will, if for no other reason than that the banks were owned not by *gringos* and other foreigners but by Mexicans—rich Mexicans, avaricious and probably dishonest Mexicans, but Mexicans nonetheless.

On December 1, the red, green, and white sash of office was placed on the shoulder of the 47-year-old De la Madrid. "We live in an emergency situation," he stated in his inaugural address. "The situation is intolerable. I will not allow the nation to disintegrate in our hands. We are going to act with decision and firmness."

He repeated that austerity and honesty would be the watchwords of his administration. Mexicans had been hearing that throughout their history, of course, but De la Madrid bore down on it so hard that even the most skeptical might have been pardoned for thinking that he meant it. He said he would enact new laws to deal with corruption. Conflict of interest would for the first time become a criminal offense. "Either you govern or you do business," he said. "Public office should be no one's booty." He established a general auditing office to oversee public expenditures and named a former Finance Minister to head PEMEX. The man was said to be rigorously honest, but in Mexico that was often said when someone assumed such a post and seldom said when he left it.

The next day, De la Madrid took a step that López Portillo had shrunk from. He doubled the price of gasoline sold in Mexico from 54 cents to $1.08 a gallon, thus cutting consumption, increasing revenues, and leaving more available for export. He announced a birth control campaign. Its objective, he said, would be to reduce the rate of growth still further—from 2.5 to 1 percent by the end of the century.

Finally, De la Madrid stated, although not emphatically, that Mexico would not change its policy toward Cuba and Nicaragua. It was not "a romantic attitude," he said. Cuba did not bother Mexico and had the right, as did the other countries in the region, he said, to determine its own destiny without outside interference.

18

Reagan Hangs Tough

IN THE MONTHS following the elections of 1982, the Salvadoran guerrillas seemed to be confused and divided. It might have been the moment for the United States to support proposals for discussions between them and the new Salvadoran government. Mexico, Venezuela, Colombia, and Panama, which called themselves the Contadora Four—the name derived from the Panamanian island resort where they first met—had offered their assistance. However, Reagan took a sterner line. In April, 1982, he approved the recommendations of a high-level planning group of the National Security Council.

Titled "U.S. Policy in Central America and Cuba Through F.Y. '84 [fiscal year 1984, beginning October 1, 1983], Summary Paper," it came into the possession of Raymond Bonner, my old colleague on *The New York Times,* a year later and was published in *The Times* on April 7, 1983. As Bonner wrote, "The document provides insight into the policy-making analysis at the highest levels of the United States Government." The introduction states:

> We have an interest in creating and supporting democratic states in Central America capable of conducting their political and economic affairs free from outside interference. Strategically, we have a vital interest in not allowing the proliferation of Cuba-model states which would provide platforms for subversion, compromise vital sea lanes and pose a direct military threat at or near our borders. . . .

Under the heading "The Current Situation," the paper found that "the deterioration in our position so evident 6 to 12 months ago has been halted." It went on to cite the elections in El Salvador; Honduras, in which a civilian figurehead was elected after a long period of military rule; the Ríos Montt coup in Guatemala; and the "minicoup" in Panama that brought to power, although behind the scenes, "a new, more dynamic and more pro-U.S. National Guard commander."

The military situation in El Salvador had improved to the point that the guerrillas could not achieve a "near-term" victory, the paper stated. Their strength was estimated to remain at 4,000 to 5,000 combatants. However, Cuba and Nicaragua were said to have the ability to increase their support of the guerrillas and of "terrorist groups" in Honduras and Costa Rica. Mexico, the paper said, continued to back the extreme left "with propaganda, funds and political support." In Nicaragua, the Sandinista government was seen as being "under increased pressure as a result of our covert efforts and because of the poor state of their economy."

The paper set out 15 objectives. One of these was the "isolation" of Mexico and the Social Democratic parties of Europe from any role in Central America while an attempt was made to persuade them that negotiations wouldn't work. Another was the belated enactment of the trade-and-aid package known as the Caribbean Basin Initiative, for which Congress had shown little enthusiasm. A third was the increasing of economic pressure on Cuba. It also recommended the carrying out of the provisions of National Security Decision Directive 17 of November, 1981, which provided $19.5 million to arm and train anti-Sandinista Nicaraguans, mainly former members of the National Guard, in Honduras.

To attain these objectives, the planning group decided that $1 billion a year would be needed "through and probably beyond" the 1984 fiscal year. Appropriations for the 1983 fiscal year would fall about $300 million short of that figure, the paper noted. It urged the White House "to make a maximum effort" to get the funds from Congress.

Meanwhile, Fidel Castro had twice tried to begin talks with the United States on the Caribbean and Central America. In December, 1981, as later became known, Secretary of State Alexander M. Haig, Jr., met with Vice-President Carlos Rafael Rodríguez of Cuba in Mexico City. In March, 1982, Castro told General Vernon E. Walters, an Ambassador at Large and former Deputy Director of the CIA, that Cuba was ready to address every issue outstanding between the two countries. Castro regarded the response from Washington as unacceptable, but he was not quite ready to give up. In late March, a group of 10 American academics, public policy experts, and journalists was invited to Havana. Castro, whom the visitors agreed to identify only as "a senior Cuban official," set out the Cuban position.

Leslie Gelb, the national security correspondent of *The New York Times,* was a member of the group. His account of the meeting was published on April 4. Gelb quoted the senior official as saying that Cuba as well as the United States bore responsibility for the tension between the two nations and that he now wished to start talking about ways to achieve "mutual restraint." He further stated that Latin America as a whole was not ready for socialism and that Cuba was willing to promote "democratic change." He acknowledged that Cuba had supplied both Nicaragua and the Salvadoran guerrillas with arms, but he added that shipments to Nicaragua had ceased more than a year earlier and that transshipments of these arms to El Salvador had ended "more recently."

"[The Salvadoran guerrillas] are not fighting to establish a socialist regime, although some would like it," Castro stated. "They don't think they can reach communism now, and they are trying to find a progressive democratic system."

Although he criticized Soviet policy in Poland and Afghanistan, he stated that Cuba's ties with Russia were "unbreakable." This "socialist solidarity" did not rule out Cuba's pursuing its own foreign policy initiatives, he said. In any case, he stated, the Soviet Union did not wish to seriously damage its relations with the United States over what it saw as the comparatively minor question of El Salvador and Nicaragua.

The Reagan administration dismissed Castro's proposals as a feint to set up the United States for the old one-two in Central America. To others, it seemed that exploratory talks could do no harm and might do some good, especially since a solution to the Central American tangle was more likely to be found in Havana and Moscow than in Managua or the hills of El Salvador.

Many possible reasons were offered for the Cuban *démarche.* One was that the Soviet Union was becoming weary of subsidizing Cuba to the extent of $3 billion a year and did not wish to take on other clients in the hemisphere. The Congressional Joint Economic Committee, in a report on Cuba that was released at about the time the delegation was returning from Havana, suggested that the continuation of the United States' embargo merely served to keep Cuba tightly between the paws of the Russian Bear.

In June, Haig, who had become accustomed to winning arguments with the White House staff by threatening to resign, did it once too often. To Haig's scarcely concealed discomfiture, Reagan was persuaded to accept it before the general could change his mind. He was replaced by George P. Shultz, who had served as Secretary of Labor in 1969–70 and as Secretary of the Treasury in 1973–74. Shultz had the reputation of keeping his head when all about him were losing theirs, and for being modest and easy to get along with. It was Haig's conspicuous lack of these qualities that had led the President to decide that he could get along without him.

Some months later, my request for an interview with Haig was turned down by his agent, Norman Brokaw of the William Morris office. Speaking from his office in Beverly Hills, Brokaw said, in effect, that his client was not interested in giving away what he was able to sell.

As spring became summer, the Constituent Assembly of El Salvador, under the leadership of its president, D'Aubuisson, pushed through a law canceling Phase II of the land reform, dealing with farms of 100 to 499 hectares, and also suspending Phase III, the "Land to the Tiller" program. The action on Phase II scarcely mattered since there had been no intention of putting it into effect. However, the suspension of Phase III was certain to cost the government support in the countryside. Reports that thousands of peasants were being illegally thrown off land for which they had titles by the original owners began reaching the capital.

In June, the Ramón Belloso Battalion, 1,000 strong, returned from 16 weeks of training at Fort Bragg, North Carolina, as did 500 newly commissioned lieutenants who had earned their bars at Fort Benning, Georgia. However, complaints from their American advisers began to be heard. They said the Salvadorans refused to learn anything from the sad experience of Vietnam. Instead of patrolling and ambushing at night in groups of 10 to 50 men, they operated in large formations, in daylight, and took the weekends off.

These tactics, moreover, were costly in terms of casualties. The Ministry of Defense reported not long afterward that 1,073 troops had been killed and 2,584 had been wounded during the preceding 12 months. That was a rate of more than 15 percent for the army as a whole and probably double that for combat formations. The figures for the next 12 months, running through the middle of 1983, gave every indication of being at least as high. An added complication was the fact that conscripts were required to serve only two years. In the second half of 1983, the discharge rate was scheduled to rise sharply, indicating a considerable loss of whatever combat efficiency had been achieved.

In July, Aristides Royo, the president of Panama, with whom I had spoken as he dedicated a fishpond, resigned. Royo said that he had a throat ailment for which he had been advised to seek medical treatment abroad. Colonel Rubén Darío Paredes, the commander of the National Guard, thereupon picked Royo's vice-president, Ricardo de la Espriella, as his figurehead chief of state.

In Guatemala, Ríos Montt dismissed his two colleagues in the junta and ruled alone. He had evolved an antiguerrilla campaign called Beans or Bullets, but it looked as if the army were more generous with the bullets than the beans. The best guess was that Indians were being murdered at a rate of 500 to 1,000 a month.

In September, at long last, two men were charged with the murders of Michael P. Hammer and Mark David Pearlman, the American land reform advisers, and José Rodolfo Viera, the head of the Salvadoran land reform agency, in January, 1981. The suspects, both corporals in the National Guard, reenacted the crime. They said that the murders had been ordered by their superior officers, Lieutenant Isidro López Sibrián, a former aide of D'Aubuisson's, and Captain Eduardo Alfonso Ávila, a nephew of a judge of the Salvadoran Supreme Court, and that Hans Christ, one of the Sheraton's owners, who had previously been implicated, was present.

Sibrián was arrested, but he was freed almost immediately, on the ground of insufficient evidence, by a judge who wanted to go on living. Ávila fled, reportedly to Guatemala. The two corporals remained in jail. That latest example of Salvadoran justice roused Ambassador Hinton to a public response. Hinton, who had never been accused of being a bleeding heart, delivered a bitter lecture at a meeting of the Salvadoran-American Chamber of Commerce. He spoiled everyone's lunch by stating that the Salvadoran judicial system was "rotten" and called the death squads as great a threat to the survival of the country as the guerrillas.

The State Department had approved Hinton's speech, but the White House hadn't. An unnamed official issued a public rebuke, saying that "high public rhetoric was frequently counterproductive."

As the ground dried, the war resumed for the third year. In October the guerrillas again overran Perquín, the village in the northeast corner of the country, and Suchitoto, the much larger town 25 miles north of San Salvador. The self-criticism sessions appeared to have worked. The guerrillas were feinting in one direction, drawing off government troops, and attacking in another. They were more aggressive, better armed, and better led. The "oil spots," areas in which they moved freely by day, grew in number and size. More frequently now the guerrillas were capturing government formations of 10, 20, or 30 men. The guerrillas quickly freed their prisoners, making it tempting for troops to avoid endangering their lives in a tight place by surrendering and giving up their weapons and equipment.

In November, Edén Pastora, formerly known as Comandante Cero, announced the formation of the Revolutionary Democratic Alliance, with Alfonso Robelo, the former junta member with whom I had spoken in Managua, as his right-hand man. Pastora, who had never been a Marxist, asked the United States to stop backing the Somocistas. He said that the forces he led would be sufficient to oust the Sandinistas.

In December, Reagan paid his first visit to Central and South America. His mission—to try to drum up support for a Central American policy that excluded from an active role every nation in the hemisphere except the United States—was not an easy one, especially when he was visiting four countries and meeting with six chiefs of state in five days.

"My eyes are dazzled by the progress of the Brazilian nation," Reagan said at a state dinner. He then announced a $1.2 billion loan, increasing that country's external debt to $90 billion, the world record. He flew on to Bogotá. President Belisario Betancur, who was that rarity in Latin American politics, a popularly elected and democratically inclined president, made his toast at a state banquet the occasion for raising a sensitive issue—that was the United States' refusal to be seated at any bargaining table with Cuban or Nicaraguan representatives.

"Why couldn't we do away with this exclusion in the inter-American system?" he asked.

Reagan flew on to San José, where he met with President Luis Alberto Monge and Acting President Magaña of El Salvador. Air Force One next set down at San Pedro Sula down in United Brands territory on the Atlantic coast of Honduras. Reagan met separately with President Suazo Córdova and Ríos Montt, the Guatemalan *caudillo*. Reagan said that Riós Montt had been getting "a bum rap."

During the autumn of 1982, Congress began to worry about the Somocistas it was paying the bills for in Honduras. They weren't interdicting any arms shipments at all, and they seemed to spend a lot of time on the wrong side of the border. The *contras* and their CIA handlers did not seem to grasp their limited role. To clarify matters, Congress adopted overwhelmingly in December an amendment to the appropriations bill for intelligence activities. It bore the name of its sponsor, Representative Edward P. Boland, a conservative Massachusetts Democrat who was the chairman of the House Intelligence Committee, and prohibited the administration from providing funds "for the purpose of overthrowing the Government of Nicaragua or provoking a military exchange between Nicaragua and Honduras."

In January, 1983, the chief of the Salvadoran forces in the department of Cabañas, northeast of the capital, refused to accept a posting to Uruguay as military attaché—a traditional form of exile. He demanded instead that García, the Defense Minister, resign. The officer, Colonel Sigifredo Ochoa Pérez, who was known as an unusually aggressive and effective leader, ordered his 1,200 troops to fire on anyone who tried to enforce the order. After four days, a compromise was worked out. Ochoa agreed to a transfer to the Inter-American Defense College in Washington. He departed in triumph, still demanding that García step aside.

The incident caused some home truths about the Salvadoran military to start sinking in. The most important was that it was still just another Third World army and was likely to remain one. Commanders received their appointments and the graft that went with them, more often than not, through a complex web of family, political, and military patronage. Ochoa and other officers in their middle forties believed that García and his contemporaries, who were eight to 10 years older, were using the war as an excuse to hold on to their posts long after they would have been required, in peacetime, to retire. What was worse, García had been shown to lack the power to punish a colonel on active service for mutiny—a problem to which Duarte had alluded in our conversation more than a year earlier.

The guerrillas, a few weeks later, marked the second anniversary of the premature final offensive by striking at a half dozen objectives, among them the San Carlos Barracks in San Salvador and Santa Ana, the metropolis of the western third of the country, which until then had been a quiet area. The heaviest attack was directed at Berlín, a town of 30,000 in Usulután Province 70 miles east of San Salvador. A force estimated at 500 occupied it for four days.

In early February, 1983, the guerrillas overran Suchitoto yet again. The American military advisers were particularly angered, I was told, by this reverse. They had been fruitlessly imploring the Salvadoran high command for two years to clean out the base area on the slopes of the Guazapa Volcano from which the attack was launched.

Shortly after his meeting with Reagan, Ríos Montt said that only a mopping up of his guerrillas was required. That may have been an exaggeration, but the Guatemalan rebels had clearly been less successful than their Salvadoran comrades. He also pledged to hold elections for a national legislature early in 1984 and to install its members in March of that year on the second anniversary of the coup that brought him to power. On the strength of that, early in January, Reagan lifted the embargo on arms sales, specifically to permit Guatemala to buy $6,300,000 in spare parts for helicopters and those little A-37B jets that were still being used against suspected guerrilla strongholds in the mountains.

In March, making a detour on his way to the meeting of the Conference of Latin American Bishops, which was being held in Haiti, John Paul II paid the first papal visit to Central America. It turned out to be one of his most difficult missions. When the trip was being planned, for example, the Vatican threatened to drop Nicaragua from the itinerary unless the five priests in the Sandinista government resigned, as they had been ordered to do by their archbishop.

The priests, supported by the government, refused, and it was the Vatican that accepted a compromise. Resignations would not be insisted on, but the Reverend Miguel d'Escoto, the Foreign Minister and the highest-ranking priest, agreed to be absent from the country during the Pope's visit, attending an opportune Third World conference in New Delhi.

In January, while the Nicaraguan problem was being negotiated, Archbishop Alfonso López Trujillo, the secretary-general of the conference, was made a cardinal. López Trujillo was a political and religious conservative, and his promotion could only be interpreted as a papal endorsement of his views. By contrast, John Paul waited until a few

303

days before his departure from Rome to confer upon Bishop Arturo Rivera y Damas the title of archbishop of San Salvador.

The Pope's visit to Managua turned the rest of the trip into something of an anticlimax. At the airport, he was harangued for 25 minutes by Daniel Ortega, the coordinator, or head, of the ruling junta. Ortega declared that "the footsteps of interventionist boots echo threateningly in the White House and the Pentagon" and that the Nicaraguan people were being "martyred and crucified every day." He added, "Our experience shows that one can be both a believer and a revolutionary and that no insoluble contradiction exists between the two."

John Paul was then introduced to senior figures in the government. One of them was a gray-haired man wearing a peasant shirt and baggy blue trousers. As the Pope extended his hand to be shaken, the man removed his beret, knelt, and tried to kiss the Pope's ring. The Pope, realizing that the official was the Reverend Ernesto Cardenal, the Minister of Culture, pulled away his hand.

"You must straighten out your position with the church," the Pope was heard to say.

The major public event of the visit was an outdoor mass in the empty center of the city. Behind the platform from which the Pope was to officiate, an enormous billboard had been erected. On it were depicted the martyred heroes of the Sandinista revolution. Facing the Pope was another billboard, about 100 feet long and 20 feet high, that showed a throng of peasants, workers, and soldiers. It bore the statement *Juan Pablo Bienvenido a Nicaragua Libre Gracias a Dios y la Revolución* ("Welcome to Free Nicaragua, John Paul, Thanks to God and the Revolution").

Anywhere from 300,000 to 500,000 persons had arrived from all over the country to attend the mass, but the best seats seemed to be reserved for those who came under government auspices and carried the red and black Sandinista banners. These were the members of the "People's Church" that had been created by the Sandinista government in opposition to the "reactionary" hierarchy.

In his homily, the Pope defended the established church. He stated that it was "absurd and dangerous to imagine that outside—if not to say against—the church built around the bishops there should be another church, conceived only as 'charismatic' and not institutional, 'new' and not traditional. . . ."

As he was speaking, microphones and bullhorns connected to the central amplification system materialized in the hands of members of the People's Church. They began chanting in chorus, *"Poder popular! Poder popular!"* This meant, more or less, "Power to the people." The Pope several times angrily shouted, "Silence."

The next day the Vatican radio station reported, "Those who were nearest to the Holy Father noticed his spiritual discomfort, especially for the aspect of the profanation of the holy mass. Furthermore, the great crowd of faithful were not only kept at a distance but did not have megaphones or access to microphones."

In San Salvador, where his visit passed without incident, the Pope knelt at the tomb of the martyred Archbishop Romero in the crypt of the unfinished cathedral. He went further, describing the archbishop as "a pastor celebrated and venerated by his flock who tried . . . to stop the violence and to reestablish peace." Archbishop Rivera y Damas said that his words fell "like rain on the desert."

The Pope's welcome in Guatemala was scarcely warmer than it had been in Nicaragua. For weeks, the fundamentalist sects had been referring to him in sermons, publications, and radio broadcasts as "the Great Beast of the Apocalypse" and the "Antichrist." Ríos Montt had rejected his appeal for clemency for six men condemned to death for unspecified crimes by a secret court he had established.

In March, Reagan addressed the National Association of Evangelicals, an organization representing 40 fundamentalist denominations, most of which were busy saving souls in Latin America. He described the Soviet Union as "the focus of evil in the modern world" and urged his audience "to pray for the salvation of all those who live in totalitarian darkness." In a speech before the National Association of Manufacturers, Reagan stated that the strategic interests of the United States in Central America made it impossible to ignore the danger of a seizure of power there by forces allied with the Soviet Union. If the guerrillas won in El Salvador, he went on, revolution would spread down the isthmus to the Panama Canal and up through Mexico to the very borders of the United States.

Because of this imminent peril, the President said, he would ask Congress for an emergency appropriation of $298,000,000 for the region. This sum appeared to be the $300,000,000 that the National Security Council, in April, 1982, had said would be needed. He had followed its advice by delaying his request for the money, and, on his own, perhaps, he had knocked off $2,000,000, bringing the price down to the familiar $2.98, plus six zeroes.

Of this amount, the President said, El Salvador would receive $110,000,000 in military aid, bringing the total for the year to $136,000,000, and $67,000,000 in economic aid for a total for the year of $227,000,000, and a grand total of $363,000,000. (The figure for 1982 was $260,000,000.) With El Salvador's population estimated at 5,000,000, that worked out to $72 for every man, woman, and child in the country, more than most of them saw in a year.

With so much at stake in El Salvador, and with only 10 percent of the Salvadoran army having had the benefit of American training, Reagan continued, he was thinking about removing the self-imposed limit of 55 advisers who were assigned to the country. The President explained it to his business audience as essentially a money-saving proposition. Either the advisers would be sent to El Salvador or the Salvadoran troops would have to be sent to the United States, which would be much more costly.

To reassure his audience, Reagan posed a ringing rhetorical question. "Are we going to send American soldiers into combat? The answer is a flat 'no.' "

In late March, the focus of interest in Central America shifted abruptly from El Salvador to Nicaragua. A military force estimated at 500 to 1,500 men, depending on who was doing the estimating, and composed mainly of former members of Somoza's National Guard, entered Nicaragua from Honduras and reportedly set up bases in the western mountains. These were the *contras* that the CIA had been organizing and training for more than a year. The Sandinistas, holding their army of 25,000 in reserve, mobilized militia units to confront the invaders.

In the weeks that followed, both sides issued vivid communiqués describing ambushes, cannonades, and pitched battles. The *contras* said that they were greeted like long-lost brothers by the oppressed peasantry. The Sandinistas charged that the *contras* burned, raped, robbed, and murdered without mercy. On the Atlantic coast, Miskito Indians, also armed and trained by the CIA, were reported to be skirmishing on the Nicaraguan side of the Coco River.

The State Department refused to confirm or to deny that the United States was helping the invasion force, although by then it was an open secret that it was. A spokesman said, "There has been rising opposition to the government of Nicaragua, including within Nicaragua itself, and clearly these opposition elements are making their pressure felt."

The House and Senate Intelligence committees didn't care for that reply. Daniel Patrick Moynihan, the deputy chairman of the Senate panel, said that by permitting the *contras* to enter Nicaragua, the administration appeared to be violating the provisions of the Boland Amendment. A member of the House committee, after a quick trip to Central America, said the administration was not "in full compliance with the law."

Jeane Kirkpatrick, whose influence at the White House was flowering, denied the accusation. There was no violation, she said, because the *contras* were only trying to harass the Nicaraguan government to the point that it would stop aiding the Salvadoran rebels. There was no *intent,* she went on, to overthrow the government.

Other questions went unanswered by Mrs. Kirkpatrick or by anyone else in the administration. For example, if the function of the *contras* was to stop the flow of arms from Nicaragua to El Salvador, and if the arms were indeed being run across Honduras in anything like the volume stated by the administration, how had it been possible for a force of at least 1,000 men and perhaps three times that many to fail for more than a year to intercept, as far as anyone knew, a single rifle?

For that matter, how was it possible for the Sandinistas to send arms by small planes at night, as the administration contended, for an even longer period without the loss of a single aircraft, even in a crash, in Honduras or El Salvador? Hundreds of flights would have been required to make this method a significant source of supply. The same question arose in connection with purported shipments by sea, inasmuch as electronic intelligence ships of the United States Navy patrolled the Gulf of Fonseca.

Only two answers seemed possible. One was that the Russians had provided the Sandinistas with boats, planes, trucks, and burros that were invisible to both radar and the naked eye. The second, and more likely, was that the Sandinistas were telling the truth when they said that they had made no significant arms shipments to the Salvadoran guerrillas since the winter of 1980–81.

Reagan also turned his attention briefly to Grenada, an island nation of 100,000 in the Caribbean 80 miles off the coast of Venezuela. Alone among the former British colonies of the region, Grenada had been afflicted with bad governments since gaining its independence in 1974. First there had been a corrupt, repressive and eccentric former labor leader named Eric Gairy. He was overthrown in 1979 by Maurice

Bishop, whose father had been murdered—most probably on Gairy's orders.

Bishop, a Marxist, established close relations with Cuba and the Soviet Union. Soon thereafter, Cuban workers and Russian machinery arrived on the island and construction began on the 10,000-foot runway of an international airport. Bishop noted that it was impossible to develop a major tourist industry without such an airport, since vacationers were unenthusiastic about changing to the small propeller planes that were all that the old airstrip could accommodate.

Reagan pointed out that the airport could be used by Soviet military aircraft as well as tourist-carrying 747's. Although he offered no evidence on this point, he went on to say, "The Soviet-Cuban militarization of Grenada can only be seen as power projection into the region."

In El Salvador, the war was still going badly, but the army's right wing and D'Aubuisson's ARENA party finally scored a victory by ousting García as Minister of Defense. The Pentagon had also been seeking his removal for months, but if it had hoped that an aggressive young colonel like Ochoa, whose mutiny in January had precipitated García's sacking, would get the job, it must have been disappointed. It went to General Eugenio Vides Casanova, the commander of the National Guard. The change seemed unlikely to be for the better. García, who had held the post for nearly four years, had worked reasonably well with the Duarte and Magaña governments, defended the land reform, and kept the army out of the election of 1982. Vides Casanova was, at best, an unknown quantity.

In mid-April, the Christian Democrats became the first party to choose a candidate for the presidential election. As expected, it was Duarte. He said that the main campaign issue would be social and economic security—"all the elements that give people confidence they will have opportunities and justice." ARENA was regarded as certain to nominate D'Aubuisson. The question was whether the smaller parties of the right would support him, thus making him a serious threat to Duarte, or would split the vote by choosing their own candidates.

If the Salvadoran armed forces had demonstrated many times a capacity for wounding themselves more seriously than the enemy, the guerrillas demonstrated in April the same talent in more extreme form. First, there was a report from Managua that the deputy commander of the Popular Forces of Liberation, the oldest and largest of the guerrilla groups, had been brutally murdered in her home there. She was a former schoolteacher named Mélida Anaya Montes and had been known by the nom de guerre of Ana María. The Sandinista government said that the crime had been committed by CIA assassins.

Cayetano Carpio, the 63-year-old commander of the faction, was photographed at the funeral. He was reported to have just returned from a trip to Libya. A week later, Carpio, too, was dead. He was said to have committed suicide a few days after the funeral. It seemed to be an unlikely end for a lifelong revolutionary who had survived many harsh imprisonments, who had been, since 1970, a terrorist and guerrilla commander, and who had every reason to suppose that his forces were closer to winning their war than to losing it. Within another week, however, a spokesman for the Popular Forces of Liberation had given an account of the linked murder and suicide that banished disbelief if for no other reason than it bared a murderous split in its ranks.

The man who spoke for the guerrillas was Salvador Samayoa, a man whose background was very different from Carpio's. He had been a professor of philosophy at the National University and the Minister of Education in the first junta. As Samayoa related the story, Carpio had broken emotionally when he learned that the woman who had been one of his closest comrades and, by other accounts, his mistress had been murdered not by the CIA but on the orders of another trusted associate, Rogelio Bazzaglio. Bazzaglio was reported to have confessed and to have said that he had acted "for the good of the revolution." His motive, Samayoa said, was ideological. From the beginning, Carpio had been committed to the Maoist principle of *guerra prolongada,* Prolonged People's War. However, in recent months, according to Samayoa, Carpio and Miss Montes had been weighing a compromise with the other factions in hopes of finally achieving unity of strategy, tactics, and command. Bazzaglio, who opposed any dilution of the true faith, was said to have killed Miss Montes so that the compromise would die with her. If Carpio had not been abroad, Samayoa suggested, Bazzaglio might have tried to assassinate him instead.

In April, 1983, the President made his most eloquent appeal for support for his policy before a joint session of Congress that was televised in prime time.

"El Salvador is nearer to Texas than Texas is to Massachusetts," he said. "Nicaragua is just as close to Miami, San Antonio, San Diego and Tucson as those cities are to Washington."

That was true enough, but when he got to explaining how important, besides being so close, Central America was, Reagan might have told what Huck Finn would have called a couple of stretchers. For example, he said that "two-thirds of all our foreign trade and petroleum pass through the Panama Canal and the Caribbean" and that the Caribbean was "our lifeline to the outside world." In fact, only 13 percent of shipping to and from ports in the United States goes through the canal, according to the canal commission. The Department of Commerce says that 66 percent of the nation's ocean trade, primarily oil, grain, and other bulk cargoes, does indeed go through New Orleans, Mobile, Houston, Galveston, and other Gulf ports, but the Caribbean and the nations of Central America lie far to the south.

The President went on to talk about the progress that El Salvador was making on the road to democracy, despite the guerrillas, and about how Nicaragua had been going in the opposite direction since the Sandinistas came to power. He quoted Cayetano Carpio's statement to the effect that both the Salvadoran guerrillas and the Sandinistas were fighting "for the total liberation of Central America."

Was it necessary, Reagan wanted to know, for democracies "to remain passive while threats to their security and prosperity accumulate" and for the United States to accept "the destabilization of an entire region from Panama Canal to Mexico on our southern border? . . . I do not believe that there is a majority in the Congress or the country that counsels passivity, resignation, defeatism in the face of this challenge to freedom and security in our own hemisphere."

At the same time, he tried to calm persons who thought the region might turn out to be another Vietnam. "There is no thought of sending American combat troops to Central America," he said. "They are not needed—indeed, they have not been requested there. All our neighbors ask of us is assistance in training and arms to protect themselves while they build a better, freer life."

That sounded fairly categorical at first hearing, but it was a different and trickier formula than the "flat 'no' " that he had used in his speech to the National Association of Manufacturers a month earlier.

The networks gave a third of the 35 minutes the President had received to the Democrats for a reply. The party spokesman was Senator Christopher Dodd of Connecticut. Dodd began by saying that all Americans were united in their opposition to the establishment of Marxist states in the region. But by putting its emphasis on force to prevent this from happening, the administration, he said, had created "a formula for failure."

"In El Salvador, the rebels have offered to negotiate unconditionally," he said. "Let us test their sincerity. We certainly have the leverage to move the government to the bargaining table. . . . And every major ally of ours in the region—Mexico, Panama, Venezuela and Colombia—is anxious for such a step to be taken and has offered, I might add, to make the arrangements. . . . These same nations have volunteered to bring Nicaragua into negotiations—and Nicaragua has agreed to talk. Instead . . . this administration is conducting a not so secret war inside that country."

Reagan had said in his address that he would appoint a special ambassador to seek peaceful solutions in Central America. He picked a Democrat for the post—Richard B. Stone, a former one-term senator from Florida. After being beaten in the primary in 1980, he had been a highly paid lobbyist for 12 months for Guatemala's brutal and corrupt Lucas García regime.

Congress did not seem to share the President's concern. The House Foreign Affairs Committee voted, 36–1, to increase aid to El Salvador for the 1983 fiscal year by only $8,700,000 instead of the $50,000,000 that Reagan had asked for. Moreover, to get the money, the Salvadoran government would be required to start negotiating in good faith with the Democratic Revolutionary Front. Even the Senate Foreign Relations Committee, which was controlled by the Republicans, voted only $20,000,000, although without conditions. Reagan responded by asking, in effect, if Congress was prepared to accept responsibility for the loss to communism of everything south of the Rio Grande.

In May, Enders and Hinton were dismissed. The two hard men, handpicked by Haig, had turned out not to be hard enough. Enders, it was whispered, had been too quick to knuckle under to Congress, too arrogant in his dealings with the White House, and too willing to negotiate with the Salvadoran rebels and the Sandinistas. The immediate cause of his dismissal, however, was his refusal to permit the release of a second White Paper on El Salvador. The first, issued two years earlier, had notably failed to demonstrate its thesis that the Salvadoran uprising was an example of indirect aggression by the Soviet Union acting through Cuba, and Enders was said to have considered the second version no better. It was made public on the day that his firing was announced, confirming, by general agreement, his opinion.

Speaking of Enders's ouster, Representative Clarence Long of Maryland said, "He was probably caught trying to do the right thing."

At that, Enders landed on his feet. He became Ambassador to Spain, where he replaced a man who had been dismissed from the same assistant secretaryship by the Carter administration because of a perceived lack of enthusiasm for the human rights program. However, Hinton, the shrewd, stringy Hoosier, seemed to be on his way to the same boneyard as Robert White, Lawrence Pezzullo, and many other diplomatic wheelhorses who didn't pull hard enough to the right. He was 60 years old and had served in the State Department for 37 years. White House sources were quoted as saying that he was a good man who had been burned out. Four months after his recall, he had not received another assignment, and it appeared that he would have to retire.

With the firing of Enders and Hinton, William P. Clark, Reagan's National Security Adviser, and Jeane Kirkpatrick, the Ambassador to the United Nations, took charge of policy in Central America. Clark, a Reagan crony who had managed to flunk out of Stanford twice and out of a trolley-car law school in Los Angeles, would no longer be embarrassed by Enders's raised eyebrows when he asked to be reminded what country Tegucigalpa was the capital of.

Nor would there be anyone to rouse Mrs. Kirkpatrick, who was generally thought to do Clark's thinking for him, from her reveries of blood and fire. She was, for example, one of the few persons to have had a good word to say for *la matanza* in El Salvador in 1932 and for Hernández Martínez, who carried it out. In a paper published by the American Enterprise Institute in 1981, she wrote, "To many Salvadorans [none was named, but D'Aubuisson was certainly one] the violence of this repression seems less important than the fact of restored order and the 13 years of civil peace that ensued."

A conversation that I had with her not long before the dismissals left me feeling rather unsettled. The affectation of her speech, her unconcealed impatience with slower thinkers or with those who did not entirely share her opinions, and a barely concealed pugnacity all put me in mind of Maggie taking after Jiggs with skillet in the classic comic strip "Bringing Up Father."

Mrs. Kirkpatrick struck me as having a sinister as well as a comic side, and in more than her thoughts on *la matanza*. In August, for example, in a speech to Nicaraguan émigrés, she stated that there were members of Congress, whom she did not identify, "who would actually like to see the Marxist forces take power in El Salvador." Thirty years before, in similar circumstances, Senator Joseph McCarthy said that he had the names of the guilty on the piece of paper he was holding right there in his hand.

In any event, she and Clark had lobotomized the State Department's institutional memory, and Enders's replacement was certain to be more tractable. He was Langhorne A. Motley, an Alaskan land developer who had been rewarded for his contributions to the Reagan campaign by appointment as Ambassador to Brazil. Political ambassadors were nothing new, of course, but it was most unusual for one to be appointed to an assistant secretaryship. Hinton's post, at least, went to a professional, Thomas R. Pickering, the Ambassador to Nigeria, but he was without experience in Latin America and was thus unlikely for many months to make a nuisance of himself.

The last of several talks I had with Enders took place a couple of weeks before his dismissal, and by hindsight, at any rate, I could sense that his career barometer was dropping. Enders slouched on his sofa, his feet on the coffee table, his socks drooping, his fingers tented as he spoke, but he seemed even more uncommunicative than ususal. The department press officer who monitored the meeting took more notes than I did, fearful perhaps of missing any whiff of subversion.

If there was gloom at Foggy Bottom, the sun was shining radiantly over the Executive Office Building, the mellow Victorian pile adjacent to the White House, where I met with a senior member of the staff of the National Security Council. He tried to unload on me a report that Carpio had been murdered and much other old rope, but the red and green telephones on his desk rang frequently, showing that he, unlike Enders, was still in touch.

From there, on an impulse, I walked to the Vietnam Veterans Memorial. My route led me, as it happened, past the headquarters of the Organization of American States. It is a pleasantly schizophrenic building. The exterior is the usual columned white marble wedding cake, but the interior is done in Hispanic style. Palms and other tropical plants flourished in a garden under the glass roof of the rotunda, and birds sang merrily, but it hardly seemed like the nerve center of inter-American relations.

The memorial, by contrast, is as simple and stark and as terrible as the fact of the 57,939 deaths it commemorates. The names are incised in chronological order from 1959 through 1975 on panels of polished granite that forms a shallow V. Near the vertex, I found the name of a soldier whose death I had written about 16 years before. Each side of the memorial is 246 feet eight inches long. If there were one for dead Vietnamese, civilians and soldiers, North and South alike, or for the dead of El Salvador, Guatemala, and Nicaragua, it would have run for a mile or more.

The White House's apparent lust for armed intervention in Central America worried even some senior officers in the Pentagon. In June, the chief of staff of the army, General Edward C. Meyer, who was only a few weeks from retirement and could speak freely, stated, "If I thought the 82d Airborne's going there would be a solution to the problem, I would probably recommend that right now, but I don't think it would be. There has been a crying need to pull together the economic and political as well as the military arms of government so that we're applying coherent programs. . . ."

Reagan defended his policy before friendly audiences, mostly in the Sun Belt. In Jackson, Mississippi, he told a meeting of Republicans that they could expect a tidal wave of refugees from south of the border if Central America were lost. He didn't have to mention that their skins would not necessarily be white. At a rally of Cuban émigrés in Miami, he cited with approval Theodore Roosevelt's famous dictum, "Speak softly and carry a big stick." It was the sort of thing Reagan had grown up hearing. T.R., after all, left the White House in 1909, only a couple of years before Reagan's birth, and remained a hero until his death in 1919. Like Roosevelt, Reagan rode for exercise. He also watched his diet, sawed wood and cleared brush on his Santa Barbara ranch, worked out regularly with dumbbells, and was reported to have added three inches to his chest measurement. It was a regimen of which Teddy, the advocate of "the strenuous life," would certainly have approved.

A couple of weeks later, in a speech to the convention of the International Longshoremen's Association, a union not renowned for democracy or honesty, Reagan announced that Henry A. Kissinger would head a bipartisan commission to recommend long-term goals for Central America. Members of Congress had urged its creation, but Kissinger seemed an odd choice to head it. For one thing, Reagan, in his unsuccessful contest for the Republican presidential nomination in 1976, had repeatedly criticized Kissinger as the architect of the policy of détente with the Soviet Union. Kissinger had also been quoted to the effect that he had never found much to interest him in Latin America. His one major venture in that area, the overthrow of the Allende government in Chile, was unlikely to enhance his standing in the region. On the other hand, Kissinger was unquestionably a star turn on the diplomatic stage, and he could make the commission seem important if anyone could. Quickly affected by the spirit of *mañana* that afflicted the region, he announced soon afterward that the committee would delay its report from December, 1983, to February, 1984. He said he didn't think that anything "irreversible" would happen in the meantime.

The Contadora nations, more sensitive, perhaps, than Kissinger to the fact that hundreds of soldiers and civilians were being killed each week in El Salvador, Guatemala, and Nicaragua and that death, too, was irreversible, continued to meet and make proposals that Washington continued to snub.

On July 16, *The New York Times* published another secret working paper from the White House. It said the situation in Central America was nearing a critical point and continued, "It is still possible to accomplish U.S. objectives without the direct use of U.S. troops (although a credible threat, such use is needed to deter overt Soviet-Cuban intervention) provided that the U.S. takes timely and effective action." The paper urged that Congress be asked to increase aid to the Salvadoran government in fiscal 1984 from the $86,300,000 that had been previously sought, and which Congress had shown no disposition to grant, to at least $120,000,000.

Only two days later, a presidential spokesman announced that maneuvers on a vastly greater scale than any ever held in Central America would begin within the next few weeks and continue for six months. Four thousand American troops would practice assault landings and jungle warfare in cooperation with the Honduran army in the area around Puerto Castilla. Aircraft carrier battle groups, cruising off both coasts, would launch mock air strikes, and just in case anyone failed to recall the term "gunboat diplomacy," the recently recommissioned battleship *New Jersey*, an anachronism for more than 40 years, would be training her 16-inch guns on flea-bitten harbors, just as she had done, to no apparent purpose, in Vietnam.

The next day, which was, coincidentally, the fourth anniversary of the Sandinista victory, Nicaragua offered to take part in broad Central American peace talks. Daniel Ortega, the coordinator of the ruling junta, responding to a proposal made by the Contadora nations a week earlier, said that he was ready to sign a nonaggression treaty with

Honduras, to freeze arms shipments to the Salvadoran rebels, and to join in a prohibition against the use of the territory of any of the Central American states as a base from which to attack another.

At his press conference, on July 21, Reagan said that Ortega hadn't gone far enough. The Sandinistas, he said, were "in violation, literally, of a contract that they made with the Organization of American States." Since he was referring to the promises of democracy, elections, and so on that the Sandinistas made after taking power, he presumably meant "figuratively." In any case, the Sandinistas might have replied that they weren't doing badly in comparison with many members in good standing of the Organization of American States. Reagan went on to say that it would be "extremely difficult" to stabilize Central America as long as the Sandinistas remained in power and that he "hoped" it would not be necessary to impose a naval blockade.

Facing a hurricane of criticism by the public, by the press, and even among hitherto loyal supporters in Congress, the President stated a week later that the United States wanted "no larger presence" in Central America. However, he refused to give comfort to those who feared the United States was heading for another Vietnam by categorically stating that combat troops would not be sent to the region. Recalling the dictum of the second Roosevelt, he said, "A President should never say 'never.' "

The next day, July 28, the House voted, 228–195, to end all covert aid to the Nicaraguan *contras* by September 30. Republican leaders put part of the blame for the defeat on the fact that they had not been informed that the maneuvers would take place before they were publicly announced. A White House spokesman stated that aid to the *contras* would continue until the bill became law, which seemed most unlikely, given the Republican majority in the Senate and the certainty of a presidential veto.

On the day after the vote, Fidel Castro said he would abide by any agreement reached by the Central American states that called for the withdrawal of advisers and an end to arms shipments. Reagan said he would give Cuba "the benefit of the doubt," but nothing that happened after that indicated that he had.

The White House confirmed, on August 3, a Nicaraguan announcement that an American destroyer, one of the warships taking part in the maneuvers, had trailed a Soviet freighter bound for Corinto, Nicaragua's main Pacific port, for two hours at a distance of 2,000 yards and had inquired by radio as to her cargo and destination. The query was not illegal, but it seemed pointless since Washington already had this information. Reagan had mentioned the ship at his press conference, saying that she had transited the Panama Canal and was carrying a military cargo, including at least two helicopters.

Meanwhile, as the Kissinger committee was getting ready to begin its hearings, an interview with him appeared in *Public Opinion,* an obscure magazine of conservative temper, in which he sounded like the Kissinger of old. "If we cannot manage Central America," he was quoted as saying, "it will be impossible to convince threatened nations in the Persian Gulf and in other places that we know how to manage the global equilibrium."

In El Salvador, the first phase of what was called the National Campaign Plan began in early June. Its objective was to expel the guerrillas from one area at a time and to station sufficient troops there to keep them from returning while the civil authorities repaired roads and bridges, reopened schools, built clinics, and did all the other things that were tried for years on end in Vietnam to win, as the saying went, the hearts and minds of the people.

The plan was tried first in San Vicente, southeast of the capital. As more than 3,000 troops marched in, the guerrillas, predictably, departed. Photographs showing smiling civic-action workers distributing corn and beans to grateful *campesinos* and treating their children's rashes began to appear in the press. They could have been taken 25 years earlier near Danang or Nhatrang. Advisers who only a few months earlier had been criticizing the Salvadorans for fighting a nine-to-five war now praised them for their puissance and for their sensitivity in dealing with the peasants. Within a month, also predictably, the army's attention had begun to wander, and in August the guerrillas wiped out a 40-man reconnaissance platoon only five miles from the province capital.

At about the same time, the Salvadoran government released the military casualty figures for the 12-month period ending in July—2,292 dead and 4,195 wounded and 326 missing. In the previous 12 months it had been 1,073 killed and 2,728 wounded. These were very large totals for an army of 22,000 or so, but the American military group, always optimistic, said they indicated a new offensive spirit rather than the guerrillas' superior skills and courage. If the guerrillas' casualties had approached those of the armed forces, the rebellion would have been over.

317

Although out of the line of fire, the Constituent Assembly had still not finished drawing up the new constitution, the task for which it had been elected nearly 18 months earlier. The difficulties arose over two articles that would prohibit further expropriations of land. The Salvadoran Communal Union, which said it had a membership of 100,000 small farmers, charged that the land reform laws that were already on the book were being increasingly flouted. It stated that more than 10,000 farmers had been illegally evicted from the holdings they had received under Phase III, the "Land to the Tiller" program. Union leaders were said to have received death threats, and ARENA, D'Aubuisson's party, had opened an office, for its own sinister purposes, next door to the union's headquarters. The union's charges could not be dismissed as Communist-inspired. It received funds and guidance from the AFL-CIO's American Institute for Free Labor Development, or AFILD.

In July, the Salvadoran government announced that the trial of the five members of the National Guard who were accused of killing the four American churchwomen in December, 1980, was positively about to begin. That made it possible for Secretary of State Shultz to certify once again that El Salvador was indeed making progress in protecting human rights. In fact, according to the figures compiled by the Archdiocese of San Salvador's Legal Aid Office, the murder toll rose from an average of 160 a month in the first six months of 1982 to 177 a month in the same period of 1983.

According to a story in *The New York Times* at the end of July, American advisers acknowledged that the shipments to the guerrillas from Nicaragua had been no more than a trickle for several months. That may have been the reason that the *contra* army in Honduras had failed so dismally to stop the traffic. If the guerrillas were getting anything at all from Nicaragua, the advisers said, it was probably medical supplies, batteries for field radios, and the like, flown in at night in lightplanes. The guerrillas continued to capture the rifles and ammunition they needed from the army.

In Bogotá, with President Belisario Betancur of Colombia serving as the go-between, FDR-FMLN delegations met with Stone, the special envoy, and then, four weeks later, for the first time, with members of the Salvadoran government's Peace Commission. Neither side made a statement, and all that Betancur would say was that there was "a possibility" of further contacts. Nicaragua and Cuba were thought to have pushed the rebels into these meetings. The Sandinistas were feeling the heat. It wasn't so much the battle groups steaming below the horizon, the maneuvers in Honduras, or the depredations of the *contras*. These manifestations of Washington's displeasure helped the *comandantes* to rally the country. It was the economic warfare that really hurt. Washington had canceled Nicaragua's sugar quota and vetoed loans from the Inter-American Development Bank and other international institutions. Then Venezuela had turned off the subsidized oil, and Mexico made its terms less generous. Both countries had economic problems of their own, but pressure from Washington almost certainly played a part. In July, its reserves of hard currency nearly exhausted, Nicaragua asked for the rescheduling of $140,000,000 that was due on its foreign loans, some of which it had inherited from the Somoza regime.

As a result of the fiscal bind, shortages of necessities like bread, cooking oil, and soap grew worse. What little industry the country had was unable to import machinery and other goods. The government did what it could to quiet the grumbling. It speeded up the distribution of land seized from Somoza and his supporters. The beneficiaries were individual families and cooperatives rather than collective farms on the Soviet model, which had, inevitably, turned out to be models of inefficiency.

Beyond that, four years after taking power, the Sandinistas still showed no inclination to start expropriating even very large *haciendas* whose owners had not been Somocistas. All told, 4,400,000 of 7,000,000 acres of agricultural land remained in private hands. One family, the Pellas, still owned 15,000 acres and milled 52 percent of Nicaragua's sugar.

By late July, the *contras'* offensive had petered out. The former Coca-Cola executive who was the spokesman for the Nicaraguan Democratic Force, as their group styled itself, put the blame on supply problems. Reports began to appear that the *contras* feared that Reagan would be unable to return them to power. In Costa Rica, Edén Pastora, whose troops were starting to stick their toes across the border, had his own complaints. He said that the CIA was trying to push him into joining forces with the *contras* by cutting off his funds. A couple of weeks later, Pastora was back on the front line. He said he had raised the money he needed to keep fighting from Social Democratic sympathizers in Europe, but later events suggested that his benefactor had been the CIA.

319

In August, the Nicaraguan government, saying that it anticipated new attacks from both east and west as soon as the ground dried, imposed military conscription for the first time. Registration was scheduled for October 1, but no one was to be called up until after January 1, 1984. Since military service, particularly in the ranks, has always been avoided by the middle and upper classes of Latin America, it seemed likely that the decree had been issued to provide yet another incentive for such of these families as remained in the country to catch a plane for Miami.

Although the State Department had ordered the closing of Nicaraguan consulates in the United States and was making it difficult or impossible for Sandinista officials to accept invitations to speak in the United States, they were still able to make themselves heard. The September issue of *Playboy*, for example, which, like all other major American magazines, was not available in Nicaragua, carried a long interview with the Sandinista leadership.

The Reverend Ernesto Cardenal, the Minister of Culture, gave his version of what had taken place at Pope John Paul II's outdoor mass in Managua. (It was Cardenal who had knelt to kiss the Pope's ring, only to have it pulled away.) In his version, the Pope cast the first stone by permitting Archbishop Obando y Bravo to make an unscheduled speech that was anti-Sandinista in tone. In his sermon, Cardenal noted, the Pope took as its text the story of the Tower of Babel, which, of course, collapsed. Beyond all that, he said, the liturgy included a prayer for prisoners, presumably the 1,000 or more Somocistas who were still confined, but not for the Sandinistas killed by the *contras* or, as is customary, for the leaders of the country. It was these provocations, Cardenal said, that roused the crowd.

On August 20, after six months of debate, the Nicaraguan Council of State completed work on a law dealing with the organization of political parties. The measure laid the groundwork for national elections. These were scheduled for 1985, which no longer seemed so far down the road. Although the Sandinistas controlled the council, opposition forces were represented and secured many modifications in the law as it was originally drafted.

Even before the approval of the law by the ruling junta, the opposition began holding public meetings. Adán Fletes, the leader of the moderate-leftist Social Christian party, said that there was a new atmosphere of political freedom, although 35 members of his and other opposition parties were in jail on charges of subversion.

"The meetings that are going on these days would never have been permitted three months ago," Fletes was quoted as saying. "But we remember the years of [the Somoza family's] dictatorship, when there were periods of looseness interspersed with repression. Perhaps the same cycle still exists. We shall see."

At the end of the month, a group of 90 Democratic Conservatives met without interference at a movie theater in Managua. They condemned the Sandinista government and pledged themselves to oppose the consolidation of "a totalitarian Marxist-Leninist regime which is in the Soviet orbit and is rejected by the immense majority of our people." The delegates also demanded the freeing of political prisoners and the end of the government's press censorship and its "antireligious" campaign.

Early in September, the Permanent Human Rights Commission of Nicaragua, an independent body, said that the Sandinistas were incorrect in stating that the country's problems were caused by the United States. The problems were "internal," the commission said, and the negotiations would have to be held with the Nicaraguan people. The correctness of the commission's opinion was of less importance, perhaps, than the fact that it could be expressed at all. People were murdered for less in El Salvador and Guatemala.

Costa Rica, which was becoming increasingly nervous about the activities of Pastora's group, the Revolutionary Democratic Alliance, became frantic when, in a characteristically dashing stroke in late August, he sent two small passenger aircraft to bomb the Managua airport. The bombs did no great damage, but one of the planes was shot down and crashed into the control tower. A fire that seriously damaged it and the passenger terminal ensued. The next day, the rest of Pastora's air force, two old military trainers, fired rockets at oil tanks at Corinto.

Under pressure from the United States, President Luis Alberto Monge had been taking no notice of Pastora's activities. The government felt obliged to deny what no one doubted—that the planes had in fact taken off from Costa Rica. Within days, and despite the protests of the American Ambassador, more than 80 of Pastora's followers were arrested. The alliance was warned that if it continued its warlike activities, its members would be expelled. A government spokesman, with one eye on Washington, said that despite his government's loathing for the Sandinistas, it would not permit Costa Rica's neutrality to be compromised.

* * *

Costa Rica could have taken a lesson from Honduras in coolness under fire. Despite the presence of more than 2,000 American troops on maneuvers, of 300 American advisers, including 120 members of the Special Forces, of swarms of CIA agents, of perhaps 5,000 armed Nicaraguans and 1,000 armed Salvadorans who were in training at Puerto Castilla, President Suazo Córdova and General Gustavo Álvarez Martínez, who actually ran the country, enthusiastically greeted each new arrival.

Their fervent anticommunism may have had an aspect of self-interest. Washington was unable to do enough for the country with which it was now standing shoulder to shoulder. Military and civilian aid was arriving on every ship, and it seemed not unreasonable to suppose that senior officials and officers were getting their share. In addition, the construction of camps, radar stations, and other military necessities provided contracts for the private sector and work for the unemployed.

The creation of a new and powerful Honduras had the support not only of the ruling National party but also of the Liberals. In fact, the only opposing view to be heard in the Congress was expressed by its one Christian Democratic member. He kept pointing out to everyone's annoyance that the country's constitution required legislative approval for the stationing of foreign troops in the country. While it would doubtless have been granted, it had not even been sought.

Honduras's intelligentsia grumbled that its poor, backward, but relatively placid land was being dragged to the slaughter, and students marched in protest. The *campesinos*, however, seemed content to ignore their country's new destiny. Such disturbances as occurred in the countryside had to do with the snail's pace at which publicly owned land was being distributed. Agricultural and industrial workers struck for union recognition, which those who toiled for United Brands and Standard Fruit had enjoyed for 30 years.

The Honduran oligarchy and military chose to treat strikes and the squatting of *campesinos* on land that was under private ownership as manifestations of a dangerously revolutionary spirit and to render summary justice on occasion. In comparison with El Salvador or Guatemala, the number of deaths and disappearances was very small—perhaps 40 or 50 a year—but it had once been close to zero.

In Guatemala, Ríos Montt's troubles began to increase after the

Pope's visit. When an official of one of the centrist parties stated publicly that the president was using his office to help the evangelicals, Ríos Montt, forgetting to turn the other cheek, jailed him for four days. His televised sermons had begun to grate. Guatemalan men did not want to be lectured about marital fidelity. Public employees didn't enjoy homilies on bribery and extortion. People began to say that Ríos Montt was *loco*, and rumors circulated that a coup was imminent.

The more powerful causes of discontent, however, were Ríos Montt's refusal to call elections and his imposition of a 10 percent value-added tax—a levy that, for once, fell more heavily on the middle and upper classes than it did on the poor. In June, under pressure, he announced that legislative elections would be held in July, 1984, and that a presidential election would take place a year or two after that.

Ríos Montt seemed to be sounding a valedictory note when he told an American journalist in early August, in language that recalled Jimmy Carter's, "I have peace in my heart because I have not been a dictator, I have not been an assassin, I have not been a bully." A few days later, he was quoted in the press as saying that neither the United States nor the Soviet Union had the best interests of Central America at heart. What they wanted, he said, was "geographical positions, strategic positions, positions for combat."

On August 7, as later became known, Brigadier General Oscar Humberto Mejía Victores, the Minister of Defense, visited the aircraft carrier *Ranger* off Guatemala's Pacific coast. The next morning, while Ríos Montt was at the Guatemala City airport waiting to fly to the carrier, a group of officers, headed by Mejía, took control of the country.

Mejía represented a return to the sort of leadership that Guatemalans were accustomed to. He had been the Deputy Minister of Defense in the murderous and rapacious government of Lucas García, Ríos Montt's predecessor. Mejía said he would restore democracy and call elections that would, presumably, be as honest as those in the past. He abolished Ríos Montt's secret court, which, it turned out, had ordered the execution of all of 15 persons. If history was any guide, its functions were likely to be reassumed by the death squads, and on a considerably broader scale.

One pledge by Mejía could be believed. That was his statement that he would "fight by any means to eradicate Leninist Communist subversion which threatens Guatemala's liberty and sovereignty." That suggested that the Indian massacres, which may have declined somewhat under Ríos Montt, would remain an important technique for the restoration, in Mrs. Kirkpatrick's words, "of civil peace."

Representative Clarence Long noted that he had spoken with Mejía about the army's treatment of the Indians. "I got nowhere with him," he said. "The more I talked the redder he got. He almost set fire to his collar."

The State Department welcomed Mejía's assurances that democracy was imminent and rejected with scorn any supposition that the coup had been plotted during his visit to *Ranger*, which, the department said, had been nothing more than a routine—that word again—courtesy call. My information indicated that it was at least possible that Washington, displeased by Ríos Montt's comments and worried about his loss of popularity, had perhaps stopped restraining his enemies.

A week or so after taking office, Mejía said, "The problems of Central America must be resolved by the Central Americans . . . [but] the United States is the only country that can help us to combat the guerrillas in the region."

Mexico watched developments in Guatemala with a certain unease. Relations between them have not been cordial since independence, when Chiapas, which had been part of the captaincy general of Guatemala, decided to join Mexico. Guatemalan politicians still demand its return from time to time. In recent years, tens of thousands of refugees, mostly Indians, have fled across the border to escape the Guatemalan army's policy of *tierra arrasada*, or scorched earth.

Since at least some of the refugees were guerrillas or sympathizers, Mexico not only had to provide a minimum of help but also had to worry about the possibility that its own Indians in Chiapas and the other southern states might catch the infection. Some senior officers in the Mexican army and police were reported to believe that Mexico ought to emulate Guatemala by taking harsh measures against the revolutionary left. The Mexican army had been kept weak and divorced from politics since the late 1920's, but there was no guarantee, particularly at a time of economic distress, that it would be willing to remain so.

As the Mexican economy continued to weaken, the electorate became angry enough for once to break its habit of voting for the PRI. The party was wise enough to permit this anger to reflect itself, in diluted form, at any rate, at the polls. In elections in July in five northern states, the reinvigorated opposition parties cut deeply into the PRI vote, costing it no fewer than 13 mayoralties, including that of Ciudad Juárez, across the Rio Grande from El Paso, Texas, and Durango, and five of the 61 seats in state legislatures that were being contested. The beneficiary was not, as might have been supposed, the left, which remained generally disorganized and impotent, but the conservative National Action party, the PAN.

Two days after the election, the government took action to strip Jorge Díaz Serrano, the former head of PEMEX, of his senatorial immunity so that he could be tried on charges of receiving kickbacks of $34,000,000 on the purchase of two tankers. After his dismissal by López Portillo for cutting export prices without permission, Díaz Serrano had received a PRI nomination for the Senate, a designation that could always be purchased for ready money, and in 1982 was duly elected. Since no senator had been deprived of immunity in more than 30 years, his purpose, it seems safe to say, may have been primarily to stay out of jail.

Under house arrest in his suburban mansion, Díaz Serrano expressed confidence in his ultimate vindication. At the same time, he praised the government that was hounding him so unjustly. "It demonstrates the decisiveness and severity of the authorities," he told the *Wall Street Journal*. That was interpreted to mean that as a loyal party man, he would not implicate López Portillo or anyone else, would be found guilty, serve a brief sentence in the warden's house, and be quietly released. By the beginning of August, Díaz Serrano was awaiting trial in a comfortable suite at a prison outside the capital. He was running the sports program and saying that he hadn't felt so good in years.

The government also announced that it was investigating the finances of Carlos Hank González and Arturo Durazo Moreno, the former mayor and police chief, respectively, of Mexico City, both of whom were spending their time abroad—González in his residence in Greenwich, Connecticut. Salvador Barragán Camacho, the president of the oil workers' union, accused a colleague, Héctor García Hernández, known as *El Trampas*, the Trickster, of a $6,600,000 fraud. *El Trampas* thereupon took up residence in his condominium in McAllen, Texas. However, he was kidnapped and returned to Mexico City. In custody, he, in turn, accused Barragán and another union leader of stealing $130,000,000. *El Trampas* said he was certain of the amount since he had been the go-between in the transaction.

López Portillo, the man the country most wanted to see behind bars, was spending most of his time in Paris, convenient to the numbered

Swiss bank accounts everyone presumed he had, rather than at his splendid estate on the outskirts of Mexico City.

Two European businessmen were quoted in *The New York Times* as saying they had actually been able to make a sale to PEMEX without paying a bribe. "It was like doing business with the Norwegian state oil company," one said.

In August, Reagan crossed the border to meet with De la Madrid. The conversation was described as friendly, but the comments the participants made at its conclusion suggested that Mexico was not prepared to modify its views on Nicaragua and El Salvador.

De la Madrid later declared, "In the face of social underdevelopment now aggravated by a profound economic crisis and by shows of force which threaten to touch off a conflagration, we must urgently respond with a firm vocation for peace and solidarity." He also recalled Mexico's "history of bitter struggle for national independence" as well as its "invasion and dismemberment." He was too polite to mention who had done the dismembering.

Reagan commented, "We believe that people should be able to determine their own solutions, and that is why we've responded to calls for help from certain of our Latin American neighbors."

In September, Reagan signed without ceremony what remained of the Caribbean Basin Initiative that he had proposed more than two years earlier. Congress had approved the $350,000,000 in aid, most of which went, as with the Alliance for Progress, to private businesses in the United States to pay for exports to the beneficiary countries. As he had requested, Congress removed duties on many imports from the region, including electronics, toys, fruit, and flowers, which had been low to begin with, but kept them on shoes, leather goods, and textiles. However, it killed the most important provision of the initiative, which granted tax advantages to Americans who set up businesses in the region. What it passed instead was a personal income-tax deduction for persons attending business conventions there.

Mexico announced a few weeks later that the peso would be devalued again, but gradually over the coming 12 months to reduce its value from 150 to 197 to the dollar, thus saving the country from the shock of a larger devaluation every couple of months. This reassured the world's bankers to the point that a week later, at the grand conclave of the International Monetary Fund in Washington, they approved an $8.3 billion debt-restructuring agreement.

The hardest blow of all fell in October, when De la Madrid let it be known that the size of the country's oil and gas reserves had been exaggerated by including fields in the Gulf of Mexico that would be far too expensive to develop without an enormous increase in fuel prices. The figure for economically recoverable oil and gas equivalents was reduced from 72 billion to 60 billion barrels. According to experts quoted in the *Wall Street Journal*, a further reduction to 50 billion barrels was possible. They also stated that, since bankers regard oil in the ground as sound collateral, the López Portillo government had purposely overstated the figure to increase the government's borrowing power.

Nothing that the Reagan administration did or said through early October, when this book went to press, suggested that De la Madrid had gotten through to the President.

For example, in what the administration described as a major statement, Fred C. Iklé, the Undersecretary of Defense for Policy, took an uncompromising line in a speech in Baltimore. "Let me make this clear to you," he stated. "We do not seek a military defeat for our friends. We do not seek a military stalemate. We seek a victory for the forces of democracy. . . . The President's policy for Central America has not been given a chance to work," Iklé continued. "Congress has denied the President the means to succeed. . . . We must prevent consolidation of a Sandinista regime in Nicaragua that would become an arsenal for insurgency. If we cannot prevent that, we have to anticipate the partition of Central America. Such a development would then force us to man a new military front line of the East-West conflict, right here on our continent."

Reagan stated soon afterward that the Soviet Union had repeatedly violated the agreement of 1962 that ended the Cuban missile crisis by sending "offensive weapons" to Cuba. However, critics pointed out that the agreement has been interpreted from the start as applying only to nuclear weapons. A White House spokesman responded by saying that Reagan was only discussing "its spirit."

The Kissinger committee, meanwhile, had been hearing eminent witnesses make predictable statements. Former Secretary of State Cyrus R. Vance, who served in the Carter administration, said that the problems of Central America were "essentially local in nature" and that efforts to find a political solution had been inadequate. Former Secretary of State Haig said, "Our problem in Central America is first and foremost global, second regional, with focus on Cuba, and third it is local."

In Bogotá, low-level representatives of the Democratic Revolutionary Front met yet again with members of the Salvadoran Peace Commission. President Betancur declared, "The dialogue for peace in El Salvador has been directly initiated."

However, Francisco Quiñónez, the head of the commission and a member of one of the country's most powerful oligarchy families, said the meeting was "a total disappointment," and the possibility of negotiations had reached "the point of crisis." He repeated the government's standing offer to participate in the coming presidential election and said that the date, tentatively late February or early March, was "negotiable." He rejected the *frente*'s proposal that the next meeting be held in El Salvador, which would have enhanced its standing as an opposition movement.

A *New York Times*-CBS poll, released on September 29, 1983, indicated that Reagan had not yet persuaded the public of the merit of his policy. Indeed, 47 percent disapproved of his handling of foreign affairs, an increase of 11 percent since a poll in June, 38 percent approved, and 15 percent didn't know what they thought.

The poll put the emphasis on the Korean airliner and Lebanese crises, but as it pointed out, "The overall pattern of opinion . . . parallels in large measure earlier polls on American involvement in Central America. Those polls indicated that the public had doubts about American commitment in the region, did not favor further escalation, feared that the situation might come to resemble Vietnam and did not feel that the Administration position had been explained well. As in all foreign-policy questions, the level of information held by the public was modest."

At the General Assembly of the United Nations in early October, Humberto Ortega, the Nicaraguan junta coordinator, charged that the Reagan administration had "declared war" on Nicaragua and was following "the policy of the big stick, the policy of gunboats, the policy of terror." The toll thus far, Ortega said, was 717 Nicaraguans killed and $108,500,000 in property damage. He told reporters later that Nicaragua would continue to get weapons anywhere it could.

President Betancur of Colombia boldly violated the oldest traditions of the United Nations by making a speech that was eloquent and literate. The members, after recovering from the shock, gave him a standing ovation. Betancur introduced himself as "the second of 22 children of a semi-literate Colombian peasant family . . . an old university professor who has stared hunger in the face, slept on park benches and taken any kind of work to survive."

He went on to state, "A few hours' journey away from us here at headquarters lies a seething continent . . . [that is] currently the epicenter of events which in one way or another makes us all actors in its tragedy. Violence, tensions, incidents, underdevelopment and injustice are all symptoms of a crisis in which coexistence and self-determination have been forgotten and which sees the superpowers shamelessly interfering in lands where peasants leave their sowing to take up alien arms and to dig their own graves."

In El Salvador, as the campaigning season, both political and military, approached, one of the old established death squads swung into action. It was the Maximiliano Hernández Anti-Communist Brigade, which bore the name of the man whose reputation Mrs. Kirkpatrick was trying to rehabilitate. From September through early October, it took public responsibility for the murder of the highest-ranking member of the Democratic Revolutionary Front still residing in San Salvador, 18 union officials, and a couple of professors. The Jesuit residence at the Central American University was bombed, and five other professors were kidnapped.

It was noted that five of these persons had been murdered shortly after being denounced by D'Aubuisson as dangerous leftists. The *Wall Street Journal* reported that Pickering, the new Ambassador, had tried to point out to him the serious consequences of idle talk. A couple of days later, a State Department spokesman said, "We have consistently deplored political violence regardless of its origin and, in the context of reports over the past few weeks, do so again in the most categorical terms. . . . It is particularly deplorable that political violence in El Salvador has been directed against those moderate groups that have accepted the risks of supporting democratic reforms."

When Hinton expressed himself in similar terms in a speech in November, 1982, he and Enders, who had approved it, were publicly rebuked by the White House. It was one of the first of the events that eventually led to their dismissal.

At the end of September, Rubén Zamora, in Managua, stated that the Salvadoran guerrillas, who were beginning their fifth year of open warfare, were close to achieving unity of command. The death of

Cayetano Carpio, the leader of the Popular Liberation Forces, was thought to have removed the last major obstacle. American intelligence sources said that if this occurred, Joaquín Villalobos might become the supreme leader. He was the head of the People's Revolutionary Army, which, the sources said, had become the largest of the guerrilla factions. Villalobos, the man who in 1975 either murdered or ordered the murder of Roque Dalton, the revolutionary poet, was rated as the most talented of the guerrilla generals.

Zamora was barred from the United States. The pretext was that a comment of his about the murder of the American military adviser— that such things were bound to happen as long as the advisers remained in El Salvador—suggested a callous disregard for human life. The actual reason, it seemed safe to say, was to keep him from giving interviews or appearing on television panel shows.

The start of the trial of the accused killers of the four American missionary women, which had been announced as imminent in July, still showed no sign of getting started early in October, leading the Senate Appropriations Committee to make its own cut in the Salvadoran military appropriation. Senator Arlen Specter, a Pennsylvania Republican, who introduced the bill, said, "I just got fed up. When the Salvadoran Attorney General spoke to me in Spanish in August, the only word I understood was *mañana*."

In Nicaragua, the *contras* resumed their offensive at the end of September. A force of 1,000 men attacked Ocotal, a town about 15 miles from the Honduran border, but was repelled on the outskirts. The *contra* commander, a former National Guard captain, stated later that it was more heavily defended than he had expected. According to a report in the Washington *Post*, the CIA wasn't in a mood for excuses. It told the *contra* leadership that it wanted to see the bearskin on the wall.

The New York Times reported in early October that the Cessna 404 that was shot down while bombing the Managua airport had been registered with the Federal Aviation Administration earlier in the year as the property of the Investair Leasing Corporation. Its president was the former head of a company that was known to be a CIA front. At about the same time, it became known that the CIA had been flying supplies to El Salvador to the *contras*. Meanwhile, Cuban officials were said to have met several times in Mexico City and in Panama City over the preceding two months with representatives of Edén Pastora in an attempt to end his breach with the Sandinistas.

In northern Honduras, in the jungle along the Patuca River, Honduran troops were said to be skirmishing with guerrillas. The government said that the guerrillas, who were also Honduran, had entered the country from Nicaragua. There was no telling if the report was accurate or merely providing another pretext for sending Honduran troops into action against the Sandinistas.

In mid-October, the *contras*, attacking from Honduras by boat, seriously damaged Nicaragua's largest oil storage depot at Corinto, finishing the work that Pastora had begun. The town had to be evacuated while the fires were put out. The government said 3,200,000 gallons of gasoline and other fuels had been destroyed. The nation's only other tank farms—at Puerto Sandino, on the Pacific near Managua, and at Puerto Benjamín Zeledón on the Atlantic—were badly damaged in attacks in September.

The Sandinista government called these actions "criminal" and sent a note of protest to the State Department. A few days later unnamed Reagan administration officials acknowledged that the CIA had picked the targets and planned the attacks. A day or two later, the Kissinger committee, winding up its six-countries-in-six-days tour of the region, met with Daniel Ortega, the junta coordinator, in Managua. Kissinger stated obscurely, "We should not have to choose between peace and democracy in Nicaragua."

As it happened, Langhorne A. Motley, Enders's replacement, was just completing his own visit to Managua. He said that he thought the Sandinista government was "serious" in its endorsement of the peace proposals of the Contadora group. At the same time, he said, "I felt a genuine anti-Americanism, which may be understandable."

EPILOGUE
Another Vietnam?

THE BIG QUESTION in the United States may be whether it is getting itself involved in another Vietnam War in Central America, but down there it's like asking if the Pope is a Catholic, or are we having tortillas and beans for lunch today. By late October, 1983, there were at least 40,000 dead, and counting, in El Salvador; 10,000 to 20,000—one could only guess—in Guatemala; 40,000 in Nicaragua during the rebellion against Somoza, and another 1,000 since the United States began fighting its proxy war there.

Fifty-five American advisers were stationed in El Salvador, and at least 200 in Honduras, not to mention the 4,000 American troops maneuvering there and the CIA agents lurking behind every tree. In Costa Rica, engineers of the American army were laying out roads to the Nicaraguan border. A government official stated that his country, the only one in Central America free of the curse of militarism, needed a real army to protect it from the Sandinistas. American aircraft were flying reconnaissance and supply missions on behalf of the Nicaraguan *contras* from bases in the former Canal Zone, violating the spirit of the canal treaty with Panama. Direct costs had risen to $500,000,000 a year and could only continue to increase.

Central America in the autumn of 1983 could be said to resemble Vietnam a year or two before the first American combat units arrived there in 1965. There was fighting in El Salvador, in Guatemala, and in the border regions of Nicaragua. The United States had not yet supplied its Central American allies with the "advanced systems," the prodigal use of which in Vietnam gladdened the hearts of defense contractors and generals alike. There were few warplanes or helicopter gunships, no "smart" self-guided bombs, no plastic shrapnel that is invisible to X rays, no white phosphorus, no napalm, or hardly any, and

332

no Agent Orange. The combat was sporadic, fought at close range with light infantry weapons, and often from ambush. In Nicaragua and El Salvador, the allies of the United States seemed to be getting the worst of it. In any case, far more civilians than troops were being killed.

The United States was installing powerful radar in Honduras in an effort to pinpoint at last those arms shipments from Nicaragua to El Salvador. Its use recalled the "electronic fence" that was installed at enormous cost along the demilitarized zone between the two Vietnams. The difference was that troops and supplies actually came down from the North, while this new Ho (as in "Honduras") Chi (as in "Chi whiz, Colonel, they're out there somewhere") Minh (as in "Minhagua") Trail seemed to exist only as a pretext for continuing the war against Nicaragua.

The Reagan administration, it has been said with some justice, appeared to be trying to refight and win the Vietnam War in El Salvador. If so, it was going about it oddly, in very much the same way that led to that disaster. (One wondered, in any case, why it bothered. Revisionist historians—fantasists might be a better word—had already demonstrated to their own satisfaction that the United States would have infallibly won the Vietnam War if American public opinion had not been misled by the press into demanding its premature withdrawal.) The United States had allied itself with a weak government dominated by a generally corrupt and incompetent military caste. The generals and colonels led, mostly from the rear, an army of conscripted peasant boys, some as young as 14, against highly motivated guerrillas. The Salvadoran elite, their children, and their servants, meanwhile, lived in safety in Miami and elsewhere, just as rich Vietnamese had sat out the war in Paris.

Washington justified its intervention in El Salvador as it had in Vietnam. It had said then that it was helping a struggling democracy defend itself against an implacable foe that was the cat's-paw of "monolithic communism" and that moreover, South Vietnam was the first of a row of Southeast Asian dominoes. Two dominoes, Cambodia and Laos, did indeed fall, but only after being dragged into the war by the United States, just as Costa Rica and Honduras were being dragged into the Central American conflict.

To prove that El Salvador, like South Vietnam, was actually an emerging democracy, the United States imposed a new constitution, staged elections, and halfheartedly backed a land reform. All this was done in the midst of a full-scale rebellion and without regard to the fact that the rich in both countries had refused, even in periods of relative peace and prosperity, to permit even the most innocuous reforms.

If the Reagan administration's version of reality transformed El Salvador into South Vietnam, Nicaragua became North Vietnam mingled with the Cuba of the Bay of Pigs invasion. The Sandinista government was accused of having been the vector of the revolutionary ideas that ignited the Salvadoran rebellion, as though El Salvador had not had its own Communist-led rebellion 50 years earlier. Nicaragua was also charged with being the way station for the shipment of arms from the Soviet Union by way of Cuba to the Salvadoran guerrillas, which was certainly true on a small scale, but only through the first months of 1981, and with providing their leaders with a safe haven in Managua, which no one denied.

The chosen instrument of American harassment, terrorism, and, one can be excused for believing, eventual direct intervention was an army led by and largely composed of former members of the one organization feared and hated by all Nicaraguans—Somoza's National Guard. In that respect, it closely resembled the Bay of Pigs invasion force, which was dominated by former members of the army and secret police of the ousted dictator, Fulgencio Batista. The composition of both forces guaranteed their failure and discredited in advance the efforts of the United States.

If the United States were, as it appeared to be, already knee-deep in the Central American *tremedal*, or quagmire, and sinking fast, it was headed for another disaster—on a smaller scale than Vietnam perhaps, but a great deal closer to home.

The time was long past when a regiment of marines could overawe Nicaragua. The fury and fatalism of Spanish and Indian blood, disciplined by a hardening Communist ideology and a nationalist cause, all but guaranteed that such a war would become a bloody and protracted guerrilla conflict. It would also, in all likelihood, merge across Honduras's narrow Pacific corridor with the Salvadoran insurgency, would almost certainly lead to harder fighting in Guatemala, and might ignite uprisings elsewhere in the region and southern Mexico. Whatever peace was finally restored would be the peace of desolation.

The Reagan administration, on one pretext or another, had rejected repeated offers for negotiations by Cuba, Nicaragua, and the Salvadoran insurgents and had given no encouragement at all to the efforts of the Contadora group—Mexico, Panama, Venezuela, and Colombia—to bring the Salvadoran government and guerrillas to the bargaining table. The administration said that it was following a "two-track" policy of supporting the Salvadoran government and the Nicaraguan *contras* while trying to negotiate with their opponents. However, the negotiations appeared to be a sham, since the only terms that were being offered came close to being unconditional surrender.

This policy appeared to have a fatal handicap. The credulity of Congress and the public of which Kennedy and Johnson took advantage in escalating the war in Vietnam no longer existed to anything like the same degree. Reagan's policy had faced substantial and growing opposition from the start, and it was more difficult to charge, as had been done in the Vietnam years, that it was Communist-inspired.

For that reason, Reagan had been forced to go even more slowly than had Johnson in Vietnam in increasing the American involvement in Central America. This "turning of the ratchet," in the terminology of the Vietnam period, was the same tactic for which the Republican right had criticized Johnson, and it had allowed both the Salvadoran rebels and the Sandinistas time to strengthen themselves and to rally international public opinion on their behalf.

If, on the other hand, Reagan was merely planning to continue the proxy war in the hope that he would eventually frighten the Sandinistas to death, he was, in the view of every expert with whom I spoke, deluding himself. He was also casting the United States in the ignominious role of the rich bully who hired someone else to do his fighting for him—and against an impoverished and devastated nation with scarcely a hundredth of its population and not a millionth part of its military power.

It was also possible that the administration's soothsayers were incorrect in their prediction that hard-line Marxist-Leninist states were the only possible outcome if the Sandinistas were permitted to remain in power and the guerrillas eventually triumphed in El Salvador. The Sandinista *comandantes* were all Marxists of one sort or another. Despite their protestations to the contrary, it was unlikely that they ever intended to share power in any real way with the non-Marxists whose help was crucial in defeating Somoza. The history of Communist movements the world over, including that in Vietnam, suggested that the Salvadoran guerrilla leaders would deal in the same way with their non-Communist auxiliaries.

However, that did not necessarily mean that either group was committed to building its nation with Soviet or Chinese blueprints. The Sandinista leaders had pledged from the day they entered Managua that they intended to retain a mixed economy and a participatory government. More than four years later, it could be argued, that promise had been bent but not broken. If the *comandantes* eventually made a sharp left turn, the unremitting hostility of the Reagan administration would have provided them with an excellent excuse for having done so.

Not that the *comandantes* were altogether blameless. They seemed to take a particular pleasure, in the manner of Sandino himself, and of Arbenz, Castro, and many other Latin American leaders of the left, in pulling feathers from the eagle's tail. However, they were, after all, generally young, flushed with victory, doctrinaire in outlook, and entirely inexperienced in the practical problems of government—as is nearly everyone in Central America who does not happen to be the friend or relative of a *caudillo*.

Even their elder statesman, Tomás Borge, was only in his forties, and it was scarcely reasonable to suppose that a man who had spent 20 years fighting or in prison would immediately extend the hand of trusting friendship to the country that had helped keep the Somoza tyranny in power until only a month or two before it was overthrown.

At that, the United States could almost certainly have retained considerable influence over the Sandinistas if it had been willing to show to them a fraction of the patience it had shown, for example, to the Salvadoran government in waiting for it to bring to trial the murderers of the missionary women and the land reform advisers. Mexico and Venezuela had demonstrated that the aid and trade that the Soviet Union seemed unwilling to provide could be used to gain concessions from the Sandinistas, but the Reagan administration declared economic war on Nicaragua as soon as it took office and within a year had begun to organize a military campaign against it.

The Reagan administration was dealing with El Salvador and Nicaragua in much the same way that Eisenhower had dealt with Guatemala, Kennedy with Cuba, Johnson with the Dominican Republic, and Nixon with Chile, and for the same reason. All these countries were seen as the immediate objectives of a Soviet master plan to dominate Latin America. Since even the notion of a Communist-dominated El Salvador and Nicaragua might not exactly strike terror into American hearts, a new version of the domino theory was devised—that

Nicaragua and El Salvador, in the sardonic words of Robert White, the dismissed Ambassador to El Salvador, were the soft underbelly of Kansas.

The Contadora group, their near neighbors, took a different view, believing that Nicaragua and El Salvador were important to the security of the hemisphere mainly as object lessons. They demonstrated what happened when countries were misgoverned past the point of endurance. Not one Contadora nation could be described as even remotely leftist in outlook. All of them had generally friendly relations with the United States and were its debtors to one degree or another. They knew infinitely more about the region than anyone in the State Department or the White House and shared a common language, religion, and culture. If they were not frightened, it was difficult to see why Washington should be. The Contadora nations thought it odd that the Reagan administration had not welcomed an opportunity to disencumber itself of one of the many problems it had shown itself incapable of dealing with.

"There are two problems," a diplomatic representative of one of these countries told me in mid-October. "One is Reagan's fear of communism. The other, and it may be the more important, is that he is unwilling to give up the monopoly of power and influence that the United States has exercised in Central America for the past 100 years. The legitimate interest of the Contadora nations in Central America is increasing. Yours [the United States'] is declining now that the security of the Panama Canal had been guaranteed. And I can assure you that we no more want Russian bases in El Salvador or Nicaragua than you do.

"Matters have developed very far, and in the wrong direction," he said in discussing the difficulty of finding a negotiated solution. "We do not think that it is possible or desirable to turn the clock back in El Salvador and Nicaragua. There is no certain formula for peace. All we can do is to try to create the conditions under which it might be achieved. Even the start of negotiations would at least reduce the chance of a regional war, which worries all of us very much."

Contrary to Reagan's frequently expressed opinion, he went on, negotiating a place for the *frente* in the Salvadoran government would not be tantamount to permitting it to shoot its way in.

"I can't say I blame the *frente* for not wanting to take part in elections before other matters have been negotiated," he said. "Not when

337

the government couldn't protect them from being murdered by the death squads.''

There was one main reason, the diplomat said, why he and his colleagues in the Contadora group were not particularly worried about the possibility of a Marxist-Leninist Nicaragua or El Salvador.

"Latin Americans are too individualistic ever to permit a truly Soviet style of government," he said with a smile, "perhaps too individualistic for any type of government. Even now Cuba, although its government is exactly the same on paper as the Soviet Union's, is actually very different—repressive but more relaxed.''

The United States' policy toward Cuba, he went on, helped make settlement in Central America difficult to achieve.

"You have been attacking Castro economically or militarily since 1961, and what have you accomplished besides driving him closer to the Soviet Union? What is the point of that?''

In any case, he went on, it was clear that there was little support in the United States, Latin America, or Western Europe for the Reagan administration's present policy. Direct intervention would leave the United States entirely isolated, and even mutually hostile Latin American states would be brought together against it, as Argentina and Cuba were against the United States and Britain during the Falkland Islands war.

As with Vietnam, I noted, having the United States bogged down in Central America would please the Russians as much as having the Russians bogged down in Afghanistan pleased the White House.

"Yes," he said. "Nicaragua might easily become your Afghanistan—and ours.''

Not long afterward, I asked a State Department official to explain to me, in terms that a child of 12 could understand, why the Reagan administration had ignored the frequent Cuban offers to negotiate its differences with the United States across the board. Even if they turned out to be irreconcilable, I asked, what harm could it do to try? The bluster and lack of content of his reply suggested that, as far as the administration was concerned, the question was essentially religious rather than political and therefore not susceptible of rational solution.

There were, conceivably, two unstated and relatively sensible reasons for the intransigence of the United States. One was that Washington didn't mind seeing the Russians spending $1 billion to $3 billion a year, depending on who was doing the estimating, to keep Cuba afloat economically. The other was that the ending of the trade embargo and the veto on development loans might start making Castro's government look a bit less unsuccessful.

Whether or not the Sandinista government was a branch office of what Reagan called the Soviet "empire of evil," it seemed clear enough that the United States had no case, political or moral, for trying to destroy it or, for that matter, for using its existence, or that of Castro's Cuba, as an excuse for continuing to prop up the repressive and corrupt governments of the region.

Jeane Kirkpatrick once drew a distinction between "authoritarian" and "totalitarian" regimes. The former she deemed worthy of the support of the United States, whatever their faults, because they were subject, theoretically at least, to reform. The latter, which, conveniently, all happened to be Communist, because they were frozen in wickedness, were not.

"Authoritarian" might apply to countries like Saudi Arabia or South Africa. Their laws were unquestionably harsh, including, as they did in the first instance, the lopping off of limbs, public flogging, and stoning to death, and in the second, the frequent exemplary hanging of black persons who were found attempting to saw through their chains. Even so, it could not be denied that these penalties were generally imposed in courts of law.

However, "authoritarian" had to be stretched pretty far to apply to Guatemala, El Salvador, the Nicaragua of the Somozas, or, to go farther afield to another former Spanish colony, the Philippines of Ferdinand Marcos. These governments resembled nothing so much as ongoing criminal conspiracies on the order of the Mafia. Neither the rule of law nor any semblance of social justice existed. The men in the black hats always won. The sole function of such states was to permit the governing class to enjoy the untrammeled exercise of power and to steal as much as possible for as long as possible from the governed. For the United States to regard thieves and tyrants as friends or allies was an absurdity. For them, the United States was a safe-deposit box, a storm cellar, and nothing more.

If Washington had been even slightly interested in promoting democracy, it would have overthrown Somoza at the same time it overthrew Arbenz, and Stroessner of Paraguay at the same time as Allende. The "destabilization" of the Sandinista government would be less repellent if it were matched by a similar action in Haiti. The vampirish hereditary despotism of the Duvaliers, father and son, has been fastened to its jugular since 1957, reducing it to a level of poverty and oppression without parallel in the hemisphere, and has forced political fugitives and starving peasants by the tens of thousands to flee to the United States.

About the only preconception with which I began this book was that in the words of Winston Churchill quoted earlier, democracy was the worst form of government except for all the other forms of government and that orthodox Marxism-Leninism was just about the worst. After two or three years of post-revolutionary euphoria, the people of countries ruled by its tenets almost always found that they had exchanged one set of masters for another, and that the new ones were in some respects, at least, crueler and more demanding than the old. Beyond that, only to the extent that it permitted itself to become less orthodox and more humane, as in Yugoslavia and Hungary, say, was Marxism-Leninism able to grow food or make goods efficiently, to create wealth, to stimulate rather than to repress the arts, or to expand the volume of human happiness generally. Even its undoubted benefits came at too high a price. What, after all, was the point of learning to read and write when the state controlled the press and steamed open the mail?

For that reason, and to confound the handwringers who chose to believe that the United States' role in Central America, and everywhere else for that matter, had been irredeemably wicked, I perhaps went too far in finding explanations for its actions. Not that I quite shared the anti-Communist faith of the unnamed father cited by Reagan in his famous address to a convention of evangelical preachers in March, 1983. The President quoted him approvingly as saying, "I would rather see my little girls die now, still believing in God, than have them grow up under communism and one day die no longer believing in God."

My own view was that I would have had to think that one over for a while but that I was certain I would prefer being mildly ill in New York, say, than blooming with health in Moscow, Peking, or Havana. More to the point, nothing I had seen and heard in Central America had persuaded me that more than a small minority of its people wanted hard-line communism, but that even fewer wanted a continuation of the gangland governments they had known. What they wanted, it seemed to me, was a government that at least let them believe that they were not altogether helpless and that life was not altogether hopeless. Hope, in various tangible forms, could have been the United States' most valuable export to Central America, and it seemed a pity that the Reagan administration had placed it under an embargo.

An astonishing number of persons in Central America admire the United States and long to emulate it. To them it is the great good place, and they cannot understand why it seems to reserve democracy for on-premises consumption. Nor can they understand why the United States chooses to remain ignorant of or to ignore the political fevers, the pains and problems that rack them for years at a time, and then, when its interest is briefly aroused, to suppose that, like physicians of the 18th century, it can cure them by bloodletting.

Not that Reagan's uncompromising approach should have aston-ished anyone. He was the most ideologically rigid and the least well-informed man to occupy the White House in modern times. He was the smile-and-shoeshine salesman of the weird notions, suggestive in many ways of the tenets of the John Birch Society, of the coven of Cali-fornia Croesuses who put him into politics in the first place.

Beyond that, the Reagan administration's obsession with Central America kept it from giving adequate consideration to a far graver dan-ger elsewhere in the hemisphere. That was the likelihood of serious political and social upheavals in Mexico, Brazil, Argentina, and Chile as a result of the austerity measures imposed on them by the International Monetary Fund. Unemployment was rising, living standards were being depressed, and worse was certainly to come.

As far as Central America was concerned, I declined to make a choice between the crooks and the commissars. Although it was late in the day, another approach was still worth trying. If I were President, I might indeed send troops to El Salvador, but their mission would be to arrest D'Aubuisson and his crowd and send them to Paraguay or Patagonia. The oligarchs directing the death squads from the comfort of their Miami mansions would be invited to follow them. Army com-mands would be given to the considerable number of reformist offi-cers still on duty or in exile. The National Guard and the security ser-vices would be disbanded. Duarte's supporters and others of demo-cratic sympathy would be armed and formed into a militia to protect the representatives of the *frente* during negotiations. As to Nicaragua, it seems at least possible that the combined persuasive powers of the United States, Mexico, Venezuela, its other continental neighbors, and, perhaps, Cuba might induce the Sandinistas to show a decent regard for the rights of those citizens who disagreed with them, to preserve a mixed economy, and to agree not to permit the establishment of Russian bases. The United States, after all, had always been Nicaragua's leading customer for sugar, coffee, and the like, and could hold out the promise of the reconstruction and development loans that were so badly needed. Meanwhile, the *contra* armies ought to be disbanded, their members given suitable decorations and permission to live in the United States, which can easily find room for a few more Latin-Americans of the rightist persuasion in the Miami area.

More than 20 years after the failure of the Bay of Pigs invasion, it seemed perverse for Washington to go on pretending that Castro's Cuba didn't exist. The negotiations that were begun during the Carter Administration with the objective of normalizing relations should be resumed. A particular effort should be made, it seems to me, to get to know the younger generation of Cuban officials. Castro, after all, won't be in power forever.

Since none of this, or anything remotely like it, seems likely while Reagan or a like-minded successor occupies the White House, one can only hope that the American people in their wisdom will entrust the ship of state to a skipper who doesn't think it is a gunboat. Someone who is aware, perhaps, that as long ago as 1953, Milton Eisenhower, who undertook several missions to Latin America on behalf of his brother the President, warned that armed revolution was inevitable there unless basic changes were made in its political and economic systems.

". . . as I traveled around and saw the situation," he wrote, as quoted in his book *The Wine Is Bitter*, "namely a few fabulously rich people in a country, small if any middle class, and oceans of poor, miserable, illiterate people living constantly at the starvation level, I became exceedingly worried, and I felt that orthodox aid would do no more than strengthen the prevailing order."

In the 30 years that followed, the aid *was* orthodox, when it was given at all, and the prevailing order *was* strengthened, or so it seemed, and conditions *have* worsened.

Milton Eisenhower, a wise and humane man, once described what he saw as the proper role of the United States in dealing with Latin America. He might not have been altogether happy about including Nicaragua and Cuba in his formula, but I think that he might have done so. (Nixon once said the same thing, but I don't think he is ready to moderate his views.) Anyhow, Milton Eisenhower's formula went like this: *Un apretón de manos para todos pero un abrazo para nuestros amigos.* That is, "A handshake for everyone but an embrace for our friends."

AUTHOR'S NOTE

FOR THE BENEFIT of readers who have noticed, perhaps with suspicion, the absence of footnotes and other scholarly apparatus, let me say that my approach to the subject matter has been journalistic, which is to say informal. I have, nonetheless, tried to be fairminded in my descriptions of events I witnessed, in rendering the interviews I conducted, in my interpretation of events, and in the use I have made of material taken from the daily press, primarily *The New York Times*, periodicals in both English and Spanish, and official documents. The books that I found most useful are mentioned in the text.

Index

345

357

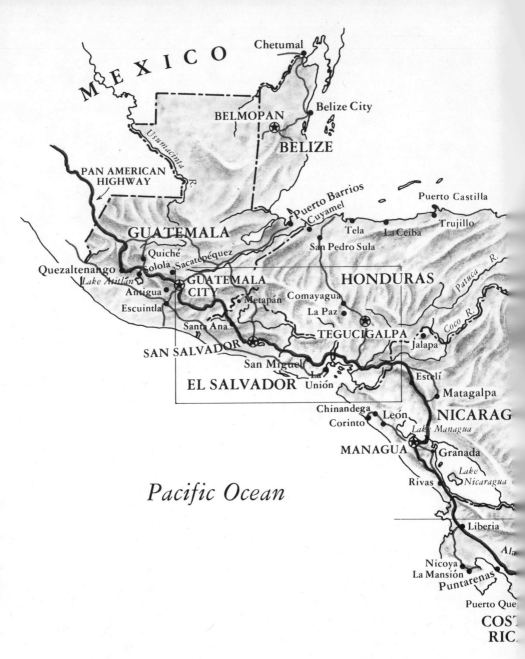

Chetumal

MEXICO

BELMOPAN
Belize City
BELIZE

PAN AMERICAN
HIGHWAY

Usumacinta R.

Puerto Barrios
Puerto Castilla

GUATEMALA
Cuyamel
Tela   La Ceiba   Trujillo
San Pedro Sula

Quiché
Quezaltenango
Colola Sacatepéquez
Lake Atitlán
GUATEMALA
CITY
HONDURAS
Patuca R.

Antigua
Comayagua
Coco R.

Escuintla
Metapán
La Paz

Santa Ana
TEGUCIGALPA

SAN SALVADOR
Jalapa

San Miguel
Estelí

EL SALVADOR   La
Unión
Matagalpa

Chinandega
Corinto   León   NICARAG
Lake Managua

Pacific Ocean
MANAGUA   Granada

*Lake
Nicaragua*
Rivas

Liberia

Ala

Nicoya
La Mansión
Puntarenas

Puerto Que

COS
RIC

Central America

0   50   100   150   200
SCALE OF MILES

———————   Roads